The Weak Body of a Useless Woman

WOMEN IN CULTURE AND SOCIETY   *A series edited by Catharine R. Stimpson*

The Weak Body of a Useless Woman

MATSUO TASEKO AND THE MEIJI RESTORATION

Anne Walthall

The
University
of
Chicago
Press
Chicago &
London

ANNE WALTHALL is professor of history at the University of California, Irvine.

The University of Chicago Press, Chicago 60637
The University of Chicago Press, Ltd., London
© 1998 by The University of Chicago
All rights reserved. Published 1998
Printed in the United States of America

08 07 06 05 04 03 02 01 00 99   1 2 3 4 5

ISBN: 0-226-87235-1 (CLOTH)
ISBN: 0-226-87237-8 (PAPER)

The University of Chicago Press gratefully acknowledges
the generous contribution of the Suntory Foundation
toward the publication of this book.

Library of Congress Cataloging-in-Publication Data

Walthall, Anne.
    The weak body of a useless woman : Matsuo Taseko and
the Meiji Restoration / Anne Walthall.
        p.   cm. — (Women in culture and society)
    Includes bibliographical references and index.
    ISBN 0-226-87235-1 (cloth : alk. paper). — ISBN 0-226-87237-8
(pbk. : alk. paper)
        1. Matsuo, Taseko, 1811–1894. 2. Women intellectuals—Japan—
Biography. 3. Nationalists—Japan—Biography. 4. Women political
activists—Japan—Biography. 5. Women poets, Japanese—Biography.
6. Japan—History—Restoration, 1853–1870. I. Title. II. Series.
    DS881.5.M323W35   1998
    952'.025—dc21   98-16365
                                                              CIP

♾ The paper used in this publication meets the minimum requirements of the
American National Standard for Information Sciences—Permanence of Paper for
Printed Library Materials, ANSI Z39.48-1992.

I dedicate this book to my brother and Beth and my parents.

Contents

Illustrations

Foreword

In 1862, Matsuo Taseko, a fifty-one-year-old peasant woman, traveled from her home in the mountains of central Japan to Kyoto, then Japan's political and cultural capitol. Perhaps only people who know Japanese history can grasp the daring of her journey. She was, a younger man remembered, "tall and slender, and she had piercing eyes. She was not easily intimidated, and she could assume a great deal of dignity when she chose. If any of the young men did something improper, she never hesitated to correct him. Many lived in fear that she would find out what they had been up to, and they stood in awe of her as though she were their mother. She was no ordinary woman." Anne Walthall has now written a major biography of this extraordinary figure.

Taseko was born into the Takemura family, members of a literate, entrepreneurial, affluent peasant class. Her father was a village headman, a job demanding a strong ethos of service that combined the duties of tax collector, notary, public works administrator, law enforcement officer, and protector of religious ritual. At eighteen, Taseko married Matsuo Motoharu, then twenty-three. He also became a village headman. They had ten children, seven of whom survived to maturity. The marriage seems to have been happy and successful. Taseko, Walthall suggests, raised silkworms to contribute to the family income. She was habitually hardworking and attentive to her family's well-being.

If this were all, a biography of Taseko might be no more than a case study in nineteenth-century Japanese social history. She has, however, a compelling, twofold claim on our attention. First, she was a writer. During her life, working with the intricacies of classical literary traditions, she composed sixteen to seventeen hundred poems that she recited and exchanged with other poets. In the 1880s, the diaries of her stay in Kyoto in 1862–63 were published. She wrote letters as well. Significantly, she signed them "Takemura Tase," the name by which her contemporaries knew her. "Takemura" was, of course, her natal name. The characters she used for "Tase" stand for "many" and "energetic." Modern naming practices have both substituted her husband's family name for hers and regularly added the suffix "ko," which means child, to "Tase." "Thus," Walthall points out, "(they) serve a double duty: they attach a woman to her husband's house and belittle her maturity" (p. 64).

As a Japanese woman writer, Taseko had predecessors. Established by aristocrats, a tradition of writing women had existed since 794. Moreover, her mother's line had bred women writers, the best-known of them her great-grandmother. Taseko had far fewer models for the activities that constitute her second claim on our attention: her membership in a xenophobic revolutionary political group, the Hirata school, based on the teachings of Hirata Atsutane (1776–1843). A nationalist and nativist, Atsutane taught that Japan had a "distinct, sacred, and unique" identity (p. 12) rooted in antiquity. Outside influences—be they Buddhism or Western commerce— were to be hated, distrusted, and spurned. Fusing religion and politics, the emperor was a "manifest deity" whose rule was to be supreme (p. 12). The Hirata school, having struggled for the overthrow of shogun power and the restoration of imperial potency, celebrated the Meiji Restoration of 1868, a watershed event in modern Japanese history.

As an activist in the Hirata school, Taseko recruited new members, gave money and encouraged others to do so, wrote poems, and then, in 1862, embarked upon that trip to Kyoto. As a peasant woman, she was an anomalous and often frustrated figure. In a long poem, which gives Walthall the title for this book, she airs "my regrets at having / the weak body of a woman / and I enumerate / all the ways / in which I am useless" (p. 231). Ironically, as Walthall points out, the radical conservatism of her movement would never have fundamentally altered her marginality as a peasant, no matter how affluent she might be, and as a woman, no matter how forceful she might be.

Nevertheless, Taseko's Kyoto trip also reveals the possibilities of a complex woman's self-transformation and self-invention. As poet and activist, she made her way by means of charm, conversational skill, deference to her social superiors, talent, vigor, and courage. Her age also permitted her a certain freedom and mobility. She could serve as "guarantor, go-between and information conduit for the revolutionary underground" (p. 352). In 1863, police and troops moved against the Hirata disciples. After several weeks as a fugitive, she reluctantly began her journey home to the rural provinces.

In 1868, after the Meiji Restoration, Taseko supported imperial forces as they consolidated the emperor's power. The next year, she returned to a Kyoto in upheaval. There she exercised some influence in the "jockeying for position" in a new central government (p. 286). She also found a place, and friendships with other women, in the household of a noble prominent in the Restoration, Lord Iwakura Tomomi. In 1869, the court moved to Tokyo, which she then visited from time to time until 1881. Although she did well socially, although she accrued credit for having supported the Restoration, the Hirata school lost its status and power in Japan's newly established bureaucratic state and modern society. Its true believers grew disillusioned with the consequences of their victory.

Taseko's husband died in 1879. She also lost her sons and a younger cousin who had been her intellectual companion. Toward the end of her own life, her eyesight failed, and she was never sure if her brush actually met paper while she was writing. Nevertheless, she was a cheerful, comfortable, unconventional matriarch who wrote her poetry, welcomed friends and students, conversed richly, raised silkworms, and worked to further her family's interests through the arranging of good marriages. In 1892, she received imperial recognition, two years before she died of cancer at the age of 83.

The Weak Body of a Useless Woman balances prodigious, scrupulous scholarship with a sophisticated, impressive approach to the challenges of writing the life of a woman who wrote her own life. Because Taseko's gender kept her from playing a formal public role, she could not shape great public events. She was as much acted upon as actor. However, her life was neither passive nor confined to a private sphere. Walthall persuasively shows how public and private overlap and interpenetrate, how they become inseparable spheres. Moreover, Walthall shows how extensively the writing of women's history enlarges history itself. The biography of Taseko enhances our understanding of the Meiji Restoration and modern Japan.

Walthall knows that a notable life is at once actual and virtual. That is, a person acts during a life span from birth to death. A peasant woman, for example, writes poetry, joins a political movement, goes to Kyoto. After that person's death, the posthumous process of memory-making takes over. In 1903, Taseko received great public recognition when she was granted court rank, one of only six women to be so honored among thousands of men. Simultaneously, her historical persona was being nurtured by a nationalistic scholar, Inoue Yorikuni, who supported the Hirata school. In the politics of memory-making, she was "captured for the conservative side" (p. 333).

So located, Taseko was depicted as a conventional woman. Over the years, various narratives about her emerged, their interpretations dependent upon the larger social and political context in which they were conceived. A key point of disagreement among them, Walthall notes, was whether Taseko was warrior enough to wear men's clothing during her revolutionary battles. Despite their position on the question of cross-dressing, the narratives focused continuously on her as a maternal figure. No matter how unconventional she might have been, she was to sustain the Japanese woman as mother, a symbolic role that she no doubt would have applauded. As Walthall ends her narrative, she wonders if Taseko would have approved of it. Aware as Walthall is of how much the historian will never know, will never discover, can never interpret, she refuses to speculate further. What will be certain to every reader is that *The Weak Body of a Useless Woman* is strong, useful, and invaluable.

Catharine R. Stimpson
New York University

Acknowledgments

This project originated in a request by George Wilson to join a panel on Bakumatsu Japan at the 1989 annual meeting of the Association for Asian Studies, a previous proposal having been rejected, he was told, because all of the participants were men. I agreed to be the token woman on the condition that I be allowed to present a paper on Matsuo Taseko. For the next two summers I went to Japan on Faculty Research Grants from the University of Utah Research Committee to find materials relating to her life and times. Progress was slow until I became the Director of the Tokyo Study Center for the University of California Education Abroad Program which put me in Japan for large blocks of time and sent me on regular trips to Kyoto. Upon my return I was able to finish my research and write this book owing to a University of California President's Research Fellowship in the Humanities and a grant from the Joint Committee on Japanese Studies of the Social Science Research Council and the American Council of Learned Societies with funds provided by the Ford Foundation and the National Endowment for the Humanities.

I have benefited enormously from the help of many people. In Japan Kitajima Eiko smoothed my way, providing crucial assistance and advice. To her, her husband Manji and to their son Shigeki and his wife Kimie go my warmest appreciation and thanks. Matsuo Yūzō, Kitahara Takeo and Hazama Jōji shared family documents with me, and Sakurai Ban helped me read Taseko's poetry. Others who helped me find materials and made useful suggestions include Patricia Sippel, M. William Steele, Linda Grove, Kate

Wildman Nakai, Fukaya Katsumi, Hosaka Satoru, Miyachi Masato, Sue-
moto Yōko, Takayama Yoshiki, Araki Yoshito, Shiba Keiko, Shioda Takashi,
Yoshida Saburō, Kondō Akiko, Ishikawa Masaomi, Takemura Shōhei, Miwada Yoshiko, the members of the Kinsei Joseishi Kenkyūkai and the staffs
at the Iida city library, Waseda University library and the Toyooka History
and Folklore Museum.

Portions of chapter 1 were previously published in "The Cult of Sensi-
bility in Rural Tokugawa Japan: Love Poetry by Matsuo Taseko," *Journal of
the American Oriental Society* 117.1 (1997): 70–86. Portions of chapter 9
have appeared in "Off with Their Heads! The Hirata Disciples and the
Ashikaga Shoguns," *Monumenta Nipponica* 50.2 (Summer 1995): 137–70.
Portions of the Introduction and chapters 1 and 2 will also appear in
"Matsuo Taseko and the Meiji Restoration: Texts of Self and Gender," in
Hitomi Tonomura, Anne Walthall, and Wakita Haruko, eds., *Women and
Class in Japanese History* (Ann Arbor: Center for Japanese Studies Univer-
sity of Michigan, in press). All are printed here with permission.

In the United States, Constantine Vaporis made photocopies of the entire
text of Taseko's biography and writings when I lacked access to major li-
braries. Peggy Pasco directed me to the literature on feminist biography.
Steven Carter gave me a crash course on classical poetry. A number of people
have read and commented on portions of this manuscript: Chieko Ariga,
Sherri Bayouth, Marjorie Beale, Thelma Foote, Hu Ying, Susan Klein,
Lynn Mally, Robert Moeller, Kathy Ragsdale, and the Early Modern Reading Group at the University of Michigan. Alice Fahs and Herman Ooms
read the entire manuscript. Kären Wigen and an anonymous reader for the
Press provided thoughtful and suggestive comments. Rod Ivan Nelson gets
the credit for the figures. Eric Carter and Jeff Holtzman helped with the
maps. Finally I hereby acknowledge my faithful companions, Ina and Wako.

Introduction

What a wee little part of a person's life are his acts and his words! His real life is led in his head and is known to none but himself. . . . Biographies are but the clothes and buttons of the man—the biography of the man himself cannot be written. MARK TWAIN [1]

Matsuo Taseko was born a peasant in the mountains of central Japan in 1811. She married at the age of eighteen, gave birth to ten children of whom seven survived to adulthood, raised silkworms, and helped her husband manage his family's affairs. Her fame, however, derives not from her roles as wife and mother. Instead, at the age of fifty-one she created a new dimension to her life by going to Kyoto where she joined the movement to revere the emperor and expel the European and American barbarians. Because she was a woman, her admittedly minor contribution to the turmoil that eventuated in the Meiji Restoration of 1868 made her a hero; had she been a man, her deeds would have drawn less notice. She spent a mere six months in Kyoto, but the experience marked her to the end of her days. Even after her death in 1894, she continued to attract acclaim by patriots and pundits.

I first encountered Taseko in the pages of Shimazaki Tōson's great historical novel about the Meiji Restoration, *Before the Dawn*.[2] Tōson's goal was to understand why his father had gone mad. To this end he recreated the world his father had lost: Magome post station (thanks to this novel now a popular tourist site), the coming of the Western powers and the shogun's inability to cope with them, and the intellectual climate of the region heavily dominated by the study of Japan's ancient history. Called Aoyama Hanzō in the novel, Tōson's father epitomized an amorphous class in the countryside known as *gōnō*, rural entrepreneurs, a class of which Taseko too was a member. The rural entrepreneurs had sufficient education to administer their villages and exchange poetic sallies with court and samurai officials. They had the knowledge to debate national issues, but their formal status as members of the peasantry kept them shut out of politics. In crafting his story, Tōson peopled it entirely with figures known to his father, making it as much collective biography as historical novel. Taseko surfaces only six times, always in reports which Hanzō receives. She is never more than a peripheral character, never more than a figure of hearsay.

Before the Dawn was written in the early 1930s when emperor-centered nationalism was taken for granted by the author and his readers. The people of the Kiso and Ina valleys who fill its pages fervently believe that restoring the emperor to direct rule will recreate an ancient unitary state predicated on strong bonds between gods, emperor, and human beings. Their desire to bring about the political transformation necessary for this to happen represents a drive to change history from the bottom up, and Taseko's presence demonstrates that it involves women as well as men. The tragedy depicted in the novel lies in Hanzō's realization that his dreams have been frustrated by a new state intent on centralizing power and instituting sweeping institutional changes from the top down. This vision of the mid-nineteenth century continues to affect the way history is practiced and taught in Japan today, and Hanzō, whose disillusionment with the new Meiji state drives him insane, elicits considerable sympathy.[3]

Taseko's reputation has fared less well. In today's Japan she is famous, or perhaps I should say notorious, for her xenophobic ultra-nationalism. She has never been portrayed with the same depth or complexity as the men who brought about the Restoration. Instead she has been seen solely as a model housewife and patriot, for she became famous only within the narrow confines of action taken on behalf of the state. When I began my research in the Ina Valley, the people I met were suspicious of my interest in a woman who in their eyes was a right-wing emperor-worshipping nationalist. The editor and referees for an article I wrote in Japanese insisted that in both the introduction and the conclusion I issue a disclaimer repudiating Taseko's politics.[4] Their demands are significant, for they provide evidence of how she has been presented in books written about women's history and the Meiji Restoration.

Let me say at the onset that I am not interested in justifying xenophobia and emperor-worship, nor am I particularly interested in explaining them, if understanding means to excuse. On the other hand, scholars who have analyzed the movement to "revere the emperor and expel the barbarians" (*sonnō jōi*) tend to downplay the second half of the slogan and explain the first as "a desire to change Japan in order to right society's wrongs."[5] I think both halves must be taken to mean what they say. At least for Taseko, a hatred of all things foreign and a religious reverence for the ruler constituted important dimensions of her political identity. They were driving forces in her life and in the lives of many others around her as well as particularly unfortunate consequences of the nineteenth century commerce between nations.

I HAVE SUBTITLED this book *Matsuo Taseko and the Meiji Restoration* in a deliberate challenge to a male-centered genre of history writing that demands the public story of the public life. In the now classic *Sakamoto Ryōma and the Meiji Restoration*, Marius Jansen traces the path whereby a decentralized government led for 260 years by the Tokugawa shoguns was replaced by a centralized government under the titular rule of the Meiji emperor that fended off foreign domination and built a powerful modern state. Jansen and other historians of his generation eschew ideological motivations and class-based concerns to construct a unified narrative that focuses on politically-minded samurai from the large southwestern domains. After a series of often bungled assassinations and failed coups d'état, these individuals quickly realized that they had to use existing institutions to overthrow the shogun's government, known as the *bakufu*. They started out as young and marginal members of the ruling class who denounced their social superiors for being lazy and incompetent wastrels. By the time they had achieved their goal, they had become statesmen. The reforms they instituted achieved Japan's modernization less through grass-roots initiative than elite directive.[6] Taseko became famous because she came to know some of these men. Hers is not a success story; it disrupts the sequence of events, confuses public and private acts, foregrounds ideology, and makes sense only in terms of her class and gender.

Following Japan's disastrous military adventures of the 1930s and 1940s, historians there have been uncomfortable with hailing the Meiji Restoration as a triumph, and they argue vehemently over who was responsible. Some find the motive force for change in the popular energy generated by the "semi-proletariat" in peasant uprisings calling for *yonaoshi*, liberation from the status quo.[7] Others indicate one avenue for understanding the dilemma faced by Taseko's friends and neighbors by pointing to a failed bourgeois revolution. In this view, the chief actors and major culprits are members of the emerging middle stratum, the rural entrepreneurs in the countryside and the merchants in the cities who have not yet developed a strong class consciousness before fear of domestic unrest and the foreign threat forces them into an alliance with disaffected members of the decaying feudal aristocracy. A third approach analyzes not economic classes per se but the culture created by the politically attuned, if politically impotent, whose thirst for information drives them to expand their communications networks across Japan. Miyachi Masato argues that a focus solely on the men who surfaced at the forefront of political events ignores the political and social constituents that make their deeds possible. The Japanese people could be mobilized to make changes only when a sufficient number of them from various social backgrounds, united in their need for news, really understood the problems facing their country.[8] Taseko's milieu provides a case study in the operation of these networks.

Recently, scholars outside Japan have also begun to take different approaches to understanding how the Meiji Restoration came about and to study people who might have affected its outcome besides the samurai from the southwestern domains. Some have dug deeply into Japanese society to expose the aspirations of its most victimized male members expressed in peasant uprisings.[9] Another approach examines motives and encompasses a variety of impulses, including those that led people to dance in the streets chanting "Ain't it great" (*ee ja nai ka*) as the government came tumbling down.[10] A third treats intellectual history. It focuses on thinkers who destroyed their ethical heritage in trying to recreate it and traces the discontinuities and dead ends lurking behind the ideas that enabled men to make the Restoration a political reality.[11] Each of these perspectives on the Meiji Restoration focuses on specific social forces and tells its story by necessarily omitting others. So long as there is no master narrative, it seems to me there is room for a woman's story of the Restoration as well.

Some readers might wonder why I insist on emphasizing the place of the Meiji Restoration in Taseko's life. As a formative episode, it colors all that came after it, but only through hindsight does it shape what happened before. Taseko spent her first fifty years in a quiet rural backwater. I do not want to discuss the different stages of her life as daughter, poet, wife, entrepreneur, and mother only in terms of how they led up to a brief moment in 1862, for they ought instead to be taken on their own terms. All too often historians of early modern Japan so perpetually keep one ear cocked to the distant rumble of revolution that they slight the importance of prior events. It is after the fact that they can define specific trends and events as having been a prelude to something else. For the people living through them, political incidents in particular can be well-nigh irrelevant. This is especially true for the contrast between national developments and private joys and tragedies. In Taseko's case, for example, the birth of her favorite cousin in 1825 probably had more significance at the time than the shogun's announcement that foreign ships were to be driven off without hesitation, a move that signaled his government's determination to close Japan against the barbarian menace. Nevertheless, her story could not be told were it not for her involvement in the most significant public events of her day.

The work of two men is particularly germane to this study of a peasant woman. H. D. Harootunian has examined the transformation of nativist thought—the study of Japan's indigenous history and culture in deliberate contradistinction to scholarship in Chinese subjects—as social and political discourse. Drawing on the work of Louis Althusser among others, he analyzes the process whereby nativism comes to take on an ideological function as its practitioners, the well-to-do peasants, switch from the apolitical study of ancient literary texts to the interpretation of Japanese history and religion. As such, nativist discourse supports the status quo in encouraging people to work hard and leave the business of governing to their rulers. It also "imagines an order vastly different from the polity it sought to support." [12] Harootunian accounts for the internal logic of nativism's powerful ideological impact on elite commoners; my retelling of Taseko's life shows how she and her friends put nativism into practice and made it into a social movement. For them it was "a veritable new religion, replete with prayer-books, devotional manuals, and a highly distinctive map of sacred places." [13]

The leading historian of the grass-roots nativists is Haga Noboru. Beginning with his graduation thesis, a study of the nativists in Taseko's valley, he has written copiously on the rural entrepreneurs and the ideas they imbibed from a wide range of teachers. His interest in nativism's social function within the context of peasant society and its impact on people's lives has led him to dusty archives in old farmhouses in an attempt to trace the connections between business practices and intellectual pursuits. [14] Insofar as he sees early-nineteenth-century nativism as distinctly populist, however, he tends to disregard how its message of racial homogeneity reinforced the political hierarchy. Many nativists, Taseko among them, were disappointed with the political configuration that replaced the Tokugawa bakufu, but the piety that lay at the core of their world view and their support of the emperor-centered state offered them no means of resistance.

This book examines the history of the Meiji Restoration through Taseko's eyes and those of her friends and relatives. Historians have pointed out that commoners as a whole or even the rural entrepreneurs as a class never supported one side over the other in the conflict between shogun and emperor, nor did they participate actively in the Restoration. Instead individual commoners may be found on all sides, and many remained neutral.[15] This holds equally true for most daimyo and samurai. Neither Taseko and her compatriots nor the men who ended up leading the Restoration represented general trends among their peers. Each experience must be assessed on its own terms.

THE REFUSAL to allow any class or individuals pride of place in the Meiji Restoration might make it appear that all things being relative, the reader should simply pick the history that best suits her predilections. Why then read this book? To clarify my reasons for placing a woman at the center of this historical narrative, I start with a highly original article by Joan W. Scott. She points out that women's history began as a seemingly "innocuous supplement" to established history; it was both an addition and a substitute. Like social history, it assumed that the reality of lived experiences, whether of workers, slaves, children, or other marginalized groups, had intrinsic interest and importance. So long as it focused on the separateness of women's experiences, however, it risked being ghettoized in the historical profession and historical practice. The goal thus became to integrate women back into history, based on the premise that their presence would force historians to recognize the insufficiency of a project that in focusing on men tells only half the story. "Women are both added to history and they occasion its rewriting; they provide something extra and they are necessary for completion, they are superfluous and indispensable."[16] By placing Taseko in conjunction with the Meiji Restoration, I refuse to separate her life from the reverberating public events of her time. Just as retelling her story as she lived through it makes no sense without explaining events extraneous to her, so too this biography does more than simply provide an additional perspective on events. Instead it changes the way they are perceived.

Biographies of exemplary men typically demonstrate either how they changed the course of history or how they represented the trend of their times. This biography does neither. Taseko played a small part in the Meiji Restoration, and that she acted on the political stage at all makes her an anomaly among the women of her day. By choosing her as the focus for this book, I am deliberately confounding prevailing assumptions regarding the criteria for choosing a life as an object of study. I am less interested in what effect she had on the course of events than on what effect events had on her. This amounts to turning the standard justification for biography inside out. Regardless of whether she personally affected her era, it is clear that the opportunities afforded her in her encounter with the men she met in Kyoto made it possible for her to act in ways that fall well outside the conventions of female behavior.

This study could not have been written had Taseko not deliberately remade herself into a political figure. She did so, moreover, in a way that is often overlooked in studies of Japanese women. We know that women participated collectively in social protest.[17] Many are the stories about individual women who aided husbands and lovers in bringing about the Meiji Restoration.[18] These wives and mistresses found themselves involved in politics through their allegiance to their men; their primary loyalty was attached to individuals rather than to ideologies or causes.[19] Taseko in no way fits these patterns. She went to Kyoto accompanied only by a servant and spent little time with women once she arrived. Far from following her husband, her intellectual interests were clearly separate from his. Her cousin Inao was a significant intellectual influence, but he never went to Kyoto to prove his loyalty to the emperor. She acted on her own. Most women, and men too, did not.

Because what Taseko did with her life must be deemed unconventional, the utility of writing her biography in terms of women's history is mixed. Dissatisfied with research projects that lead to large scale models of social life, some feminists argue the need to see the individual variety in women's lives, to reconstitute "the meaning of women's social experience as women lived through it."[20] Much has been written about the life cycle of Tokugawa farm women and the constraints imposed by texts such as "The Greater Learning for Women" (*Onna daigaku*); we know less about how women actually maneuvered within these limits and the leeway they had to craft themselves. Even within the rural entrepreneurial class to which Taseko belonged, women's experiences varied depending on their distance from the shogun's capital at Edo and the particular traditions of their families' households.[21] Without the added dimension of individuality and the opportunity to explore how specific women responded to their own situations, however, new knowledge about life patterns risks reducing their experiences to new stereotypes. Unless they can be separated from the ceaseless and exhausting routine of housework, all too often "the lives of women make no sense. . . . [T]hey seem devoid of significance."[22]

In recent years, feminist biography has addressed this issue by recounting the lives of women (some ordinary, some unconventional) who had hitherto achieved little or no recognition. Edwin McClellan's elegant and original work, *Woman in the Crested Kimono*, might be considered allied to this genre. It depicts a merchant class woman who marries a samurai doctor and then suffers through the vicissitudes of the Meiji Restoration. While leading a conventional life outside the public domain, Io combines an outspoken personality with a strong will that makes the crucial difference to her family's survival.[23] Other examples include Elizabeth Perry's work on Belle Mosko-

witz, a woman who had considerable impact on New York state politics, and
Marjorie Shostak's life history of Nisa, a !Kung woman. With the notable exception of Laura Thatcher Ulrich's *A Midwife's Tale*, most biographies focus
either on women who tried to shape their own lives through autobiographi-
cal writing or twentieth century women whose lives are to some extent accessible through interviews.[24] These works have an intrinsic interest for
women in showing how others have experienced joy and dealt with sorrow.
They also demonstrate that there is much more to the past than politics.
From a woman's perspective, much of what passes for history is no more
than "a uniform drama of masculine posturing."[25]

Life histories have their detractors. Some neglect, as I do, "the married
women who stayed home rearing children and tending to family affairs."[26]
By privileging the individual over the collective, the biographer risks giving
"intellectual sustenance to the political celebration of individualism now
reigning in the atmosphere of neo-conservatism."[27] To define a woman as a
uniquely singular subject is to accept masculine norms of individuality and
the capitalist myth of autonomy. This danger is compounded when we remember for all that she challenged the bonds of conventional feminine behavior and participated in an opposition movement to the government of her
time, Taseko patriotically supported the nation-state. In the classic contradiction replicated in many women who themselves speak to political issues,
she ultimately rejected the possibility of political action for women.

Feminist theory has challenged male-centered approaches to autobiography, life history, and biography, but usually in the context of the Western
tradition. It emphasizes how the male (auto)biography sets up criteria of
analysis—eminence, for example—that are largely irrelevant for female
(auto)biography. A question left unanswered is whether this Western approach defines issues in ways that might inadvertently replicate the conditions of domination under which Japanese women lived. Joan W. Scott's
recent work on the history of feminism in France, for example, deliberately refuses the mode of the heroic biography and the notion that personal life stories offer sufficient explanation for individual action. Instead she sees the
women who are the subjects of her book as sites where political and cultural
conflict are enacted. No matter what they do, women are the product of the
social forces that situate them.[28]

The various contexts that circumscribe a life cannot, however, fully explain individual initiative; they cannot explain why Taseko and Taseko alone
decided to go to Kyoto. To paraphrase Karl Marx, she made her own story,
even if not under circumstances of her own choosing. Women writing on
women in Japan, such as Esashi Akiko, reject the model of the larger-than-

life public figure, but their position vis-à-vis the personal is slightly different. They see a political danger in allowing women to be completely embedded in the all too traditional contexts of daughter, wife, and mother.[29] To take a trivial but illuminating example, finding a late-nineteenth-century photograph of a woman by herself is almost impossible. They are invariably shown as part of a family group.[30] Extracting a woman from the social forces that condition her outlook and behavior thus becomes the biographer's most challenging task.

What makes a biography readable is human interest, which is something that public life spectacularly lacks. Esashi Akiko admits that an unconventional life is more intriguing for the writer than an ordinary one, and it is more likely to hold the reader's attention as well. She argues, however, that a woman too far out of the ordinary does not make a good subject because her political or religious role may so far overshadow the private woman as to render her invisible.[31] In Taseko's case as well, it is all too easy to focus exclusively on her public life to the exclusion of her private moments, to read qualities of public character into personal anecdotes and to assimilate her deeds to stereotypes of the hero. Only by examining her every dimension is it possible to uncover something akin to an individual.

Let me give an example. When I first started reading Taseko's love poetry with a scholar I met in the Ina Valley, I discovered that our readings of this poem, titled "to my beloved" (*koi no kokoro wo*) differed dramatically:

Onore nomi	How long will my smoldering passion
taenu omoi wa	my ceaseless longings
kawaraya no	burn within me
itsu made shita ni	like the flame kept banked
Kuyuri waburan	in a kiln for firing roof tiles.[32]

This poem features the author in an unusually prominent position, made explicit in its very first word. It is definitely Taseko's body that was filled with longing, but what was she longing for? Before I showed Mr. Sakurai this poem, he had read biographies that emphasized her learning, her life as a good wife and wise mother, and her devotion to the emperor. Nothing having prepared him for the possibility that she might have written love poetry, he suggested that perhaps the poem expressed her attitude toward scholarship. "We know she enjoyed her studies, indeed she had become quite a scholar before her marriage. As a young bride, however, she was probably too busy to do what she wanted. The poem could refer to her unfulfilled desire to spend more time with her books."[33] This was his formulation of what a respectable woman could say; so much for my assumption that she was talking about sex.

Taseko is one of six women honored with posthumous court rank for her role in the Meiji Restoration—not a large number compared to the thousands of men who have been so honored.[34] Like other women who participated on their own in major historical events, such as Vera Brittain, whose record of what she did in World War One was later either ignored or judged to be insignificant, Taseko's place in the turmoil of the 1860s has been slighted by historians when it has not been simply forgotten.[35] Women were not supposed to be concerned with the violent world of politics and power, but Taseko refused to remain confined to the woman's chronology of marriage and rearing children, of circulation among men. Like other women who remade their lives in old age (for example, Simone de Beauvoir), she had to write her own story; she did not have access to the "quest plot" that provides the pattern for the life stories of famous men.[36] This lack of what a sociologist would call role models means that it was much more difficult for Taseko to act as she did than it was for the men she met in Kyoto and, like other extraordinary women, she has largely been relegated to silence.

MY REASONS for writing about Taseko are quite different from the concerns of previous biographers and most probably Taseko's own conception of her life. In creating role models for their wives and daughters, they divide her life in two: her publicly recognized support for the emperor and her often stereotyped function as wife and mother. I want to know the private life of a woman who managed to defy what I understand to be the norms of behavior prevalent at her time by acting in public space. In trying to grapple with how these two sides fit together, I have become increasingly dissatisfied with the binary distinction between private and public. Rather than dichotomizing these two terms, they might better be seen as overlapping and interpenetrating. In a society such as Tokugawa Japan in which hereditary status was the crucial determinant of a person's position in society, the creation and maintenance of kinship ties was in itself a political act. Mary Elizabeth Berry has shown how the arranging of marriages and adoptions between daimyo families was an integral part of the machinery of government.[37] Within the context of rural society as well, being a wife and mother had public implications. In some ways Taseko's role in the Restoration represented a fusion of public and private. During the chaotic years of the 1860s, she carved one niche for herself analogous to the niche that women of her class filled in rural society. She made friends with men, worshipped with them, and wrote poetry. Her work as hostess, liaison, information conduit, guarantor, and facilitator replicated the kin work and social services performed by women that underlie and support the public arena.[38] There was, however, a significant difference. Prior to the 1850s, the political realm had been largely confined to the shogun and his top advisors. Thereafter a new public sphere in which national policy was debated and influence sought expanded rapidly and became more heterogeneous.[39] During this window of opportunity, gender demarcations blurred just enough for Taseko to meet with men heretofore strangers to her with whom she discussed politics and engaged in political intrigue. She laid claim to and was recognized as an imperial loyalist, a role with no analog in the society she had left behind.

The public sphere that developed in the 1850s had antecedents in arenas besides the debates among samurai over foreign policy. By drawing on the work of Jürgen Habermas, it makes sense to look for these in the prepolitical realm of letters populated by people in the commercial classes without formal access to national decision-making circles, remembering always that the presence of women must complicate the picture.[40] Taseko was a peasant, but she was a rich peasant. Her male relatives brewed sake, lent money, and served in local government as well as tilling their fields and supervising their tenants. Despite a lack of teachers, they tried to educate themselves in the Chinese classics, Japanese classical poetry, and Japanese history as well as agronomy. Some historians have sneered at their "pseudo-samurai pretensions . . . symbolized by swords, surnames, and rudimentary scholarship."[41] The military government nevertheless sold them the right to these marks of samurai status, and their commitment to scholarship was at least as deep as that of the samurai who received secure if modest stipends for standing guard at their lord's gate. No matter what they made their focus of study — some preferred the Confucian classics, Western learning, swordfighting, or the eclectic moral teachings of Ōhara Yūgaku and Ninomiya Sontoku — they combined their intellectual interests with a practical purpose: the strengthening of their villages and their families' position within these villages both economically and morally.[42]

Taseko's access to what might be deemed the literary public sphere came through her practice of classical Japanese poetry. It was an arcane art, drawing on the language and sensibility of the imperial court seven to nine centuries earlier. Allusive variation on earlier poems being the hallmark of the practitioner's skill, it required the time-consuming memorization of many models found only in expensive books. Unlike the Western poetry tradition in which the archtypical poet was decidedly male, some of the most renowned Japanese poetry had originally been written by the aristocratic women of the Heian court, 794–1180, thus establishing a precedent for the women of

Taseko's day.[43] Insofar as the rural poetry circles tried to mimic as closely as possible this rarefied world, they became in a sense "gender-free zones" where what mattered most was the ability to write an appropriate poem. Although Taseko has never been considered a great poet nor did she write memorable verse, her practice of poetry provided her with a lifelong vocation. She preserved her literary production in a series of anthologies, she used her desire to study poetry as one excuse to go to Kyoto, and she received recognition as a poet from the nobles she met in Kyoto as well as her kin and neighbors. Along with Nomura Bōtō and Ōtagaki Rengetsu, she is acclaimed one of the three female poets of the Restoration movement. Her poetry thus became her most visible and long-lasting contribution to the political public sphere.

In Taseko's case, acting politically did not represent a linear development arising out of her earlier poetry writing, nor did the poetry circles in which she was raised mutate spontaneously into political fora. Both required the intervention of the new ideas and new organizational structure found in the Hirata Atsutane school. Atsutane, 1776–1843, wrote voluminously on Japan's ancient history, preached the belief in a distinct, sacred, and unique Japanese identity, and taught that the emperor was a manifest deity. He hated any outside influence that had corrupted the Japanese tradition, especially Chinese philosophy and Buddhism. His followers espoused the unity of religion and politics to guarantee a utopian and communitarian social order, only to learn that the changes wrought by the Meiji Restoration were not at all what they had expected. This philosophy provides the world view for Aoyama Hanzō, the protagonist in *Before the Dawn,* but Tōson is more interested in Hanzō's collapse in the face of the new westernizing Japan than in the pragmatic steps taken by Hanzō's friends to cope with political dislocation and the frustration of their dreams. Some men retreated into the Shinto priesthood; others invested in new technologies or, like Taseko's grandson, tried to increase their villages' productivity by building levees to control flood damage. Following her first exposure to Atsutane's ideas in her forties, Taseko continued to draw on his categories of thought to the end of her days. Her membership in his school ultimately ensured that even she would be remembered publicly in the political realm.

IN TELLING this story of Taseko's constraints and opportunities, her thoughts and actions, I have developed a strategy of juxtaposing analysis and narrative. The first and longest part of this book examines her first fifty years in a series of shifting contexts: the creation of her identity as a poet, the politics of her time and place, her activities as wife and mother, her role in the political economy of the household, her participation in the nativist movement in the Ina Valley, and the texts that she read as a nativist scholar. The second and third parts tell the story of her political "moment" in the 1860s when she plunged into the stream of history. For her the Meiji Restoration was a truly revolutionary experience that reoriented her life trajectory in a way unimaginable in the decades before. The last part dissects the patterns of her old age and the way she has been portrayed in history and memory.

I reject the assumption underpinning traditional forms of biographical narrative that "lives, however chaotic, are lived in a continuous, unilinear, well-ordered and coherent manner," that what a person does late in life is necessarily prefigured by what went before.[44] Constructing a narrative tends to smooth out discontinuities. One that follows a chronological framework implies a linearity where none in fact existed, subordinates explanation to what happens next, and makes it appear that Taseko's actions at any one stage in her life were preordained. This even tenor begs to be disrupted. I want to emphasize the disjunctures between the contexts of Taseko's early life and her later activities. Furthermore, I want to warn the reader that gaps remain, no historical records exist to fill them, and they are not to be filled with inventions that conform to convention. Instead I point them out, offering the rough edges of a life in digressions and fragments, rather than a seamless web stretching from birth to death. Taseko inhabited a number of communities. Her life shows that these were the products of work and struggle, they were inherently unstable, they had to be reevaluated in relation to her own political and personal priorities, and they are not always retrievable.

To write Taseko's biography, or indeed any biography, raises issues of evidence and veracity. Frustrated at the paucity of sources available for the study of Tokugawa women, I first decided to study Taseko because at least some of her writings have been published. Yet despite what I have been able to find, I am all too well aware of how little I know about her life and her response to the circumstances within which she maneuvered. What remains are episodes, some no more than moments, others of longer duration, the narrative equivalent of snapshots and home movies. How does the biographer acknowledge the role that chance has played in preserving documents? Carolyn Heilbrun has argued that all "biographies are fictions necessary to the biographer" because the results of our scholarship are never so conclusive as we might wish them to appear.[45] No two biographies of any single individual are ever the same, and my portrayal of Taseko is quite likely unrecognizable to the people who told her story in the past.

Taseko died over a hundred years ago, and the people who knew her are also long gone. All that remain are her diaries, letters, poems, and the mate-

rials collected by others, in particular the biographical studies produced by
Ichimura Minato, historian par excellence of the Ina Valley before World
War Two.[46] Tōson interviewed him and used his book on the history of loyalist thought for *Before the Dawn*.[47] I owe him an extraordinary debt for having published and preserved Taseko's work, interviewed her children and
grandchildren, and depicted in so many ways the culture of the Ina Valley in
the early nineteenth century. At the same time, I wish he had done more.
Living with her descendants, he had no need to describe her daily routine,
and he paid no attention to the household economy that sustained her intellectual life. He also had no wish to embarrass anyone by digging up old
scandals. Exposing one's relatives means exposing one's self, at least according to Esashi Akiko, and Minato was nothing if not discreet.[48] He was interested in Taseko not as a woman but as a patriot who brought fame to his
valley. For that reason many of the questions I would have asked were left
unspoken. Furthermore, his own commitment to the emperor system of
prewar Japan meant that h e always saw Taseko in its terms. For the purposes
of my project, his work thus constitutes both a bridge and a barrier.

The pride of place that informs Minato's work and that of other local historians is different than the motivations of a scholar from outside. In her land-
mark study of how the Ina Valley went from a thriving manufacturing center
and transportation network in the eighteenth and early nineteenth centuries
to a political and economic backwater by 1920, Kären Wigen points out that
the historians she consulted refused to admit the extent of the valley's economic decline even in the face of the evidence that they themselves had collected.[49] I have found myself reading Minato's biographies against the grain,
questioning his most vehement assertions, and reinterpreting his conclusions
in the light of my own perspective. I have read widely in local histories and
gone through family archives to supply the economic and social context that
he took for granted. I have tracked down other biographies, especially those
of the women Taseko knew. I suspect that much of what I learned he would
have considered beneath notice. My work is for my time and place, just as his
was for his. I use my materials to offer a new perspective that informs one of
many conceivable accounts of Taseko's life.

Minato always refers to Taseko by her first name, but he usually calls
men by their surname or family name, and in this he follows an almost universal custom: "Jane Austin was sometimes Jane, but John Milton was never
John."[50] Taseko's fellow disciple of the Hirata school and longtime friend
Hazama Hidenori kept a daily account of whom he met on his trips to Kyoto
and Tokyo. Taseko was either Tase or Taseko; men were Morooka, Gonda,
Ikemura, and so forth.[51] Servants and children were, like women, called by

their first names. In Japan the family name comes first, as in Hirata Atsutane, but a woman's claim to it is contingent. For most of her life, Taseko went by the name Takemura, the designation for her natal house. In the Meiji period, 1868–1912, the state decreed that married women take their husband's names, in clear distinction to earlier practice, and for that reason biographies of Taseko are always titled Matsuo Taseko. Rather than call her either Take-mura or Matsuo, I plan to refer to men by their first name as well, even though I am certain it will jar the sensibilities of many readers knowledgable about Japan. I do so deliberately, for practical reasons in that many of the men I discuss shared a common surname, and for political reasons in the name of equality.

In writing a biography of Taseko I am defining achievement according to the male, public world, but it is in this world that Taseko herself sought recognition.[52] All too often the definition of the exceptional woman is one capable of a type of political behavior most often practiced by men. Taseko's intent was of a rationality men can understand, unlike the female founders of new religions who gained the power to speak publicly only when possessed by a god. According to Carolyn Heilbrun, "woman's selfhood, the right to her own story, depends upon her ability to act in the public domain." Women who do not are "deprived of the narratives, or the texts, plots, or examples, by which they might assume power over—take control of—their own lives."[53] They remain anonymous, denied the chance to be heard outside the intimate space of the domestic realm. It is nevertheless important not to end up with a derivative history built from male modeling that obfuscates what Taseko as a woman actually did or the obstacles that women, not men, have to overcome. Sidonie Smith has argued that if a woman "presumes to claim a fully human identity by seeking a place in the public arena, she transgresses patriarchal definitions of female nature by enacting the scenario of male selfhood."[54] It is because Taseko went to Kyoto in that autumn of 1862 that she has become the subject of biography, but what she did and what she said did not simply replicate what men did and said. By creating a public self she, not they, risked a loss of reputation, risked the distinction of becoming unfeminine.

Out of the materials given her by the chaotic events leading up to the Meiji Restoration, Taseko remade an ordinary life with its lack of outwardly dramatic incident into an eccentric story, she insinuated its lines into the lives of male actors and in so doing she crafted an identity other than the one submerged in marriage. In some ways she acted as heroically as men such as Sakamoto Ryōma, for she had to overcome the constraints not only of class but gender as well. She had a much smaller impact on political events than he did, but that was for lack of opportunity. At a time when political action was monopolized by men, her unconventional usurpation of the male prerogative is not to be denied. And, as Nancy K. Miller has said, "to justify an unorthodox life by writing about it is to reinscribe the original violation, to reviolate masculine turf."[55] In the sense both of who has been written about and who has done the writing, at least within the English speaking world, the Meiji Restoration has constituted masculine turf.[56] Let us now proceed to violate it.

PART ONE   *Life in the Ina Valley*

CHAPTER ONE

The Making of a Poet

Mourning for Kitahara Yorinobu who died in 1862:
At the window for education
in our village
I remember the words you spoke,
"Look, there's the place."
MATSUO TASEKO [1]

On the twenty-fifth day of the fifth month of 1811, Takemura
Sachi gave birth to a girl named Taseko.[2] It was the rainy season, with the heat of summer soon to follow, but in the village
of Yamamoto south of Iida in the Ina Valley, the nights remained cool. Sachi was thirty-eight. Her husband, Tsunemitsu, then forty years old, had been adopted to succeed her
father as head of the household. Taseko had only one sibling,
a brother born seven years earlier. Taseko's grandmother was
already dead, and her grandfather died when she was four.
She thus spent most of her childhood in a family smaller than
was typical of the peasant households for her time.[3]

In 1811 the shogun was still Tokugawa Ienari, who reigned
for fifty years until 1837 and fathered fifty-five children. A
few days before Taseko was born, a crew from a Russian ship
landed on an island off the coast of Hokkaido and stole provi-

sions from a village. To retaliate, the Japanese captured the ship's Russian captain, Lieutenant Commander Vasilii Golovnin, and held him for over two years before exchanging him for a Japanese merchant who had been trapped by the Russians. In 1817, 1818, and 1822, British ships came to Uraga near the shogun's capital of Edo, and his government, the bakufu, began planning defensive measures by fortifying the coast.[4] Only vague rumors penetrated the countryside, however. For Taseko, the implications of these encounters would not become apparent for many years. Of more immediate significance for her as a child and young married woman was the social and cultural milieu of the Ina Valley.

The social order in Taseko's day was predicated on hereditary social inequality. The samurai rulers lived in cities, and they expected merchants and artisans to live there too. The countryside was the sole preserve of the peasants, whose function was defined as the production of life's basic necessities, mainly food and preferably rice. Despite a trend for poor peasants to sneak off to cities in search of better employment opportunities and young men or women to work outside their villages for a few years before marrying, the military elite officially forbade people moving from one occupation to another or from one locality to another through a system of population registers and village laws.[5] You were what your parents were. No matter how wealthy a family in the countryside might become (and Taseko's family was wealthy by the standards of the time), it could never deny its peasant roots, and neither its men nor its women ever completely escaped taking a turn in the fields. The rulers expected village headmen to know how to read directives and calculate taxes, but did not take responsibility for teaching them. In education as in so many other areas, the peasants were on their own.

The Ina Valley generally saw adequate harvests, and the mountains supplied raw materials for handicrafts and cottage industries. Trains of packhorses passed through Yamamoto carrying local products to the castle town of Iida and from Iida to markets in the major cities of Nagoya, Kyoto, and Osaka. In the village adjacent to Yamamoto a small government office attracted visitors from across the valley. Inns and a flourishing row of shops sold them regional specialties and daily necessities. A thriving (if tiny) red light district provided entertainment.[6]

Taseko grew up during a time of peace and prosperity. The village elite, of whom Taseko was one, enjoyed a standard of living that would have amazed their ancestors, despite conflicts with tenant farmers and other villagers over rents and tax assessments. Under-employed and ill-paid samurai railed against the luxurious ways of city merchants and wealthy peasants.

The period of her youth is known by the era name of "Bunka-Bunsei" (1804–1829), which may be translated as "becoming cultured" and "civi-

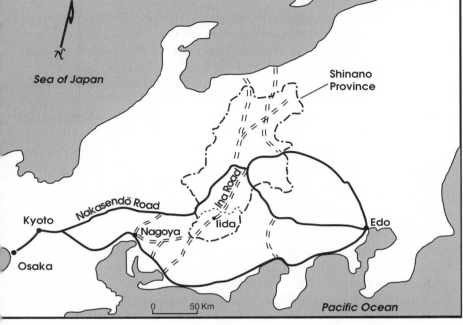

Map 1. Central Japan, 18th - 19th centuries, showing principal transport routes.

———————— Official highways   –·——·– Shinano Provincial boundary

= = = = Major private packhorse routes   ·········· Shimoina county boundary

lized rule"—appropriate titles for an age known for the florescence of literary arts. What is more, these arts spread from the urban setting hitherto their home to the countryside, sinking roots in mass culture and being nourished by it in turn.[7] Writers and artists of all sorts discovered that castle town merchants and even rural entrepreneurs were willing to pay for instruction and performances. It was said that Iida, not far from Taseko's birthplace, was the sole city in the mountain province of Shinano where traveling kabuki troupes could be assured of a two-day stay.[8] In the 1830s, local boosters paid one thousand *ryō* for performances by the Edo kabuki actor Ichikawa Danjūrō, who played to full houses for over ten nights.[9]

Learning to read and write put Taseko among the 10 to 15 percent of women who achieved literacy in the early nineteenth century. She gained not only a social skill that widened her horizons, but also opportunities to reinvent herself in ways ignored by previous biographers intent on confining her within the mold of the model housewife. She most probably began learning these skills as a child. (One of her friends from late in her life, Miwada Masako, claimed that as a young girl she loved to read romances.[10]) Both of her parents were literate, and the Takemura family owned a great many volumes in both Chinese and Japanese—so many that they filled two floors at the back of the storehouse. In one account it is said that her father disapproved of scholarship for women. He scolded Taseko when he found her engrossed in books and snatched them from her. Another anecdote relates how the Takemura's library was forbidden to all but the master of the house. Once when he visited it, he saw signs that someone else had been pulling books out at random, and then he found Taseko, reading away in a corner. She was munching parched beans rather than waste time with meals and even with her father towering over her, she could not take her eyes off the page. Her Takemura descendants claimed that as a child she much preferred her books to sewing or having fun. She was not terribly particular about housework so long as it got done quickly enough to give her time to read.[11]

This snapshot of Taseko says more about the conventions of early life for a poetry prodigy than what Taseko actually did, but it is the only anecdote that recalls her childhood. Starting at age eleven, she went to her father's relatives in the Kitahara household to further her education. It was not uncommon for children to be farmed out to other families before they were married, either to apprentice themselves to a trade or to learn self-discipline away from the indulgent eyes of parents. Spending part of each year away from home gave them the opportunity to build character and learn new skills. As the Takemura's first born daughter, being well-educated in the subjects appropriate for a woman would have enhanced Taseko's value in the marriage market and her family's prestige vis-à-vis its neighbors.

Taseko's education at the Kitahara's included household management, sericulture, etiquette, and deportment under the watchful eye of Kiso, her cousin's wife. Every night she sat down to spin with the women, and she was not allowed to stop until she had turned an entire bundle of cotton into thread. She most probably learned how to weave cotton as well, for most farm households produced all the cloth they needed for daily wear. The sewing techniques she acquired stood her in good stead for the rest of her life. Like all housewives of her time, not only did she make every item of clothing worn by herself and her family, she would also take it apart before washing it, dry each piece smooth on a board and then sew it back together.

In the course of learning basic domestic skills, Taseko showed herself to be frank, stubborn, and shrewd. One evening early in the new year all the women were gathered together, and Isa, Kiso's mother-in-law, wanted a massage. Each took her turn giving her one except for Taseko, who continued to doze by the fire. "She's lazy," scolded Isa, and she certainly showed a lack of deference for the aged. Ichimura Minato, the biographer who heard this story, excused her behavior by saying, "she cared nothing for trifling details and always did what she thought best." [12]

Taseko studied reading, writing, and poetry through the guidance of Kiso's husband Yorinobu. Fortunately for her, he had wide-ranging interests in the natural sciences as well as Japanese and Chinese poetry. He had a particular fondness for geography and astronomy and colored his own map of the world which he hung where his students could always see it. He taught 111 pupils over the course of a lifetime otherwise devoted to serving as a village official, erecting levees against flooding by the Tenryū River, and digging wells. In 1849 his students donated a large picture of a horse in his honor at a local temple. Taseko, then married and thirty-eight years old, was one of twenty-nine women who helped pay for it.[13] Yorinobu's mother Isa wrote classical poetry and exchanged poems with the literati who visited their house. His father had liked haiku, having written several thousand couplets by the time he died.[14] Yorinobu followed his father in fancying himself a haiku poet as well as a devotee of classical poetry. A conscientious village official with a ribald sense of humor, he composed the following poem for a party at which Taseko was present in 1853 (*momo* means both peach and crotch):

Mukutsukeki	That lewd shape
onna sugata ya	of a woman—
momo no hana	peach / crotch blossoms.[15]

Taseko's schooling was informal and ongoing, much of it the catch-as-catch-can variety. Her book learning most likely began before she started spending the winters at the Kitahara's, and her pursuit of poetry continued after she married in 1829. Men and women in Tokugawa Japan had quite different capabilities when it came to reading and writing, or so it was assumed. Most women seldom used more than a handful of Chinese characters because they weighted down the paper in a way considered to be unfeminine. Taseko never wrote more than a few hundred in her letters, poems, and diaries. Judging from the texts she read, she must have learned to recognize several thousand over the years. She knew arithmetic, although no evidence remains for how she used it in her daily life. The contours of her education followed no set curriculum, encompassed no specified body of materials. From the vantage point of the present, it is not possible to say what she learned in her teens and what she learned later.

Taseko did not grow up to be a beauty. Her biographers have noted that her

FIGURE 1. Matsuo Taseko in old age. Portrait by Gekko, an itinerant painter from Nagoya. Courtesy of Matsuo Yūzō.

complexion was dark, and her face was round, not oval. She had a high forehead, long curved eyebrows, and small, bright eyes. Her nose was shapely above an unremarkable mouth. She was tall for a woman of her day and large boned.[16] In short, she was more sturdy than delicate. From her portrait it would appear that what made her attractive was the smile at the corners of her eyes, and the eyes themselves, lively and intelligent. No peasant with any regard for his family's future wanted a wife who was too beautiful. Such women were assumed to be flighty and extravagant. As Yorinobu's son was later to point out, it was better for a wife to be clever.[17]

Taseko was brought up to ornament her mind rather than her body. In an age when sumptuary laws forbade luxurious fabrics and fancy jewelry to all but the most exalted members of the society, education replaced material possessions as markers of the family's position in society. The samurai in the ruling class might use a reputation for erudition to improve their chance of advancement.[18] Merchants and farmers involved in the commercial economy needed practical knowledge in accounting. For wealthy peasants, scholarship became an activity the government could neither tax nor seize.[19] As early as the mid-sixteenth century Luis Frois pointed out that in contrast to the Europe of his day, "a noble woman of Japan without the ability to write would lose status."[20] By Taseko's time, this statement could well have been made about women in the families of rural entrepreneurs. Taseko never had the opportunity for an advanced course of study in medicine or the natural sciences. Instead she developed an interest in a subject that had already captured the hearts and minds of many local intellectuals in the Ina Valley— classical poetry.

TASEKO'S BACKGROUND had well prepared her for her life as a poet. She came from a line of locally notable writers, at least on her mother's side. The most famous was her great-grandmother Sakurai Chie, born in 1724 to a samurai family who later resided in Yamamoto. While Chie was still in her teens, she and her father took a trip to Kyoto where she studied with a number of well-known poets. Her siblings having died young, her father married her to the son he had adopted as his successor. She had twelve children before her husband died in 1785. Her eldest daughter Michi married Takemura Kiyomitsu and became Taseko's grandmother. Once freed from household chores by her grandson's marriage (her son having died young), Chie went back and forth to Edo, studying with one of the leading poets of the time and passing on what she had learned to the wives of the daimyo. In an essay on Ina Valley poets, the daimyo for Iida praised her skill. Back in Yamamoto she and her grandson hosted poetry meetings that might last several days. Chie died in 1813, two years after Taseko was born, but many of the men and women who counted themselves her disciples remained in and around Yamamoto.[21] When Taseko married, she took one of her great-grandmother's scrolls to hang in her new home.

By writing in the style of classical poetry (*waka*), rural entrepreneurs aspired to standards of cultural refinement far removed from everyday village life. In contrast to the seventeen-syllable haiku with its distinctly plebeian cast, the thirty-one syllable waka produced within the confines of the imperial court exuded an unmistakably rarefied aura. Samurai and merchants too acquired polish by participating in this common national pastime, which was dominated by aristocratic canons of taste and held culturally in thrall by the Heian past of the tenth century.[22] It was a badge of status. For the rural entrepreneurs, a knowledge of classical poetry mitigated the status gap between them and their political superiors, distinguished them from the ordinary peasants who lacked their advantages of education and economic resources, and provided a common bond with other families engaged in similar activities. Because female poets had participated in creating this genre, its practice enabled later women to overcome gendered imbalances in the acquisition of social and political capital and gave them a voice within the elite circles of rural society.

The conventions of classical poetry were more difficult to master than those for haiku, but they provided Taseko with a correspondingly greater standing in the eyes of her friends and neighbors. Up to the early eighteenth century, the specialized knowledge required to appreciate the poems found in the court anthologies of the tenth through the fourteenth centuries had remained the private preserve of various aristocratic families, and their monopoly tended to increase its value. "The aristocrats did not see it as constituting the avenue to a national literature. Instead it belonged to them because their ancestors had written it."[23] The great nativist scholar Motoori Norinaga criticized the aristocrats for trying to keep it a secret; Sakurai Chie utilized the "complicity between the 'cultural' and 'economic' currencies" when she used her wealth to buy an education in poetry writing.[24]

To display cultural competence in writing classical poetry, Taseko needed first of all a familiarity with the lexicon derived from the first three court anthologies beginning with the *Kokinshū* compiled in 905. She also had to learn classical grammar, including particles and agglutinative auxiliary verbs that gave poems their emotional force and the rules governing the use of the syllabary.[25] Finally she had to have a thorough knowledge of the classical poems themselves, including those in the *Shinkokinshū*, which was compiled in 1206 and is usually acclaimed as the greatest of the anthologies.

No poem was worth writing if it did not draw on at least one previous poem and often more, not just in terms of material and phrasing, "but to raise the atmosphere—something of the situation, the tone and the meaning—of the original."[26] Even a text as early as *The Tale of Genji* was "saturated with fragmentary quotations from other poems,"[27] and nineteenth-century poems were mostly pastiche. Of course both the writer and reader had to have memorized enough poetry to make the pastiche recognizable. Literary reverberations served to create an ongoing dialogue with the past, to "enhance and enrich the poems with the kind of resonance that a 'brand new poem' cannot hope to create within the small confines of *waka*."[28] They also had an immediate social purpose. The poetry produced by the rural entrepreneurs made sense only to people who possessed "the cultural competence, that is, the code into which it is encoded." [29] No ordinary peasant and few women could afford the enormous investment of time and energy required to acquire this competence, that is, to master the diction, grammar, and examples of classical styles necessary to know before composing or appreciating a single poem.

It is possible that one of Taseko's early teachers was her cousin Sakurai Haruki, Chie's great-grandson and heir to the Sakurai house. In 1810 he went to Kyoto where he joined the school of Kagawa Kageki, a talented teacher and one of the leading poets of his day. Kageki taught a classicism rooted in the first of the imperially commissioned anthologies, the *Kokinshū*. Despite his desire to infuse poetry with natural emotion, he believed that both diction and theme "should adhere to an essentially closed artistic canon, one that relied strictly on precedent." [30] Haruki's attempt to learn poetry writing in the appropriate classical style met with scant recognition. Takabatake Shikibu, a Kageki disciple who befriended Taseko in Kyoto in 1862, was one of several women listed in the "Maegashira" class just below the top three classes in a 1839 sumo-style ranking of Kyoto-based poets, but Haruki made it no further than helper (*sewa yaku*). He is excluded from a list of Kageki's most important disciples that was compiled in the twentieth century. [31] After his father had squandered the family's fortune on donating the paving stones between the Kaminari gate and the temple at Asakusa in Edo, Haruki left the Ina Valley for Edo, never to return. Before his departure in the 1840s, however, he had established himself as a notable local poet. [32] Taseko often wrote variations on poems from the *Kokinshū*, and the most likely way for her to have studied this anthology was with her cousin. [33]

Taseko had few opportunities for instruction in a subject so recondite as classical poetry. Unlike her great-grandmother, she had no chance to study in Kyoto before her marriage at age eighteen. The itinerant teachers who came through the Ina Valley in the early nineteenth century met only samurai administrators in Iida and a few commoners with strong ties to the ruling class as government purveyors. The masters from afar lectured on poetry, officiated at poetry meetings, and corrected the poems presented by the locals. In return they allowed themselves to be entertained at boating and flower viewing parties where the sake flowed freely. Starved for erudition, the samurai, merchants, monks, doctors, and wealthy entrepreneurs from the nearby villages flocked to meet them. One such aspirant was Fukuzumi Kiyokaze. Having heard what various proponents of the schools fighting for supremacy in Kyoto and Edo had to say, he developed his own opinions on what constituted a proper poem and passed these on to his disciples. He reserved his strongest invectives for Sakurai Haruki's teacher Kagawa Kageki,

FIGURE 2. Fukuzumi Kiyokaze with the shaven pate of a Buddhist monk. From *Ina sonnō shisō shi*, opposite page 106.

calling his poems "unbearable," "unsuitable," "irritating," and "commonplace." [34]

Kiyokaze became the crucial link between Taseko and the classical tradition transmitted by itinerant poets. Born in 1778, he was adopted by an apothecary in Iida who also lent books, served as ward elder, and purveyed medicine to the daimyo. His father and grandfather taught him poetry, his grandfather having been friends with Sakurai Chie, and he honed his skills by meeting every poet who came through the Ina Valley as well as devoting long hours to the study of poetry on his own. He often visited the Matsuo house, sometimes staying for days at a time and always talking with Taseko about poetry. "Buddhism discourses on the three worlds to guide people," he wrote on a portrait of himself. "Confucianism sets up the five virtues to teach people. Only in our country is there no teaching; our only way is that of poetry. Through poetry we come to know the pathos of things and expose our emotions. Those who understand this well should be able to rule the realm." [35] Classical poetry was predicated on an unresolved conflict between the spontaneous expression of feeling and the civilizing program. Whereas in China this program and the poetry that embodied it tended to be moral and regulatory, in Japan the court aristocracy best symbolized the process of refinement and the program relied more on taste.[36] Kiyokaze put great store by form, and he was quite particular when it came to grammar and the use of the syllabary. "There are some words that you should hesitate to employ," he wrote in a handbook for his disciples. "The *Man'yōshū* and the *Kokinshū* contain words you may use and words you should not lest your poetry sound vulgar. Of all the imperial anthologies, none can compare to the *Shinkokinshū* in beauty and elegance."[37] It is no wonder that he quarreled with Sakurai Haruki.

In the traditional Japanese arts, practitioners affiliated themselves with a single school, and the choice of teacher then determined the form and content of their practice. In tea ceremony, for example, such is still the case today. Taseko studied with Kiyokaze and wrote many poems in the *Shinkokin* style. Despite his tirades against other anthologies and teachers, however, she never confined herself to his school. In the fluid world of early nineteenth century poetry circles, the relations between teacher and pupil were not so restrictive as they had been earlier, making it easier for a poet to move from one teacher to another and to choose from a variety of different styles.[38] Even within the circumscribed world of the Ina Valley, a number of teachers (all male after Chie's death) competed for disciples. The poems that Taseko wrote as a young married woman in her twenties and thirties drew on a variety of texts. She had wide ranging interests within the confines of the form, and she made her own choices when it came to writing poetry, freely mixing snatches of poems that represented separate literary movements. To the end of her life she continued to allude to the different traditions associated with the court anthologies and other texts as well. Her voice was never so distinctive as modern poets who strive self-consciously for individuality, but neither did it simply reflect whichever teacher happened to come her way.

Writing poetry opened up Taseko's social world. Poetry meetings and the circulation of poems enabled her to strengthen her connections with her relatives in places as far away as Nakatsugawa on the other side of the Kiso range and meet people, primarily men in nearby villages, who shared her interest in poetry. Some, such as Ōhara Kagehiro (born in 1836), were much younger than herself, and others such as the Katagiri brothers were her contemporaries.[39] Through Kiyokaze she met Hara Mayomi from Seinaiji, a man with whom she remained friends until his death. The pursuit of cultural refinement provided an arena where rural entrepreneurs living scattered across the countryside could come together. The space for such activities was governed by its own rules that permitted the suspension of some of the conventions operating in the world outside, including those that kept women absent from the company of men or silenced them in their presence. The court anthologies provided evidence that women had figured prominently in the creation of the poetic tradition, thereby justifying their inclusion in poetry circles and locally produced anthologies. What mattered more than the social construction of normative roles was the ability to write and appreciate classical poetry.

Kiyokaze had beautiful calligraphy and he loved poetry meetings:

Koto no ba no	There's nothing like getting together
makoto no michi wo	at a poetry meeting
fumu hito to	with people who tread
uta no matoi ni	the true path
tsudoite shika na	of composing song.[40]

For the new year's poetry meeting of 1846 that he held at the Kitahara house, the alcove in the formal sitting room was decorated with a portrait of Hitomaro, Japan's great poet from the seventh century. In front of the portrait was a reading stand and beside it, a stack of poem cards. The first topic of the day, "plum blossoms," had been sent to the guests in advance. Upon entering the room they came forward one by one, examined the portrait, placed their poem on the reading stand, took a fresh poem card and found their seat. When everyone had arrived, they arranged their writing supplies in front of them and waited for the next topic to be given out. This was "the snow goose." Each wrote two poems that she then brought to Kiyokaze to be corrected before returning to her seat to wait quietly for a reading of all the poems by Kiyokaze and his two chief disciples.[41] The record does not say, but surely this solemnity was followed by a little sake!

After her marriage, Taseko was a frequent participant at the poetry meetings held by her Kitahara relatives. Her cousin Inao celebrated her presence one year with a poem patterned closely after a *Kokinshū* poem, "my beloved friends / tearing myself away from / your company this / evening is painful as / rending fine Chinese brocade":[42]

Omoudochi	My beloved friend
matoi suru hi wo	the days when we get together
aya niku ni	and you can join our number
taranu wa kimi ga	are unfortunately
kasu ni zo arikeru	not nearly enough.[43]

Taseko herself wrote any number of poems for these poetry meetings and also many more expressing her regret at having had to miss them for one reason or another. She blamed her absences on hindrances (*sawari*), a term that covers everything from an impassable river to family responsibilities to menstruation. One letter aired her envy of those who had participated, but raising silkworms had kept her too busy to attend.[44] "I have been collecting the poems abandoned at our regular meetings and tried two or three of them with the tip of my brush," her neighbor Katagiri Yukitomo once wrote after she had missed a gathering. "Please allow me to add some of your rare and unusual poems."[45]

Like Yukitomo, Kiyokaze collected poems written by others. As a culmination to his years of teaching, he edited a poetry anthology of his disciples' work. Seventy-five people contributed to this project, eight from Nakatsugawa and the rest from the Ina Valley. Among their number was Taseko with a poem titled "a love lodged in snow":

Ato wo dani	Even though it is just a trace
kesa wa katami no	this morning I saw it as
miru mono wo	a lover's keepsake,
hi kage sasu nari	the white snow in the garden
niwa no shirayuki	already lit with sunlight.[46]

Kiyokaze probably saw fit to include this poem because the first and last lines can be identified with two different poems in the *Shinkokinshū*. The lines in the middle appear in any number of different anthologies, so much so that the poem's only originality lies in their selection and arrangement. This jumble of allusions does not so much layer the poem with resonances to other works that contribute to a larger meaning as it juxtaposes different moods and images. For example, the first line repeats the first line of a poem by Izumi Shikibu mourning that a connection so recently consummated has left nothing but a trace on the grass.[47] By itself, it provides a nicely complementary set of circumstances for Taseko's poem. The last line is also the last line of a poem by the Buddhist priest Jakuren describing how the snow has piled so deeply in his garden that no one comes to visit.[48] Taking a line from one poem and putting it into another poem that reversed the meaning of the first was a standard poetic tactic that added layers of complication through negation. Taseko later revised the poem by changing the last line to "thin snow." Doing so replaced the allusion to the *Shinkokinshū* with an emphasis on the imagery of traces soon to vanish like love itself.[49] For a collection edited by Kiyokaze, however, it was better to use phrases hallowed by association with the most perfect of the court anthologies than to strive for coherence.[50]

Kiyokaze could have selected one of Taseko's many poems written on the changing seasons, another important category in the classical court anthologies. Instead he chose a poem written from the point of view of a woman whose lover has just left after spending a clandestine night of passion. This kind of relationship was typical of the court aristocrats of the Heian period, but not the wealthy peasants who were Kiyokaze's clients.

In the aestheticized world created by Kiyokaze, it was perfectly appropriate for Taseko to escape her role as wife and mother by imagining herself in love with a man not her husband. She even wrote poems to her friends that played at seduction. "When I paid a visit to Yamamoto in the second month, I sent this poem to Mayomi in Seinaiji:"

Sugi tateru	Even if there is no gate
kado naranaku mo	where the cedar stands
Yamamoto ni	in Yamamoto at the foot of the mountain
kimi wo matsu koto	a woman awaits her lover
imo wo matsu koto	a man awaits his lover.[51]

Mayomi had so thoroughly memorized the *Shinkokinshū* that if anyone recited the first five syllables from any of its 1,980 poems, he could immediately respond with the next seven. To lure him to her, however, Taseko used a different text. The first line and a half and the word *yama moto*, which literally means "the base of a mountain," come from a poem in the *Kokinshū* inviting a friend to pay a visit to "the gate where the cedars stand."[52] The poem is clearly an inducement for Mayomi to come write poetry with Taseko while she was visiting her parents and while her husband, presumably, stayed in Tomono. Despite the tenor of the poem, it is not necessarily an invitation to make love.

Taseko had more space to explore relationships with different men both figuratively and literally than is commonly assumed for women in early modern Japan. Each of her poetry collections contains poems clearly labeled "love," "to my beloved," "the morning after," "clandestine love," and "rejected love." I do not want to suggest that she had a lover. Many of her poems were written on topics decided by Kiyokaze, and he assigned them because each classical court anthology devoted many chapters to love. Not just the composition of poetry but the quality of the experience itself was a staged event even though the very ideal of "the poetic," implying something spontaneous as the guarantor of the genuine, ran at cross-purposes with the idea of staging. To feel genuine emotion depended upon the poet's ability to generate selves suitable for each and every poetic occasion, that is, to conjure up multiple personalities. Within the narrow confines of conventions established nine hundred years earlier, the practice of poetry allowed Taseko the opportunity to experiment in her mind with identities other than that which she had been assigned by her station in life.

Taseko followed the example of the ancient courtiers, who loved best when the object of desire was absent or about to become so. Little better captured the keen appreciation for the transience of the moment that defined the aristocratic cult of sensibility than the poignancy of parting and the uncertainty of ever meeting again. She was thus allowed to experience a mood and a set of emotions once the property of the nobility. By selecting and mingling phrases from various court anthologies, she could put herself in their place, and this she did over and over again. One verse titled simply, "written on the topic of love" (*koi no uta tote*) drew on a technique found in the *Kokinshū* of extending the meaning of a poem through a series of double entendres.

In this poem, allusion is made to how the pattern woven into mats resembled waves (*nami*). The first syllable for that word can stand for "not" (*nashi*). To refrain from (*inamu*) is also the first part of the word for mat (*inamushiro*). The first line about an expected meeting that had not come to pass comes from the *Kokinshū*. The oldest of the poetry anthologies, the *Man'yōshū*, provided the rice sleeping mat spread by a man wishing he did not have to sleep alone on his travels, and the *Shinkokinshū* supplied the imagery of dewy tears:

Au koto wo	Why do you refrain from making love to me
nado inamushiro	because we didn't put our sleeping mats
	together last night
kawasaneba	those woven mats that look like waves,
hiruma namida no	the tears on my dewy sleeve that I used for
	a pillow
tsuyu no tamakura	haven't yet had time to dry.[53]

This poem fits squarely within the received tradition of women writing poetry to reproach a lover for failing to come. Poems like this say nothing about the "facts" of Taseko's relationships with other men; she was addressing not a flesh and blood referent but the classical tradition. They nevertheless expose the kind of affairs that she staged in her imagination.

The emphasis on her presence in contrast to her lover's absence, and her passion in contrast to his coldness, constitutes a recurring motif in Taseko's poetry. For this next poem she begins with a line from a *Shinkokinshū* poem entitled "clandestine love:" "Vanish completely / like the clouds that hang upon Mt. Shinobu's peak / endure until this yearning heart / is gone without a trace."[54] Composed by a male courtier for a poetry writing contest in

1202, it refers only obliquely to the pain of unrequited love. While not as physically direct as a modern reader might expect, Taseko's poem is still more passionate than its model:

Kiene tada	Just vanish completely
tsurenaki hito wa	why should I burn inside
shiranu hi no	with a secret fire consuming my heart
kokoro zukushi ni	if that cold-hearted man
nani ka moyu beki	doesn't know anything about it.[55]

This poem is full of negatives: the feelings that would not die, the unfeeling lover, and the hidden fire. Taseko used these images to describe a secret passion even though she included the poem in an anthology meant to be shown to others.

In her poetry, Taseko crafted the identity not of a faithful wife but of a passionate if often spurned lover. The following poem, titled "love despite being unable to make love" contains phrases drawn from classical poetry that point to a particularly titillating concatenation of circumstances. In it Taseko alludes to a famous poem from the Buddhist section of the *Shinkokinshū* titled "an injunction against illicit relationships." "Heavy enough / are your sleeping garments / without the weight / of another evening robe / from someone not your wife!"[56] By the eighteenth century the specific term for nightclothes used in this poem had come to imply a woman who committed adultery. Taseko's poem borrows not only this term but also the verb, "to lie on top of each other."

Kaku bakari	Would my sleeves
sode ya shioren	be so completely drenched
sayogoromo	were it that time before
kasanenu saki no	when our evening robes
hedate nariseba	had not yet lain on top of each other?[57]

Taseko must have known the implications of the poem to which she alluded so clearly. It is hard to escape the conclusion that she was confessing to adultery.

The affair (or affairs) glimpsed in these poems were most likely a complete fantasy. Stimulated by her studies in the classical poetry tradition and encouraged by her teachers to establish an intuitive empathy with the feelings expressed in the poems of antiquity, Taseko created one of the types of poetic persona available to the women of her time and thought herself into a place and time far distant from her own. By capturing a piece of a past known only through literature she placed herself in a situation scandalous in her own day, yet without suffering any consequences. Through reading and writing poetry, she thus produced a personal space in an imaginary world that gave her a chance to fashion an identity, to craft a self and a subjectivity, and to explore its ramifications and permutations. While she went about her everyday tasks, in her life of the mind she experienced the emotional intensity of heartbreak and the secret thrills of illicit love. As Anne Allison has pointed out, subjectivities depend on the social setting. Not all are equally encouraged and rewarded, or, in the case of a historical personage like Taseko, remembered.[58]

AS A WOMAN Taseko had to overcome considerable obstacles in her pursuit of poetry, but they were not necessarily the same as those faced by young women desiring an education today. Her chief problem was a lack of instructors and texts. After Kiyokaze died in 1848, when she was thirty-seven, she and her friends had no one to call teacher. They circulated poems for correction among themselves—Taseko appears to have gotten as many requests to critique them as anyone else—and they were always on the lookout for a good instructor. For a time Taseko studied through a correspondence with Ishikawa Yorihira, a minor poet who lived in Kakegawa in Tōtomi, and introduced her husband's brother to him.[59] Yorihira arranged for them to send their poems with pilgrims going to the Akiha shrine, where they would be left until another pilgrim came along who was going to Kakegawa. His replies followed the same route. "I beg of you most earnestly please to keep sending me your poems in order for me to respond to your feelings that have such grace and refinement to them," Yorihira wrote. "Please read this realizing just how deeply I've been moved. . . . There's something else I want to say. I'm delighted with the cotton padding you sent me now that the weather has gotten so cold. My wife too would like to convey her greetings. Please give my regards to the person with whom you share your heart."[60]

Books of poetry were few and expensive and had to come from Kyoto or Edo. Little was published in Shinano aside from a few sheets of haiku, medical texts, histories of temples, stories of battles, and maps.[61] The Matsuo family library contained a number of imperially commissioned poetry anthologies as well as books today considered part of the literary canon such as *The Pillow Book* and *The Tale of Genji*. Surely Taseko read them, else how would she have been able to allude to them in her poetry?[62] She kept an introduction to writing poetry (*Shogaku wakashiki*) and a compendium of poems from the imperial court (*Waka kuretakeshū*) as well as other poetry collections next to her desk.[63] About the time her eldest son married, she acquired a commentary on *The Tale of Genji*. According to one anecdote, she happily sold her dowry to buy it—a depiction of her thirst for knowledge that says more about the way she is remembered than her finances.[64] Costly though books were, this work would not have cost more than a few *ryō*, a sum well within Taseko's grasp. The equivalent of several months wages for a day laborer, it would have been unthinkable for most peasants. (By way of comparison, an eighty-dollar book today would take less than three days to earn at minimum wage.)

One way for Taseko to get books was to borrow them from her cousins in the Kitahara house. According to a ledger Inao made of the books he lent beginning in 1849, she borrowed six books on poetry in a two-year period, including both volumes of *Tales of Ise*, a collection of stories related to Ariwara Narihira, the great ninth-century aristocratic poet and lover. *Tales of Ise* could be read as "a handbook for poets, one that demonstrates better than any other the attitudes and occasions that should inspire poetry, and the manner in which poems should be written." [65] Taseko also borrowed a book of poetry compiled in 1847 titled "One hundred poems by one hundred virtuous women" (*Retsujo hyakunin isshū*). Each poem comes complete with a brief biographical sketch containing some Chinese characters with the readings glossed on the side that explain why the woman is noteworthy. The women range from Heguri no Chisato who made sure that her son, the eighth-century diplomat Hironari, always surrounded himself with well-born companions, to Kaji, a late seventeenth-century courtesan from Kyoto's famous Gion district.[66]

Despite her difficulties in getting books and instruction, Taseko managed to acquire the knowledge of Japanese classical literature to write between 1,600 and 1,700 poems over the course of her lifetime. Unlike her great-grandmother Chie, she deliberately collected her poems into a series of anthologies beginning with *Sakakigusa* (Sacred Tree Miscellany), written between her marriage in 1829 and Kiyokaze's death in 1848. Of its hundred poems, twenty-nine explored the topic of love. The last is titled simply, "Poems from 1882 and beyond." She sometimes revised her poems from one collection to another, perhaps changing only a syllable, perhaps an entire phrase. In addition, she wrote poem cards for friends and acquaintances. Particularly in the later years of her life when her activities in the 1860s had brought her a certain measure of renown, she received many visitors who wanted samples of her poetry. For her, classical poetry thus became a lifelong vocation and one source of identity.

Commonly held assumptions about the proper course of study for women apparently did not hinder Taseko so long as she confined herself to *waka*, a poetic form associated with Japaneseness and aristocratic women. Chinese poetry, on the other hand, was long held to be the domain of men. In contrast to the wide range of subjects pursued by her cousin Yorinobu, her own field of scholarly endeavors was extremely limited. Yet the whole notion that a woman might compose poetry as though she had an illicit affair, write a sexy invitation to a man not her husband, go to poetry parties and other gatherings where alcoholic beverages would be served without her husband's company, and explore a set of identities outside her ordinary life as wife and mother is so alien to twentieth-century notions of the Tokugawa period that it is simply ignored. Taseko's poetic pastimes suggest that young commoner wives did not feel the same constraints as samurai women who faced greater pressure to stay indoors, devote themselves solely to their husband's interests, and submerge their desires in their family's welfare, nor did they have to be so careful about who they met, when and where. Her great-grandmother's career suggests that after they had finished raising their children, even some samurai women had considerable leeway to do what they wanted.[67]

The opportunities for Taseko to furnish her mind with book learning should not be exaggerated. Not everyone approved of literacy for women, and educators thought that too much knowledge was dangerous. "It's all right for women to be illiterate," wrote the late-eighteenth-century philosopher and bureaucrat Matsudaira Sadanobu. "For a woman to have knowledge can cause great harm. They don't need learning at all, and it's enough that they can read books in the syllabary."[68] Rural entrepreneurs felt considerable ambivalence when it came to the literary arts. "If you become addicted to Chinese poetry, you might turn into an outlandish foreigner," one village official wrote. "If you take pleasure in reading love poetry, you will start chasing after prostitutes and in any case you will neglect your occupation."[69] When Taseko went to Kyoto in 1862 using her desire to further her studies in poetry as an excuse, a neighbor maligned her thus:

Nyōbō no	It doesn't do
amari uta yomi	for a wife
ikanu mono	to write too much poetry
teishu wo shiri ni	for she'll keep her husband under her butt
Shikishima no michi	to pursue the art of composing verse.[70]

The first two syllables of *Shikishima no michi* (Japanese verse) is a double entendre; it can also mean *to spread* (*shiku*). The line thus translates literally as "she'll spread her buttocks over her husband," or euphemistically as "she'll keep her husband under her thumb." The meaning is clear: as an overly-educated woman, Taseko had reversed the proper relationship between husband and wife within the household.

CHAPTER TWO

Taseko's Political Heritage

The sky dark
with the threat of falling snow
dimly through
the trailing mist
rise mountains near and far.
MATSUO TASEKO, late 1840s[1]

Taseko lived most of her life in the Ina Valley. Carved by the Tenryū River that rises in Lake Suwa, it cuts northwest to southeast through the mountains of central Japan. On the west bank where she was born rice terraces meet the foothills in the Kiso mountain range. There is much less room for paddy fields on the east bank where she spent her years as a married woman because the lower reaches of the Ina range fall practically to the river. Behind them the lofty Akaishi mountains present a formidable barrier in a jagged ridge line that tops ten thousand feet at the peaks. The valley is marked by paddies, hummocks, hills, and plateaus carpeted with verdant green in summer and cut by fast running mountain streams that both provide irrigation and dump quantities of boulders into the river bed. On the largest and most southern of the plateaus stands the castle town of Iida. Thereafter the valley ends abruptly at the Tenryū narrows, a gorge where few ham-

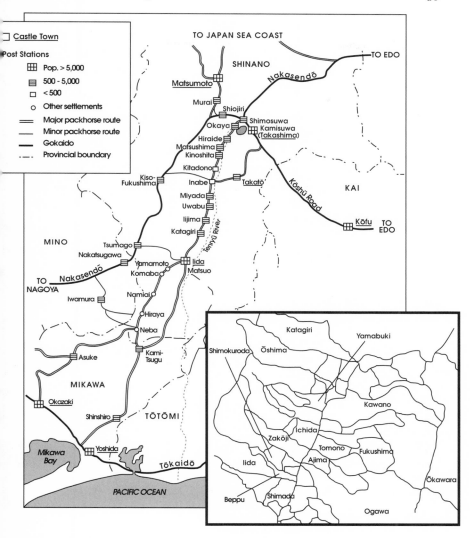

MAP 2. The Ina Valley.

lets perch precariously on the sides of cliffs along the ravines that feed the river. South of Iida travelers would either cross the Kiso range going toward Nakatsugawa or take the narrow Ina Road past the Namiai Barrier, then follow one of its forks to the coastal highway at Toyohashi or Nagoya.

The Ina Valley of today is not what it was in Taseko's time. Yamamoto village where she was born is now a southern suburb of Iida city, its main street crowded with banks and businesses. The fastest way across the mountains is through a thirteen-mile tunnel, the longest on the central expressway that links Nagoya with Lake Suwa and continues on to Tokyo. This expressway carries cars, buses, and trucks above and to the west of the old highway for horses that ran through the center of the valley. Concrete buildings and dams, asphalt roads, and a train line have further changed the texture of the landscape. Even the fields are different. Instead of small odd-shaped plots, the rice paddies have corners and straight edges. Many have been converted to orchards for peaches and apples. In the late 1880s Taseko's grandson started work on a levee that confined the Tenryū River to a channel between banks of stone now reinforced with steel nets and concrete, and rice paddies cover what was once a flood plain. The mountains still rise in their implacable majesty, but their lower slopes have been turned into tree farms. The tiny hamlet of Tomono has been absorbed into the amalgamated village of Toyooka, and local place names like Maizaka (dancing slope), once the subject of Taseko's poetry, remain only a memory:

Maizaka wa	Waves of mist
nami no kasumi no	trail over
tanabikite	Maizaka, the dancing slope
tsuki naki nobe ni	on fields unlit by the moon
matsu kaze zo fuku	the wind blows through the pine.[2]

While Taseko was growing up, the only town she knew of any size was Iida. Despite having fewer than ten thousand inhabitants, it had no competitors to its claim to being the most important political and cultural center in the southern reaches of the valley. Laid out on a street grid in the imperial mode, it gained local fame as "a diminutive Kyoto of the mountains."[3] In 1868 Taseko's friend Iwasaki Nagayo wrote a poem celebrating its beauty:

Yama mireba	Looking at the mountains,
yama iya takaki	the mountains are so high
kawa mireba	looking at the river,
kawa tōshiroshi	the river is vast
. . . . . .	
sumuraku no	A good land
yoroshiki kuni	where living is easy
. . . . . .	
uraguwashi	The town is so beautiful
sato zo ura	it pulls at my heart
guwashi kuni zo	The province pulls at my heart.[4]

In addition to the castle compound for the daimyo and his chief retainers on a narrow plateau overlooking the Tenryū River, Iida contained large and thriving commercial districts, one clustered west of the castle that dealt in commodities both wholesale and retail and one along the Ina Road that dealt in transport. Surrounding the merchant quarters were residential sections for the exclusive use of the samurai.

The Iida castle town took advantage of natural features for its defenses, but it was by no means sealed to outsiders. It contained a number of government offices for other jurisdictions, including one for an intendant who managed the shogun's lands in the Ina Valley. He seldom visited the area, leaving the office to be run by his underlings.[5] A shogunal bannerman (*hatamoto*) by the name of Chimura Heiemon also had an office conveniently located there to manage the lands that he held in trust for the bakufu.[6] In 1868 he called on Taseko for help in getting the imperial government to ratify his credentials. His office manager was Ichioka Masatomo. Masatomo's younger siblings were Onari, who was to join the Hirata school under Taseko's sponsorship, and Tami, who was to become Taseko's daughter-in-law.

In Taseko's day the provincial boundaries for Shinano and the natural barriers in the Ina Valley had little to do with political jurisdictions. In the sixteenth century, one of Japan's great generals Takeda Shingen had demonstrated the difficulty of digging a determined and resourceful military leader out of the natural mountain fortress of central Japan. Realizing that today's friends and relatives may all too easily become tomorrow's enemies, the Tokugawa shoguns planned carefully to avoid a similar situation by dividing the valley's political geography between different domains and different types of domains. Their rulers, the daimyo, might be defined as bakufu allies for having supported the Tokugawa side at the battle of Sekigahara in 1600, or outsiders who had not, or even the shogun's distant relatives, but by the nineteenth century, they had all developed close kinship ties. Their retainers replicated these connections, undercutting what at one time had been discrete political units with overlapping residential patterns and their own web of marital relations and friendship. Bakufu prohibitions to the contrary, they sometimes married the sons and daughters of wealthy peasants, as when Taseko's grandmother Sakurai Michi had married Takemura Kiyomitsu.

The political divisions that carved up the Ina Valley were sometimes important, sometimes irrelevant. For women going about their daily tasks, these divisions could easily be ignored, but for men in their administrative roles, political jurisdictions defined to whom taxes would be paid and to whom to turn for assistance in disputes with neighboring villages. They provided a public identity. Taseko's kin all served as village headmen. They had the opportunity to negotiate with members of the ruling class in their official capacity and to exchange poems and sake cups with them on social occasions. Without official duties to perform, most women had no reason to appear before the authorities unless they were criminals. In this as in other ways, Taseko was to prove an exception.

Born in the Iida domain, Taseko's father was adopted by the Takemura family who lived in a different jurisdiction. Their village of Yamamoto had two overlords. Two-thirds of the village families paid taxes to the Kondō family of bakufu bannermen who had close kinship ties to the daimyo who ruled Iida. The other third paid taxes to the Matsudaira of Takasu, a junior branch of the shogunal relatives headquartered at Nagoya. The Kondō family built a headquarters in Yamamoto in 1754, but with lands generating a putative yield of 5,000 *koku* (1 *koku* equals 5.1 bushels of rice), it had the privilege and the burden of spending half of its time at the shogun's knees in Edo just like the daimyo whose lands were worth over 10,000 *koku*. Taseko once wrote a poem for Masatoshi, the last of his line to rule Yamamoto:

Tsuki hana no	Among the admirable villages
akatsu no sato ni	that you administer
kimi masa wa	first of all for you
Ina no Yamamoto	there should be the fields of
no to ya arenamu	Yamamoto in Ina.[7]

The division of Yamamoto between two different jurisdictions makes it hard to get a fix on either the village size or its population. Some records show its yield at 792 *koku* whereas in others it is listed at 1079 *koku*. In the late eighteenth century the population of that portion of the village controlled by the Takasu family varied between 293 in 1777 and 233 in 1794. Population registers for the rest of the village exist only in fragments. In 1871 the Kondō portion of the village had a population of 600. A number of villages showed population increases in the early nineteenth century, making extrapolation a guessing game, but it would appear that during Taseko's childhood, its total population was around 800 to 900. All population registers show fewer women than men.[8]

To manage its parcels of land scattered throughout the lower Ina Valley, the Kondō relied on the same Sakurai family that Taseko numbered among her ancestors and cousins, including the poet Haruki. With the exception of the Takemura family, the Sakurai married samurai. Haruki's grandson was adopted by Kubota Jirōhachi, who was to buy the position of Kondō intendant when the Sakurai family went bankrupt. Jirōhachi exchanged poems

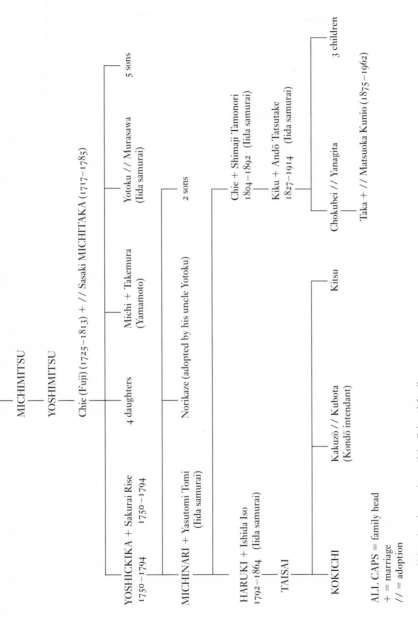

TSUNAYOSHI (died in Iida in 1570)

MICHIMITSU

YOSHIMITSU

Chie (Fuji) (1725–1813) + // Sasaki MICHITAKA (1717–1785)

YOSHICKIKA + Sakurai Rise   4 daughters   Michi + Takemura   Yotoku // Murasawa   5 sons
1750–1794   1750–1794   (Yamamoto)   (Iida samurai)

MICHINARI + Yasutomi Tomi   Norikaze (adopted by his uncle Yotoku)   2 sons
             (Iida samurai)

HARUKI + Ishida Iso (Iida samurai)   Chie + Shimaji Tamonori   (Iida samurai)
1792–1864   1804–1892

TAISAI   Kiku + Andō Tatsutake   (Iida samurai)
                                                                        1827–1914

                 Kakuzō // Kubota   Kiisu   Chokubei // Yanagita   3 children
KOKICHI   (Kondō intendant)
                                                                        Taka + // Matsuoka Kunio (1875–1962)

ALL CAPS = family head
+ = marriage
// = adoption

FIGURE 3.   Abbreviated genealogy of the Sakurai family.

with Taseko, and his son Kenkichi carried news of her to a mutual friend in Ōmi Hachiman in 1865.[9]

Taseko spent her married life under the jurisdiction of the Takasu domain. Founded in 1700 during an expansive period in the history of the Tokugawa rulers of Nagoya, it had a nominal tax base of 30,000 *koku*. Its territories were scattered, however, and much of its income was derived from lands that it held in trust from the bakufu. 15,000 *koku* of its land was in the Ina Valley, split into four parcels interspersed between Iida and bakufu bannerman lands. The headquarters in Takesa, a small hamlet next to Yamamoto, was staffed by village headmen who worked there in rotation. One of them was Taseko's husband. Having been founded late as a branch of a senior domain and holding much of its land only on sufferance from the bakufu, the Matsudaira rulers of Takasu had no castle. They commuted back and forth between their headquarters in Mino and their mansions in Edo along with the other daimyo. Without a clearly defined domain to administer, they preferred Edo. It was to be there that Taseko would meet and discuss politics with the domain lord in 1855.[10]

LAW AND CUSTOM restricted politics to small groups of hereditary officials and administration, even at the village level, to men. No matter how large or small a domain, the daimyo and his leading advisors made policy, which they then disseminated to lower ranking samurai and thence commoners in top-down directives. Scholars have recently demonstrated that these policy makers sometimes simply appropriated proposals by peasants or merchants and passed them off as their own.[11] In the small fiefs ruled by bakufu bannermen, peasants such as Taseko's father and brother took an increasingly prominent part in determining government budgets, blurring the line between ruler and ruled.[12] Ordinary peasant men, on the other hand, had neither the time nor the qualifications for office.

Being a woman, Taseko suffered far greater disabilities. Widows without grown sons might represent their households at village meetings, but they never performed any official function. As the daughter and wife of village headmen, Taseko would have seen her father and husband depart for interviews with their superiors and readied the house for those infrequent occasions when samurai officials visited the countryside. She would have known how burdensome office-holding could be while raising her sons to follow their father. For she herself to have taken a public role, however, was unthinkable. Her only direct contribution to the family tradition of service would have been informal, consisting of aiding the needy with small acts of private charity.

As the daughter and then the wife of a village headman, Taseko took for granted the privileges of her position. The Kitahara family still proudly dis-

FIGURE 4. The Takemura family house before World War Two. From *Matsuo Taseko*, frontispiece.

plays the headman's baton, an iron rod about a foot long draped with a gold silk tassel, that marked his status much like the two swords marked the samurai. The Takemura family used every means in its power to reinforce its position in the status hierarchy. Taseko's father and then her brother rotated as headmen with another branch of the Takemura family between 1805 and 1855. Her brother also served as a salaried employee of the Kondō for ten bags of rice a year. In that capacity he had permission to wear swords and use a surname just as the samurai did. When he visited members of the Kondō family at their headquarters, he was invited to sit below them on the tatami mats that floored their audience room. Surrounded by a wall pierced with a gabled gate forbidden ordinary commoners, the Takemura mansion contained a formal sitting room reserved for the Kondō and other government officials with a privy nearby for their exclusive use. Ordinary peasants might climb no farther than the wooden verandah outside, and no samurai would ever want to set foot inside their houses unless he was chasing a criminal. The tenant farmers, called "water-drinkers" because they could neither afford (nor were they permitted) tea, had to squat on the earthen floor at the entrance whether they were visiting the Kondō's headquarters or the headman's house. That was as it should be because after all, their own huts had nothing but dirt for floors.

Village headmen put in long hours for a minuscule salary. Granted, the perquisites were considerable: the right to a larger house than the other villagers, potentially profitable control over the village assessments for corvee labor and taxes, and in theory, at least, the respect that accrued to officials. To a large extent, however, ministry to the community was its own reward. Thomas Huber has made much of the emotional satisfaction felt by the poorly paid samurai administrators who paternalistically believed that "their service was for the good of all," an attitude they shared with the village headmen.[13] Taseko grew up in this tradition. The social inequality of the status hierarchy with its components of superiority and responsibility, inferiority and deference, were as natural to her as the lack of a public role for women. She never failed to express her gratitude for the condescension displayed by her betters. Even though she never held office herself, this ethos of public service and status identity might help to explain her rationale for taking action in the 1860s.

Taseko was immersed from childhood in the world of village officials. Her father played a leading role in all village deliberations (*yoriai*), meetings from which the water-drinkers were excluded. This could be a problem because the peasants used the meetings to resolve disputes over access to mountain products and to decide who would bear the brunt of the village assessments for corvee labor. In most villages, each family tilled its own plots of land or rented them out to others. The village collectively managed the nonfarm lands that provided grasses and leaves for fertilizer as well as the firewood and various materials for household furnishings that might make the difference between relative comfort and hardship. In 1855 Yamamoto was rent by a dispute over access to the mountain. Despite an informal settlement, the villagers continued to quarrel until another agreement was signed the following year. It stated that only landholding peasants would be allowed to cut down trees, but thirty-five other families would also have the right to harvest grasses and leaves.[14] As a landholding family, the Takemura needed to protect its rights to the village commons; as a family of village officials it was also forced to realize that it could govern the village only by compromising with the tenant farmers.

Taseko's father and brother also had the burdensome task of selecting men to help carry baggage, because Yamamoto was situated so close to the Nakasendō, the official highway in the neighboring Kiso Valley. As the coastal road grew more congested, more and more officials and even some daimyo switched to the interior mountain route. There they joined the imperial emissary to Nikkō, the castellans for Osaka and Nijō, the Kyoto governor, priests, senior councilors, magistrates, and other important figures who preferred the Nakasendō either because it took them closer to where they were going or because it had easier river crossings. No post station had a large enough population of porters and packhorses to carry all that official travelers required, and the stations along the narrow Kiso gorge were particularly ill-equipped. Porters were paid a pittance for their efforts, and it by no means made up for the time they spent going to and from the post station. Rather than working their fields, they found themselves traipsing off across the mountains and wearing themselves out in labor that had nothing to do with farming. No one traveled in the winter when snow blocked the passes, so instead travelers took advantage of the spring and autumn, when the weather was delightful, the scenery spectacular, and the peasants at their busiest. There were other problems as well. Village officials complained that helping with transportation not only brought the peasants hardships but changed their character for the worse. It exposed them to big city ways, taught them irresponsibility, and imbued them with a love of drink, quarreling, and gambling.[15] In other words, it gave ordinary peasants and tenant farmers a chance to get out from under the thumb of village officials and explore the wider world of the highway with its red light districts and low-life thugs.

While Taseko was growing up, her father expended much time and energy on meetings and petitions in trying to mitigate the burdens that providing porters placed on Yamamoto. Two years after she was born, he and officials from thirty other villages proposed that they be allowed to take a ten-year break from supplying porters and horses. In 1814 village representatives carried the petition to the magistrate in charge of roads in Edo. The following year the bannerman himself proposed that the corvee be reduced by 50 percent. After all, some of the villages were in his fief. Insofar as providing labor for the bakufu's highways constituted a kind of tax, it limited the amount that he could collect for himself. The magistrate responded by sending two investigators to inspect all the documents the villagers had collected. Their stay cost the villages 316 *ryō*—a hefty sum even when split thirty-one ways. The result was that the magistrate agreed to reduce the regular assessment by half for twenty years.[16] When Taseko went to Kyoto in 1862, she thus took a road well traveled by porters and packhorses on their way to provide labor for the Nakasendō.

Taseko's relatives and neighbors in Yamamoto were not opposed to making extra money by renting out their horses to transport baggage. They just wanted to do it on their own time, not too far from home, and for a reasonable fee. Packhorses traveling up and down the Ina Valley quickly proved popular with merchants. Private operators not only charged lower rates than the transport agents on the Nakasendō, they were also willing to carry goods long distances, thus reducing the risk of breakage and saving time and money. The post stations soon complained that they were losing customers. Charging private business higher fees subsidized the expenses of the officials who paid little if any of their own cost. Lawsuits and countersuits followed, but in the end the Ina Valley authorities sided with their peasants against post stations on the other side of the mountains, and the private operators continued to flourish. They carved stone monuments in honor of the horse-headed merciful Buddha (Kannon) and left them scattered across the valley where they may still be seen today. A popular song testified to the prosperity brought by the packhorses:

Takesa Yamamoto	When the iris blooms
maguso no naka de	in the middle of the horse manure
ayame saku	at Takesa and Yamamoto,
to wa shiboraja	no one is squeezed [for cash].[17]

Dealing with the conflicting demands that arose in the competition between government officials and private entrepreneurs over limited transportation resources put a considerable strain on Taseko's relatives. It has been argued, in fact, that the primary impediment to the economic development of this region was the bakufu's demand that villages such as Yamamoto help the post stations on the Nakasendō with transport.[18]

TO THE NORTH of Iida and within the Iida domain lay the village of Zakōji, where Taseko spent her teens with her Kitahara cousins. It had ranked low in the land surveys of the late sixteenth century, but improved levees along the river made it possible to open new fields to rice cultivation.[19] With a putative yield of 2,050 *koku*, it was twice the size of either Yamamoto or Tomono, and with a population in 1853 of 720 men and 699 women, managing its affairs required two headmen. The Kitahara family achieved the status to be one of seven families qualified for this position in the 1750s. In 1807 the bakufu had ordered Zakōji to start providing porters and horses to the four post stations on the Kiso Road above Nakatsugawa. From the 1830s through the 1850s, Yorinobu and his son Inao went back and forth to the supervisor's office at Kiso-Fukushima and even as far as Edo trying to lessen the burden this responsibility had placed on their village. They thus had many opportunities to travel, meet people from other areas, buy books, and talk with scholars. On one of his trips to Edo in 1832, Yorinobu went to Shinagawa to view the gun emplacements being built by the bakufu for coastal defense.[20]

It was most likely through her well-traveled and well-informed Kitahara cousins that Taseko would have learned of the crises facing Japan in the 1830s and 1840s. Massive crop failures began in 1833 and reached a nadir in 1836–1837. Although villages in the Ina Valley saw their population decline in those years, they suffered far less than the Northeast, which endured successive years of cold summers. Even western Japan experienced incidents of mass starvation. Town and country alike witnessed an unprecedented wave of civil disorder. Furious at what he deemed a failure of will on the part of bakufu leadership, a retired policeman named Ōshio Heihachirō led a peasant army on Osaka that burned a quarter of the city in an effort to save the people. Inao so revered Heihachirō that he collected as many of his writings as he could and carefully preserved a sample of his calligraphy.[21]

Conditions appeared no better on the foreign front. Following forays by British and American ships into Japanese waters, even into Edo Bay, reports reached Japan of China's humiliating defeat at the hands of the British in the infamous Opium War of 1840. Like many daimyo, the shogun tried to deal with the twin problems of domestic unrest and foreign encroachment through administrative reform.[22] Despite being an outside daimyo traditionally denied access to bakufu decision-making circles, the Iida lord was appointed *wakadoshiyori*, a position akin to Home Minister.[23] In 1843 he accompanied the shogun on a costly pilgrimage to Nikkō, shrine to the dynasty's founder. For that occasion, he ordered Inao to come to Edo to swell his retinue.[24]

Like other village headmen families, the Kitahara identified themselves self-consciously with their office. "Should we not say that the headman, who is the head of the commoners, is superior to the retainers who are the hands and feet of the nobles," one village official from Tosa exclaimed.[25] The Kitahara took equal pride in their achievements and saw themselves as inferior to no one. "No matter what one's occupation, fundamentally all are equally worth doing," Inao was to write in 1877. "There is no distinction between high and low, mean and noble. The only people to be despised are the lazy."[26] As village government became more complex, Yorinobu's father had begun keeping a diary in the late eighteenth century to transmit his administrative techniques and experiences to later generations, a tradition continued by Yorinobu and Inao. They also tried to preserve other documents created by their ancestors with the understanding that they owed their fortunate position to the people who had gone before. By thus seeking to clarify what it meant to be a village official and the responsibilities of their office, they created a status identity that stressed public service on behalf of the community.[27]

In a society in which prestige depended on bloodlines, Taseko's Kitahara cousins took pride in an illustrious lineage that went all the way back to the Minamoto through a branch that had settled in Shinano. Since Minamoto is one of the four surnames that designate emperor's sons cast out of the line of succession, the Kitahara thus asserted an origin coeval with the founding of the Japanese state. Only in the sixteenth century did its genealogy achieve enough precision to specify when the head of the main line died (Sadanori was killed in battle in 1575). The eleventh family head built the house in 1716 where Taseko spent her teens and where the family still lives today. By the late eighteenth century, during an age when social and geographic mobility was officially prohibited and most peasant families only had two or three children, we find the Kitahara having many children.[28] They married them to people in other domains (sometimes at a considerable distance away), they married them to urban merchants, and they married them to samurai.[29]

The first head of the Kitahara house to begin the tradition of having large families was Taseko's grandfather. He had thirteen children, four by his first wife and nine by his second, of whom three died in infancy and one died at the age of eight. The remainder married into important families in and around Iida where they developed a network of kinship connections that symbolically validated the prominence the Kitahara family had achieved in local affairs.[30] One example of these linkages was the adoption of Taseko's father by the Takemura family in Yamamoto. The demands of kinship meant that in one instance, a Kitahara daughter married her uncle.

The generation of Taseko's cousin Yorinobu, the eldest son of her father's older brother, provides further illustration of how the Kitahara used marriages and adoptions to validate their status in rural society. Yorinobu's mother was Ichioka Isa, daughter of the intendant for the Chimura bannermen in Iida. Born in 1792, Yorinobu was twenty-one years older than his youngest brother Shigemasa. His first daughter was just four years younger than her uncle, and they grew up together until Shigemasa left to be adopted by the Ichioka family, who ran an inn for daimyo (*honjin*) across the mountains in Nakatsugawa. He replaced his elder brother, who had died while his son was still an infant. This infant later became Taseko's son-in-law. Yorinobu's sisters married well. The eldest, Mino, married Maijima Masayuki, head of one of the oldest and most powerful peasant families in the Ina Valley who lived in Ōkawara village on the same side of the river as Tomono. Ōkawara was ruled by the Chimura bannermen, making it likely that the marriage was arranged by her mother's relatives. The other sister, Nui, married Kubota Jirōhachi in Iida. He later became the intendant for the Kondō bannerman family in Yamamoto.[31]

Yorinobu started his career as a village headman in 1818 at the age of twenty-eight, four years before Taseko started studying with him, and he continued to serve with only short breaks until his son Inao took over for him in 1852. His duties included going to Iida Castle on the fourth day of the new year to pay his respects to the daimyo, and he might well have other audiences throughout the year. In 1823, for example, he presented the daimyo with a poem on early flowering plum blossoms.[32] When the bakufu called

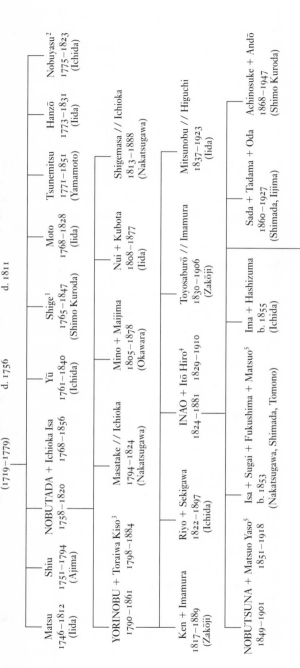

MITSUSHIGE + Fukuzawa Gihei's daughter + Kitahara Toshi from Shimo Kuroda

Children who died before marriage are omitted.

Names in parentheses are marital or adoptive villages.

[1]Shige married her uncle Kitahara Kanzaemon.

[2]Nobuyasu married his first cousin in his grandmother's family, the Imamaki.

[3]Kiso's father was a retainer to the Chiku Hatamoto family with headquarters in Ajima.

[4]Hiro's father was a village headman and sake brewer in Takami village, now part of Komagane.

[5]Yaso was Taseko's youngest daughter. Taseko's youngest son Tameyoshi was Isa's third husband.

FIGURE 5. Abbreviated genealogy of the Kitahara family.

for proposals on how to deal with the foreign threat following Commodore Perry's arrival in 1853, Yorinobu complied by drawing up a complete strategy for coastal defense. Being a commoner, he was never able to get the men who made national policy to take it seriously. His major achievement was building a new levee along the Tenryū River in the 1820s. Word of his civil engineering expertise led the domain to put him in charge of digging irrigation wells in a nearby village. For his work in flood control and the opening of new rice paddies, he and Inao received permission to use a surname and wear the two swords of a samurai.[33]

Yorinobu managed the marriages of his seven children into prominent families. By placing his oldest daughter into one of the Imamura families in Zakōji that had the qualifications to be headmen and having his third son adopted by the other, he made sure that this locally important office would be dominated by his descendants.[34] Yorinobu's youngest daughter died when she was fifteen. The older one married an official at the Ichida market just north of Iida on the Ina Road. The youngest son was adopted by a wealthy dry-goods merchant in Iida. Yorinobu expected his eldest son Nobutane to succeed him, and every year he listed Nobutane's age as well as his own at the beginning of the family diary, completely ignoring his wife and his other children. Nobutane showed an early interest in the arts. At the age of seventeen he got an introduction from his uncle in Nakatsugawa to a samisen instructor in Kyoto, only to be murdered on the road. His place was then taken by Inao.[35] Born two years after Taseko started boarding at the Kitahara house, Inao became her closest associate and life-long friend. They shared literary and intellectual interests, and they had their children marry each other.

Taseko had many opportunities to observe Yorinobu in his role of village leader. She saw him promoting the welfare of his community, and she knew that he spent his life ministering to its needs. When he died, she sent Inao the following poem:

Awate kishi	Having come away in such a hurry,
kokoro bakari zo	I suffer nothing but
nagekarure	regret at
manabi no oya no	this final parting from
tsui no wakare ni	the one who taught me so much.[36]

The efforts Yorinobu put into building levees and wells demonstrate his commitment to improving local conditions. It is true that his deeds benefited the Kitahara house, but Yorinobu believed implicitly that he knew what was best for his village and the peasants under his charge. Inao inherited this de-

FIGURE 6.
Kitahara Inao in the guise
of a Shinto priest. Courtesy
of Kitahara Takeo.

votion to the public weal and the assumptions that went with it. Unfortunately for him, this paternalistic approach to village affairs had fallen out of fashion by the 1850s. It is well known that the families who had come to dominate their villages by the end of the eighteenth century suffered increasing difficulties in maintaining their position just a few decades later.[37] Inao was to learn that while community service ought to have been supported by house interest and family honor, it might well conflict with both.

In the Kitahara family history, Inao is revered for his devotion to emperor and state, but he started having trouble with some of the Zakōji villagers beginning with his first year as village headman. The problem was that while the public works for flood control launched by Yorinobu had benefited disproportionately the families with lands close to the river, everyone in the village was expected to help pay for them. Peasants from the upper elevations started making their discontent known in 1852 when they refused to raise

their flag at the shrine for the village's tutelary deity during the annual festival or participate in the lion dance. In 1856, representatives of peasants from
the upper elevations questioned the assessments for flood control. Inao
recorded his version of what had happened in his diary:

1856/4/20. The representatives for the higher elevations wanted to in-
vestigate the records. Without support from the village officials, their
efforts were laughable.

4/25. The representatives have continued their investigation for five
days. The petition that they presented to the sixteen village officials is
so unreasonable as to be ludicrous.

5/1. Last night representatives of the higher elevations came to discuss
the expenses for water control incurred last winter. Eight of their
leagues are refusing to pay their assessments either for last winter or this
spring. Gonshichi made a rude and outrageous remark, so I hit him.[38]

Inao's father might have been able to get away with thrashing a peasant,
but the times had changed. At least in this instance the ordinary peasants and
tenant farmers were unwilling to be treated like children, subjected to what
they perceived as the arbitrary whim of men who claimed to be their betters.
Another meeting was held at the house of one of the men qualified to be
headman three days later. There it transpired that the representatives for the
higher elevations had gone first to the other headman for an explanation of
the assessments, then not satisfied with what he had said, they paid a visit to
Inao. Inao had a different story. Gonshichi called Inao a liar, prompting Inao
to attack him in a fit of rage. The peasants from the upper elevations announced that to strike their representative was the same as beating them all.
They refused to accept Inao or the other headman's authority any longer.

The 1850s and 1860s were difficult for Zakōji. Quarrels between Inao and
the higher elevations led to his being barred from serving as headman for ten
years. Another man filled his term, but he died suddenly in 1860. Iida officials appointed other candidates, only to have them back out pleading illness.
The quarrels over assessments and the general disinclination to serve as
headmen left the village without formal leadership. The headman appointed
in 1863 with Inao's younger brother as his apprentice tried to resign the next
year citing family difficulties. His request was denied. An attempt to mend
the rift in 1865 by appointing a new headman specifically for the lower elevations fell apart when the representatives from the higher elevations learned
that part of the deal was for Inao to be reappointed headmen the following
year. Despite their opposition, he returned as headman in 1866. Even when he

was out of office, he continued to play a major role in village affairs until his son was old enough to replace him and the change in the national government gave him a wider scope for his talents.[39]

None of Inao's nor Taseko's biographies mention this incident lest it bring shame to a family still locally prominent, and Inao is always portrayed as a paragon of virtue. His fight with Gonshichi casts him in a different light. He becomes a more complex individual, one less perfect, but more human.

HAVING BEEN raised by village headmen, Taseko then married a village headman. Like Zakōji, Tomono village had a system of rotating officials. The Matsuo family was one of a handful with the qualifications in terms of lineage and income to fill the office. When Taseko became a bride in 1829, her husband was just twenty-three and his father was still living. Both went by the name Sajiemon on official documents. A loan certificate from 1833 in her husband's handwriting suggests that he had already taken over the name and the official responsibilities that it entailed just four years into their marriage.[40] In 1833 and 1838 he petitioned the Takasu domain for permission to borrow back fifteen *koku* of rice from the tax payment following massive crop failures, in order to give the peasants something to eat. By the 1840s he was handling the demands for porters and packhorses for the Nakasendō that began to be assessed on the village in 1828. He also took his turn serving at the Ina Valley headquarters for the Takasu domain in Takesa, next door to Yamamoto.

Taseko's husband had to work hard at being a village headman. His most significant responsibility was making sure that the land tax got paid. He had to divide the village's assessment among the peasants, collect each person's allotment, and work with officials from other villages to deposit it in domanial storehouses. Governmental directives came incessantly, and those marked urgent would have to be relayed by messenger to the next village even in the middle of the night. He had to manage the ferry crossing at Tomono. He had to keep the river channel clear, build levees, supervise the repair of roads and bridges, and notarize the documents that flowed across his desk, including bills of sale, certificates for people leaving the village, and the population registers. When peasants wanted to make an appeal to higher authorities, he wrote it out in the exacting format of the time. He had to mediate disputes, repair the damage done by natural disasters, reward good behavior, assist travelers, cope with robbers and arsonists, take his proper place in the yearly round of religious observances, and entertain visiting dignitaries.[41] He had power, but the buck stopped with him.

The Tomono tenant farmers and peasants with little land—the "small" peasants—started questioning the way the village officials apportioned irrigation water and the records showing landholdings in 1824. Unwilling to risk disorder, the Takasu domanial authorities pressured the village officials to come to an informal agreement. The officials developed a set of regulations, but the headman for the year refused to cooperate. In desperation the small peasants threatened to appeal to Takasu. Rather than deal with all the thorny issues that an illegal petition would have raised, the authorities again urged mediation, this time involving headmen from other villages, including one from Yamamoto. The result was to open up village procedures that had heretofore been kept secret. The small peasants chose their own representatives to inspect the records showing how much the government assessed in taxes and corvée. These representatives were to witness the division of village expenses and labor for public works projects. Most importantly, the entire village worked out a survey of village lands, then made sure that each family received a written copy of its holdings that matched the records kept by the village officials. Sales of land were to be witnessed and recorded by the village officials. "The village officials and the small peasants are all in complete agreement. Henceforth no one will make the slightest complaint, the villagers agree to work together in harmony and no one will ever do anything to cause trouble." [42]

By clarifying procedures the 1827 agreement indeed staved off further conflict between the village officials and the small peasants. In this dispute over accountability and accessibility, everyone received something. The village leaders could no longer claim the privilege of handling village affairs in secret, and the small peasants now had to take responsibility for holding on to their property. The survey performed as part of this agreement set a bench mark for future land transfers. When Taseko's husband bought land in the 1830s and 1840s, he could do so safely, knowing that size and yield had already been openly determined by agreement of the entire village.

Taseko's relatives suffered relatively minor problems compared to the village officials in Minamiyama, a village south of Tomono. In 1859 the bakufu had recently transferred this area from its own control to the Shirakawa domain, and to the peasants' distress, Shirakawa officials were determined to remedy what they saw as bakufu laxity. Pushed by the small peasants, village representatives met first with an intendant, then with a magistrate stationed at Ichida, the market town where three Kitahara children had gone in marriage. When the magistrate rejected their petition, the crowd angrily decided to press its own demands on the domain: a return to bakufu rule, the restoration of government subsidies for irrigation and ferry boat use, the dropping of charges against previous protesters, and the installation of new, more sympathetic officials to be put in charge of their affairs. Iida domain officials tried to get them to return home, to no avail. In the course of this uprising, the village officials lost all credibility with the small peasants and tenant farmers. After the peasants finally went home, they continued to pick quarrels with the local leadership.[43]

Taseko's relatives were horrified by these events, but they were not directly involved. If anything it encouraged them to look to their own position. Inao strengthened his ties to the Iida government by making a special contribution to its coffers called "thank you money" in exchange for becoming an official distribution agent.[44] Just a few months earlier he had joined the Hirata school—only the second person in the Ina Valley to do so. The Hirata school was particularly appropriate for village officials because it preached the innate harmony between people who worked together in nature. Its disciples believed that the qualifications necessary to be a good headman went far beyond simply collecting taxes, to exacting standards of honesty and probity.[45] Regardless of how poorly Inao got along with the men from the higher elevations in Zakōji, he continued to identify himself with the tradition of ministry to the community that he had inherited from his father.

In actual practice, commitment to community service was limited to men and men of the village official class. Under ordinary circumstances, their wives raised sons to this ethos and served the family's interests. The only way women might contribute to the village welfare was by providing charity out their kitchen door, and this activity became increasingly important as a way for village officials to win respect and approval.[46] Yet had Taseko not come from this class with its "status identity, status pride, and status missions,"[47] it is unlikely that she would have acquired the range of vision to tackle issues beyond her immediate realm. Her 1862 trip to Kyoto, made with the secret hope of offering what little assistance she could to the emperor, might have arisen out of this tradition of public service, but lest such a conclusion be drawn too hastily, let me point out that no other village official's wife ever dreamed of doing what she did.

CHAPTER THREE

Married Life

Now that I have become the wife
I longed to be
I sleep every night
accustomed to the bedding
under the harvest moon.
MATSUO TASEKO, before 1845[1]

One fine spring morning in 1828, the villagers in Yamamoto
were preparing the rice paddies to receive the young seedlings. Among them was a slender girl of seventeen, dressed in
a short belted robe that ended above her knees. Her job was to
guide the horse pulling the rake that broke up clods of earth
and left the ground level.[2] A young man from Tomono had
crossed the Tenryū River and walked all the way to Yamamoto
to catch a glimpse of her. She presented such an attractive
sight to him that he agreed to accept the proposal to join the
Takemura and Matsuo families in marriage. No one knows
whether Taseko herself had anything to say in this matter, nor
is there any hint that she met her future husband before the
night when she arrived at his house as his bride. It is even possible to doubt whether Motoharu actually paid this visit to
Yamamoto, since the tale was told many years after his death

by one of Taseko's cousins.[3] For the man telling the story and the biographer who published it, however, it clearly established the appropriate relationship between husband and wife.

"To become a woman is a process in no sense fixed," claim modern feminist scholars.[4] Women today confront a bewildering array of choices throughout their lives, from the types of toys they enjoy to educational programs, employment opportunities, and travel. Even marriage and the family, once considered the natural culmination of a woman's becoming, is less a given than an option. In contrast, the lifecourse trajectory followed by premodern women appears much more rigid, much less open to deviations either chosen by the woman herself or forced upon her by circumstance. It is consequently considerably duller. Marriage in particular is a condition so universally acknowledged and so obvious as to become invisible.[5] What is there to say about Taseko other than that she married at eighteen, bore ten children of whom seven lived to maturity, and helped her husband restore the family's fortune?[6]

Writing about a woman's life is not a fixed process either. Taseko's biographies composed before World War Two made a determined effort to fit her into categories defined by the term "good wife, wise mother" (*ryōsai kenbo*). To that end they collected stories showing her to be hardworking and nurturing. She devotedly served her parents-in-law until both died within eight years of her marriage. Afflicted with chronic stomach trouble, her husband had her massage him for thirty minutes every morning before he could bear to stand up. "She set the servants at their tasks and promoted agriculture and sericulture through example. Her dedication so impressed her neighbors that they all wanted to have their daughters trained in her household."[7] These books simply ignored contradictions between what she was expected to be and what her own writings, especially her poems, suggest that she did. She had a much more multifaceted character than she is usually allowed, and it was created through a variety of activities from household chores to travel and drink. If we begin with the assumption that Taseko "lived in a world as complex, fluid, and riddled with ambivalence as the world of today," then her life becomes much more interesting and believable.[8] The path that she followed was by no means as obvious or as unilinear as it might appear at first glance.

Taseko's marriage was arranged to suit the interests of the Takemura and Matsuo families. Insofar as the heads of these families were always male, descent was reckoned through the patriline. In Shinano villages by the 1750s, lineages (*dōzoku*) that once knit families both rich and poor into a single if fictive kinship system had given way at least among the wealthy to connections of marriage and adoption between houses symmetrical in status and often many miles apart.[9] In such a system women played a crucial role as a medium of exchange in linking two families for their mutual prosperity and prestige.

In going to the Matsuo family, Taseko may have married slightly beneath her. The Takemura family had an illustrious lineage that it traced back to one Takemura Inaba, a retainer of the Iida castellan, Banzai Nagatada. After Nagatada died in battle in 1562, Inaba and another warrior tried to escape to the Kiso Valley with Nagatada's son and heir. They got lost, and the infant starved to death. Having fulfilled their obligation to their master's house, the two men returned to the Ina Valley where they set themselves up as farmers. Their descendants maintained their military pretensions not only through remembering their ancestors' exploits but by occasionally marrying into warrior families, as with Kiyomitsu's marriage to the daughter of Sakurai Chie or Mitsunaka's marriage to the sister of Kubota Jirōhachi, the man who had replaced the Sakurai in serving the Kondō family of bannermen. For them the status barriers erected between commoners and samurai were indeed permeable.[10] One mark of family continuity was having the head of household use the character *mitsu* (waxing, as the moon) for his given name, although I have been unable to trace this custom back any farther than Taseko's grandfather and it ended with her son.

Although descent was always reckoned in the male line, for several generations the Takemura family was de facto matrilineal, owing to the custom of adopting sons-in-law. Taseko's mother Sachi had two younger brothers. One was adopted by a family in a village some distance from Yamamoto, and the other was set up as a branch family. Creating a branch family in this fashion was only possible when the family had enough land that even after its division, both the main line and the new family would have viable enterprises.[11] Taseko's father lost not only his family name in marriage but had to take a new given name as well. When Taseko's brother had no children, he adopted Taseko's son and married him to a woman four years his senior. They had only one child, a daughter, for whom they adopted a husband. For the third generation in the junior branch of the family, Jirōkichi adopted his sister's son and married him to his cousin's daughter. While these women probably had no more say than Taseko regarding who they would marry, at least they remained in a familiar household.

A bride snatched from her parents' loving arms to live among strangers was a stock figure of misery in Japanese literature, but an adopted son-in-law faced an equally difficult adjustment. Both had to accommodate themselves to others and withstand the critical and constant gaze of their in-laws. For a woman to remain with her parents gave her distinct advantages, allowing her to be much more assertive within a wider range of action than would nor-

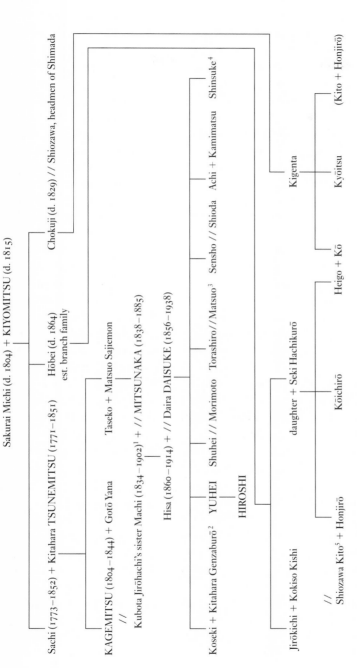

FIGURE 7. Abbreviated genealogy of the Takemura family.

[1]Taseko's older brother adopted Machi, then married her to Taseko's second son.
[2]Genzaburō was adopted to succeed Kitahara Nobutsuna and Yasao, Taseko's daughter.
[3]Torashirō was adopted by Tameyoshi, Taseko's eldest son.
[4]Shinsuke was allowed to establish a branch family.
[5]Jirōkichi adopted his daughter's son and his cousin's daughter to marry and succeed to his house.

mally be the case. If Sachi conformed to type, Taseko would have grown up with a strong role model. Life was more uncertain for a second or third son. It is not known exactly when Tsunemitsu married Sachi and took her family name, but it was probably not many years before Taseko's brother was born in 1804. Since Tsunemitsu was born in 1771, that would put his age at marriage at around thirty—old for the better-off men of his time. His nephew Yorinobu probably married in his mid-twenties, and Taseko's husband was twenty-three.

While newly prominent families might reconstruct their lineage to fit their circumstances, the Matsuo did less of that than the Takemura or the Kitahara. Beyond a vague claim to descent from the Seiwa Genji family, also called the Minamoto, it did not trace its origins to a gallant warrior ancestor. From what little is known about its genealogy, it did not marry into warrior households and of the first seven generations of household heads, the death dates are known for only two. It did not monopolize the position of headman, and in fact before the 1700s it is hardly notable at all. It apparently fell on hard times at the end of the eighteenth century, and the most substantial indications of wealth come after it acquired Taseko. The match presumably came about through the Kitahara family. Taseko's cousin Yorinobu listed her future father-in-law among the relatives in attendance at a wedding for which he was the go-between in 1822, and he included Tomono in his round of new year's visits long before Taseko ever married there.[12] The surviving records unfortunately provide no clue as to how this connection came about.

Genealogies do not always tell the whole story when it comes to marriage and kinship. Taseko's husband Motoharu was raised not by Seko, his birth mother, but by a step-mother. Seko later married into the Imamura family of Zakōji, where she bore a daughter named Kuniko, Motoharu's half-sister. We know of her existence only because once when she came to visit her brother, Taseko wrote a poem about her:

Nakanaka ni	My sleeves have become
sode was nurekeri	exceedingly damp
umi wo koshi	at parting from one
kawa wo watarishi	who goes across the sea
hito no wakare ni	who traverses rivers.[13]

The Matsuo family genealogy includes Seko and Kuniko not at all. How Seko came into the family and why she left remain a mystery.

Because Taseko's marriage involved three prominent families, it is somewhat better documented. We can assume that the Takemura family sent Taseko off in style. The marriage took place at night on the twenty-fourth day of the second month of 1829, and Taseko's retinue would have left at dusk to complete the journey of slightly under twelve miles. Following the custom of the time, her parents would have remained at home with their presence represented by the go-between, Motoharu's teacher from Tomono.[14] Ordinary peasant brides had to walk to their new house, but Taseko probably rode in an enclosed palanquin such as the one used by the Matsuo family brides on display at the Toyooka History and Folklore Museum across the river from Iida. At one time restricted to members of the ruling class, these conveyances had been appropriated by wealthy peasants with the proper lineages and record of government service, who used them for special occasions as a mark of distinction within village society. "Even though it was supposed to be spring," Taseko said later, "it was still cold and spring in name only with a thin layer of snow on the ground. A bush warbler calling faintly in the distance seemed to be urging me to come."[15]

Taseko's family probably supplied the goods used in the marriage ceremony as well as a dowry. When Yorinobu's sister Mino had married into the wealthy Maijima family just eight years earlier, the Kitahara family sent along the offerings that invited the gods to bestow the couple with prosperity, longevity, and progeny. These were a sea bream, a dried cuttlefish, two sheets of kelp, and a barrel of sake. They also supplied formal men's attire for the groom. Gifts of a boxed fan, a fish, and a roll of ramie cloth went to each Maijima relative. As the bride's uncle Taseko's father received two hundred pieces of gold; the Kitahara aunts received hair ornaments and white face paint or in some cases a roll of cloth. The Maijima's servants received a barrel of sake, the clerk got a wrapper (*furoshiki*), and the cook got two bundles of paper. All of this was in addition to the personal possessions expected to last Mino a lifetime: the two enormous chests, the rolls of hemp, cotton and silk cloth, the robes and obi, the combs, bodkins, hairpins, scissors, needles, a gargling bowl, seven hundred sheets of ordinary paper plus colored sheets for writing poems, thirteen colored woodblock prints, medicine, oil, and a weight used in pickle making. All told the wedding cost the Kitahara family well over twenty *ryō*, far beyond the imagining of ordinary peasants but not out of line with what wealthy peasants in other areas spent.[16] Surely the Takemura family would not have wanted to embarrass Taseko by sending her off with anything less.

According to the custom of the time, a woman's dowry was hers and hers alone. Her parents would make sure that all the durable objects were stamped with their family crest, thus demonstrating that they belonged to the family and it could take them back in case of divorce. The use of the crest also implied that the woman herself continued to be part of her natal family even after the marriage. In 1843 Taseko's husband married one of his sisters to a man in Tomono. In return he got a document stating, "At this time we are taking in your sister as a bride. This constitutes proof that we have indeed received the amount of twenty *ryō* that she brings with her. We will make sure that it all gets handed over to any heir she may have in the future. If by some chance there is a divorce, we will without fail return to you the money she brought with her as well as all of her belongings." [17] The Civil Code of 1898 outlawed this practice; thereafter both the woman and her trousseau belonged legally to her husband for him to do with as he pleased. [18]

The Civil Code of 1898 also put an end to the practice of a woman keeping her family name after marriage. In some regions, commoners had long since dropped this custom because the husband's family was responsible for the wife's gravestone, and it did not want other names mingling with its own. In the area near Nagoya where a number of families professed the nativist tradition, however, women retained their natal names even after death. [19] (In public only samurai and a few elite commoners such as Kitahara Yorinobu had permission to use surnames, but in practice and among themselves, most commoners identified themselves with family names.) Among her contemporaries, the woman we know today as Matsuo Taseko was called Takemura Tase. This is the name by which she usually signed her letters, and it is the name she was to give in pledging to become a disciple of Hirata Atsutane. "Tase" is not a common name and the characters that she used to write it, "many" (*ōi*) and "energetic" (*ikioi*), suggest a forceful personality. Occasionally she called herself or allowed others to call her Taseko. Only in the modern period is she always assigned "*ko*," the suffix meaning "child" attached with monotonous regularity to women past and present until the last decade or so. [20] Thus modern naming practices serve a double duty: they attach a woman to her husband's house and belittle her maturity. In Taseko's case, they may well have obscured her sense of autonomy in the eyes of modern historians.

Even after marriage Taseko continued to involve herself in Takemura family affairs. For a sturdy walker, it was possible to make the round trip between Tomono and Yamamoto in a single day. [21] Her poems show that she visited her parents on a regular basis and her few remaining letters to them suggest that she paid a great deal of attention to what they did. Just as her father built on his connections with his parents' house by sending his daughter there to be educated, so did she continue her relationship with him, both through visits and by sending her second son to be adopted by her brother. One of her favorite poems (crafted in numerous variations) alluded to the love shared between daughter and father. "Once when I was young, my father gave me a bamboo staff saying I should use it in the future:"

Tarachine no   The knotted bamboo
michi no mamori to   from my father
kuretake wo   to protect me on my way
chitose no saka no   has become a staff to lean on
tsue to nashikeri   throughout the vicissitudes of my life.[22]

While the ninth century emperor Kōkō was still the Crown Prince, he presented his aunt with a silver staff for her eightieth birthday. For her poem Taseko used the same fourth line found in the *Kokinshū* poem that acknowledged the gift: "Is this the handiwork / of the awesome gods? thrusting it before me / I can forever cross / the hills and valleys [vicissitudes] of my life."[23] It has become increasingly clear in studies of family and household in Japan that regardless of the patrilineal ideology, married women maintained close ties to their parents, siblings, and siblings' children.[24] Taseko's letters and visits to the Takemura house ended only with her death.

This does not suggest that Taseko was anything but pleased to be associated with the Matsuo family. While she was in Kyoto in 1862, she delighted in visiting the shrine commemorating the site where sake was first brewed in Japan precisely because her husband was a sake brewer. She took great pride in the accomplishments of her son and grandson and the glory they reflected on the Matsuo name. She herself had numerous responsibilities. She raised silkworms to provide an additional source of income for the family; she bore children to assure its future.

For the first twenty-odd years of her married life, Taseko was either pregnant or caring for infants. If, as was commonly assumed, sexual frigidity caused infertility, she must have been passionate indeed.[25] Fortunately the Matsuo family had the wherewithal to raise the seven out of her ten children who survived childbirth and the first dangerous weeks thereafter. Taseko had only two children before her mother-in-law died, leaving her with the entire responsibility for running the household before and after the remaining eight were born. It is possible that she got help from her daughter-in-law when she bore her youngest daughter a year after her eldest son married in 1850. Farm families in eighteenth- and early-nineteenth-century Japan were notoriously small; even after 1868, when a population boom began, they averaged less than six in size.[26] The increase in the Matsuo family was probably made possible by the expanding economy of the early nineteenth century and Taseko's contribution to the family's income.

Taseko's children provide a textbook example of how the political, social, economic, and cultural networks created by rural entrepreneurs reinforced each other through marriage alliances. Her eldest son married Ichioka Tami

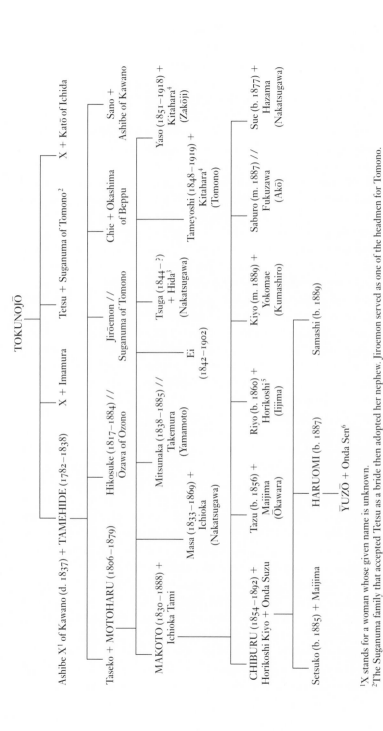

TOKUNOJŌ

Ashibe X[1] of Kawano (d. 1837) + TAMEHIDE (1782–1838)

Taseko + MOTOHARU (1806–1879)   Hikosuke (1817–1884) // Ozawa of Ozono   X + Imamura   Jirōemon // Suganuma of Tomono   Tetsu + Suganuma of Tomono[2]   Chie + Okashima of Beppu   X + Katō of Ichida   Sano + Ashibe of Kawano

MAKOTO (1830–1888) + Ichioka Tami

Masa (1833–1869) + Ichioka (Nakatsugawa)   Mitsumaka (1838–1885) // Takemura (Yamamoto)   Ei (1842–1902)   Tsuga (1844–?) + Hida[3] (Nakatsugawa)   Tameyoshi (1848–1919) + Kitahara[4] (Tomono)   Yaso (1851–1918) + Kitahara[4] (Zakōji)

CHIBURU (1854–1892) + Horikoshi Kiyo + Onda Suzu   Tazu (b. 1856) + Maijima (Ōkawara)   Riyo (b. 1860) + Horikoshi[5] (Iijima)   Kiyo (m. 1889) + Yokomae (Kumashiro)   Saburo (m. 1887) // Fukuzawa (Akō)   Sue (b. 1877) + Hazama (Nakatsugawa)

Setsuko (b. 1885) + Maijima   HARUOMI (b. 1887)   Samashi (b. 1889)

ȲUZŌ + Onda Sen[6]

[1] X stands for a woman whose given name is unknown.
[2] The Suganuma family that accepted Tetsu as a bride then adopted her nephew. Jiroemon served as one of the headmen for Tomono.
[3] Hida Kurobei was the headman for Nakatsugawa.
[4] Tameyoshi and Yasao married a sister and brother.
[5] Chiburu and Riyo married a sister and brother.
[6] Yūzō and Sen are first cousins once removed.

FIGURE 8. Abbreviated genealogy of the Matsuo family.

from Iida, whose family had long served as the intendant for the lands managed on behalf of the bakufu by the Chimura family of bannermen in the Ina Valley. Tami's great-grandfather claimed responsibility for introducing silk spinning techniques into the Ina Valley by bringing skilled workers from Kyoto to teach local women. Both her father and her older brother were known for their erudition, and her younger brother was to escort Taseko part way on her journey to Kyoto in 1862.[27] It appears that Taseko and Tami got along quite well, bound together as they were by their common devotion to the prosperity of the Matsuo house. In one letter from 1885 Taseko wrote that Tami had wanted to pay a sick call on her brother-in-law Mitsunaka, but "even though she really wanted to go, she didn't because her absence would have caused me so much trouble."[28]

Taseko married two of her daughters and one of her granddaughters to local notables across the mountains in Nakatsugawa. First Masa married her second cousin, Ichioka Masaji in 1849. "We've gotten together with Nakatsugawa," Taseko announced in a letter to her cousin Kitahara Inao. "Today we are planning to initiate talks. We hope they will go in an agreeable direction, and since we want things to go well, I beg you please with all my heart to come help us out."[29] Taseko's third daughter married Hida Kurōbei, the headman of Nakatsugawa and an important man in his own right. Her granddaughter Sue married Hazama Washio, heir to a family of sake brewers and cousin to Taseko's friend Hazama Hidenori. The Kitahara had been the first to establish the connection across provincial boundaries. Once it had been made, Taseko and the Matsuo family used it to build their own links to families who were likewise village officials and entrepreneurs. Living on a major post station on the Nakasendō, these families were also in a position to be well-informed on national politics.

Sending her daughters across the mountains did not mean that Taseko's ties to them became attenuated. After all, what was the point of finding a useful family with which to establish a marriage connection were it not to be maintained? Like many women Masa returned to her mother when she gave birth to her own children, thus giving Taseko an early glimpse of her grandchildren. When one of them died, she wrote a number of poems expressing her grief:

Natsu goro mo	Even this summer
kitsutsu asobishi	I came to play with the child
omokage no	now how can I ever forget
kasanete ima wa	all my different memories
wasurarenu kana	of that face.[30]

FIGURE 9.
Matsuo Suzu, née Onda.
Wife of Taseko's grandson
Chiburu. Courtesy of
Matsuo Yūzō.

Taseko's letters sometimes mentioned past and planned visits to Nakatsu-gawa. She was to spend months at a time there, even into the 1880s.

Taseko's second daughter Ei was born a deaf-mute. Her handicap pre-cluded any chance of a suitable marriage, so she remained in the Matsuo household until her death at the age of sixty, eight years after her mother. Taseko taught her sewing to occupy her time and to provide her with gain-ful employment. She is chiefly remembered for her fondness for practical jokes. On my recent trip to the Matsuo house, Taseko's great-great-grand-daughter-in-law, Sen, told me how Ei once played a nasty trick on Sen's aunt Suzu (Chiburu's wife) by taking away a ladder Suzu had used to climb into the attic. Suzu long remembered the sight of Ei grinning maliciously up at her. She blamed the fright she received for her son Haruomi's timidity, she having been pregnant with him at the time.[31]

Taseko's other children replicated kinship ties already established by the

振千尾松　孫嫡の子勢多　　　　　　　誠　尾松　男長の子勢多

子ゝや原北　女末の子勢多　　　　　　誠為尾松　男末の子勢多

FIGURE 10. Left to right, top to bottom: Taseko's grandson Chiburu, her eldest son Makoto, her daugher Yaso, and her youngest son Tameyoshi. Courtesy of Matsuo Yūzō.

Takemura family. Her second son became the head of the Takemura house and two of her children married the children of Taseko's cousin and closest friend, Kitahara Inao. Yaso, her youngest child, married the head of the family, giving her a position of great prestige especially once her husband took a leading role in local affairs and even became a member of the National Diet. Her brother Tameyoshi remained in the Matsuo family. He was finally allowed to marry Kitahara Isa, who had been married twice before. Judging from one of Taseko's letters that mentioned Isa in passing, the marriage had taken place by 1884 when Tameyoshi was thirty-six. The couple apparently had no children for they adopted one of Taseko's great-grandchildren from the Takemura family. Even though Tameyoshi eventually controlled a portion of the family's assets under his own name, he did not set up the branch family that took over the Matsuo sake-brewing enterprise until 1899 at the age of fifty-one.[32] At some point, relations with the main family so soured that neither speaks to the other.

TASEKO'S COMMITMENT to the Matsuo family resulted in the household's economic prosperity and progeny who went on to play important roles in public service. Raising them and managing the household economy creates the appearance that she spent the thirty years before 1862 doing the nondescript tasks performed by most peasant women. In fact, however, her life course teetered between the domestic affairs consigned to her by marriage and the opportunities brought her way through religious observances, poetry practice, travel, and the tea ceremony. Despite her responsibilities in running the household, she occasionally had time to have fun.

According to her great-grandchildren, Taseko spent her young married life a fervent Buddhist. Whenever neighborhood priests appeared with their begging bowls, she invited them in for a feast. Sometimes she would have a whole crowd come to read the sutras, then set out trays of food in return for their efforts. She always went to the temple services in a neighboring village, and after Tami married into the household, the two of them would go together. Once she took in a child whose parents could not feed him, then paid the expenses for him to become an acolyte.[33] Setsuko and Haruomi told this story as an example of how their famous great-grandmother always threw herself wholeheartedly into the practice of her beliefs, thus demonstrating a consistency of enthusiasm if not purpose. Regardless of whether she was in fact as single-minded as her descendants claimed her to be, these anecdotes also suggest that before her encounter with the nativist teachings of the Hirata Atsutane school, Taseko shared the common belief of most women of her time in the saving power of Kannon, the Buddha of Mercy.

With few exceptions, every household in Tokugawa Japan belonged to a Buddhist temple that took charge of funerals and memorial services. These practices placed the family in a continuum that stretched back to the ancestors and forward to future generations.[34] The temples also offered opportunities to pray for this-worldly benefits, good health and prosperity chief among them. Many priests were highly educated and able to hold their own in poetry meetings and tea ceremonies. They left a lasting imprint on rural society, from the help they provided the poor and downtrodden to the cachet they lent the gatherings of the rural elite.

In 1853, the same year that Commodore Perry first arrived to open Japan to modern foreign intercourse, Taseko and her husband hosted a poetry meeting for her cousins Kitahara Yorinobu and Ichioka Shigemasa as well as a Buddhist priest and a painter from Okazaki, a post station on the coastal highway. Motoharu's younger brother and two of Taseko's neighbors, Hara Toshiko and Hara Motoko, rounded out the party. The group collaborated on a poetry and picture anthology, "The scent of the wild mountain rose" (*Yamabuki no kaori*) to commemorate their gathering, and the manuscript remains today in the Matsuo house. Most of the poems celebrate the beauties of nature and the changing of the seasons. In one exchange, Motoko accuses her lover of being fickle, and Taseko protests her steadfastness. In another, Taseko proposes "talking about the ancient days promised us by the gods." The men respond with assertions that the essence of Japan is inviolable because the gods have pledged to protect it. The sketches show the moon rising over a pine forest, a shrine in a grove of trees, the wild mountain rose in bloom, and a group of men and women frolicking at a picnic.[35] This is a far cry from the solemn gatherings presided over by Taseko's teacher Fukuzumi Kiyokaze, but even in this more relaxed atmosphere, the practice of poetry served to gentrify the occasion and the participants.

In 1649 the bakufu had issued a rescript to peasants nationwide urging them to be deferential to their superiors, diligent in their agricultural pursuits, and frugal in their everyday lives. Even in the nineteenth century, this set of hoary hortatory injunctions continued to take pride of place on the village notice boards. The statement applicable to women was as follows: "No matter how good the quality of your wife, if she likes to drink tea and go on excursions and sightseeing, she should be sent away. You should refrain from sake and tobacco as much as possible."[36]

The bakufu routinely issued orders without taking any steps to follow through. Insofar as it habitually overreached its capabilities, the Japan of this time has been called a "flamboyant state."[37] Nowhere is its vainglory more apparent than in the contrast between what it told commoners they should

FIGURE 11. Drawing from the collective poetry collection, "The Wild Mountain Rose." Courtesy of Matsuo Yūzō.

do and what the commoners actually did. Taseko was not a conscious rebel, at least not in the practice of her everyday life, but she regularly transgressed bakufu regulations with impunity.

Some entrepreneurs opposed the practice of tea as a waste of time and money inappropriate to the rural way of life. The rituals accompanying preparation and service were time-consuming to learn and perform. They implied a "keen attention to deportment" and a physical discipline that required leisure to obtain.[38] What had farmers to do with the aesthetic sensibility and spiritual qualities that made drinking tea appropriate for a Zen monastery? The objects necessary to make the ceremony a momentous occasion took considerable effort to acquire, and the expense could be ruinous. On the other hand, the tea ceremony gave peasants an excellent excuse to get together. As with the poetry meetings, it provided a space where likeminded people with enough money could meet and talk about business, philosophy, politics, or whatever else interested them. It had been forbidden to women in medieval Japan, but by the early nineteenth century that barrier too was coming down, even in the countryside. When a traveling instructor named Kawase Shūbaku from Wakayama spent some time in Tomono in the early 1860s teaching the art of the tea ceremony, Taseko proved an eager student.

Taseko's biographers have paid as little attention to her interest in tea ceremony as to her writing of love poetry. This kind of "frivolous exercise" meshes ill with the model of patriotism that she became in the early twentieth century. Yet a short poetry anthology from 1862 includes the heading, "when Mr. Kawase said he was ready to begin teaching tea ceremony, we formed a group and had a drinking party to celebrate:"

Osamareru	A sign that the age
miyo no shirushi wa	is well governed,
uchiyama no	we are having a party to celebrate
ki no me ni soete	using the tree buds
kotohokai suru	from the imperial court.[39]

Let me point out that sake, not tea, was the celebratory drink, even for people planning to hold tea parties thereafter. Taseko quickly became quite fond of this practice.

As this was the time when Taseko was learning to write long poems, she wrote one for her teacher in which she told the story of how he had originally been a samurai in Edo. "When things annoyed you, and you came to hate the world, you left your position." He went to Kyoto to study the art of tea before his peregrinations brought him to the Ina Valley. "Delighted at your visit everyone came together in a group for one or two days in the reflected glow of the sun. During the hours we spent together our surroundings fell away. While I was with my teacher, I thought nothing of the time." Instruction was held in winter, the off-season for agricultural workers. With the coming of spring and the rising of the rivers "may you prosper more and more." [40] Taseko wrote another poem to commemorate the occasion when she was allowed to be the hostess for a tea ceremony held at the Kawase residence.[41] Having become an aficionada of the drink, she was to visit a temple near Mt. Takao boasting the oldest tea nursery in Japan during her stay in Kyoto in 1862.

As for drinking sake and smoking tobacco, Taseko's diaries provide ample proof that she did both.[42] According to her great-granddaughter, she always had two or three cups of sake for a nightcap, preferably accompanied by a few vegetables.[43] A least once she gave some to her cousins at the Kitahara house:

Sakahokai	At this festive drinking party
ushi nomi mae no	it is good to imbibe
miki mo yoshi	the sacred sake in front of my teacher
haru no kage no ni	Here in the spring shadows
kotohokihoki to	we are having a celebration.[44]

On another occasion when a friend had brought her some fish, she ended a poem with the lines, "I had some sacred sake to accompany that large flat fish and then I slept extremely well." [45] Samurai women expected to maintain a sense of decorum drank considerably less than peasant women. Coming as she did from a family that brewed sake, it would have been more surprising had Taseko not indulged at all.

Besides her many trips to visit relatives and participate in poetry meetings, Taseko went on a number of excursions, and she always traveled in the company of her husband. Some might find this odd, since most Japanese today travel in same-sex groups. This custom has its roots in the Tokugawa period, when women travelers faced many more obstacles than men, from government regulations to avaricious boatmen.[46] What was more unusual was that Taseko left home with neither a mother-in-law nor a daughter-in-law to look after her young children. Somehow she balanced the responsibility for running a household with the freedom to leave it in the hands of servants.[47] Like some couples today, Taseko and her husband bucked convention and found such pleasure in each other's company at a relatively young age that they several times shared the rigors of the road together.

Taseko's first opportunity to travel came in 1845 at the age of thirty-four, just a year after the birth of her third daughter. She and Motoharu set out in the eighth month, following the course of the Tenryū River to Lake Suwa, then heading through Matsumoto for Zenkōji, a popular Buddhist temple in the city of Nagano. After spending a day worshipping at the temple, they went on to Naoetsu on the Sea of Japan. On the way home they stopped by the To-gakushi shrine, located amidst jagged mountain peaks. The entire journey took a little over two weeks. On one night near the end of the journey they planned a moon-viewing party at Obasuteyama, the mountain of abandoned old women.[48] According to one nineteenth-century guidebook, Obahime, the ugly elder sister of the surpassingly beautiful Konohananosakuya, fell ill on their way to Sarashina and decided to remain behind at this lovely locale.[49] Ever since a *Kokinshū* poem described the moon over this mountain, it had been favored by travelers. Taseko wrote three poems, the first two complaining that the moon was obscured by clouds, the second alluding to her feelings for her husband:

Kokoro aru	At the sleeve
hito no tamoto ya	of my beloved
ika naran	what will the future bring
Obasute yama no	watching the moon
tsuki wo nagamete	on the mountain of abandoned old women.[50]

Once in a while the formal conventions of classical poetry fit the reality of the poet's situation. This poem might reflect Taseko's concern for her husband's shaky health and her awareness of life's transience. It less likely suggests that she herself feared abandonment in the aristocratic mode of cast-off women.

One of the pleasures of traveling was composing a travel diary complete with poems that linked the traveler's experiences to poetry written at the same sites in the past. Poetry marked the difference between the ordinary world and the adventure of seeing new places; it "transformed tedious travel into an elegant, romantic journey; moreover, the result could be shown to friends and acquaintances."[51] In contrast to diaries of everyday life, records of journeys always featured poems.[52] Taseko's first effort in keeping an account of her days came on this trip. Whereas many diaries depicted the joys and rigors of the trip in realistic detail,[53] Taseko's poems generally bemoaned the hardships of the journey and her regret at leaving her family and friends behind. These were highly appropriate subjects for poetry written in the classical mode drawing on a courtly tradition that saw travel as exile—but out of synchrony with a trip that the people of her time anticipated with great delight. Here is Taseko on the road:

Furusato wo	On a borrowed pillow
wasurenu aki no	in autumn unable to forget
kari makura	my home town
omoi zo marasu	the cries of the cicada
matsu mushi no koe	drown out my thoughts.[54]

As long as she used the classical poetic code to construct her experiences, it must be said that her memory of the sounds she had heard were as much an object of culture and history as of nature.[55]

Taseko's diary does not contain an empirical verification of her trip but an evocation of the sights and sounds named in classical poetry. At one point she admits that the area was not especially desolate, but she had heard a quail cry. Since quail inhabit overgrown fields and abandoned houses, the poem had to be a sad one, even though it was written in the most lively of post towns:

Fukakusa no	Even though Fukakusa is not a village
sato wa sarade wo	overgrown with weeds
sabishiki wo	plaintively
uzura naki nari	calls the quail
aki no yūgure	at dusk in autumn.[56]

Despite the red glow of lanterns inviting travelers to stop for a drink, dusk was the time of day associated most closely with the melancholy of autumn. Besides, quails and sadness had gone together ever since one appeared in *Tales of Ise,* written in the tenth century.[57]

Two years later Taseko and Motoharu set out for Mt. Akiha, site of a

temple and shrine complex founded in 709. "My beloved husband thought
to make a pilgrimage and invited me to go along. 'Let's make it today,' he
said, and so we left our home village at six in the morning on the twenty-
eighth day of the first month."[58] The first night they stayed in a village on
the other side of the pass famous for its monkeys. "It is really interesting the
way monkeys ape people," she remembered in a poem. For the second night
they stayed at a house that did everything in the ancient style, "including the
parched boiled rice [described in *Tales of Ise*] cooked in quantity in a Chinese
rice tub. That night the five of us did not sleep a wink. While waiting for the
dawn by the light of flaming torches, we all laughed our heads off." Taseko
wrote a number of poems about this experience, one remembering the fun
and laughter, another alluding to the poetic tradition of staying awake out of
longing for an absent lover, and a third bemoaning the lack of sake for a
nightcap. She ended the episode with a poem composed by her husband not
as an exercise in imitating the poetry found in the court anthologies but as a
joke. It gave yet another reason for not being able to sleep:

Watchira wa	Awakening all alone
yabure futon yori	on a torn futon
kono takibi	by the light of the torch
hitori mezamete	let us now
shishi gari wo sen	chase the lice from our clothing.[59]

By noon on the following day they had reached Mt. Akiha. They rested
for awhile at the base of the mountain, catching glimpses of Mt. Fuji through
breaks in the clouds. A climb up the mountain brought them to the temple's
main hall, which was dedicated to the Buddha of Mercy. "There were crowds
of people there, including some unusually beautiful women. We took in everything worth seeing, then went back down to the inn where we spent the night."
The next day they visited more temples before taking a badly maintained
road through the mountains, sampling the regional delicacies as they went.
The journey that had started out as a pilgrimage ended with a visit to Ishikawa Yorihira, a poet living near present-day Hamamatsu. "We chatted for
awhile, then he gave us some of his poems written on poem cards. We all
spoke freely without reserve. He brought out tea and snacks for us and we
spent a long time talking about sundry matters not realizing how late it was
getting. Finally we took our leave and rushed back to our lodging in a great
hurry."[60] Following this trip, Taseko began a correspondence with him, using the shrine as a relay point for the letters entrusted to pilgrims.

Unable to prevent commoners from traveling at all, the bakufu restricted their excursions to visiting relatives, going on pilgrimage, and staying at hot springs for their health. Through the loophole afforded by these exceptions stepped thousands of people who took full advantage of the opportunity to enjoy a world far removed from their everyday life in what Constantine Vaporis has called a "culture of movement."[61] The two trips that Taseko and Motoharu took in the 1840s featured pilgrimages and poetry. Taseko never mentioned the restrictions that bedeviled women travelers, particularly the difficulty of getting through and around government barriers. Perhaps such subjects were deemed out of place in a diary devoted to recapturing the sensibility of the past; perhaps she and her husband thought so little of evading the barriers that they passed beneath notice. When Taseko and Motoharu traveled to Edo in 1855, however, the world had changed. The shogun had been forced to negotiate with foreign powers beginning in 1853, and foreign ships sailed more and more frequently into Japanese waters. The people they met were no longer simply innkeepers and poets, and their conversations ranged beyond the refinements of classical verse to contemporary affairs.

The Edo trip was a lively affair. Taseko and her husband were joined by three women: Kitahara Inao's mother Kiso; Hara Toshiko from Tomono, who had joined them in composing a poetry anthology in 1853; and their youngest daughter Yaso, then just four years old. Two servants attended the group. The journey took forty-eight days, including a stop at Zenkōji on the way home. Inao noted their departure in his diary and gave the purpose of the trip as sightseeing. He wrote a number of farewell poems expressing his yearning to go with them, but unlike Motoharu, he considered himself far too busy to take time off.[62] For the Matsuo family, with Makoto having been married for five years and a grandson already under the roof, the trip may well have celebrated Motoharu's retirement as household head and village official. Taseko too had no need to curtail her fun by rushing back home now that a daughter-in-law took care of the house.

The truly remarkable event in this trip to Edo was the interaction between Taseko and the daimyo of the Takasu domain, Matsudaira Yoshitatsu. An austere and dignified man, Yoshitatsu had married a younger sister of the renowned reformer Tokugawa Nariaki, and through her imbibed Nariaki's reverence for the imperial court and his fear of the foreign threat. Motoharu had served at the domain's branch office in Takesa. For him not to have paid a courtesy call at the daimyo's compound while they were in Edo would have been rude. Given the status and gender hierarchy of the time, it could hardly have been expected that a peasant woman such as Taseko would be invited to meet the lord as well. Morosawa Yōko posits that Motoharu had previously loaned the domain money, and Taseko probably brought expensive gifts.[63] "We spent some time in the Takasu lord's mansion at Ichigaya," Taseko recorded in a poetry anthology. "We were viewing the garden when he asked me for a poem so I extemporized one on the spot:"

Midori sou	There against the green
taki no shiraito	the silver thread of the waterfall
kuri kaeshi	continually renews itself
musubi wa kimi no	scooping up the water over and over
chiyo no kazu kamo	numbering the thousand years allotted to my lord.[64]

Using the excuse that he wanted to view a peasant child up close, Yoshitatsu urged Taseko to bring Yaso with her when she paid her next visit. Taseko demurred. Yoshitatsu repeated his request. At last Taseko agreed. When they appeared at the compound's gate, Yoshitatsu deigned to see them immediately and showered Yaso with presents. Even in old age she still remembered them and the large crane's nest in the garden.[65]

Taseko and Motoharu arrived in Edo just a little over a year after the shogun had signed friendship treaties with the United States and the European powers. Taseko had written a poem calling on the same divine wind (*kamikaze*) that had defeated the Mongols to sweep away this new threat.[66] The daimyo had been ordered to prepare coastal defenses, which they could ill-afford to do, and the Takasu domain had ordered tiny Tomono to send four men to Edo to serve as guards.[67] With the opening of Hakodate and Shimoda to trade with the Dutch, Japan's long-time trading partners, other nations started trying to do business there as well, to the disquiet of bakufu officials. In their visit to Edo, Taseko and Motoharu must have learned a great deal about foreign affairs. It even appears that Taseko discussed not just poetry but politics with Yoshitatsu. If such was the case, it suggests that peasant women in the early nineteenth century faced fewer barriers to the expression of their opinions than did women in the modern period. I must admit I was skeptical when I first read about this incident. Yoshitatsu wrote several poems for Taseko, however, including one that is hard not to link to the defense of Japan:

Mononofu no	Reading the palm
te ni tori mireba	of a warrior
misuzukaru	you can see the good quality
Shinano no mayumi	of the straight bows from Shinano
shina yoku ari keri	where they cut fine reeds.[68]

FIGURE 12.
Taseko's husband Matsuo
Motoharu. Courtesy of
Matsuo Yūzō.

Having received this proof of her conversations with the daimyo, Taseko and the rest of her group finished their sightseeing in Edo and returned home.

Motoharu's last trip with his wife was in the fall of 1859, to the Kusatsu hot springs high in the mountains between the Kanto plain and Niigata. He suffered most of his life from a stomach ailment, and he had heard that the waters there were particularly beneficial for his affliction. The trip took just over a month, including a two-week stay at the baths. On the way home, he and Taseko made a detour to pay their respects to Zenkōji once more, the last time Taseko is known to have visited a Buddhist temple for the purpose of worship. Then they spent a day in Kami-Suwa at the home of Matsuzawa Motoko, the widow of a peddler named Yoshiaki. He had been well known in the Ina Valley as a salesman of precious metals and shell ornaments, and he had early joined the nativist school of Hirata Atsutane. Like Atsutane, Yoshiaki had learned the Korean writing system, claiming that it was originally Japanese, and used it to write poetry.[69]

Motoko was also a disciple and a noted poet. "Mere words cannot express my joy at your unexpected visit to me," she wrote after Taseko had returned home. "To have parted from you after only a single night of talk at this busy time has left me depressed all day, and I have not been able to sleep for thinking about it." She filled her letter with poems and begged Taseko to send some of hers:

Au to mishi	At the dawn
yume no sametaru	that awakens me from a dream
akatsuki no	in which we met
kokochi nomi shite	all that remains in my heart
akanu kimi kana	is an unfulfilled desire for you.[70]

For Taseko and Motoko, love poetry served as the model for expressions of friendship. Just as nineteenth century American women were accustomed to more passionate displays of affection than women today find seemly among friends, so too did women in Japan fill their letters with mutual protestations of intense desire.[71]

Motoharu went on to live another twenty years after this trip to Kusatsu, but he never left the Ina Valley again. Apparently the respite afforded by his journey was only temporary, and as he grew older he found himself too feeble to travel. He was a gentle man, well-versed in Chinese poetry with a taste for fine calligraphy. His photograph shows him with the beard of a scholar, too engrossed in his Confucian studies to take the time to shave. Once he had turned the household enterprises over to his son, he and Taseko shared a lovely retirement cottage in one corner of the Matsuo garden. In an undated letter to her cousin Inao, Taseko mentioned that he "is just as he was some days ago, and he has not yet returned to normal."[72] They had been married for fifty-one years when he died in 1879. After his death, Taseko wrote a poem in his memory, titled, "Having parted from the person with whom I had been joined for a long time:"

Haru aki no	We spent our time together
koto no ba kusa wo	exchanging poems
sashi soete	in spring and autumn
kimi ga kokoro no	I will not forget the depths
hodo zo wasureji	of my lover's own heart.[73]

CHAPTER FOUR

The Farm Family Economy

"In praise of silk worms"
Think of our country
our country permeated
by light
from the jeweled thread made by
the silk cocoons of Japan.
MATSUO TASEKO, n.d.[1]

Had Taseko not come from money, she would never have gone to Kyoto. No matter how quick her mind, she would have spent her life as so many farm women did, mired in illiteracy and struggling from before dawn till after dusk to keep her family alive.[2] Mapping the conditions and changes in her economic position is thus crucial for understanding how she was able to do what she did. It is also nearly impossible. Ichimura Minato, the only historian to make a serious effort to tell her story by collecting her written works and interviewing people who knew her, cared more for her spiritual development than her material circumstances. He pointed out that her husband had many illnesses that weakened his constitution and he suffered habitually from stomach trouble. While he was incapacitated, "Taseko performed remarkable achievements in managing the household. The family's income gradually increased. Everyone near and far praised her virtue. She improved the morals of her district and served as a model for the masses." [3]

Ichimura took Taseko's money for granted, and as a school teacher and local scholar living in the lower Ina Valley, he may not have thought it appropriate to pry into the financial histories of his neighbors and associates. I wanted more precise information. On my first trip to the area, I paid a visit to the Matsuo house. Matsuo Yūzō and his family graciously showed me Taseko's portrait, her poems and diaries, and the gifts she had received from the imperial family. When I asked about family records, however, I was told that they had long since disappeared. Sometime before World War Two the Matsuo family had split acrimoniously. Yūzō thought that his cousins might have something, but he had no idea where they lived. I discovered much later that they resided just a few doors away. Yūzō would never have introduced me to them, so from his point of view it was better that they and all the family records had disappeared.

I set about trying to piece together a more general overview of the region's economic development and Tomono's place in it. In this I relied heavily on Kären Wigen's *The Making of a Japanese Periphery, 1750–1920,* which contains a case study of the lower Ina Valley. Then I started coming across scattered references to the Matsuo family documents in postwar publications. Tomono is now part of Toyooka, and the Toyooka village history referred repeatedly to the Matsuo archives, even printing some samples. I wrote the Village Education Committee to ask where they were. The head of the Village Historical Society replied that the family had placed four boxes in storage with the Toyooka History and Folklore Museum, but the contents would not interest me—they had to do only with village business and that mainly from the late nineteenth century. The indefatigable researcher leaving no stone unturned, I made an appointment to view the boxes one Sunday afternoon in the little-used ramshackle building that houses a display of local artifacts. The boxes contained no summary listing of the Matsuo holdings, nor any documents concerning sericulture which was, after all, women's work. Instead I found the 1827 resolution to the quarrel between village leaders and small peasants omitted from the Toyooka village history, perhaps because it jibed ill with a tradition of the harmonious village community. I also found a number of bonds attesting to the Matsuo family's role as a moneylender in the 1830s and 1840s, providing indirect evidence that perhaps Taseko did indeed make a significant contribution to building the family's fortune.

The Matsuo were not simply wealthy peasants; they were rural entrepreneurs known in Japanese as *gōnō.* This amorphous class fit ill within a status hierarchy that defined commercial activity as the preserve of urban areas, but then again, it did not exist when that hierarchy was being created at the end of the sixteenth century. Even though its appearance is sometimes used to argue for increased economic differentiation in peasant communities, in fact Japanese villages had always contained both those with wealth and privilege and those without.[4] Some rural entrepreneurs, such as the Maijima family in Ōkarawa, were originally rusticated warriors who transformed their erstwhile retainer bands into hereditary dependents and set them to work tilling the fields. Others, such as the Kitahara, might claim an ancient lineage that befitted their dominant position in the early nineteenth century village, but they had remained unremarkable in village affairs before the last half of the eighteenth century. Only then did they start serving as village headmen, building up their connections to the ruling class, creating documentary evidence of their erudition and lineage, and promoting the economic enterprises that made them rich within the context of peasant society.

The Matsuo family in the early nineteenth century reaped the rewards of a commercial development that spanned two centuries. With the coming of peace after the protracted warfare of the sixteenth century, rulers learned that the only way to increase their income was to find more effective means of exploiting their domains, first through heavier taxes, then the development of specialized products that could be marketed in urban centers, especially Osaka and Nagoya. Peasant and samurai agronomists developed better strains of rice that suited a variety of ecological systems and refined the tools used to till the fields and bring in the harvest. They also promoted the planting of secondary crops and more efficacious fertilizers and fertilizing methods. Had they done nothing more than force the land to produce higher yields, however, they would soon have reached a point of diminishing returns, plus idle surplus labor. The decisive difference was using this labor to turn agricultural products into something else.

Rural entrepreneurs cannot claim the entire credit for the transformation of some areas into the early modern equivalent of industrial zones. According to Edward Pratt, urban merchants dominated "the elaborately articulated system of inter-regional and national trade."[5] Iida's daimyo in the seventeenth century fastened on paper hairdressing ties (*motoyui*) as a suitable industry to generate export income for the domain and supplement the meager stipends that provided less than a livelihood for the lowest ranking members of his retainer band. He enticed skilled artisans to settle in his domain, and he smoothed the way for the sale of their products outside. The start-up capital came from urban merchants, and production centered on the castle town and its suburban villages, including parts of Zakōji.

The major impetus to the commercial development of the Ina Valley was the transportation system using peasant packhorses for carrying goods, a system that by-passed the official transport agents who ran the post stations. Peasants were first allowed to use their horses to transport goods to market, only to start carrying commercial products on their return trips. By the eighteenth century they were carrying baggage farther and farther afield and competing with post-horse operators in the Ina and Kiso Valleys. Domanial attempts to regulate the packhorse drivers proved futile in the long run because Iida's prosperity and indeed the prosperity of the entire valley came to depend on this relatively cheap and reliable means for moving cargo.[6] Iwasaki Nagayo, the man responsible for introducing Taseko to the teachings of Hirata Atsutane, wrote a long poem about Iida that featured these animals:

Asahi ni wa	At dawn
yao ma hiki ire	8oo horses are pulled into the city
yūbe ni wa	at dusk
sen ma hiki ite	a thousand leave
hito sawa ni	myriad people
michi ari	fill up the roads
mono sawa ni	myriad goods
tatawashi kereba	take up all the space.[7]

Many of these horses and people came from outside the Iida domain. In the pursuit of profit, scant regard for administrative divisions was paid as people, goods, and services flowed back and forth across the landscape.

The transformation of the Japanese economy before the introduction of mechanized production in the 1870s proved crucial to Japan's industrialization. The rise in agricultural production, the spread of cottage industries, the concentration of capital in the hands of rural entrepreneurs and urban merchants, and the production of goods for distant markets have led historians to characterize this period as one of "protoindustrialization."[8] In contrast to industrial production, most manufacturing occurred in the countryside. There, laborers and tenants could be put to work under the watchful eye of the village entrepreneur, who was also a large landholder and an official.[9] Underpinning economic development was what Hayami Akira has called an "industrious revolution." This cultural transformation oriented commoners and many samurai toward bettering their lives through economic endeavors and rational calculation.[10] Important too was the creation of an ethos of honesty and accountability. Striving for numerical accuracy in business dealings constituted the basis for trust, and with trust came revolving credit associations that might take ten or more years to pay out. In the absence of a legalized and regulated banking system, these credit cooperatives (*kō*) both spurred the circulation of capital and developed habits of mind conducive to efficacious business practices.[11]

The process of protoindustrialization took different forms in different areas. Cotton cultivation and processing came to dominate the region around Osaka; wooden combs became a specialty product of the Kiso Valley. Protoindustrialization was not unilinear. The paper-making that proved profitable in Zakōji village in the eighteenth century became less so in the nineteenth. Even within a single area, location determined which villages would benefit most from commercial opportunities; within a village, different historical experiences and opportunities meant that some families got ahead while others did not.

In the Ina Valley, the western banks of the Tenryū River had wider and more fertile rice fields than the eastern plus better transportation facilities via access to the Ina Road, and the earliest commercial development tended to concentrate there. Only with the spread of sericulture did villages on the east bank such as Tomono come into their own.[12] Still, in terms of economic competition, Tomono village suffered several comparative disadvantages. It was on the wrong side of the Tenryū River, outside the sphere of Iida's influence, attached to a domain whose land was scattered across two provinces, and governed by rulers who provided little guidance for the development of local industry.

The official village yield for Tomono (575 *koku*) did not change at all between 1601 and 1871. The tax collected by the authorities varied more, from 242 *koku* when it was still under bakufu control in the seventeenth century to 258 in 1683 when the switch was made to Takasu control. In 1737 it went up to almost 276 *koku*. By 1871 it had declined to 210 *koku*. Each year the village also paid an additional tax of between one and three gold *ryō*. These figures make it appear that taxes were high: from 42 percent under the bakufu to 48 percent in 1737 then dropping to 37 percent in the nineteenth century. A land survey at the end of 1871, however, "revealed that nationwide roughly 30 percent of the nation's farmland had eluded the eye of the revenuers."[13] In 1872 Tomono admitted to producing 630 *koku* of rice, only a 10 percent increase over 1601. But in addition it produced 410 *koku* of barley, 83 *koku* of wheat, 73 *koku* of soy beans and 129 *koku* in other grains. None of these were as highly rated as rice, and simply adding them to the official yield would not give a true picture of the disparity between the village's official yield and what it actually produced. Assuming that other grains were worth approximately one-third the value of rice gives a total yield of 861 *koku*, nearly 50 percent over the official yield, and an effective tax rate of 24 percent. In addition the village produced mulberry for paper and silkworms, silk cocoons, thread, charcoal, firewood, lime, and 600 sticks of dried persimmons.[14]

Taxes declined for Tomono in the nineteenth century, but the population showed an increase. Some village populations in the lower Ina Valley almost doubled between 1700 and 1850. Kären Wigen sees in this evidence of the salutary effects of proximity to transportation networks and the development of protoindustry.[15] Given the importance of long-term trends in tracking the significance of population growth, it is unfortunate that the existing records for Tomono cover only a twenty-six-year span, from 1821 to 1847. Even within such a short period, however, there was a remarkable 17 percent increase. The crop failures and famines of the 1830s that devastated northern Japan created only a slight bobble in an otherwise upward trend. Equally noteworthy is that the average number of people per household increased much less, going from 5.2 in 1822 to 5.5 in 1847. The nationwide trend, in contrast, showed a stagnant population in the early nineteenth century, and mountain villages not far away lost population, in some cases dramatically.

Tomono did not have the district's largest households in the early nineteenth century; that honor went to a nearby paper-making village that averaged 5.9 members, but it still had larger households than predominantly agricultural villages. Yamamoto, for example, had an average household size of only 4.5 in the 1840s. Wigen attributes the Tomono pattern to "some combination of rising birthrates, prolonged retention of offspring within their natal households, and an increase in live-in hired help."[16] The Matsuo family typified the first two of these trends; no documents say anything about the servants who must have lived in the house as well.

Neither the Matsuo family documents nor the Toyooka village history report how much land the family owned. A list of village shrines compiled in 1744 shows that the head of the family (always called *Sajiemon* in public documents) had a tiny shrine—about one foot square—inside his compound where he worshipped the family's tutelary deity. In this he was not unique. Only well-off peasants could afford a compound and only those with a suitably impressive lineage had the right to their own shrines. Sajiemon also had two other shrines in forest plots for the worship of the mountain god. He alone in the village maintained more than one of these small shrines, and from this I infer that he alone had more than one plot of woodlands. He also supported the local Buddhist temple that served three villages. In 1701 he bought land worth 16 *ryō*. Of that land, he donated a little over one *tan* (ap-

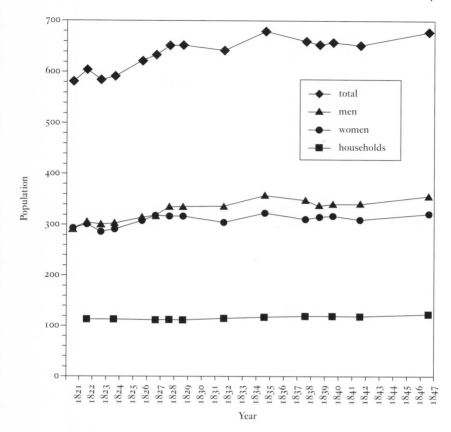

FIGURE 13. Population trends in Tomono, 1821–1847.

proximately a quarter acre) for temple expenses. In 1740 he among others contributed to new buildings, including a bell platform and a two-story tower with ten pillars and a thatched roof. The bell was rung first in memory of his parents, suggesting that he had made the largest donation.[17] These fragmentary records of religious contributions do no more than hint that the Matsuo family was perhaps one of the largest landholders in the village by the first half of the eighteenth century.

The only other document to provide a clue regarding the Matsuo family land holdings comes from 1896, two years after Taseko's death. It shows a tax payment on land under cultivation of 7.351 yen.[18] Given that the land tax at that time was 2.5 percent of the land's value, this would mean that the Matsuo family owned agricultural land worth 294.04 yen. It must have had other taxable income, however, because Taseko's grandson ran for the National Diet in 1892. To be eligible or even vote required payment of at least 15 yena year in direct national taxes, and only about 1 percent of the population qualified.[19] The Matsuo family also owned a section of river plain that had no assessed value because it could not be kept under cultivation. This may be where it ran its ferry boat operation. It is quite possible that the family increased its landholdings after the institution of the new land tax in the early 1870s made landlordism more profitable.[20] For that reason it is not possible to say how much land it owned while Taseko was mistress of the household.

Land alone did not provide the basis for the Matsuo family's wealth. Instead, the family derived a significant if fluctuating portion of its income from sake brewing. As with any other manufacturing enterprise, approval had to be obtained from the authorities, who would then issue a permit to brew a specified amount. These permits could be divided, bought, and sold. In the late 1740s Sajiemon bought an 80 *koku* permit from Den'emon in Ajima, just downstream from Tomono but in a different domain. He also bought Den'emon's sake-making equipment and sake storehouse for a total of 40 *ryō*. (One *ryō* was worth approximately 4000 *mon*. A day laborer earned 100 *mon* a day.) With this, Sajiemon could brew 3,584 gallons a year from 728 bales of rice. In the 1780s, however, a series of crop failures and famines led the bakufu to order sake brewers to reduce their output. By 1788 Sajiemon found himself allowed to produce only 26.6 *koku* on his 80 *koku* permit. He then sold the permit in 1794 to a man in Iida, yet another example of how commercial practices nullified domanial boundaries. To sell this permit he sent a petition to the Takasu government office stating that he had discussed the matter with the other villagers and no one had raised any objections. The village officials signed the petition, indicating that a sake brewery concerned not just the individual but the village as a whole.[21]

Selling the 80 *koku* permit did not mean that the Matsuo family stopped brewing sake. By the 1820s they were back in business, this time with a permit to brew 20 *koku* or 896 gallons a year. At a retail price of approximately two *ryō* per *koku*, this netted them a gross income of forty *ryō* on the Edo market. Prices in the countryside may have been lower. The bakufu ordered sake brewers to reduce their production by one third in 1829, and Sajiemon brewed only 597 gallons. The crop failure of 1833 meant that he got permission to brew just over 298 gallons while the retail price rose to over three *ryō* per *koku* in 1834 and five *ryō* in 1837.[22] These restrictions were lifted in the 1840s. Once when a friend of Taseko's came for a visit, he praised the sake he was served with a poem:

Umashige ni	This is so delicious
kami mōkuramu	even the gods would drink it
tsune wa naru	the great sake
Matsuo no nushi no	produced on a regular basis
ie no ōzake	at the Matsuo house.[23]

By 1861, the family was again brewing about 60 *koku* or 2,688 gallons a year at five *ryō* per *koku* retail.[24] A crop failure in 1869 led to the temporary cessation of sake brewing before the permit system was abolished in 1871. Thereafter, and even without the official protection afforded by government-issued permits, the Matsuo sake brewery continued to flourish. It ultimately provided the capital for Taseko's youngest son to set up his own business in 1899.[25]

The Matsuo family got another source of revenue from managing a ferry boat operation on the Tenryū River. The Takasu domanial authorities had originally mandated the provision of ferry boats for official visits to its villages on the eastern bank. Village headmen also used them going to the government office in Takesa next to Yamamoto. Since each domain required its own access to the east bank, boat crossings peppered the river. Once they came into operation, they naturally proved popular with commoners as well. By the early eighteenth century, cormorant fishing boats large enough to transport the bales of rice used to pay the land tax had replaced dugouts. In 1828, the year before Taseko crossed the river to be married, the Tomono villagers built an earthen wharf to make getting in and out of boats easier. Each boat master held a share in the village ferry limited stock corporation. In 1829 one of these masters fell into debt and sold his share to the Matsuo family for 5 *ryō*. In 1830 a different master sold another share to the Matsuo family for 5 *ryō*, 1 *bu*. With a trip across the river costing a mere 32 *mon*, there must have been a high volume of traffic to make these shares worth buying. Unfortunately the records provide no indication of the total number of shares or how many the Matsuo family owned in addition to the percentage they received as managers.[26]

In 1866, when Taseko's son was questioned by the bakufu regarding the family's occupation, he stated that it cultivated its land, brewed sake, raised silkworms, and supervised a ferry boat operation.[27] Nothing in the Toyooka village history suggests otherwise. In the boxes containing the Matsuo family documents, however, I found eighteen examples of Taseko's husband acting as a moneylender to peasants in his own and nearby villages who put up bits and pieces of land as collateral for the loans, and I found another eighteen documents showing that he eventually acquired land that had previously been mortgaged to him and others. Perhaps because money lending constituted such a conventional sideline for a sake brewer, stretching back to fourteenth century Kyoto,[28] Taseko's son simply forgot to mention it to the authorities.

The first loan dates from 1833, four years after Taseko joined the household. Mankichi from Ajima borrowed 5 *ryō* at an interest rate of 10 percent with both principal and interest to be repaid within the year. Motoharu made three loans at the end of 1834, for a total of over 8 *ryō*. In all cases the interest rate was 10 percent and the loan was for one year. The reason for borrowing the money was to make up arrears in the land tax. The bonds listed the land put up as collateral and made the following promise:

> If by any chance I experience the slightest delay in repaying this money, my guarantors from my five-family group will take responsibility for managing the mortgaged land, and they will definitely repay the balance themselves by the stated day. . . . It is absolutely not the case that this land has been used as collateral for any other loan. . . . Once having repaid the interest and principal, if I need to borrow money again in the future, please lend it to me.[29]

These were not legal documents, and whether they could have been enforced in a court of law is open to question. In any case it would have cost Motoharu more than it was worth to collect a bad debt. For that reason he turned to the five-family group to guarantee compliance. Each village was supposed to be divided into such groups whose members were collectively responsible for each other's good behavior. If anyone of them committed a criminal act, the authorities might well punish them all. What had thus started out as a mechanism of political control, in this instance at least, became grease for the wheels of commerce.

The 1830s saw serious crop failures even in the Ina Valley. Despite the best efforts of village officials to win tax relief, many peasants found themselves short at year's end. One peasant who managed to squeak through the end of 1834 found himself borrowing money in the first month of 1835, to cover arrears on the 1834 taxes. He received one loan for 10 *ryō* that he promised to repay within the year at 8 percent interest using crop land as collateral and another for 5 *ryō* 2 *bu* again at 8 percent interest with a repayment period of three years against his house and all of his household furnishings. For only three other people did Motoharu allow an interest rate of 8 percent. This might suggest that these borrowers were able to make personal claims on him enjoyed by none others. In 1838, however, we find Gentarō receiving one loan of 10 *ryō* at 8 percent and another of 20 *ryō* at

10 percent. In both cases he was already paying tenant fees and the land tax, so the principal and interest would have to come out of the remainder of the harvest and within the year. For a peasant already in trouble, only an excellent harvest and a strong rice market would have enabled him to pay off all his obligations.

Motoharu lent out larger sums of money than most peasants would have been able to keep on hand, but the scale of his operations was in fact minuscule. The most he ever loaned in any one year was 35 *ryō* in 1838. For four years his lending was in the single digits. This was small potatoes compared to a village headman from the Nishijō village of Mino province in the polder region of the Kiso-Nagarai-Ibi watershed; he lent 300 to 500 *ryō* a year up to 1831 and then started lending over 1,000 *ryō* a year in 1837. He financed this remarkable expansion by borrowing money within a network of wholesale credit organized by village officials and rural entrepreneurs.[30] The Matsuo family records provide evidence of borrowing only once, when Motoharu borrowed 33 *ryō* 1 *bu* from the Takasu domain, with a one-year repayment period at 8 percent interest.[31] He borrowed this money in 1838, following a series of disastrous harvests, and the domain may well have supplied it to keep peasants from going bankrupt. If this is the money he then lent to Gentarō and another man, he made a profit of 2 percent on 23 *ryō*, and nothing on the loan of 10 *ryō*. With this exception it appears that Motoharu generated his funds out of his family's internal operations. Perhaps he became a moneylender simply because he had sources of revenue unavailable to other peasants at a time when they needed help.

Acting as a moneylender did not draw Motoharu farther into the banking world where money is used to make money. Instead he bought land, sometimes from the same men to whom he had already lent money. His land transactions follow a slightly different pattern from the loans. They occurred mainly in the 1840s and suggest that the sellers, already weakened by the crop failures of the 1830s, had been unable to make a recovery. After years of indebtedness, their only recourse was to sell off a few plots here and there. In no case was any parcel bigger than a quarter acre and one was only 144 square feet. The price ranged from 26 *ryō* 2 *bu* for 7 parcels including top grade paddy, a house, and a plot of brush in 1832 to 1 *ryō* 2 *bu* for a tiny dry field in 1847. In many cases the bill of transfer contained the notation that the seller had the option of buying the land back within a twenty-year period. It also stated that the seller had removed his name from the land in the record of village holdings and Motoharu was welcome to record it as part of his property. This was in accordance with the village agreement worked out in 1827. Finally the seller promised that neither he, his relatives, his descendants, nor anyone else would ever raise the slightest objection to the sale.

Matsuo family moneylending and land purchases, 1832 – 1847

	LOANS	PURCHASES
1832		26 *ryō* 2 *bu*
1833	5 *ryō*	
1834	8 *ryō* 1 *bu*	7 *ryō*
1835	21 *ryō* 2 *bu*	
1836	4 *ryō*	
1837	10 *ryō*	8 *ryō* 2 *bu*
1838	35 *ryō*	
1839	13 *ryō*	
1840	2 *ryō*	13 *ryō*
1842		11 *ryō* 2 *bu*
1843		16 *ryō* 1 *bu*
1844	3 *ryō*	19 *ryō* 2 *bu*
1845		27 *ryō*
1847		1 *ryō* 2 *bu*

These transactions imply that the Matsuo family expanded its landholdings in the 1840s by taking advantage of the decapitalization suffered by less fortunate villagers in the 1830s.

Three years after Taseko's marriage and the same year that Motoharu made a major land purchase, the Matsuo family started building a new house and compound. Completed in 1838, it enclosed an area of 114 *tsubo* or 4,100 square feet and cost 75 *ryō*.[32] It took a long time to build, perhaps having been delayed by the poor conditions of the 1830s. When it was finished, the family had a home that rivaled a court noble's in size though not in status. On one side Motoharu landscaped a garden with rocks and trees. He and Taseko moved to a retirement cottage called *Senshinkyō* (Hall for cleansing the heart) that opened upon it in 1872. There Taseko could delight in watching the changing of the seasons:

Yuki yori mo	A view more dazzling
nagame mabayuku	than the snow.
niwa no omo ni	Today is the day to praise
chireru sakura wo	the cherry blossoms
metsuru kyōkana	fallen on the garden.[33]

After World War Two, land reform reduced the family's income. When the village required a new road, the retirement cottage and part of the garden had to be sacrificed to provide an easement.

FIGURE 14. The Matsuo family house before World War Two. Courtesy of Matsuo Yūzō.

There is no way to know whether the information presented above covers all of Motoharu's transactions. The Matsuo family records for loans and land purchases consist solely of loose pieces of paper, and over the course of years some might easily have gotten lost. I found only two other records of this type, both dating from the late 1850s and both in a different handwriting, probably that of Taseko's son, also called Sajiemon. In 1857 he lent Yanokichi 15 *ryō* and took from him land worth 10 *ryō* to cover his debts. Yanokichi was to pay him off at 4 *ryō* 2 *bu* a year for ten years, a total of 45 *ryō* which means an interest rate of 20 percent. Two years later this Sajiemon bought fourteen parcels of land for 120 *ryō*, the largest single purchase the family ever recorded. In 1859 the opening of the ports to trade with the west had already brought about a certain degree of currency fluctuation and inflation, but not enough to account for a four-fold increase in purchasing power over 1845.[34] If the family generated internally the funds that it loaned out, where was the money coming from?

I think that what made the crucial difference to the Matsuo family economy in the nineteenth century was sericulture. I argue further that Taseko brought the requisite techniques with her when she married, indeed, the marriage may have been arranged precisely because she had skills the family needed. After all, it was brewing only one-fourth the sake it had brewed in the eighteenth century and in some years it was not allowed even that much. No matter how much land it owned, it needed a nonagricultural enterprise to generate the capital to loan to peasants hard hit by the crop failures of the

FIGURE 15. The Matsuo family retirement cottage before World War Two. Courtesy of Matsuo Yūzō.

1830s when sake brewing was at its nadir, plus build a new house at the same time. I must admit that my evidence is close to nonexistent. Sericulture was women's work, and no Matsuo family document makes any reference to it at all. The diary kept by a headman near Edo shows clearly that his wife and mother managed their own enterprises separately from his own, and it may be that Taseko did the same.[35]

First let me suggest the possibility that the Matsuo family did not raise silkworms until after Taseko had arrived as a bride. Sericulture played such a major role in Japan's industrialization that it is easy to overlook the competition it faced from other industries before the opening of Yokohama in 1859. The Iida domain lord had first called for the planting of silk mulberry trees in 1672, and the bakufu's decision to close Japan to silk imports from China in 1685 meant that by the turn of the century Iida was sending raw silk directly to the looms of the Nishijin weavers in Kyoto.[36] Except for Iida and the villages in its vicinity west of the Tenryū River, raising the silkworms and spinning the filaments drawn from cocoons into thread (sericulture and filature) did not become popular by-employments. Villages even as close to Iida as Yamamoto did not develop these industries to any degree, and the east bank were even less likely to devote much land and labor to raising silkworms.[37]

When Taseko was eleven years old, she was sent to her father's family, the

Kitahara, for her education. Her biographers have been quick to assume that her goal was to study poetry with her cousin Yorinobu, but she may equally well have raised silkworms under the tutelage of his wife Kiso. The Kitahara produced 15 *kan* or 131 pounds of silk cocoons in the fifth month of 1822, the year Taseko first spent time there, and sold them for 2,650 silver *momme*. Sixty *momme* equaled about one *ryō*, so the sale yielded the equivalent of 44 *ryō*, 1 *shu*, a tidy sum. The next year the harvest was down to 10.7 *kan*.[38] The Kitahara family raised more silkworms than most families in the area around Iida. In the early nineteenth century, the average yield was between 3.7 *kan* of silk cocoons, or 32 and a half pounds, and 7.2 *kan*, or 63 pounds. Few managed to produce so much as ten *kan*.[39] The Kitahara family apparently sold most of its cocoons to brokers who then put them out to women in and around the castle town to be spun into silk. Spinning had to be done in hurry, lest the larvae turn into moths and ruin the cocoons. Taseko too learned spinning, and even late in life, she continued to produce her own cloth.[40]

Most families tried to raise two crops of silkworms. In the lower Ina Valley, the first crop in the spring took approximately 43 days, then spinning took 10, and by that time the second set of silkworms had hatched. In the warmer weather, they took only 27 days to reach maturity and spin their cocoons. "Lots of silkworms can be found in every province," one rural entrepreneur from western Japan declared in 1803. "This is a woman's enterprise and does not require input from men so it can be performed with the labor not needed for cultivation. Because it brings in lots of money, it is the most important product that benefits the peasants and profits the state." A writer commenting on conditions in the Ina Valley in the late 1780s pointed out that collecting mulberry leaves had to be done just when grasses were being chopped up for fertilizer and raising silkworms did in fact require labor otherwise available for food production.[41] Sericulture only made sense for families desperate for by-employments or for families high enough on the economic scale to hire labor and absorb the inevitable fluctuations in yield.

Raising silkworms was a time-consuming, labor-intensive enterprise fraught with risk. A family had either to borrow money from a broker to buy the cards with eggs glued to them (one card cost 2 *ryō*) or they had to provide this capital themselves. They had to plant mulberry trees, perhaps replanting woodland plots once given over to paper mulberry or persimmons, or placing the trees on the ridges between the rice paddies where they might shade the rice and stunt its growth. It was also possible to buy leaves. Once the worms hatched (and they preferred the first balmy days of spring when a family was at its busiest preparing the fields), they had to be fed constantly with tender leaves. Any number of agronomy handbooks explained the art of raising silkworms, and there was considerable debate over whether and how much to chop up their food. Silkworms increased their body weight ten thousand times during their brief life. For gains like this, they had to eat voraciously and continually except for four periods of sleep. Simply piling leaves on the trays where they fed was not enough. Too many leaves would smother them; too few and they would go hungry and die. They also had to be kept clean and their droppings removed, because a silkworm will eat anything that lies near its mouth. While they are eating, the din of their chewing can be heard for miles. The smell is reminiscent of nothing so much as a very dirty chicken coop.

Taseko spent a lifetime raising silkworms. In an early letter to Kitahara Inao she apologized for missing his monthly poetry meeting because she was so busy feeding them that she had time for little else. "Once the silkworm season is past, I will be looking forward to an occasion when we can really have a good talk." [42] Following the opening of the port at Yokohama in 1859, sericulture expanded rapidly in the Ina Valley, and when Taseko was home, she played her part. She had a standing invitation to visit the new imperial capital in Tokyo in the 1870s, but she refused because she was needed at home to chop mulberry leaves. [43] Silk production grew steadily, and Taseko finally allowed herself to be talked into moving to Tokyo with her grandson in 1881. They spent just a year there before sericulturalists suffered a string of disasters. A conflict between foreign merchants and the Yokohama baggage handlers depressed the market in 1881, and the next year saw a drop in the value of Western silver. The United States' recession in 1883 lowered demand, while at the same time the Japanese government decided on a drastic deflation of the currency. Silk producers increased output to compensate for lower prices, and Taseko hurried home to help. She continued writing about how busy she was raising silkworms even in her last decade.

Production figures for Tomono and four other villages, 1881–1883 [44]

YEAR	SILK COCOONS	PRICE/*KAN*	THREAD	PRICE/*KAN*
1881	2,080 *kan*	5.21 yen	156 *kan*	63.0 yen
1882	2,520 *kan*	4.50 yen	150 *kan*	53.3 yen
1883	2,573 *kan*	3.00 yen	225 *kan*	40.0 yen

In the course of her lifetime Taseko saw tremendous changes in the manufacturing of silk thread. In the 1850s a new device for reeling thread made its appearance, one that turned the reeling frame with a foot treadle instead of by hand. In the 1870s the reels were hooked to screws driven by water wheels and placed in factories. By being turned faster at a more constant rate of speed they produced finer, stronger thread with greater luster and greater market value. The first factories were small. Three years after they appeared in the lower Ina Valley, Taseko's nephew Suganuma Heihachirō opened the first in Tomono in 1876. He employed twenty workers. By 1883 he had made a profit of 1,080 yen on capital of 3,780 yen with thirty basins heated with steam and a labor force of thirty-one women and four men, the biggest operation in the village at that time. A much smaller outfit was run by Katagiri Gintarō, the son of one of Taseko's poetry-writing friends, employing only seven spinners in 1880. These independent operators gradually lost out to larger corporations with better access to urban financing, especially those established in the industrial core around Lake Suwa. As long as Taseko lived, however, she could always sell her silk to factories in her neighborhood. The Matsuo family never involved itself in the mechanized production of silk thread even though the fortunes to be made were in filatures, not sericulture.[45] Taseko's antipathy to all things foreign may have been one factor, but the male members of the family might well have preferred the reliable if modest profits that came from brewing sake.

It bothered Taseko not a little that the silkworms she so lovingly cultivated made the thread sold to foreigners. In the late 1850s an overcapacity had developed in the production of thread, and export promised a way out. The European silkworms having fallen victim to blight and Chinese production being disrupted by the Taiping Rebellion, for a brief period Japan had the world silk market practically to itself. Thread was cheaper in Japan than in the West, and that too increased its appeal for foreign buyers. In 1859 a merchant from a village near Iida made a sizable sale of 1,092 *ryō* by shipping 12 packs of silk to Yokohama. One of Taseko's friends, a doctor from Nakatsugawa who spent some years in Tomono, was said to have made a fortune, 2,400 *ryō*, on just one trip.[46] In 1860 foreign merchants paid 440 to 470 dollars for 100 catties (132 pounds); by 1865 the price was 830 to 850 dollars. Some economists feared that exports would exhaust the country's resources, and silk might well disappear from Japan. At one point the bakufu issued a temporary ban on selling silk to foreigners, claiming that silk was Japan's sole national resource, the price domestically had risen too high, the amount available for domestic weavers had declined too much, and people would undoubtedly come to regret the mercenary impulse of a moment. On the other hand, the bakufu also profited from the trade by charging a hefty fee of half a *ryō* per *kan* on all exports.[47]

For people such as Taseko, who wanted to revere the emperor and expel the barbarians from Japan's sacred soil, selling the country's treasures to the barbarians was no better than selling them the country. Iwasaki Nagayo wrote a number of poems expressing his rage at the situation:

Ōkimi no   The evil men who gather
mikokoro shirade   at the market in Yokohama
kokoro sae   have not the slightest sympathy
Yokohama no shi ni   with our emperor
tsudou akibito   and how he feels.[48]

Another of Taseko's friends threatened a merchant in Iida with the vengeance
of heaven for trafficking with foreign traders.

Taseko wrote and rewrote a number of poems lamenting the export of
silk. She sent them to fellow Hirata disciples, one a samurai from Chōshū
and the other a fertilizer merchant in Ōmi Hachiman:

Yo no naka no   It is disgusting
ito no midare no   the agitation over thread
ayashiku mo   in today's world.
sumera mi-kuni no   Ever since the ships
matamanasu   from foreign countries
kaiko no mayu wo   came for the jeweled
koto kuni no   silkworm cocoons
fune no kuru yori   to the land of the gods and the emperor,
chihayaburu   people's hearts,
hito no kokoro no   awesome though they are,
hiki haete   are being pulled apart
kaburu uretasa   and consumed by rage.
utsusekai   The superficial
kara no emishi ga   foreign barbarians
shirogane no   pile up mountains
yama wa nasu tomo   of silver,
hi no moto no   but even I, who am not
masura takeo ni   a brave warrior
aranu mi mo   from the land of the rising sun,
ware wa horisezu   I do not want their money,
madoshiku ari tomo   I would rather be poor.

Envoy
shira ito wo   The families of Japan
kaburu no mi-ka wa   who take responsibility for white thread
yo no naka no   with all this confusion
midare mo itodo   in the world
kurushi karikeri   have suffered more and more.[49]

Taseko uses an old word for China to stand for the barbarians in this poem, eliding foreignness with Japan's ancient source of civilization, now seen as an alien and empty tradition.[50] The Japanese themselves are called awesome, *chihayaburu*, a term usually reserved for the gods. The barbarians offer quick profits, but Taseko takes the moral high ground and rejects their money. Despite her refusal to trade in silk, however, it had made her family and friends rich. Would it not be ironic if the export of thread from cocoons she had raised provided the means for her to participate in the movement to revere the emperor and expel the barbarians?

Documents in the Matsuo family collection and Taseko's letters give no more than hints of where the family made its money. Although he lived well enough to employ servants and raise a large brood of children, the head of the family either did not see fit to keep the kind of diary or account book that rural entrepreneurs working on a larger scale used to control their business enterprises, or else it has disappeared. This was not a time when careful records had to be kept; the government never inquired into the finances of any individual family and even the village as a unit might increase productivity with relative impunity. All we can know for certain is that Taseko had the money to use for her own purposes. Without control over her own sources of income, she would never have gone to Kyoto, supported nativist projects, and entertained her friends with tea and talk.

CHAPTER FIVE

The Nativist Encounter

Treading the road
marked
by cherry blossoms in full bloom
I long to see
the way of the ancients.
MATSUO TASEKO, 1880s[1]

A stranger appeared in the Ina Valley in the autumn of 1852.
Despite his indifference to his personal appearance and a severe stutter, he was a handsome man with a broad forehead
and glowing eyes.[2] He liked Iida's lively streets and the bustle
of commerce so he decided to stay a while. Perhaps through
a peddler with connections in Edo, he managed to strike up
an acquaintance with men willing to introduce him to their
circles as a teacher of Japanese classical drama. One of them
was Ichioka Masatomo, brother to Taseko's daughter-in-law
and intendant for the Chimura family of bakufu bannermen in
Iida. Seven months later in the third month of 1853, Taseko's
cousin Kitahara Inao met the newcomer at the house of a
samurai in Iida. Finding each other congenial, they talked late
into the night. The man was Iwasaki Nagayo, and he was des-
tined to have a profound impact on the intellectual life of
Taseko and her friends.

Nagayo was born in 1807 in Edo where his father apprenticed him at the age of seven to an instructor in the Konparu school of Noh to learn the flute, drum, and dance. For two years he received a stipend for his performances from the daimyo of Awa before severing the connection to allow more time for his studies.[3] He also acquired sufficient skill in the tea ceremony to teach it to willing disciples. He studied poetry and literature with Motoori Ōhira, the successor to the great philologist and interpreter of ancient Japanese texts, Motoori Norinaga, then became a disciple of Hirata Atsutane in 1839. In Iida, he made a living teaching the art of Noh to wealthy commoners, both merchants and peasants, who wished to acquire an elegant pursuit once the property of the daimyo. In 1855 he and his disciples put on a Noh performance at a local shrine. Only men were allowed on stage, but Taseko might well have been in the audience. Her later poetry occasionally featured allusions to Noh drama, suggesting that she had imbibed something of his teachings. Having been without a resident poetry teacher since Fukuzumi Kiyokaze died in 1848, she and others like her gladly accepted his instruction in poetry as well. Nagayo made his reputation proselytizing for the Hirata school, but he did not sponsor his first disciple until 1859. Either he hesitated to push his intellectual agenda, or the people he met were indifferent to his message until social upheavals such as the Minamiyama riot and turmoil surrounding the opening of Yokohama to foreign trade forced them to seek new solutions to their problems.

Nagayo was to spend most of twelve years in Iida. He continued to travel, going as far as Nakatsugawa and Suwa in search of pupils and making two trips to Echigo on the Sea of Japan. There he visited the grave of Ikuta Yorozu, also a disciple of Hirata Atsutane, who had died leading an army of the poor against domanial troops following the crop failures and famines of 1837. At one time he fell under the suspicion of the Iida domanial authorities for his work proselytizing the Hirata school and was forced to move out of the castle town. He left for Kyoto in 1863, returning only once in 1868. By becoming a protégé of the Shirakawa family of court nobles in charge of Shinto affairs he ended up a priest at the Naniwa shrine in Osaka where he wrote many Shinto prayers as well as continuing his practice of Noh. Toward the end of his life, he kept a large dog constantly at his side in a filthy room. There he would drink with whomever came to see him. When his visitors complained about the dirty cups, he would reply, "the sake's not polluted so why worry about it." He knew nothing about finances. The shrine's accounts ended up in complete chaos, but it never bothered him at all.[4]

As a poet Nagayo rejected the elegant classical expressions found in the court poetry anthologies in favor of Japan's most ancient poetry collection, the monumental *Man'yōshū*. This text had been the object of considerable scholarly interest since the seventeenth century. Written in an archaic mixture of Chinese characters used as often to represent sounds as concepts or names, it took painstaking philological analysis by men whose prodigious memories served them in lieu of computers before its long forgotten language began to make sense to contemporaries.[5] Nagayo used and taught vocabulary from the *Man'yōshū;* he also tried to write some of his own poems using Chinese characters for their sound alone in place of the syllabary derived from them used by most Japanese of his day. Thus an 1862 poem at one time in the Matsuo family collection described the descent of the heavenly grandson to rule over the Japanese islands entirely in Chinese characters. (None of the men who wrote in this style seem to have appreciated the irony of using a foreign writing system to celebrate Japanese uniqueness.) Nagayo was known for his skill at improvising poetry, especially long poems. Once he took up his brush and sat down before a piece of paper, the words were said to pour out of him.[6] They did not always make sense, at least according to a Japanese historian to whom I showed a poem he wrote about the American bombardment of Shimonoseki in 1863.[7] No matter, they expressed what Nagayo felt at the time. He sang the praises of the beautiful Ina Valley and applauded the prosperity of Iida manifested in the strings of packhorses that surged through it every day.

Taseko may well have started her study of the *Man'yōshū* before she ever met Nagayo. One of the books she borrowed from her Kitahara cousins in 1850 was *Michi no suga no ne* (The roots of the sedge by the road) composed by an obscure contemporary writer, Andō Nukari. Born in 1815 in northern Japan, he was supposed to become a mine supervisor like his adoptive father, but he left home to wander Japan as an itinerant poet. He affected an extreme eccentricity in dress, tying his robe with a rope, and he was known to refuse to come in out of the rain.[8] In 1850 he ended up in Nakatsugawa where he tutored Taseko's cousin Ichioka Shigemasa, met Shimazaki Tōson's father, and wrote poetry in praise of the area. It is probably through Shigemasa that this poetry collection landed in the Kitahara house where Taseko found it.

Nukari's poetry must have come as a considerable surprise to Taseko. His poems were not written in the decorous thirty-one syllables she had studied all her life. Instead they ran on for pages. With one exception they were written in Chinese characters; only the pronunciation gloss at the side indicated that this was Japanese poetry. Students of the *Man'yōshū* such as Nukari and Nagayo called for a revolution in the style and content of poetry. Rather than judge a poem according to its technique and its allusions to the rarefied sensibility of the Heian court, they emphasized the sincerity of the poet's emotions in immediate responses to actual experience.[9] While some long poems spoke of love, the form more often served as a vehicle for formal public laments and provided the space for elaborate depictions of events in the real world. Reclaiming the *Man'yōshū* ultimately made it possible for poets to talk about politics.

Taseko never met Nukari. His poetry introduced her to the *Man'yō* style, but the man who guided her study was Nagayo. On his travels around the area, he stopped most often in Zakōji to visit the Kitahara house where Taseko first encountered him at a gathering to discuss poetry and contemporary conditions. Following that first introduction, he also visited Tomono and the Matsuo family. Everywhere he went he presided over poetry meetings and corrected the participants' poems. Even his short nature poems drew on the *Man'yōshū* for their poetic inspiration and an archaic vocabulary that sought to capture the sensation of the moment:

Koto no ba no	The fields filled with flowers
hana tsumu nobe wo	noted in the ancient poems
misuzukaru	put me in mind of
Shinano to nomi mo	nothing so much as Shinano
omoi keru kana	where they cut fine reeds.[10]

"Misuzukaru" is a pillow word for Shinano derived from a set of *Man'yōshū* poems in which Priest Kume asked Lady Ishikawa to wed him and she responded favorably.[11] For Nagayo the pleasure was in recognizing the continuity between past and present represented by the wildflowers, then recreating the linkage by placing words no longer current in a contemporary poem.

Accepting Nagayo as her teacher meant that Taseko had to reorient her interests and scholarship. In the years before his arrival, she had memorized many poems from the sophisticated court anthologies and read at least portions of *The Tale of Genji* and a commentary written on it. Through Nagayo she learned that according to Atsutane, *The Tale of Genji* was a lascivious work, and the artifice of court poetry ill-behooved anyone who wished to express her true feelings as sincerely as possible.[12] She soon began to write earnest, even naive poems that inserted the gods into the changing of the seasons. Her vocabulary expanded to include the archaic polysyllabic words found in the *Man'yōshū*, though she refrained from writing poetry entirely in Chinese characters. Despite Nagayo's influence, however, she never abandoned the poetic techniques of her youth, and she delighted in writing elegantly crafted poems using classical images to the end of her life. She had added another collection to her repertoire; she did not abandon the old simply because a new mentor disapproved.

Nagayo taught not just a newly archaic style of poetry but a specific doctrine. Without his leadership, the Hirata school of nativist studies might never have made the inroads that it did among the commoners of the Ina Valley. The Iida domain lord admonished his warriors not to become Hirata disciples. Most of his retainers, it was said by scholars in the 1930s, knew nothing about the history and beliefs of their own country but instead pursued the study of Chinese thought. Some were even convinced that practicing poetry would bring about their family's ruin.[13] In other regions the rural entrepreneurs studied Chu Hsi Confucianism or the eclectic teachings of the agronomist Ōhara Yūgaku. Tomono's neighboring villages produced over thirty adherents of the heterodox Confucianism promoted by the Mito school that emphasized reverence for both the emperor and the status hierarchy. A samurai of low rank, Atsutane put most of his energy into a futile effort to enlist daimyo and other powerful figures in his cause. Nor was he able to attract many urban dwellers in the three metropolises. Instead his most dedicated adherents were those who through the opening of new rice paddies or their engagement in commerce and industry were rapidly becoming influential in local society. According to historian Itō Tasaburō, their interest had an effect on Atsutane's teachings. The combination of his character and the audience he attracted meant that the Hirata school was more street oriented and less bookish than other nativist schools and more engaged with religious than literary issues.[14]

Due acknowledgment must also be given to his adopted son Kanetane. Atsutane had enrolled 553 disciples before his death in 1843; twenty years later, his posthumous disciples numbered 1,330. The most precipitous rise came thereafter with 1,500 joining the school between 1864 and 1868. By 1876, a total of 4,283 people had enrolled.[15] Most were commoners, mainly wealthy peasants. Next came shrine priests and only then samurai. Atsutane claimed to be preaching history, not religion, but if his school can be seen as akin to the religious sects founded in the nineteenth century, from the Church of Latter Day Saints to Bahai to Ōmoto-kyō, then he was the equivalent to the prophets Joseph Smith, Bab ed-Din, and Deguchi Nao while Kanetane played the role of organizers such as Brigham Young, Baha Ullah, and Deguchi Onisaburō. With the exception of a few islands, by 1868 the disciples could be found in every one of Japan's provinces. The province with the largest number was Shinano (633) followed by Mino and its important post station of Nakatsugawa (362). The district with the largest number was Ina (386).[16]

Neither politics nor economics determined the intellectual climate inhabited by the rural entrepreneurs of the Ina Valley. The Hirata school did well there partly because the valley was politically fragmented without a unitary domain capable of asserting the dominance of a rival school and also because the transportation network provided local inhabitants with a steady flow of information. Nagayo's presence, however, made the decisive difference. Under his direction the school attracted disciples who took concrete measures to bolster the school's visibility and outshine their rivals in other regions.[17] The study groups might appear anywhere, but in Ina they met regularly and included women. In addition, Ina Valley disciples launched the publication of Atsutane's magnum opus, *Koshiden,* the history of the gods and ancient Japan that drew on early chronicles, Shinto prayers, and local gazetteers. They raised the money to build a shrine to nativist teachers and involved people from across the region in this project. Some disciples went to extremes. Spurred to action by Atsutane's denunciation of Buddhism, they cut off the heads of stone statues of Jizō, the protector of children, and smashed memorial tablets bearing posthumous Buddhist names before throwing them in the river. They erected new god tablets in the Shinto style and worshipped Atsutane and his predecessors along with their ancestors.[18] Despite this level of activism, even in the Ina Valley most village officials and rural entrepreneurs remained aloof. Perhaps they did not feel the same sense of crisis on the domestic or the international level; perhaps their scholarly interests lay elsewhere. The Hirata school never became a mass movement.

Kanetane realized that simply waiting in Edo for disciples to come to him for instruction in his father's teachings was not enough; he had to encourage proselytizers to go out to the countryside, and he had to involve family members. A person wishing to enroll in the school had to find a sponsor, that is, someone willing to attest to her character and interest. She then had to sign an oath, pay a registration fee, and thereafter accept Kanetane's directions for training and study. Kanetane encouraged the formation of study groups where the disciples could read Atsutane's texts on their own. He lent books to disciples who visited the school in Edo and even sent them upon request through the mail. He exchanged news items with his disciples all over the country as well as answering their questions concerning Atsutane's writings. This circulation of information enhanced the cohesion of the nativists as a group.[19] A number of disciples made copies of the membership lists. One man from a village upriver from Tomono printed a woodblock edition of the list and distributed it to other disciples as his contribution to propagating the school.[20] Taseko had already acquired a large number of acquaintances through her poetry circles; joining the Hirata school expanded it further beyond the boundaries of her valley.

Long before anyone in the Ina Valley joined the Hirata school, the poetry meetings had provided opportunities to discuss fears of domestic unrest and a concern for the country's future. Like the salons before the French Revolution, they brought men and women of different backgrounds together for political purposes. Many of these meetings took place in Zakōji at the home of Taseko's cousins, Kitahara Yorinobu and his son Inao. These two men had long been accustomed to hosting the leaders of local society, and besides, Zakōji was far enough from Iida to escape the prying eyes of samurai while still being easily accessible to the town's residents. According to Higuchi Mitsunobu, Inao's younger brother, the conversation once devoted to poetry often veered to the problems of the times and proposals for remedies. Whenever Taseko appeared at these meetings, she too had the chance to learn about what was going on in the wider world. With his wide-ranging circle of correspondents providing him with the news of current events, Nagayo played a crucial role. It was through him, for example, that shocking news—the assassination of Ii Naosuke, the highest ranking member of the shogun's cabinet—reached the Ina Valley commoners before the Iida domain retainers knew anything about it.[21]

The vast majority of the Japanese population—the peasants, merchants, artisans, and all others not members of the ruling class—were officially expected to remain ignorant of national politics. The bakufu had long-standing laws forbidding publicity about itself or any current event with political ramifications. Taseko's family and friends honored this prohibition in the breach. They needed accurate information to succeed economically. From village to town to the metropolises of Edo, Kyoto, and Osaka, overlapping webs of communication networks linked together literate men across the country. Designed to speed news of harvests and market prices, by the 1850s these webs carried reports on the foreigners' proposals, the paralysis of will within bakufu circles, and the emperor's anguish over the barbarian presence.[22] This kind of information was generally restricted to men, yet through the poetry circles and nativist cells Taseko gained access to at least some of it.

It is clear that Taseko was deeply interested in news about foreign affairs and quickly realized that she could write commentary on what she had learned using the *Man'yō* style. She wrote poetry at Commodore Perry's arrival in 1853 that summoned a divine wind (*kamikaze*) to sweep him away. She called for a return to the age of the gods at a poetry meeting in 1853, and she had discussed politics as well as poetry with the Takasu domain lord in 1855. Beginning with the assassination of Ii Naosuke in 1860, she began to write political doggerel in earnest.

Through Nagayo and perhaps other communication channels, Taseko already knew enough about what was going on in Edo to understand the sig-

nificance of Ii's death. The most powerful man in the bakufu, Ii had many
enemies. Samurai from the western domain of Chōshū hated him because he
had executed their revered teacher Yoshida Shōin, whose only crime in their
eyes was an excess of zeal in trying to rally the Japanese people against the
foreign threat.[23] Ii had also defied the emperor's wishes in signing a commercial treaty with the United States and other foreign powers. Japanese historians today like to point out that the real quarrel was not over whether to open
the country by signing the treaties, but rather who was to become the next
shogun. Was it to be Hitotsubashi Yoshinobu, 1837–1913, a man of proven
abilities and the seventh son of the Mito domain lord, or was it to be Tokugawa Iemochi, 1846–1866, younger, more malleable and from Mito's traditional rival, the Kii branch of the Tokugawa family?[24] Ii chose Iemochi, thus
in the eyes of Mito retainers adding insult to injury. On the third day of the
third lunar month in 1860, eighteen samurai ambushed Ii and his sixty-man
guard just outside the shogun's castle. He was the highest ranking official to
die at the hands of assassins in the history of the Tokugawa bakufu.

Nagayo's reports of what was happening to Japan had already outraged
Taseko and her friends; Ii's assassination simply fanned the flames. Angry at
Ii and others like him, full of sympathy for the men who had done the deed,
Taseko wrote the first long poem of her career. First she set up a contrast be-
tween the emperor who in ancient times had ruled Japan and the shogun's
short-sighted advisors:

Tori ga naru	In the eastern provinces
azuma no kuni ni	where the birds sing,
kumoi nasu	in place of the emperor
tō no mikado ni	who once had taken charge
ame no shita	of the great affairs of government
ō matsuri goto	for the realm
torimaosu	in his palace far away
kimi no kawari ni	above the clouds,
tsukasadoru	the despicable charlatans
shireese hito wa	who run the administration
hi no moto no	have abandoned the way
michi wa yukisute	of the foundation for the sun
utsusekai	and learned even from
kara ni mo narabi	superficial Chinese teachings.[25]

Japan may have received much of its high culture from China, but Taseko
called it worthless. By doing so, she implicitly condemned all knowledge de-

rived from foreign sources. In contrast to lofty time-hallowed expressions praising the emperor, she used words that grated on the ear, *shireese* (foolish, ugly) and *utsusegai* (literally the empty shell of a clam), to damn the officials who had forgotten their duty in their mad rush after foreign technology.

In the central section of this poem Taseko lauded the assassins. Drawing on graceful images from classical Japanese verse with sounds believed to have magical power, she captured her heroes' grief and resolve to take action. She then picked up the pace in depicting the attack itself:

mononofu wa	The warriors
takebe ni takebi	shout and shout,
Shikishima no	enflaming
Yamato kokoro wo	the true Japanese spirit
furi okoshi	of these myriad islands.
mi-kuni no tame to	For the sake of the country
ie wasure	they forget their families
mi mo tanashirazu	and consider their lives less than nothing.
ama kirai	The deep snow fallen
fureru miyuki wo	from a leaden sky
kurenai no	they stain
iro ni nashikeru	with crimson.[26]

Taseko concluded her poem with a statement that this deed must not be forgotten. In the envoy she summoned an ancient past when young men died at the height of their beauty and glory. It is clear that she read the assassins' motives simply as a desire to cleanse Japan of traitors who had defiled it by accepting foreign ideas. Their deaths, and some did die at the hands of Ii's guards, recalled other heroes who had died in the service of the emperor many centuries before. Beyond suggesting that administrators had been seduced away from their duties, the poem ignored the political machinations of the time: the attempt by young, low-ranking samurai to find a voice in the political arena, the diverse opinions expressed by the daimyo on how to handle the Western powers, or the troubling issue of redefining the relationship between shogun and emperor, between the bakufu and the court. Taseko was and remained an outsider in the realm of political affairs. Her poem provides a glimpse of how she and commoners like her responded to the events that shook Japan, nothing more.

From Taseko's point of view, Ii had allowed the bakufu to be threatened and humiliated by the foreigners. He entertained barbarian diplomats and profited from foreign trade regardless of the harm it brought to Japan. The barbarians proudly paraded through the streets of Edo, took over the most impressive temples for their lodgings, treated the shogun's advisors as their equals, and acted as though they were above the law. Having written a long poem lauding the assassins for their deed, Taseko also wrote short ones calling on the men around her to root out these noxious guests.

Kari harau	Perhaps we must rely on
to kama mo kana to	the sickle and the carpenter's plane
tanomu kana	to cut them down and get rid of them—
natsuono no ubara	these weeds that flourish
hayashikeru koro	in the fields of summer.[27]

This poem is perhaps less forthright that the modern sensibility would expect for an expression of rage, but most nativists preferred graceful euphemisms and circumlocutions.[28] It is notable for its distance from the classical vocabulary of the court anthologies and the vigor of its first line, which becomes the third in the English translation. By calling for the tools of the peasant and the artisan, Taseko implies that commoners too have a role in ridding Japan of the barbarians.

It was not completely surprising that Taseko ventured an opinion in the discussions held at her cousin's house on contemporary affairs.[29] Poetry had given her a voice, national affairs gave her a subject, and the Hirata school gave her an institutional framework within which to be heard. Peasant men who had been marginalized in the political world of their time found that the extraordinary circumstances surrounding the coming of the barbarians gave them a chance to express themselves to their rulers. In the cracks that opened if only briefly and only slightly in the bastion of male privilege, a handful of women who had been silenced as women found an opportunity to speak as well. It is true that few among the ruling class heard even the men and fewer still paid them any mind. For that reason, perhaps, their existence has seldom been noted in the history books.

Taseko was among the initial people to join the Hirata school in the Ina Valley, but she was not the first. That honor belonged to Katagiri Harukazu, an elder in the Yamabuki domain ruled by the Zakōji family of bakufu bannermen. Like so many of his friends and relatives, Harukazu was a peasant with warrior pretensions. He and Taseko had a multi-generational connection: his great-grandfather wrote poetry with Sakurai Chie; his grandfather was friends with Sakurai Haruki, and his grandmother came from the same Ichioka family in Iida as Taseko's daughter-in-law. Following Commodore Perry's arrival in 1853, Harukazu collected bronze bells from the three temples in Yamabuki and melted them down to make cannon. He organized a troop of gunners from among the domain's samurai, inducted peasant men into a new unit of foot soldiers, and drilled them in the use of weapons. In 1857 he went to Edo to study the martial arts. There he met Kanetane and joined the Hirata school.[30] Just before he died, he inaugurated plans for a shrine to nativism, a project that also involved Taseko.

The man who sponsored Taseko's entry into the Hirata school was her cousin, Kitahara Inao. He had joined at the end of 1859 under the guidance of Nagayo along with Hara Mayomi from Seinaiji, a man to whom Taseko had once written a love poem as an invitation to visit her. Inao deeply regretted that Atsutane had not published his most important manuscripts during his lifetime. If only they were in print, it would save the labor of copying them and make it easier to disseminate the school's message. In 1860 Inao used his own capital to issue a short text on chronology called *Kōninreki unkikō*. This text critiqued all previous attempts to establish a chronology from the age of the gods through Emperor Jimmu by tracing the imperial lineage back to Izanagi and Izanami. It was dated 1833, 2,493 years since Emperor Jimmu had founded the nation. (Tokugawa Nariaki of Mito also proposed celebrating the 2,500th anniversary of the nation's founding in 1840, and the 2,600th anniversary was in fact celebrated in 1940.) Inao distributed this text to his friends in the Ina Valley and his uncle in Nakatsugawa, but not, apparently, to Taseko.[31] Its publication is said to mark the beginning of the nativist movement in the Ina Valley.[32]

Taseko joined the Hirata school in 1861 at the age of fifty. She was one of twenty-nine women who registered as disciples, less than one percent of the total enrollment. Unlike most women who joined the school following their husbands or fathers, she was the first of her family to join; her husband never did.[33] "Having listened to Inao's talks about our sacred country, I was invited to enter the school of our teacher Hirata," she wrote as the heading for the following poem:

Ima yori wa	From now on
ashita mo sara ni	and redoubling my efforts day by day
yūdasuki	tying back my sleeves
kakete zo kami no	with strips of cotton cloth
michi wo tadoramu	I will follow the way of the gods.[34]

Yūdasuki were the white cotton strips used by shrine maidens to tie their sleeves out of the way while they were engaged in Shinto rites. The impetus for the spread of the Hirata school in the Ina Valley may have been political problems, but as with so many of her friends, Taseko sought their resolution in a renewed dedication to the way of the gods.

The pledge that Taseko signed in joining the Hirata school on the twenty-fifth day of the eighth month was written entirely in Chinese characters. The characters used for their sound alone were the same as those in the *Man'yōshū,* with one exception. This was the character for emperor, usually pronounced *sumeragi* or *ō,* functioning here as a verbal ending to provide a visual reinforcement to the message:

> I earnestly beg to receive the guidance of this teacher along the road to the ancient days of our imperial country. In accordance with the directive I have received, I wish to register my name in order to obtain instruction on how to proceed on this way. Hereafter I will study with all due respect and learn the way of the gods. I promise not to disobey the government's injunctions, not to contradict what the teacher says, and not to hold heretical thoughts. Should I betray this vow, in thought, speech or writing, I understand that the august gods of heaven and the gods of the earth knowing this and seeing this will punish me.

It was signed, "the wife of Matsuo Sajiemon, Takemura Taseko." [35]

Over three months later Taseko received a letter from Kanetane welcoming her to the school and bestowing upon her a selection of prayers and two pages of commentary:

> I have been told by your relative, Mr. Kitahara, that you wish to enroll in this school because you are devoted to the study of the imperial way. I have gratefully celebrated the receipt of your pledge and the entrance fee of 200 gold *hiki* that you sent. Please understand that since I myself am unworthy, you are to consider yourself the posthumous disciple of the teacher who was here before [Atsutane], and I have placed your fee before his spirit. I trust that hereafter you will seriously devote your energies to making progress in your studies. Please let me hear from you occasionally. Affectionately, Hirata Kanetane. [36]

One *hiki* equaled 25 copper *mon,* so she paid the equivalent of 5,000 *mon* at a time when a day laborer earned 100 *mon* a day and a maid earned 80.

Once Taseko had officially enrolled in the Hirata school, she participated regularly in the monthly study sessions held either at the house of her Kitahara cousins in Zakōji or in Tomono. "On the seventh day of the first month we are going to have the first meeting of the year at Majima's," she wrote to Inao at the end of 1861. "Majima has asked me to tell you that we very much want you to come. He will be looking forward to seeing you and so will I." Born the same year as Taseko in 1811, Majima Toshinari had specialized in eye medicine in Kyoto and Edo before moving to Nakatsugawa. In 1854 he turned his practice over to his adopted son and left for Tomono, where he stayed until 1865. An active proselytizer, he and Taseko saw to it that Tomono ended up with one of the largest clusters of Hirata disciples in the villages of the Ina Valley.[37]

The study groups provided the opportunity to read Atsutane's works, ponder their meanings, and worship in the spirit he had envisioned. The cell centered on Katagiri Harukazu, the valley's first disciple, convened on the eleventh of every month (that being Atsutane's birth day). Calling itself the "Circle of Righteous Men," it met before a portrait of Atsutane just as the earlier poetry circles had featured a portrait of the poet Hitomaro. Harukazu wrote a prayer with which to begin the meeting that both enumerated Atsutane's vast scholarly accomplishments in clarifying Japan's ancient way and sought to bring his listeners into harmony with the divine age of antiquity:[38]

> Humble but courageous men blessed by the spirit of our divine teacher,
> we resolve to carry out the true practice of the godly way passed down
> in our great country under imperial rule from the beginning of heaven
> and earth.

Harukazu purified a small alcove in which to hang the portrait, offered sacred sake for the refreshment of Atsutane's spirit, and then "the members who have gathered together partake of the leftover sake to bring us into closer fellowship with joy and laughter."[39]

Harukazu kept much more detailed records for his study group than did Inao or any of the people in Tomono. Everyone who joined the "Circle of Righteous Men" had to abide by five regulations that to a certain extent limited costs. The host (a rotating position) decided on the offerings to put before Atsutane's portrait, but they had to include no more and no less that one *shō* (two quarts) of sake. The tea was to be low grade, accompanied by nothing fancier than dried persimmons or steamed beans. Historian Itō Tasaburō has called this "the true spirit of the nativist movement" and one with the potential to transform commoners into citizens. He envisioned peasants gathering to hear the prayer written by Harukazu. When the ceremony was over, they would wet their throats with tea while discussing ancient history and contemporary problems. Toward evening, they would open the dinners that each had brought, drinking a little sake and continuing their conversation in a more light-hearted vein before breaking up after dark to return home.[40]

Why then would the ruling authorities in Iida look askance at nativist proselytizers? After all, by enjoining its followers to be diligent and accept the political hierarchy, especially within the village, the Hirata brand of nativism apparently offered support to the crumbling political order. In answer to this question, Harry Harootunian has argued that nativism tried to establish an ethical significance for agriculture and the peasants' endeavors that gave its adherents a sense of enhanced worth by positioning them squarely at the center of an equation between gods and nature. It envisioned an ideal world based on folk or popular culture as distant from the centers of power as from official ideology.[41] Japanese scholars go farther in arguing that the rural elite deliberately appropriated the nativist vision to legitimize the role they had created for themselves in intervening between rulers and peasants and to buttress their position against the problems of disorder, rebellion, and depopulation.[42] It thus made sense for Inao to join the Hirata school following his eviction from his position as village headman.

Nativism has come in for some harsh criticism. In the eyes of James White, a scholar of popular rebellion, "nativism became a tool of commoner elites in their efforts to repress the contentious tendencies of the people." It further widened the gap between them and ordinary peasants already opened by market and social forces, and was "made to order for a rural elite that had already defected from the people economically and politically, yet lacked philosophical justification for its position." In short, it represented a "concerted effort to impose a soporific false consciousness on the people."[43] In response, I argue that the vision of the harmonious village community subordinated individual desires to the good of the whole, but it did so more for the leaders who believed the nativist message than the tenant farmers. If anyone was guilty of false consciousness, it was the village elite. As Katsurajima Nobuhiro has pointed out, in justifying their social function as hereditary officials by positioning themselves at the base of a vertical hierarchy topped by the emperor, they ended up unable to envision a polity without him.[44]

The Hirata school changed between Atsutane's time and its reorganization by Kanetane. In the 1840s Atsutane and his disciples were concerned with the afterlife, and their writings had a deeply religious cast.[45] Most disciples came from Kanto and Tohoku; only four were women. In the 1860s, the threat of foreign domination as much as domestic unrest spurred commoners to find a way to become political subjects. The message they found in Atsutane's writings was that everyone in society was responsible for carrying out the duties entrusted to him or her by the emperor. Just as the shogun was responsible for the country as a whole, so too each village headman was responsible for the welfare of his village.[46] Taseko had probably been exposed to Atsutane's teachings in the 1850s, but she did not join his school until the foreign threat had forced a palpable change in the political arena.

Taseko was the first woman to become a posthumous disciple. Of the twenty-four women who joined the school after she did, fully fourteen were from Shinano and Nakatsugawa—just across the border.[47] Perhaps the men she knew made less distinction between the scholastic avenues open to men and women than those in other areas. It is equally possible that once Taseko had led the way, it became socially acceptable for other women to join as well. In this period of political confusion, they were granted a somewhat larger public role than usual for a brief time while the line between public and private dimmed. The same has happened in other revolutionary situations when an old order that had monopolized public space was forced to give way to new voices and gender demarcations became blurred.[48] With everything else up for grabs, politics too became for a time, at least, more inclusive. It is nonetheless striking that most women joined the Hirata school only after its concerns had gone beyond purely domestic issues to encompass political problems and international relations.

Taseko joined the Hirata school between the assassination of Ii Naosuke and another unprecedented event, the marriage of the emperor's half-sister to the shogun. The bakufu had experienced a remarkable decline in its own authority and seen a concomitant rise in that of the court. In a desperate attempt to use the emperor's prestige to shore itself up, it proposed that shogun Iemochi marry Kazunomiya, who was born in 1846 and thus just fourteen during these talks that would decide her fate. Since Emperor Kōmei himself wanted stronger ties to the bakufu, this proposal was difficult to refuse, despite Kazunomiya's previous betrothal to Prince Arisugawa and her distress at the match. In the end, certain court nobles who hoped that closer ties with the bakufu would lead to new opportunities for themselves managed to convince her to do her duty by agreeing to be sent to Edo in Musashi province. With some resignation she wrote:

> Oshikaraji   It's all right.
> kimi to tami to no   If it's for the sake
> tame naraba   of the emperor and the people
> mi wa Musashino no   I will gladly vanish
> tsuyu to kiyu tomo   with the dew on the plains of Musashi.[49]

Kazunomiya was not the first woman from the imperial court to be married off to distant Edo, but she had the highest rank and the times were extraordinary.[50] Rumors flew: the emperor had been coerced into letting her go; low-ranking nobles had accepted enormous bribes to promote the marriage; young radicals were going to capture her on her way to Edo and return her to Kyoto; bakufu officials planned to use her to put the daimyo in their place, then force Emperor Kōmei to abdicate.[51] Concerned that foreigners might interfere in her journey, the bakufu decided that she would take the interior mountain route to Edo, the Nakasendō.

The news of Kazunomiya's betrothal to the shogun provoked a mixed response in Taseko's circle. Her cousin Ichioka Shigemasa opposed the match, and in his poetry he suggested that the princess was too young to be sent so far away.[52] Nagayo complained of how bakufu men had treated the porters, saying that they had beaten some with green bamboo and shot those who tried to run away. "According to what the people at Nakatsugawa told me, this incident will dim the imperial prestige and we hate to speculate on what the princess must feel. . . . The one night that her retinue spent at Nakatsugawa cost 3,500 *ryō*, and it is really too bad that the princess's escort should be so greedy."[53] In contrast to his jaded appraisal, Taseko's poems offered her felicitations for the upcoming nuptials:

Nagaki yo no	This will become a precedent
tameshi naruran	for a long reign.
ōkiso ya	Along the Kiso Road
kiso no kage michi ni	shaded by the trees in the Kiso Valley
kakaru miyuki wa	winds the imperial procession.[54]

Angry though she had been at perfidious bakufu officials like Ii Naosuke, Taseko seemingly endorsed this ploy to cloak the tattered robes of shogunal authority in the mantle of imperial grace. After all, the one condition attached to this marriage was that the shogun expel the barbarians from Japan within ten years.

WITH ONE EYE cocked to national events, the Ina Valley disciples continued to promote the nativist movement. In 1862, Taseko's cousin Inao and his closest associates issued a prospectus for the publication of Atsutane's monumental *Koshiden* (Lectures on Ancient History), one of the texts Atsutane had identified as containing the central tenets of his teaching. The prospectus described how Atsutane had spent fifty years of his life forgetting to eat and sleep, ignoring cold and heat and turning night into day in his efforts to research the texts of a hundred schools and sweep away the last bit of Buddhist-laden dust from "the true visage of our divine land." Despite his prodigious labors, however, the work remained unpublished. Inao and his friends wanted to rectify the situation "in order to repay one ten-thousandth of our obligation to the country for having been blessed with peace for three hundred years." They had already raised the money to print the first volume of four chapters, but sixteen chapters remained. The prospectus was widely disseminated in the Ina Valley and the movement to publish this text gained adherents in other provinces besides Shinano. "Once everyone both above and below is able to read the true facts regarding the age of the gods, we will be able to advance the way of loyalty and filial piety to gods, rulers, country and ancestors." The sponsors' ultimate goal was to present *Koshiden* to the emperor and let him know who had made the project possible. They promised their supporters that "contributing to this publication will glorify your name throughout the ages."[55]

This promise was ultimately kept. The name of each person who contributed to the project was listed at the end of the chapter for which she had paid. When a complete edition of Atsutane's collected works was published using modern technology in 1914, this woodblock edition, including the names of the sponsors, became the standard text. The reprint edition of 1977 provides an appendix giving the names and villages of the people who first supported its publication. At the end of the third chapter in the first volume one will find the following statement: "The disciples Majima Toshinari, Kitahara Nobukata [Inao] and Iwasaki Nagayo announce that those who offer this third chapter to the god of wood are the wife of Matsuo Motoharu, Takemura no Tase from Tomono in the Ina district of Shinano plus [two others]."[56]

Publishing *Koshiden* was an expensive and complicated undertaking. The work of preparing the wood blocks and printing the chapters was done in Edo under Kanetane's direction. He and Inao exchanged numerous letters regarding how the project was to be funded. Kai disciples paid for the second volume, Nakatsugawa disciples paid for the third, then more Ina disciples paid for the fourth. Sixty-six people contributed to the project, most from Ina and Mino but others from as far away as Shikoku and Kyushu.[57] In an 1864 letter to Inao, Kanetane complained that the expenses for publishing each chapter had increased until it cost 200 *ryō* per volume. At four chapters per volume, that meant Taseko put up 16 *ryō*—a hefty sum in those days.[58] (Remember that the dowry supplied to her husband's sister had been 20 *ryō*.) Silk must have been selling very well indeed.

Taseko did more than simply contribute money to this project; she was actively involved in helping it come to fruition. "I have a request to make of you," she wrote Inao while on her way to Kyoto in 1862. "Please take care of things regarding *Koshiden* until I get back."[59] She may have been referring to more than the publication of "her" chapter. Just as Inao and his associates took credit for organizing the subscriptions for the chapter to which she contributed, so too at the end of chapter ten is the following statement: "The disciples Takemura Tase, Higuchi Mitsunobu and Iwasaki Nagayo announce that chapter Ten has been printed through the efforts of those who build their houses next to the stables of Nakatsugawa on the Nakasendō, Sugai's son Mitsutaka and Hazama no Hidenori, who feel as we do about this project."[60] Mitsunobu was Inao's youngest brother, who had been adopted by a dry-goods merchant in Iida. Taseko may well have recruited Hidenori and Mitsutaka while she was in Nakatsugawa waiting for her chance to go on to Kyoto. In any case, she was the only woman who not only contributed money to the cause but also convinced other people to do the same.[61]

As well as finding subscribers for the publication of *Koshiden*, Taseko recruited disciples for the Hirata school. "Right where I'm staying several people have said they'd like to become disciples," she wrote Inao and Nagayo from Kyoto in 1862. "I'm delighted that sooner or later they'll join the school. It seems that all the disciples are gaining in power."[62] In 1864, she sponsored Matsuoka Toshinari, a Takasu domain retainer with whom she was later to board in Kyoto. In the late 1860s she sponsored a number of people in the villages around Tomono. One was Ichioka Onari, the younger brother of her daughter-in-law. While she was in Tokyo in 1869 and working in the public sphere, eight men, many of them higher in status than she, listed their names as Hirata disciples and gave hers as their sponsor. A total of eighteen people, ranging from men in their forties to a girl under ten, joined the school through her introduction. Among her associates, only Hazama Hidenori from Naka-tsugawa and Inao sponsored more disciples than she did. Katagiri Harukazu, the first Ina Valley disciple, for example, never sponsored more than fifteen.[63] Taseko was the only woman in the Shinano–Mino area to induct other people into the Hirata school.[64]

Taseko's entry into the Hirata school also had an impact on her immediate family and friends. All three of her sons plus Chiburu, her oldest grandson, joined the school. Her granddaughter Takemura Hisa joined at the age of ten. Makoto sponsored ten disciples himself; Mitsunaka sponsored three.[65] In Tomono Taseko had taught Hara Sugako in the classical poetic tradition, but she had Makoto sponsor Sugako as a disciple. Sugako's husband had died young, leaving her with small children. For over ten years she managed the family enterprises practically single-handedly, yet she still found time to practice poetry and take an interest in national affairs.[66] One of her poems expressed the desire felt by many Ina Valley nativists to do something, anything, to resolve the crisis facing Japan:

Tachi toranu	Even though I don't have the body
mi ni wa aredomo	to take up a long sword
jiji araba	if something happened
kuni no mi-tame to	might it not be that
narazarame ya mo	I could do something for the country?[67]

NOT CONTENT with study, book-publishing, and proselytizing, Katagiri Harukazu laid plans to erect the *Hongaku reisha* (shrine to the spiritual leaders of fundamental learning). They were four: Kada no Azumamaro, a Shinto priest from Fushimi who vilified Confucian and Buddhist doctrines in order to establish the study of Japanese literature and history as a separate discipline; Kamo no Mabuchi, who tried to recapture the ancient way by elucidating the *Man'yōshū* and reviving the long poem (*chōka*); Motoori Norinaga, the first in centuries to figure out how to read Japan's ancient history texts; and Hirata Atsutane. Inao and his friends encouraged the project and promised to help with the financing. The site chosen had already been identified by Harukazu's father as one of the eight most beautiful in the region, high on a hill in a grove of pine trees overlooking the Tenryū River. Kanetane chose the name. He knew, he said, that other disciples in Satsuma and Akita had proposed building similar shrines, but none had ever materialized.

The greatest difficulty facing the shrine's proponents was acquiring the appropriate material objects to stand for and receive the spirits of the teachers. For Atsutane they requested a large phallus he was known to have cherished as a visible manifestation of the primeval creator god. A number of families, including the Kitahara and Matsuo, worshipped this god as their family deity, and they had placed stones representing female and male genitals in their gardens for the prevention of disease and to ward off death.[68] Kanetane at first refused because the other teachers would be represented by smaller, more traditional objects and the contrast could be seen as an insult. Besides, it might have an adverse effect on local customs. Only when the organizers agreed to house it in a separate building out of sight of the common people did Kanetane agree to part with it. He sent a necklace of quartz circling a sunstone for the main shrine.

It took two years to build the shrine and collect appropriate accouterments. First, messengers had to be sent at considerable expense to fetch with appropriate ceremony the objects made precious by their link with the teacher they represented. Through Taseko's connections with a Kyoto merchant, the organizers purchased a set of four bamboo screens from a family of court nobles. A large bell to be hung in front of the shrine was the gift of a disciple from Yokkaichi on the Pacific coast. Kanetane donated two horse loads of printing blocks to pay for the shrine's upkeep. Then Harukazu died suddenly at the end of 1866 while the mementos from the teachers' families were still being negotiated and the shrine itself had yet to be built. Inao and the other supporters pressed on, however, raising the framework at the end of the first month of 1867 and completing the shrine two months later.

The inauguration took place in the middle of the night, the best time to communicate with the gods. It was the largest gathering of which Taseko was ever a part: 118 people participated, and they came from all over the Ina Valley plus the region around Nakatsugawa. In addition to Taseko there were two other women, each wearing a short sword at her belt. Pine torches carried by the worshippers lit the visible and invisible worlds. The procession was led by a large banner inscribed by the bakufu bannerman whose fief included the shrine. Behind it came young men carrying a brocade banner, followed by a staff decorated with zig-zag white paper streamers. Inao carried a branch of the sacred sakaki tree. Next came a plaque inscribed with Azumamaro's spirit name, followed by the bronze mirror collected from his descendants. In the section of the procession for Mabuchi, the staff decorated with zig-zag white paper streamers was carried by Taseko's eldest son, Makoto. Her second son, Mitsunaka, carried the staff for Norinaga. Taseko's grandson Chiburu, then just thirteen, bore a shield for Atsutane. Once everyone had climbed the mountain to the shrine and the precious objects had been installed, young men performed a sword dance to pacify the spirits. Naturally, the ceremonies conformed as closely as possible to ancient rituals.[69]

For better or worse, Hirata Atsutane's teachings contributed a strongly religious cast to the study of ancient Japan. In building the Hongaku shrine, his disciples hoped to pursue the path of scholarship marked for them by their predecessors, a path originally laid out by the gods that would lead them to an empathic understanding of the ancient world created by the gods. Following the opening ceremonies (which lasted till dawn), they held a banquet and recited poetry that spoke to their joy at the accomplishment of this great undertaking and their hopes for the future. They were only commoners, but by building this monument, they felt that they had made a contribution to defining the national spirit.[70]

Since its inauguration, the shrine's fortunes have shifted with the times. Taseko continued to attend festivities at the Hongaku shrine through the 1880s. By 1897, however, all the people who had first supported it had died, and the families had scattered.[71] Interest in the shrine declined: no one came to perform the ceremonies, the path reverted to fields, the torii decayed and collapsed, and the roof fell in. The Katagiri family removed the sacred objects to their own house for safekeeping. In the late 1920s descendants of the original founders raised the funds to rebuild the shrine in the style of the Ise shrines—with no red paint or foreign additions. They put in a stone path and set up a retaining wall.[72]

Nowadays school children occasionally visit the shrine to pray for success on their entrance examinations. On the day I went at the end of April in 1994, the shrine was deserted. It is not a beautiful building with its metal roof and barn-like shape, but the view looking out over the Ina Valley toward the eastern mountains is superb. Below the shrine is a small monument erected in 1932 to commemorate the shrine's inauguration. On the front is engraved the poem Taseko wrote at the banquet following the opening ceremony:

mono iwade	Even without them saying anything
kami mo ureshi to	I think the gods
omohosamu	must be delighted
kono Yamabuki no	at this new shrine
nii miyadokoro	for them here at Yamabuki.[73]

CHAPTER SIX

Nativist Texts and the Female Reader

At the old pine tree
that has endured for a thousand years
let us talk about
the ancient days
of the gods who made us their pledge.[1]
MATSUO TASEKO, 1853

"Thank you for letting me borrow so important a book as *Tamadasuki* (The Precious Sleeve Cord) for this long," Taseko wrote her cousin Inao at the end of 1861. "I'm sure you must be worried about it because it's already well past the time when I should have returned it to you, but I'd like to keep it a little longer. I've re-read everything from the introduction through chapter five twice. Once the new year comes I'll have more time, and I beg you please to allow me to have it till then."[2] The title refers to strips of cloth used to tie back the sleeves, signifying that the wearer was embarked on a serious endeavor sanctified by the gods. Written in the vernacular with pronunciation guides provided for most of the Chinese characters, this introductory text contains the essence of Hirata Atsutane's teachings. It also includes a collection of prayers that the disciple was expected to recite every morning in worshipping the gods and the spirits. According to her daughter-in-law, Taseko continued to study it to the end of her days.[3]

Taseko started reading nativist texts at least three years before she joined the Hirata school. Inao's record of books lent to friends, neighbors, and relatives mentions the Matsuo family repeatedly, and Taseko was the most likely recipient.[4] (Her husband never showed any interest in nativism, and in two cases the record matches her letters.) While she was in Kyoto in 1868 she urged the noble-born Iwakura Masu to read "The Precious Sleeve Cord." Interviewed by her biographer Ichimura Minato early in the twentieth century, her daughter-in-law Tami recollected seeing Taseko read a number of books by Atsutane, especially "The Precious Sleeve Cord" and "The Sacred Pillar of the Soul" (*Tama no mihashira*).[5] She also read at least the chapter from "Lectures on Ancient History" (*Koshiden*) that she had helped publish. These texts resonate throughout her later poetry. They must have had a substantial impact on how she saw the world.

Was it possible that the volumes studied by Taseko offered a welcome liberation for a woman trapped in a world defined by Confucian morality and norms of conduct that demanded submission to patriarchal authority and an ignorance of politics? Historians of the nativist movement have emphasized that Atsutane celebrated fertility, procreation, and lust.[6] None of them has ever entertained the possibility of a specific message for women in the context of nativist writing, or a gap between Chinese-inspired texts that emphasized a wife's duty to her husband and others that valued maintaining harmony within the household. Any hope of finding something akin to a feminist theme, however, must remain stillborn. Unlike some of his predecessors in the nativist tradition, Atsutane thoroughly approved of Confucius, if not later scholars in Chinese intellectual history, and he believed that the inequality between husband and wife reflected the natural order. In terms of politics, he ardently supported the status quo. He even denigrated the love poetry Taseko had been writing all her life.

Atsutane did not write for women, meaning he did not write in a style that fell within what was assumed to be a woman's capabilities. He usually begins each section of the texts that Taseko read with a few intimidating lines of Sino-Japanese (*kanbun*), in which a string of Chinese characters is annotated on the left to indicate the Japanese word order. Since Japanese is a highly inflected language and Chinese is not, on the right is commonly found notations signifying verbal endings and particles. When the introductory section comprises a prayer written in Chinese characters used to represent sounds, not things (*man'yōgana*), Atsutane usually provides a complete pronunciation gloss as an aid to the uninitiated. The Sino-Japanese quotations inserted in the body of each section, however, contain little in the way of a guide to pronunciation and hence meaning. The rest of the text is written in the formal literary style that mixes characters and the syllabary. Atsutane generally provides a pronunciation gloss for the characters, especially those on which he bestows a highly idiosyncratic reading. He wanted his works to be easily comprehensible; he tried to write as clearly as possible, and to say that he repeated himself is an understatement. Nevertheless, even though he aimed his teachings at ordinary people, he wrote at the level to which men were educated, not women.[7]

For Taseko, reading Atsutane must have been a challenge. Previously she had studied poetry anthologies written largely in the syllabary (*kana*) and a limited number of Chinese characters. Even the collection by Andō Nugari, which was written in what he thought of as *man'yōgana*, had glossed each character with its Japanese pronunciation. With that kind of help, the reader need have no knowledge of characters at all. It is unlikely that Taseko learned to read Atsutane's texts on her own nor would she have asked her husband for help, because Atsutane often attacked the kind of Confucian studies he pursued. Fortunately she had friends in the vicinity to whom she might turn in addition to the study group centered on her cousin Inao.

In 1858 Taseko read a chapter from "An Introduction to Western Texts" (*Seiseki gairon*) that outlined Chinese history, discussed the transformations in the meaning of Confucianism, and compared Confucian customs in China and Japan. It thus provided a critical overview of the kinds of texts that Taseko's husband and so many other men had absorbed for intellectual stimulation and a philosophy of life. In Japan as in China, what was called "Confucian studies" (*jugaku*) varied enormously. It is not clear whether Motoharu preferred the message of Yamazaki Anzai, praised by Atsutane for having remembered that he was Japanese first, or Dazai Shundai, denigrated for his disloyal claims of Chinese superiority, or some other scholar who expounded on the vast corpus of Chinese thought. In Atsutane's eyes, they all betrayed Japan by respecting another country to the point of worship. "Almost everyone in the realm believes that one must follow the teachings of the [Chinese] sages so as not to fall into the way of beasts. This is silly."[8] Statements such as these would surely have given Taseko a new perspective on her husband's pursuit of knowledge!

The next text that Taseko studied was chapter seven of "The Jeweled Comb Basket" (*Tamakatsuma*) by Motoori Norinaga, whom Atsutane claimed as his teacher. "Today I was going to return *Tamakatsuma* which I borrowed from you some time ago," she wrote Inao in 1860. "I still have something I want to look up though, so I'll return it with my next letter. I'm afraid you're going to think it rude of me to have kept it for so long."[9]

In his writings Atsutane had praised the section in chapter seven that demanded public access to ancient texts.[10] "I think that all good things should be disseminated as widely as possible," Norinaga wrote, and he criticized by implication the oral transmission of secret teachings that the court nobility claimed as its property. "To the extent that I have achieved some understanding by thinking about ancient texts, I plan to write it all down and not hide even the least little bit. If there be anyone who would like to learn by following me, all he need do is look closely at what I have written because aside from that there is nothing else."[11] This section, like many others in this chapter, was written almost entirely in the syllabary, partly because this style of writing was deemed more elegant being more purely Japanese and partly because it made the meaning more accessible to readers. "When it comes to old words, in particular those that people sometimes make mistakes in reading, I use the syllabary every single time, even in places where the pronunciation ought to be obvious, in order to make sure that they will be read correctly. I myself know that people of lofty spirit will laugh at me, but this habit has become so ingrained that I find it difficult to break."[12]

Chapter seven contains a mixed bag of essays, some written almost entirely in the syllabary, others written in Sino-Japanese with nothing by way of a pronunciation guide. Composed toward the end of Norinaga's life, it includes selections from court diaries, corrections and supplements to his earlier writings, elucidation of old poems, especially the *Man'yōshū*, inquiries into the meaning of place names and things, scholarly debates, regional practices, grammar lessons, reflections on the past, thoughts on taste, belief, and ideas, expressions of frustration and rage, and jokes. It is truly a basket of treasures, each one polished like a jewel.

The first half of chapter seven deals largely with matters pertaining to the way of the gods. How many times should one clap one's hands at a shrine? What kind of ceremonies should be performed on a yearly basis? Norinaga proposes using texts describing the rituals performed at the great shrine at Ise as a model for contemporary observances. He points out that at many old shrines it is not always possible to know which god is to be worshipped. Sometimes the god's name does not even appear in the ancient texts, suggesting that it has been fabricated in later times. When only the shrine's name is known people will assume that to be the god's name (e.g., any of the numerous shrines labeled Hachiman, in popular terminology, the god of war, or Inari, commonly assumed to be the goddess of rice). In contrast to the shrines of old with their impressive facades and constant stream of visitors, the shrines in Norinaga's own day appear to him to be sadly decrepit. "People today have no idea how much things have changed since ancient times when all they see is what exists now."[13] This sorry state of affairs he blames on the introduction of Chinese learning. "Most educated people just read texts written in Chinese and get all their knowledge from them. Unless they read the ancient writings of our own country, they will know nothing about the shrines and the deeds done by the gods in the past." [14]

Norinaga cites many documents written entirely in Sino-Japanese. In one section he simply lists the dates for the emperor's enthronement ceremonies beginning in 888 and ending in 1212. A fourteenth-century diary allows him to discuss the importance of having tissue paper handy to wipe one's nose. Taseko might well have appreciated the other snippets of court life and Japanese history that he gleans from this record and the insights it gives him into the etymology of the word for privy, for example, but what would she have made of another citation from a twelfth-century text on how to judge documents stamped with the imperial seal? [15] It also describes the ceremonies that marked the beginning of the construction of a library in 1145, the dress worn by the celebrants, the shape of the building itself, and the kind of books it contained. In addition, it reports an imperial decree that told Buddhist priests to refrain from appropriating Shinto ceremonies. [16] If Taseko actually read these passages, rather than skipping over them, she was considerably better educated than her previous training in poetry would suggest.

A FEW MONTHS after Taseko encountered chapter seven of "The Jeweled Comb Basket," she borrowed a short text written by Atsutane that must have been considerably easier to read. This was the "Biography of the goddess Miyabi" (*Miyabi no kami godenki*), a lecture recorded by a disciple in the vernacular though with little by way of pronunciation glosses for the characters. The goddess Miyabi is more commonly known as the "Dread Female of Heaven" (Ame no uzume no mikoto), and she is notorious for having performed a lascivious dance to lure the sun goddess out of a cave where she had hidden in anger at her brother for polluting her rice fields. [17] Yet according to Atsutane, there is nothing shameful in Miyabi having exposed not only her breasts but her genitals as well. It is simply slovenly (*shitoge naku*) and unconventional (*sharaku*). The response by the gods and ordinary people ever after is laughter, "an expression of their true feelings." Even in Atsutane's day, if a woman lost her sewing needle, she need only pray privately to her personal god, lift her skirt three times and clap three times for it to reappear. Once it had returned, she was to expose her breasts three times. [18]

Despite her fame for having exposed herself, the goddess Miyabi is not the patron saint of licentious behavior. She originates dance—the lewd dances performed at drinking parties and the stately sacred dances (*kagura*) as well as Noh. Her performance to entice the sun goddess from the cave cannot be considered coarse at all. It has its own dignity, it is beautiful beyond compare, and it attracts the love and respect of the onlookers. The obscene counting song that she sings to make the gods laugh is the origin of all poetry and song, from the classical poetry written by the aristocrats to folk songs and ballads. It also originates numbers. Repeated in the right sequence, from one to ten, then one hundred, one thousand, and ten thousand, they bring long life. The goddess Miyabi thus has the power to promote longevity.[19]

Miyabi turns out to be an important deity indeed, one whose worship is, in Atsutane's eyes, sadly neglected. After the sun goddess moves into the new shrine built for her after she left the cave, Miyabi serves her faithfully. In so doing she becomes the model for men and women who serve a superior, especially the women officials who run the emperor's court. In one of his few remarks that might be read as empowering women, Atsutane points out that in ancient days, court ladies were called the samurai of the interior. "People today think that samurai just means a military man who wears two swords at his hip, but in reality the term makes no distinction between men and women. In its broadest sense it refers to everyone who works in the palace, who serves the master and takes care of his business."[20] A good servant carries out her master's wishes before he even realizes what they are. She intercedes for him to smooth his way in all his human relationships.

> A person who serves in this fashion never resents her superiors. Anyone who is sincere about offering service will delight in the good things that happen to others and grieve at the bad. . . . Depending on the time and the circumstances, she might cajole her master with banter. When it is appropriate, she should not hesitate to cause ordinary people to laugh by doing crazy things that might appear shameful to others. In short, the true meaning of *miyabi* [usually translated elegance] is friendly and harmonious relations between parents and child, husband and wife, brothers and friends.[21]

Miyabi is one of the key terms in the Japanese aesthetic vocabulary, but Atsutane puts his own spin on it. In contrast to the Motoori school, which reserves the elegant life style for the aristocracy epitomized in Prince Genji and the scholarly elite, Atsutane claims it for anyone who sincerely follows the conventional patterns of behavior for her station in life. In fact he deplores *The Tale of Genji* and all other tales of lustful men for their superficial understanding of what *miyabi* is all about.[22] "Everyone has his own way of doing things (*furi*). Men have their way, women have theirs. Nobles act like nobles, and the base have their way too." These various patterns of behavior do not arise spontaneously. They have to be learned and practiced through self-discipline (*shitsuke*) until they have become second nature. Just as the techniques studied by actors originate in the goddess Miyabi's lascivious dance, so too do the schools of etiquette (for example, the Ogasewara school) for the samurai. As far as Atsutane is concerned, true *miyabi* for men lies in being humble about their talent, not putting themselves forward and never acting in bad taste. A woman who possesses *miyabi* would neither make a show of her intelligence nor be ashamed of her accomplishments.[23]

Atsutane urges his readers to worship the goddess Miyabi every day. Not only does she grant long life and harmonious interpersonal relationships, but also success in business. "If people never forget the true meaning of *miyabi* and believe in this god, she will protect them as they rise in the world (*risshin shusse*)."[24] It would also be a good idea to hold a ceremony for the goddess twice a year. Atsutane provides detailed instructions for how it should be done, illustrated with a drawing showing four women arranging food to place before a picture of the goddess. The offerings are to include rolls of red and white silk wrapped in paper, cotton cloth, a tall dish of rice, rice cakes, three kinds of fish, two kinds of shellfish, and green vegetables. Naturally there has to be sake. Following the recitation of a prayer, the counting song sung to lure the sun goddess out of her cave is to be chanted repeatedly. Next comes the banquet: first food and drink, then singing and dancing, bawdy plays and burlesque, all performed in a way that harmonizes with the goddess. Having a good time makes her happy too.[25]

There is no evidence that Taseko ever managed to introduce the worship of the goddess Miyabi into the Matsuo house. On the other hand, she alluded to this text in a long poem presented to a retainer from the Takasu domain at his request. The introductory lines contain an abundance of pillow words found in *Man'yōshū* poems.[26] The fourth and fifth draw on Atsutane's pun that "the essential meaning of *miyabi* begins with the palace staff (*miyabito*)." *Miya* can also mean shrine. Insofar as the emperor is also a god, his dwelling constitutes both sacred and secular space:

Uchi hisasu	Where the bamboo flourishes
miyako no kata	in the direction of
sasu take no	the sun blessed capital
ōmiyabito ni	this weak woman
miyabi mote	serves respectfully
tsukae matsureru	with *miyabi* (earnestly)
tawayame wa	the people of the great palace.[27]

Of all the texts that Taseko is known to have read, the biography of the goddess Miyabi has the most positive things to say about women. The way of women is different from that of men, but it is not innately inferior. Men and women, old and young, all serve the gods and emperors and desire the love and respect of their fellow human beings. Written for the master of the house to urge him to worship this goddess for the sake of harmonious interpersonal relations, the text yet acknowledges that women have their own role to play in the household, just as aristocratic women have their own autonomous responsibilities in serving the emperor.

THE CHAPTER that Taseko helped publish from "Lectures on Ancient History" (*Koshiden*) takes a different slant. It begins with "the primordial sexual relationship" between Izanagi and Izanami, responsible for the creation of Japan and its chief deities.[28] They have just given birth to a child who is no good, the leech child, the child who cannot stand on its own. They report the result to the heavenly deities, who perform a divination to figure out what has gone wrong. The problem is that the female goddess, Izanami, spoke first. In Atsutane's interpretation, "when the woman speaks first, she betrays the nature of men and women. . . . This nature originates in the male god having been produced first and the female god having appeared second. . . . The principle that women should follow men has been a matter of course down to the present. . . . It is important to understand that this principle is not self-evident, for how could the gods act contrary to something they already knew was wrong?"[29] The act of creation thus comprises not only producing things but establishing order. As with so many norms, this one puts women in an inferior position.

Atsutane develops the theme of gender inequality in the next section, in which he focuses on how Izanami and Izanagi circled the pillar before either spoke. He decides that Izanagi must have gone to the left because the left is respected as the man's place while the right is despised as the woman's place. This passage elucidates two principles: everything comes in sexed pairs, and the male always takes the superior position. "It is quite marvelous, indeed mysterious, that even countries and mountains may be deemed male and female. Everything living, everything born down to the trees and grasses conforms as a matter of course to the principle of left and right, male and female." On male birds, the left feathers lie on top whereas female birds put their right feathers on top. The shells of male snails swirl to the left; those of females to the right. Sexing plants is one task Japanese agronomists had set themselves, and with some of their number among his disciples, Atsutane offers his own insights: "Male rice stalks when fully ripened bend to the left; females bend to the right."[30]

Having put women in their place, Atsutane moves on to discuss childbirth. It bothers him that the two most important sources for the age of the gods, the *Kojiki* and *Nihonshoki,* make no mention of the placentas that must have accompanied the birth of the eight isles that make up Japan. For this he blames Chinese accretions. In answer to those who claim that islands are far too big to have been produced inside the belly of a goddess, Atsutane insists that they must have grown from small to large just like other growing things. The fetus produced through the intercourse of its mother and father is minute. As the months pass, it takes on the shape of an infant, or, in this case, an island. It took many millennia for land produced by the gods to grow to the size it is now, making it entirely possible that it originated inside Izanami.[31] In other words, the origin of the Japanese islands resembles in principle the bearing of children, and procreation recapitulates these sacred acts of creation.

Atsutane further develops the parallels between sacred and profane acts of creation in the last section of this chapter that takes as its theme the marriage of Izanagi and Izanami and their creation of the important deities as well as all other living things. Superior beings are often called gods, but the masses are not. Since both are created by the same couple, why are people inferior to the gods? Atsutane argues that the gods did not really concentrate on individual people, they just wanted lots of them. People and gods are naturally different from the very beginning, with gods being respected and people despised, a lesson that Taseko was to take to heart and repeat even in her last poems.[32] All parents who want to raise good children should keep this in mind. If they think deeply about how to perform all their tasks successfully and serve their lord and parents faithfully, then their children will undoubtedly inherit their parents' virtues.[33]

In discussing the process of creation, Atsutane carefully distinguishes between Japan, the Japanese, and everyone else. In contrast to the main Japanese islands produced by the intercourse of the two great creator gods, all others, and foreign countries as well, originate in congealed brine later molded and shaped through the actions of gods who went roaming about the earth. They are thus fundamentally different in character, Japan being exalted and beautiful, foreign countries being base and ugly. Atsutane admits that he does not know where foreign peoples come from; perhaps the Chinese are correct in saying that they come from yellow clay. In any case all foreigners, being different from the Japanese in shape and features, are clearly inferior.[34]

It was probably entirely fortuitous that the chapter Taseko helped publish from "Lectures on Ancient History" alluded so directly to the unequal relations between women and men and between Japanese and foreigners. Atsutane's purpose in writing the book was to elucidate the history of the age of the gods and demonstrate the reality of their achievements manifested most concretely in Japanese geography.[35] He repeats much of its contents in other texts that Taseko also read, chiefly "The Sacred Pillar of the Soul" and "The Precious Sleeve Cord." Yet neither of these mentions the deformed child born because Izanami had violated the natural order in speaking first. In a poem Taseko was to write in 1864, she compared herself to this leech child and lamented that as a weak woman, she could not stand on her own.

"THE SACRED Pillar of the Soul" and "The Precious Sleeve Cord" constitute the bible and a book of common prayer for the Hirata disciples. The first provides a cosmology drawn from both Japanese myth and western theories. As with any theological work, its ultimate purpose is to explain the existence of evil and what happens to people after they die.[36] The second begins with two introductory chapters that trace Japanese history from the age of the gods down to the seventeenth century. The rest of the book contains prayers to be offered to various deities every morning, an elucidation of their meaning, explanations of the significance of each god mentioned in the prayers, biographies describing the gods' achievements, stories about people who have had direct experience with the supernatural, and concrete suggestions for leading a deity-centered life. In both texts Atsutane castigates foreigners, Buddhism, his predecessors in the nativist tradition, and his contemporaries who dared to disagree with him.

Atsutane wrote "The Sacred Pillar of the Soul" to reassure himself that neither his dearly departed wife nor anyone else would go to the polluted netherworld called *yomi*.[37] He begins with a circle representing the void inhabited by three gods. The first is the god ruling the center (Ama no minakanushi), eternal and unchanging. The others are the exalted creator deity, a male, called Takamimusubi no kami, and the sacred creator deity, a female, named Kamimusubi no kami, who are the divine embodiment of the universe's creative forces.[38] (These gods are at the same time one god, and if this sounds even faintly like Christianity, it is probably because Atsutane had studied Christian teachings brought into Japan through Chinese texts.[39]) Out of the void appears a mass that gradually starts to divide into three, each part with its own deities. The top part breaks off early and becomes heaven. The middle section, the earth, remains attached to the lowest section, the netherworld, for considerably longer. Everything that is bright and pure floats off to heaven; everything polluted and dark eventually sinks to the netherworld.[40]

The chief obstacle to denying that souls go to the netherworld after death is the famous legend of Izanami in the role of Eurydice. Most accounts say she dies when she gives birth to the fire god, but Atsutane asserts that she deliberately hides herself in the netherworld because she knows she will be soiled by childbirth. She wants both to spare her husband the sight of her and spare the earth the calamities that might arise from pollution. In rage and grief at her absence, her husband hacks up the fire god. His fiery blood flows down to the netherworld where it becomes polluted by filth. When Izanami eats food prepared with this fire, she too becomes polluted. Rather than bring pollution back to earth, she agrees to stay in the netherworld and rule over it. She is later joined by her son Susano-o. Needless to say, the pollution suffered by Izanami is recapitulated by every woman who gives birth. Atsutane entirely approves of parturition huts to keep this pollution away from the rest of the family, and he urges his readers to pay particular heed not to eat food prepared with polluted fire.[41]

If Izanami did not go to the netherworld because she had died, she had not set a precedent for the dead to go there either. When the netherworld finally breaks off from earth, it becomes the moon. Just as no ordinary earthling spirit could ever hope to rise to the high plain of heaven, so too is it impossible to go to the moon. Instead, spirits have to stay on earth. Susano-o's descendant Ōkuninushi first establishes his rule over the entire earth from his palace at Izumo. When the sun goddess announces that her grandson is to rule the world, Ōkuninushi agrees to turn invisible and rule the invisible world. All the other gods hide their shapes as well. They know everything that goes on in the visible world, which is why the pledge signed by Taseko in joining the Hirata school warns that its teachings must not be transgressed, even in thought. While a person is alive, he operates in the visible world as the emperor's subject; once he dies, his spirit returns to the invisible world of the gods ruled by Ōkuninushi. Atsutane argues that even the great teacher Motoori Norinaga must not have really believed that his spirit would end up in the netherworld, else why go to such lengths to prepare a grave site on Mt. Yamamuro and write poetry implying that his spirit would remain with his beloved mountain cherry?[42]

Atsutane blames evil on the gods of calamity (*magatsuhi no kami*). Some are produced when Izanagi purifies himself after visiting the netherworld; others arise in countries that, lying closer to the netherworld and farther from heaven than Japan, are themselves naturally polluted. These gods are not intrinsically evil; they just react violently to pollution. Insofar as the calamities that they cause succeed in ridding the world of sin and filth, they are in fact good.[43] The sun goddess in particular hates pollution. It brings out her rough or savage (*arai*) side, the side that causes disasters. Once she has been assuaged through purification, she can be restored to her gentle aspect manifested in the rectifying spirit (*naobi no kami*). The reason why the incidence of disease has increased in Atsutane's own time is because people who had died earlier are angry at having suffered. They roam around filled with bitterness and try to inflict on others what has been inflicted on them. Smallpox is a particular problem because, having been brought from a foreign land by a foreign god, the spirits of its victims have no place to go where they can rest in peace.[44] On the other hand, people do not have to turn evil even if they die unpleasantly. They have a choice. "There is nothing worse than hemorrhoids," said one sufferer. "After I die, I will become a god to help all those who suffer this affliction."[45]

Another message in "The Sacred Pillar of the Soul" is that Japan and the emperor are superior to all other nations and rulers.[46] Japan provides the seat for the sun goddess at her holy shrine of Ise. It is governed by the descendants of her heavenly grandson, and being at the apex of the earth, it lies closer to heaven than any other country. This last was apparently particularly difficult for his critics to accept, and Atsutane adduces various arguments to buttress his position. One works through analogy: there is no more reason for the earth's apex to face up (i.e., for the sun to be directly above Japan at the spring and autumn equinox) than for a man to have his face on top of his head. Atsutane also draws on foreign sources: both Chinese and Western accounts mention a great flood that in the West left only Noah's ark afloat. The lack of any mention of a flood in Japanese history proves that its position is intrinsically higher.[47] Only in Japan is it possible to learn the truth about the origin of the world; the cosmologies created in other countries might be useful for comparisons, but they are essentially incomplete. Confronted with this self-contained and self-referential explanation, the only appropriate response is belief.

Reading "The Sacred Pillar of the Soul" would have opened Taseko's eyes to a wide and diverse range of texts. Atsutane's methodology consists first of establishing the principle of the way things ought to be and then searching Japanese, Chinese, and Western documents for proof. His scholarship is not so much inductive and positivist as normative and theoretical.[48] He ruminates widely over the history and philosophy of Japan and other countries to select what the gods had originated that is therefore good and worth adopting versus what is bad and ought to be discarded. It is difficult to know what Taseko made of this. Unlike some of her male friends, she never wrote her own commentaries. She made the pilgrimage to Ise, she visited Norinaga's grave on Mt. Yamamuro, she abhorred the pollution brought by foreigners, and she wrote poems in praise of Ōkuninushi. Beyond that, she kept the life she lived in her head to herself.

"THE PRECIOUS Sleeve Cord" repeats many of the themes found in Atsutane's other writings, but it focuses primarily on human history and contemporary practice. According to him, a summary of the age of the gods demonstrates that they act out of love and compassion for the people, most concretely in fulfilling their pledge to provide food, shelter, clothing, and a beautiful, peaceful, well-governed environment. Unfortunately, too many Japanese have allowed themselves to be seduced by the novelty of foreign practices, especially Buddhism and Confucianism. This foolishness alienates the gods. The emperors of old rode horses, pulled their own bow, hunted in the mountains, and punished traitors. Ever since the reprehensible Prince Shōtoku, 574–622, however, they have neglected the martial arts, acting like the Chinese kings who care only for scholarly pursuits. Though neither should be neglected, the true Japanese way is for the military to take precedence over the literary.[49]

Atsutane wrote that as a matter of course, the more effeminate and lascivious the court becomes, the more its authority declines and the more disorder increases. Forgotten is the importance of matching name and function (*taigi meibun*), the principle established when the sun goddess sent her august grandson to rule over the islands by which all subjects are expected to obey their natural ruler, the emperor. A Japanese person can no more disclaim the emperor than the earth can ignore the sun.[50] In the roll call of traitors, the first is Minamoto no Yoritomo, 1147–99, whose disdain for the court causes his unnatural death. The emperor's attempt to regain control of the country in 1221 leads to his exile. His attendants should have committed suicide; instead they shamelessly paid not the slightest attention to his sufferings and continued writing poetry as though nothing had happened.[51] It is no wonder that politics becomes the purview of the warriors. With few exceptions, however, they all betray their duty by treating the emperor abominably and causing the people hardships. Worst of all are the Ashikaga shoguns, beginning with Takauji, 1305–58, who pretends to support the emperor only to turn against him, and his grandson Yoshimitsu, who claims to be the king of Japan in his dealings with China. He commits serious crimes of treason and leaves behind a name that will stink for all time.[52] So ends the middle age, a time of increasing chaos and suffering.

Modern times, Atsutane's own era, sees the world restored to its proper order. The great generals of the sixteenth century, Oda Nobunaga and Toyotomi Hideyoshi, respect the court, pacify the country, destroy the evil monks dug in on Mt. Hiei (the mountain to the northeast of Kyoto), and put a stop to calamity. Whereas one eighteenth-century historian had criticized Nobunaga for scolding his erstwhile lord, the last Ashikaga shogun, Atsutane argues to the contrary that Nobunaga understood his first allegiance to be to the emperor. When the times require it, the principle of matching name to function means that the public relationship between emperor and subject has to supersede the private bonds between lord and vassal.[53] In the 1860s, Atsutane's disciples were to first criticize and then try to overthrow the shogun for ignoring this principle when he disobeys the emperor's wishes to expel the barbarians. Atsutane might well have been shocked at their deeds. Founded with due respect for the emperor, the system of governance established in 1603 by Tokugawa Ieyasu, "The shining god in the east" (*Tōshōgu*), has brought peace and prosperity in accordance with the will of the gods. The shoguns are to act as the emperor's deputies forever, rule the realm, and nurture the people. Best of all, Ieyasu had encouraged the emperor and his court to pursue the study of ancient Japan. Who could quarrel with a hero who had made Atsutane's work possible?[54]

Reading "The Precious Sleeve Cord" would have given Taseko a highly idiosyncratic vision of Japanese history. Its lengthy recital of the crimes committed by the Ashikaga shoguns later led furious men to pillory their statues. In its insistence that a proper balance be maintained between the martial and literary arts, it presages late nineteenth-century depictions of Emperor Meiji as both a scholar and a soldier.[55] But in its praise for Ieyasu, it assumes that his successors are well-nigh inviolable and makes a world without the shoguns unthinkable.

According to Atsutane, the shogun and everyone else in Japan and around the world are clearly subordinate to the emperor. In that the emperor is the direct descendant of the sun goddess, he embodies her love and concern for her people. "His body is in this world but not entirely of it; as a manifest divine human (*arabito gami*) he has the power to guarantee the continuity of the state and the preservation of the divine will in the visible world even as he himself, in his very being and through rites and rituals, moves in the hidden world of the gods."[56] Although individual emperors might make mistakes (practicing Buddhism being one, neglecting the martial arts being another), in principle the emperor is sacrosanct. Loyal service to him (*kinnō*) is the highest duty. Under ordinary circumstances this service simply requires respecting the government, enjoying one's occupation, and working at it diligently.[57] In time of crisis the subject's charge is summed up in the *Man'yōshū* poem "Umi yukaba," the famous dirge that sent sailors and soldiers off to die in World War Two: "If I go to sea, a water-logged corpse I'll be. If I go to the mountains, a moss-covered corpse I'll be. Should I die for the sake of the emperor, I die not in vain."[58]

Atsutane quotes these lines in the early nineteenth century, an age of peace and prosperity when serving the emperor meant leading a god-centered life. He reminds his readers that "in everything we do we are blessed by the gods.

We must not forget that even for a moment." [59] "Every time you use one stick of firewood, one pinch of salt, one sheet of paper or one cup of water, remember that these are the blessings of the gods and be careful not to waste them or use more than you need." [60] Before eating, Atsutane always recalls the blessings promised by the sun goddess and the hard work of the peasants in raising crops. The Japanese eat correctly, in accordance with the way of the gods, each with his own tray and his food served in individual dishes. "The Chinese think they have the best table manners, but they all sit around the same table and dip food from the same bowl. . . . This is a rude and filthy way to eat." [61]

Once an individual fully realizes the blessings he has received from the gods and their abhorrence of pollution, he has the responsibility to act accordingly. It is particularly important to treat the god of fire respectfully because he had been polluted at birth. Feet being one of the dirtiest parts of the body, putting them on a small stove (*kotatsu*) or stomping out a hot tobacco ash offers an insult to the god. Atsutane was himself once punished with a stomach ache for drinking sake warmed by a fire already polluted by cooking meat. This does not happen to other people because they do not know any better. After all, an aristocrat can expect to be punished for a breach in etiquette, but not an ignorant commoner. [62] Atsutane paid particular attention to his prayers to the toilet god. The toilet being the filthiest place in the house, it is easy to forget that it too is governed by a deity. Treated with respect, he can cure ophthalmia; disdain risks eye disease. Even night soil has to be handled correctly. Once a carpenter staying with Atsutane urinated in the buckets of the old man who came to clean the toilet. The old man was furious. As long as night soil was in the toilet, it was polluted; once it had been placed in his buckets, it became fertilizer. It could even be presented to the gods. "Now that you've pissed into it, it can no longer be used as fertilizer. You're a stupid man who knows nothing of the rules for farming." [63]

A Hirata disciple does not necessarily reject techniques and practices just because they are foreign. The Chinese lunar calendar works only because the Japanese gods had taken it there in ancient times. The same is true for Western medicine in that it had originated in the teachings of Japanese gods on their visit to India. From there it migrated west where doctors added various improvements to deal with the more severe illnesses that afflict people living in more polluted regions. [64] Atsutane even praises Confucius, in particular for his elucidation of the five relationships that subordinate women to men. "Even though he was Chinese, he followed the true way." [65] Mencius is despicable, however, because his notion of the mandate of heaven fits ill with an emperor who is everlasting and inviolable. To make these value judgments, Atsutane tried to learn everything he could about other countries and he encouraged his disciples to do likewise. He was not rabidly xenophobic, nor was he an obscurantist.

Atsutane reserves his most intense vituperation for Buddhism. It arose in countries where people know no better because they are ruled by the sun goddess's savage spirit and entrusted to the gods of calamity. A Korean king made the mistake of sending it to Japan along with other tribute as a mark of respect. The gods hate Buddhism and everything associated with it. They did not prevent its entry into Japan, however because men must take responsibility for their own actions. On the other hand, parents should show their love for their daughters by forbidding them access to Buddhism; if a woman is allowed to be bewitched by Buddhist teachings, the older she gets, the more addled she becomes.[66]

Buddhism is a perverted, polluted religion that denies both the creative power of the gods of heaven and earth and human nature itself. In his "Lectures on Ancient History," Atsutane goes through considerable contortions to discover male and female pairs where none had been found before. Anyone who follows the path of being human, whether man or woman, must form half of a conjugal pair if he or she is to tread the way of the gods. The creator gods bestow people with sexual difference and lust, but Buddhists call this the root of all evil. For them to prohibit desire is like digging a deep well, then being upset when it fills with water.[67]

Even a parent should not stand in the way of lust. Atsutane tells the story of a young woman who loves a man living on the other side of a mountain. Despite her mother's and his employer's objections, she visits him every night to consummate their relationship. One night she is stopped by a starving wolf who wants to eat her. She begs to be allowed one last tryst with her lover and promises faithfully to come back. The wolf agrees, but when she returns, it is nowhere in sight. The woman stops making the journey until her longing overcomes her fear. Now, however, she always leaves food for the wolf at the top of the pass. One night a man from the village, who has fallen in love with her and gotten her mother's permission to court her, follows her up the mountain and tries to force himself on her. She says she cannot submit to him because she already has a lover whom she considers to be her husband. He threatens to kill her, she calls for help, and the wolf to whom she has been bringing food kills the man. Impressed with her fidelity, her mother and her lover's employer agree to allow her to marry her lover.[68] Even though she had defied her parent, she is blessed by the gods because she has made herself one half of a conjugal pair and refuses sexual relations with other men.

Atsutane is a great believer in monogamy, at least for women. He urges women to pledge their fidelity to their husbands through prayers to Suseri-hime, the consort of Ōkuninushi, ruler of the invisible world. Why? She had offered him a poem along the lines that because you, my master, are a man, you have many wives, but because I am a woman, I have no other man but you. A married woman should remember this poem and protect her husband. After he dies she should obey her sons.[69] Although Atsutane values sexual intercourse, he confines it within the received wisdom regarding women's roles within the family. In contrast to the prevailing practice that focused solely on patrilineal descent, however, he emphasizes the importance of knowing matrilineal descent lines as well, and he notes approvingly the priestess families that trace their lineage through women.[70]

Atsutane seldom mentions women, and when he does, it is to give men advice on handling them. Ninigi, the sun goddess's grandson sent down to rule the earth, makes a dreadful mistake in his choice of brides. Offered two sisters, the elder rock-like in her ugliness, the younger more beautiful than the cherry blossoms, he chooses only the latter and sends the first back to her father. Their father then tells him that had he taken both, his life would have lasted as long as the rocks and he would have prospered like the flowers. Because he has rejected the elder, his life and the lives of all those who inhabit the visible world will be sweet but short. Atsutane reminds his readers that it is human nature for men to despise ugly women and desire the beautiful. They should nevertheless choose a wife for her virtue, not her beauty, remembering that women are ruled by men and to have children is the way of the gods.[71] In writing precepts for his descendants, Taseko's cousin Inao later warned them on this very point. He may have been remembering this passage, or he may have reflected the prejudice widespread in farm families that too beautiful a wife brings nothing but trouble.

Atsutane had plenty to say about female disabilities. He devotes pages to the pollution caused by menstruation and the danger it poses for men. The great mythical hero Yamato Takeru allows his wife to seduce him during her menses. His sacred sword then tries to leave him because, in Atsutane's explanation, it abhors pollution. (This connection is not made in the early accounts of their encounter.[72]) Having soiled his body with menstrual blood, Takeru loses the protection of the gods and dies from a poisonous bite by the mountain god in the form of a snake when he tries to climb Mt. Ibuki.[73] Atsutane urges his readers to make sure their wives' food is cooked with a separate fire while they are menstruating and after childbirth. Women so polluted are to avoid sacred places. Men too are polluted by the birth of children, to a much lesser extent. A man and woman, having had sexual intercourse, should refrain from going to shrines for three days.[74] Given that the aim of

"The Precious Sleeve Cord" is to encourage its readers to worship the deities, warning women against shrine visits on a monthly basis puts them at a severe disadvantage in trying to lead a god-centered life.

In the last chapter of "The Precious Sleeve Cord" published late in 1869, Kanetane interjects a summation of his own views on women. Men are to be respected and women despised, a formulation commonly found in the late nineteenth century that continues to resonate down to the present. A woman should be gentle and follow her husband's orders, then when she is old, she should obey her son. This makes it difficult for her to do as she pleases and because she must take care in everything she does, her anxieties and exertions are endless. A good husband must try to be aware of his wife's feelings. Having been born a man, he should be nice to her and not give her cause for worry.[75] If Taseko read these remarks, she did so late in life. On the other hand, she was to spend a good many hours in Kanetane's presence while they were both in Kyoto. In her diary she never failed to note her gratitude for the benign condescension with which she was received.

ATSUTANE PAID scant attention to women. The occasion for writing "The Sacred Pillar of the Soul" was the death of his wife, but he wrote it as a consolation for himself. "The Precious Sleeve Cord" omits all mention of women in the history section, even Hōjō Masako, whose status as Minamoto Yoritomo's wife allowed the hated Hōjō to seize power, and Hino Tomiko, often called the greatest villain in Japanese history for causing civil war in 1467.[76] The occasional anecdotes that feature women in the other chapters either warn men of pollution or have as their larger point themes completely unrelated to them. The Hirata school did not recruit women and did nothing to make them feel welcome. The personal reasons Taseko had for joining this school must have owed less to her sex than to religious and political imperatives.

It may well be that Taseko noted approvingly Atsutane's denigration of women because it provided so perfectly a reflection of her own assumptions as to be entirely unremarkable. That she was aware of the constraints that convention imposed on her as a woman is obvious from the poetry she wrote a few years later; that she became critical of them is not. On the other hand, assuming that she read his work in the light of what he had to say about women may do her an injustice by assuming that her scholarly interests were confined to a narrow spectrum. Just because she was a woman does not mean that her concerns lay with women's issues.

A text as rich and as long as "The Precious Sleeve Cord" contains innumerable points to ponder. Perhaps Taseko's eye was caught by his treatises on sake because that is what the Matsuo family brewed, or his discussion on sericulture, or perhaps she liked best some sections that because they dealt with the supernatural escaped my notice entirely.[77] She read only a small selection from Atsutane's vast opus, but what she read, she read repeatedly and most probably piously. Like readers in early modern Europe, her reading was intensive rather than extensive.[78] For her and for her compatriots, what mattered was not how many books one had consumed, but how deeply they had been absorbed.[79]

"The Sacred Pillar of the Soul" and "The Precious Sleeve Cord" shocked Norinaga's disciples in their flat-out denial of his teachings regarding the netherworld and the history of Japanese literature. Atsutane retorted that being a disciple meant going beyond one's teacher, not just repeating what he had already said like old women mumbling prayers to the Buddha.[80] Unlike some of her friends, Taseko never took advantage of his permission to seek new avenues for scholarly inquiry. She strayed beyond the bounds of the conventions established by his writings less in what she said than in what she did.

PART TWO *Kyoto: 1862–1863*

CHAPTER SEVEN

Autumn in Arashiyama

Even though I keep looking back
in my traveling clothes
my home village
is concealed in the mist
and I am all alone on Mt. Nashino.[1]
MATSUO TASEKO, 1862

"Caught at the mercy of the autumn winds, I resolved to visit the capital to fulfill my dreams," Taseko wrote in the eighth month of 1862.[2] It was a traumatic year for Japan. The emperor firmly believed that the shogun had the responsibility to run the country, even though the latter, whose full title was "barbarian subduing generalissimo," had proved incapable of thwarting the Europeans and Americans who came with gunboats to demand trading and residency privileges. Despite his seclusion inside the palace where he pursued a heavy schedule of ritual ceremonies, the emperor had made it known that he adamantly opposed letting the foreigners set foot on Japan's sacred soil. In this he was not alone; by the summer of 1862 he had become the rallying point for many sword-wearing malcontents. Under the slogan of "revere the emperor, expel the barbarians," they flocked to Kyoto where they quarreled over foreign policy, vehemently criticized the do-nothing shogun, and assassinated men they deemed traitors to the throne.

None of this should have mattered to Taseko, and there was no reason for the trajectory of her life to intersect the reverberating public events of her time. She was not a samurai member of the ruling class. No other woman abandoned husband and family for the chaotic conditions in the capital. In an age when most people traveled in groups, even her resolve to travel with no companion other than a servant marked her as unconventional. Why did she decide to go?

In part the conjuncture was entirely fortuitous. By autumn, Taseko's work raising silkworms was over for the year, leaving time hanging heavy on her hands. Her husband was retired; her oldest son and his wife had not only taken over the family's enterprises but produced an heir. At fifty-one she was still a vigorous woman with more than enough energy for the few household chores that remained to her. Besides, she had a dream. Every student of classical poetry longed to go to Kyoto, the source of the poetic tradition, both to see the sights hallowed in poetry and to receive instruction from the court nobility. From the day Taseko set out, she composed poems for the diary she kept of her journey. It contained elements of a day book in its listings of where she spent the night and who she saw. It also took on the air of a literary project in the tradition of travel diaries stretching back a millennium in which no clear distinction was made between poetry and prose and every scenic opportunity anticipated a lyric outburst. Had she simply gone to Kyoto to study poetry, however, she and her journey would have been quickly forgotten.

Taseko had already compromised her pursuit of art for art's sake when she joined the Hirata school the year before her trip and discovered a new appreciation for Japan's history and religion. By participating in the nativist cells, she had learned about the political crisis facing her nation. Just as her study of poetry did not necessarily prefigure her decision to become a Hirata disciple, however, it cannot be said that becoming a disciple sufficiently explains her decision to leave home. Her six-month stay in Kyoto opened a fissure in the chronology of her life. It marked a performative break, allowing new possibilities hardly determined by what came before.

TASEKO DID NOT begin her journey at the Matsuo house. One day in the eighth month she crossed the river to knock at the gate to her Kitahara cousins' house in Zakōji. She was simply passing through on her way to visit her son in Yamamoto, she said, and had little time for talk.[3] A long-distance trip usually required elaborate preparations, including a farewell party that might accompany the traveler to several tea houses and sake shops before the

final parting of the ways. Either Taseko had not thought to go far when she left
Tomono, or she let no one know what she was about to do.

And so the diary of Taseko's travels begins with her departure from Yamamoto, the village where she was born. Her son and his wife were both suffering from measles, and she had spent ten days nursing them. From there
she sent a note to her cousin Inao saying that she had been planning to stop
by on her way home to pay her respects to his ailing father, but "my illness
came back. O-Machi [her daughter-in-law] said it might be better for me to
take a long trip, so I resolved to go to Kyoto, something I've been thinking
about for a long time." [4] Taseko did not specify her illness (*yamai*), but it could
so easily have been mental as physical, perhaps a certain spiritual malaise.

Before daybreak on the last day of the eighth month, Taseko prepared for
her journey by offering prayers to the village's tutelary deity and the spirits
of her ancestors, following the order of services she had learned in "The Precious Sleeve Cord." [5] She borrowed a servant from her son to serve as her escort because the roads were considered too dangerous for a woman to travel
alone. It started to rain. With a satchel tied behind her back containing a notebook, brush, ink and inkstone, an extra pair of straw sandals, maybe a change
of undergarments, and a few toiletries, she started trudging up the mountain
path toward Seinaiji pass. Along the way, she composed a poem to express
her resolve:

Ame itou	Even though it rains
fure tomo omou	furiously,
koto no ana	with something on my mind
reba ame wa mono	what's a little rain?
ka wa to tachidenu	And so I make my departure. [6]

Heroes in the Japanese tradition typically had to defy rain or snow when they
set out on the adventures that brought them fame. After all, if one is afraid of
the weather, one will never accomplish anything. Storms thus mark an auspicious beginning for great deeds.

At Seinaiji Taseko met her daughter-in-law's brother, a young man named
Ichioka Onari from Iida, who had agreed to escort her over the pass. She was
late and she had to apologize. The rain showed no sign of letting up. Perhaps
they should call on Hara Mayomi, to whom she had once written a sexy poem,
and spend the night at his house. Having visitors show up unexpectedly was
no great surprise in the days before telephones, but the visitor also ran the risk
of finding the host out, as happened in this case. Mayomi was off on his own
quest, first to a hot springs for his health, then to Edo to see for himself what

was going on in the world. After a brief rest, tea, and refreshments, Taseko and Onari continued up the mountain road in the rain. It was only a few miles from Yamamoto to Seinaiji, then another five to go up and over the pass to their next stop at Hirose. Taseko complained, "I could have barely crawled along even if I hadn't had my luggage."[7]

Taseko was starting to tire, but mountain roads provided few amenities. One tea shop sold her a snack of rice cakes broiled on a skewer and flavored with soy sauce and burnt sugar—still today a tasty regional specialty. Then she and Onari pressed on to Tsumago, a post station on the Nakasendō, the official highway through the mountains between Edo and Kyoto. There she tried to hire a palanquin. None was available. So it was up to another pass and, in the meantime, "it was approaching that depressing hour at dusk." With no place to lend them shelter and exhausted from the rain, Taseko was feeling she could not take another step when a man came by leading a horse. She asked for a ride; he refused, saying the horse was tired. "'I'll pay extra.' 'All right then, ride.' Both horse and rider ended up completely soaked."

Toshi wo heshi	With the passage of years
ashi ke mo yowaki	legs and spirit are weak.
oi uma no	I go along borne on the back
Magome no uma ni	of an old horse
se owarete yuku	a horse going to Magome.[8]

What could better capture the essence of weariness than riding an old horse at the end of a long day. This poem depicts what actually happened to Taseko in such a way as to insert her into a long tradition of dispirited travelers.

Today Magome is a favorite destination for tourists who visit its quaint shops and rest in its old-fashioned inns. By the time Taseko had arrived, lights were shining invitingly from every house. Onari announced that he had no intention of stopping even though all other traffic on the road had ceased. Dangerous though it might be to travel a narrow mountain path in the rain, the two of them trudged on, despite "the road which should have lain fair before us having turned treacherous in the moon-less night."[9]

Taseko and Onari arrived at their day's destination, Nakatsugawa, past nine o'clock at night. Their late arrival at the Ichioka house caused great surprise. "Everyone came rushing out, the mistress of the house in the lead, my daughter right behind, everyone talking at once, exclaiming at my appearance, asking questions." Taseko's answers went unheeded. Better to wait for the morrow, she thought, and exhausted from having arisen before dawn to travel thirty miles, most of it on foot, she went to bed.[10]

FIGURE 16.
Ichioka Shigemasa in the
formal garb of a post
station official. Courtesy
of Hazama Jōji.

Taseko spent the night at the *honjin*, the largest set of buildings in Naka-tsugawa. It was officially an inn for daimyo and bakufu bannermen, the chief priests of important temples, aristocrats from the imperial court, and samurai on government business. Samurai traveling on their own and commoners were expected to stay at the ordinary inns that lined the road. An imposing structure with a massive gate and entryway, the honjin comprised a compound enclosing over ten thousand square feet surrounded by a tall whitewashed wall topped with boards. Inside the gatehouse was room for transport agents; the courtyard could hold a train of packhorses; on one side there was a long house for porters; at the back was the main building with formal rooms for officials and the family's living space. The room reserved for the highest ranking visitors had an escape route out the back to the neighboring temple.[11] Taseko was among the least of its guests.

The honjin was run by Ichioka Shigemasa, one of the most prominent men in Nakatsugawa. Taseko's daughter was married to his adopted son (who was also his nephew) and Taseko's father was his uncle.[12] Born in 1813, Shigemasa had a large square face dominated by bushy eyebrows. He was a well-educated man who practiced tea ceremony and wrote poetry, both the seventeen-syllable haiku and the classical thirty-one-syllable waka. In 1841 he and a friend competed to see who could write a thousand waka within the year, and Shigemasa won. In 1855 he solicited poems to put in an anthology for his adoptive grandmother's eighty-eighth birthday, and Taseko was among the contributors.[13] As an important government purveyor (though not a member of the ruling class), Shigemasa had permission to wear swords, use a surname, and be registered as a samurai in the Owari domain for his lifetime. He had traveled widely, first to Edo when he was twenty, then to Osaka, Kyoto, Ise, and even Konpira on the island of Shikoku. Beginning in 1848 he kept a record of what was going on in the world culled from letters, government directives, and the gossip that flowed up and down the Nakasendō.[14] Well-educated and well-informed, he knew as well as anyone in the countryside what was happening in Kyoto, and he did not think it was a good place for his cousin to be going.

With the assassination of Ii Naosuke, the shogun's chief advisor, in the third month of 1860, Japan's political center had begun to shift from Edo to Kyoto, and the wedding of Kazunomiya to the shogun the following year only accelerated the trend. In the fourth month of 1862, Shimazu Hisamitsu, the de facto daimyo for the Satsuma domain on the island of Kyushu, marched on Kyoto at the head of a thousand troops. There he presented a proposal for reforming the bakufu to the imperial court. Neither Satsuma nor the court had any traditional justification for discussing a matter ostensibly of concern only to the bakufu itself, but Hisamitsu argued that the times demanded extraordinary measures whereby men of talent and ability might serve the country. He aimed at promoting harmony between Japan's various factions to present a united front against the foreigners, and he argued that to restore national prestige, men like himself had to have input in policy decisions.

While Hisamitsu and the imperial envoy he accompanied to Edo were wringing concessions from the bakufu, more radical and lower ranking samurai began a reign of terror in Kyoto. They murdered not men in positions of responsibility who had supported Ii Naosuke or promoted Kazunomiya's marriage, but their underlings. Their aim was as much propaganda as punishment. Called a "festival of blood" (*chimatsuri*) in a sacralization of violence, its agents took upon themselves the "vengeance of heaven" (*tenchū*). The assassinations began a month before Taseko set out for Kyoto, and Shigemasa was in a position to know all about them.

Aiding and abetting the political turmoil in Kyoto was the unprecedented appearance of many daimyo. The retired but still politically powerful Yamanouchi Yōdō from Tosa came as far as Fushimi just south of Kyoto in the fourth month, and his men were deeply implicated in murder and murderous plots. Mōri Takachika from Chōshū arrived two months later; his journey down the Nakasendō had been slowed by the measles spreading east from the Kyoto region where it had been brought by Shimazu Hisamitsu's troops.[15] This was likely the source of the contagion that laid low Taseko's son and daughter-in-law. Satsuma, Chōshū, and Tosa were just three of the most important domains that started moving large numbers of men into the city to offer protection to the emperor.[16] Between 1862 and 1863, the city's population swelled from its customary 300,000 to 500,000.[17] Was it really any place for a woman?

In later years, Taseko sometimes reminisced about her experiences on this journey, especially when she had been drinking. According to her Takemura granddaughter, while she was staying in Nakatsugawa, she was visited one night by Hazama Hidenori, a fellow Hirata disciple whose contribution to publishing "Lectures on Ancient History" she may have solicited at this time. They were discussing foreign affairs and the domestic situation when Taseko let it be known that she planned to go to Kyoto. Hidenori was horrified. Kyoto was too dangerous for a woman. How could she even think of going there? "What do you know of things, you're only a country bumpkin," she retorted. "I'm just a woman, but wait and see, within three years the Tokugawa rule will be overthrown."[18] It must be admitted that hindsight gave Taseko a perspicacity she did not have at the time. This anecdote suggests, however, that her friends as well as her relatives found her desire to go to Kyoto and to go by herself to be unconventional, if not foolhardy.

On the morning following her arrival, Taseko announced that she planned to continue down the Nakasendō. Her relatives objected. They refused to let her go any farther, and Taseko lamented how she "counted the days on my fingers as they did nothing but slip away." Somehow she managed to bring her daughter around to her point of view. "Given the temper of the times, it would be remiss for you to stay here any longer," Masa said, and she got the other members of the family to agree.[19] Taseko must have been an exceedingly determined, indeed stubborn, old woman to have wrung this concession from Shigemasa. It is unlikely that he was pleased, but with his daughter-in-law siding with her mother, he did not stand in her way.

Yet one more obstacle blocked her path. Ichioka Onari had promised to escort her only as far as Shigemasa's house, and he had already returned to Iida. Going to Kyoto was bad enough, going all alone was unthinkable, yet no one from Nakatsugawa had the time or inclination to accompany her. At this juncture along came Yūsuke, a young clerk from a Kyoto shop with long-standing business connections in Nakatsugawa and the Ina Valley. Yūsuke was willing to act as Taseko's escort; indeed, he said he would welcome the company of a kindred spirit. Now that her departure was imminent, her friends and relatives held a series of farewell parties to wish her luck. Delighted to be on her way after a ten-day hiatus, Taseko wrote:

Uchi hisasu	The sun-blessed capital
miyako no momiji	is adorned with
te ori tsutsu	brocade woven
nishiki kazashite	from autumn leaves,
mata kaeri komu	that have come back again.[20]

This poem discloses a token of what she anticipated in Kyoto. She was to write many poems in praise of the brilliant autumn colors covering the hills that ringed the city, and it is clear that classical literature had already taught her what to see.

It took six days for Taseko and Yūsuke to travel from Nakatsugawa to Kyoto, a distance of some 125 miles. At a little over twenty miles a day, theirs was not a rapid pace, and it allowed time for her to view the sights along the way. She wrote the following to Hidenori, whom she had left behind in Nakatsugawa: "As for the famous places along the road that you told me about at my departure, it concerned me that I was causing trouble for my companion to stop and see them all. Still I managed to get off the highway here and there."[21] Being a poet herself she was naturally interested in a tumulus associated with Saigyō, a Buddhist poet priest who lived through the turbulent twelfth century and wrote poetry "marked by a bleak and somber air, . . . suggestive of drabness, loneliness, and melancholy."[22] To commemorate her visit, she wrote her own poem in a suitably subdued style:

Adara yo wo	You cast off
sumi no koromo ni	this vain and empty world
furi sutete	in clothes dyed ink black
tabi yuku hito no	[your tumulus] must be a sad reminder for
aware ato kamo	the travelers who pass by.[23]

Buddhist priests wore dull robes as one sign that they had renounced the world, and Taseko too dressed in nondescript black. The mood induced by this sight did not last long. Soon she was on her way again, exclaiming at the ever-changing wonders of nature spread before her as she crossed hill and dale.

While Taseko respected Saigyō the poet, as a disciple of Hirata Atsutane she had learned to despise Buddhism. On the outskirts of one town she came across a large old hall in an attractive location. "Nothing grieved me more than to learn that here the great gods Ōnamuchi [another name for Ōkuni-nushi, ruler of the invisible world] and Sukunabiko [god of medicine, especially the medicinal properties of hot springs] are worshipped as the Buddha Yakushi [the healing Buddha]:"

Ōnamuchi	Who was so dastardly
Sukunabikona no	as to arrange for
ōkami wo	the great gods
Yakushi totonou	Ōnamuchi and Sukunabiko
shiko wa dare zo mo	to be called Yakushi?[24]

The native gods and Buddhist deities had been worshipped as one for centuries in Japan. Scholars argue that trying to separate the two necessarily imposed a false dichotomy on indigenous religious practices, but Taseko belonged to a school determined to purify the way of the gods from Buddhist accretions.[25] She herself worshipped only at shrines dedicated to the souls of her ancestors and the myriad deities listed in Atsutane's texts.

Taseko frequently noted her disdain for Buddhist temples and practices. At one stop Yūsuke encouraged her to view a temple to Kannon, the Buddhist goddess of mercy. "I myself inhabit the sacred country so there was nothing I had to say to this object renting a room in heaven, and I didn't leave a single line of poetry in exchange for the fire I borrowed to light my tobacco. My companion procured some incense and bowed so low that his head touched the floor, an act showing extreme fear of the afterlife." Taseko need have no such fear herself, for she had learned that the spirits of the dead went not to the netherworld (*yomi*) but to what might be described as a parallel universe. That night she examined the alcove in the sitting room of the inn. "In front of one object had been placed a drum with some other stuff, obviously belonging to that mumbling (*dabudabu*) Nichiren sect."[26] The Buddhist priest Nichiren had taught his followers to chant, "all praise to the Lotus Sutra." In time of trouble, they would work themselves into a frenzy of forgetfulness by beating the drum and repeating this phrase to the destruction of their neighbors' peace and quiet.

Traveling now on horseback, now in a palanquin, now on foot, Taseko wrote poems to commemorate her every visit to sights made famous in classical poetry. In some ways, her trip can be seen as a literary journey; the scenes that caught her eye had meaning for her precisely because they had previously been recorded by countless other poets.[27] As she got closer to Kyoto, her diary contained fewer descriptions of what she did, providing instead simply place names followed by poems, suggesting that the names themselves had the power to evoke specific associations. At Kusatsu where the Nakasendō joins the coastal highway, the Tōkaidō, she stopped long enough to see one of the eight famous views of Ōmi.

Yūbai no	The colors of the autumn leaves
momiji no iro wa	which caught the light so beautifully at dusk
kure hatete	have now darkened.
tsuki sumiwataru	The moon crosses the clear sky
Seta no nagahashi	over the long bridge at Seta.[28]

Many a famous woodblock print depicts precisely this setting. Taseko also wrote a poem at a spot said to be the tomb for Ono no Komachi, the great classical beauty and poet, and a poem in honor of Murasaki Shikibu at the moon-viewing pavilion at Ishiyama where she is said to have begun writing *The Tale of Genji*.

Although Taseko crafted her travel diary in part as a literary project, it was disrupted repeatedly by poems that capture not only her anti-Buddhist stance but also her politics. She wanted a return to the political arrangements found in ancient Japan, and she wanted them in the here and now. Whether or not she really intended to concentrate her energies on studying poetry once she reached Kyoto, she can often be found thinking about the past in the light of current events. At one place she met a bakufu official who hurriedly told her about the reforms in Edo designed to harmonize relations between the court and the military. Earlier, at a field famous for the 1183 battle in which the hero Kiso Yoshinaka lost his life, she wrote:

Kimi ga tame	On this plain there must be
mikuni no tame ni	the remains of warriors
mononofu ga	who fought striving against each other
kisoi arasou	for the sake of the sacred country
ato ya kono hara	for the sake of the emperor.[29]

It must be admitted that this poem gives Yoshinaka a national consciousness it is doubtful that he possessed at the time. Taseko's aim was to summon warriors to combat the foreigners, calling on the magical power inherent in words (*kotodama*) to make manifest what she had named. Like the Japanese in ancient times who had believed that the spirit residing within an object responds sympathetically to the reciting of its name,[30] she sang the praises of men long dead that they might rise to fight again.

Her political stance becomes even more apparent in poems written as she drew closer to Kyoto. More than anything, she wanted the emperor treated with all due reverence and the foreigners expelled. Furthermore, the slogan that expressed this desire—*sonnōjōi*—was but the means to an end: the recapturing in the present of the ancient world in which the gods had ruled through the emperor.

Tachi yorite	As I approached nearer
isa ya yomemu	somehow or other I burst into song
Kagami yama	the road to the unclouded
kumoranu miyo no	age of the gods
michi wa ari ya to	must be there on Mt. Kagami.[31]

Kagami means mirror, and in its manifestation as a mountain, it reflects the gods' awesome power. Surely it too could be summoned to produce the magic that would bring about a return to glorious antiquity.

On the fifteenth day of the ninth month, Taseko arrived in Kyoto, coming over the pass from Ōtsu, through the city's eastern mountains along a highway lined with temples and shops, across the great bridge at Sanjō, and straight to one of the biggest streets of the time, Teramachi. Today the intersection of Sanjō and Teramachi is a pedestrian mall, too narrow for the vehicular traffic that clogs the drastically widened streets around it. In Taseko's time it marked the city's busiest crossroads. Her destination lay two tiny blocks west of Teramachi and just over one block north of Sanjō, at the home of the cloth dyer Ikemura Kuninori and his shop called Iseya. As a matter of course she called on poetry to express her delight:

Tachi narabu	Oh, my joy at taking in
kewashiki yama wo	the skies of the capital
wake wakete	pierced through by
miyako no sora wo	steep mountains
abuku ureshisa	lined up in rows.[32]

Taseko arrived in Kyoto with considerably more than the baggage she carried with her. First of all, she had credit; she could draw on funds held by Kuninori with the understanding that her family in the Ina Valley would reimburse him. There is no way of knowing exactly how this system worked except for one letter in which she mentioned a priest who had brought her news from home and who needed money to continue his journey. "I've sent him over to Iseya to borrow three *ryō*. Please make sure you repay this sum to their clerk when he gets to Iida." Secondly, she had connections. "Now that

I've arrived at the capital," she wrote to Hidenori in Nakatsugawa, "Mr. Sera sometimes comes to visit me. To have these opportunities which give me such delight is something I owe our teacher and his disciples such as you, and I just wanted to let you know how happy I am."[33] Blessed with money and introductions through her membership in the Hirata school, Taseko was set to make the most of her stay.

Taseko met two men soon after she arrived in Kyoto. The first was Sera Toshisada, then aged forty-six, one of the few samurai from the Chōshū domain in western Japan who joined the Hirata school. He was temporarily stationed in Kyoto, and he explored the mountains around the city with her when his official duties permitted. He had to go back to Chōshū within a few months of her arrival, dropping completely from the historical record, and Taseko never saw him again. Her second acquaintance was Fukuba Bisei, born in 1831, which made him twenty years the younger. He was a samurai from the Tsuwano domain, also in western Japan. In the early 1870s he was to become notorious for his work in separating Shinto and Buddhism, promoting Shinto funerals, and demolishing Buddhist temples.[34] Given the antipathy to Buddhism that Taseko expressed in her poetry, she would have found him a kindred spirit. He was staying near her at an inn on Sanjō, and once they had met, he gave her permission to call on him whenever she liked.

Fukuba Bisei proved to be a useful person to know. Ten days after Taseko's arrival, he wrangled an invitation to a poetry party at the home of Shirakawa Sukenori, a court noble and hereditary administrator of Shinto shrine affairs. The Shirakawa family had been closely associated with the Hirata school ever since it asked Atsutane to revise its regulations and gave him permission to lecture to the priests under its supervision. Bisei himself was to lecture on the *Kojiki*, the "Record of Ancient Matters," the oldest chronicle that depicted the age of the gods and the origin of Japan. For a peasant woman this was an honor far beyond the bounds of normal conventions. "Truly nothing gave me more delight than to be informed that I'd be able to attend," Taseko wrote Inao. "At first I thought I should refuse, being an old woman who doesn't know anything. When I pointed this out to the others, they told me that I should go ahead and go, because as long as I intended to devote myself to my country, it'd be all right. I really felt as though I were in a dream, I was so thrilled and frightened all at once."[35]

Taseko's persona displayed a number of facets at this party. She was a patriot, a woman who had come to Kyoto to do what she could for the sake of the emperor. She was a student, anxious to learn about classical historical texts by listening to a renowned lecturer on the subject. She was a poet, and this made the day of the party an expensive one for her.

The court nobility had long been accustomed to selling its expertise in classical Japanese poetry to whomever had the cash to pay for it. Taseko paid one *bu* in gold (one *bu* is approximately a hundred days wages for a day laborer) each to Lord Shirakawa and Lord Ōhara Shigetomi, another court noble and rabid xenophobe, five *shu* (each worth one fourth of a *bu*) to attendants in the Shirakawa household, and about 75 *mon* (100 mon was a day's wages) for refreshments and hot water.[36] In return she was allowed to write a poem on the topic assigned for the day, "the long flourishing chrysanthemum." When she had finished reciting her poem, she recorded proudly that she received refreshments from the lord's own hands. She then recited another poem, this one a paean to the Shirakawa house for its unsullied lineage of devotion to the emperor.

To join such an august gathering required better attire than mere traveling clothes. With nothing else at hand, Taseko dressed herself in a robe embroidered with the Iseya crest, which she borrowed from her banker's (Kuninori) wife. Of all the poems she wrote that day, the only one in which she talked about herself alludes to her outfit:

Otomeko ga	Today I am so happy
ama no hagoromo	I have come to borrow
kari ni kite	the feathered robe of heaven
kumoi ni noboru	belonging to a young girl
kyō no ureshisa	and climb above the clouds.[37]

Above the clouds, *kumoi,* is the standard designation for the imperial palace where the emperor and all who served him lived, hidden from the eyes of ordinary mortals. The poem draws on a strikingly beautiful Noh drama about a young woman who comes down from heaven to bathe, only to have a mortal man swipe her robe. He finally returns it in exchange for watching her dance.[38]

Taseko was distinctly fawning in her approach to the nobility. She delighted in the slightest attention Lord Shirakawa paid to her, deserving as she was of none at all. In this she resembled low ranking samurai who managed to gain access to the court. "Truly nothing could give me more pleasure," Takechi Zuizan, an activist from Tosa wrote to his wife having met Ōhara Shigetomi. "For those of us of low status to travel to the heavens caused me to weep for joy."[39] (In 1865 Zuizan was to be ordered to commit suicide for "actions unbecoming his station."[40]) Taseko accepted without question the status hierarchy of her time. She stood in awe of Sukenori because of his proximity to the emperor, regardless of whether he had any talent as a poet.

This was the closest she had ever been to the rarefied circles at court. For her, or Zuizan, for that matter, to gain a sense of intimacy with men so much her betters shows just how far public space had expanded to include new social actors.

In meeting men ranked high above her in the social scale, Taseko's age proved a distinct advantage. Before the party, Bisei had told Sukenori about an unsophisticated old woman from the countryside, devoted to the imperial cause, who wrote passionate poems in the nativist tradition. Sukenori having expressed interest in this oddity, a poetry-spouting crone (*uta wo utau baba*), Taseko was told that it would be all right for her to attend.[41] Regardless of how well she composed poetry, and most of her poems from this period are at best political doggerel, that she could write at all apparently piqued his curiosity.

Unlike a younger woman, for whom just being in such august company would have been an intimidating experience, Taseko showed no hesitation in reciting her poems and drinking from the cup she was offered. Her poise can be attributed at least in part to her maturity. Deguchi Nao, founder of Ōmoto-kyō, a new religion of the late nineteenth century, began to speak in the voice of her god only after she reached the age of fifty, and the female founders of religions in the Tokugawa period were all forty or older.[42] Ethnographic interviews with women in today's Japan find that many look forward to old age. What a relief "no longer to have to keep a low profile and display feminine reserve." Instead they can be bold, drink, and speak their mind, regardless of the company.[43]

At the age of fifty-one, Taseko was already past menopause. She had reached what nineteenth-century American women heralded as a "golden interim" before they went into the inevitable decline leading to death.[44] Margaret Mead believed that once women got through their child-bearing years, they found that they had new energy and vitality, calling it "postmenopausal zest"[45]—something that Taseko appears to have had in abundance. She was indeed fortunate that the political turmoil in Kyoto had drawn her to the city at the right moment in her life to take advantage of her opportunities while she still had her physical stamina.

Taseko's next adventure came just three days after the party at Sukenori's. On the twenty-eighth day of the ninth month, Sera Toshisada came to her house before dawn for a trip west of the city to Arashiyama to see the autumn leaves. Their first stop was where a forest had once been, more ancient than the city of Kyoto itself, in the area known as Uzumasa (now the site for a motion picture studio and theme park). Taseko was delighted to discover that one of the gods to whom she paid her respects was the same she had worshipped at home as the god of silkworms.[46] According to the ancient chronicles, in the early decades of the fourth century, the Hata clan had brought sericulture techniques from the Asian mainland to Japan. They raised silkworms and paid tribute to the emperor with cloth so soft and warm that they were given the Uzumasa region as their homeland.[47] The shrine was last rebuilt in 1831, so Taseko saw it as it is today, in the shadow of the Buddhist temple that dominates the site.

Taseko's only interest in Kōryūji, popularly known as the Uzumasa temple, was an imperial tomb said to be in its precincts. She passed by the Lecture Hall, erected in 1165 and the oldest structure in Kyoto, because it contained nothing more important than a statue of the Bodhisattva Amida, who promises salvation to Buddhist believers. She scorned the Keiguin, an octagonal structure roofed with cypress bark that contains a statue of Prince Shōtoku carved by himself. (Remember that he was castigated by Atsutane for having introduced the Chinese style imperial administrative system into Japan.[48]) Kōryūji has an exceptional collection of Buddhist art, including an exquisite statue of the Maitreya, the Buddha of the future, which was carved in the late sixth century. Taseko's comment: "To learn that the temple was built over an imperial tomb just goes to show what an excessively base and wretched world this is. How lamentable."[49]

Walking farther up the road brought Taseko and Toshisada to the east bank of the broad and beautiful river that flows past Arashiyama. "The mountain glowed with autumn color. The scenery with the rafts floating down the Ōi River and the boats being poled along was beyond description." First they settled down to enjoy the view at a tea house. They had a delicious lunch with plenty to drink "and somehow or other we got into a fine mood." But the day was still young and the mountain beckoned. "You really ought to cross the 'Moon-crossing' bridge. The autumn leaves on the other side are gorgeous," the tea house attendant urged. And so they did what travelers have done before and since, traversing the long low bridge that spans the river and inserting themselves into an age-old tradition of visiting the autumn leaves.

Taseko did not go to Arashiyama simply because it was pretty; she went because she had already been taught that it was noted for its autumn leaves before she ever arrived in Kyoto. Mountains, moreover, embody deities. Even in industrial Japan, tourist agencies lure visitors to scenic spots by promoting their associations with history and culture. Simon Schama has argued that "landscape is the work of the mind," and minds have worked in different ways across time and space. In the West, for example, travelers looking for the picturesque found in rocky gorges an "agreeable horror" while the Romantics sought "reveries and fatalistic spells of self-annihilation." Alpine Club members attacked mountains with "muscular, quasi-military determination."[50] I have heard contemporary Japanese people speak of mountains as living entities, encompassing more than the sum of the flora and fauna that inhabit them. They enter a mountain (*yama e hairu*) to commune with the numen that animates it. In Taseko's mind she was making a pilgrimage to Arashiyama. It was a religious experience, for in nature she saw the countenance of the divine.

Taseko and Toshisada did not stay long on the other side of the river. They worshipped at the first shrine they found before a priest appeared and ordered Taseko out. Like many at the time, the jealous mountain god would not permit women to invade her territory. Outside the shrine at the base of the mountain Taseko found that the trees were too tall for her to reach the branches. She contented herself with picking up the leaves that had already fallen and asking the gods that their red hues be woven into her heart. The redder the heart, the more devoted the person to protecting Japan's sacred soil from foreign invasion. Taking the leaves reminded her of a classical comedy (*kyōgen*) about a man caught stealing flowers who gains his release by producing a poem. In the same vein, she and her companion playfully indulged in an exchange of poems to make up for having spied on the sacred shrine and stolen its leaves:

Yamamori yo	O protector of the mountain,
ware ni wa yuruse	Please forgive me
itazura ni	for having idly broken off
chiru wo shimite	and brought down
te ori momiji yo	a branch covered with autumn leaves
—TOSHISADA	

Oru hito no	By attaching the color,
akaki kokoro ni	the red of the autumn leaves
momiji no	to the red heart of
iro wo mo soete	the one who broke them off
kami ya yurusamu	the god will surely forgive me.[51]
—TASEKO	

Back on the other side of the moon-crossing bridge, they came to Tenryūji, a temple erected in 1339 to appease the soul of Emperor Godaigo. It was built by Ashikaga Takauji, the man vilified by Atsutane for having hounded the emperor to his death. The brilliant hues of the autumn leaves enticed them inside precincts they would otherwise have avoided. "To have seen that color just once in a lifetime was more than enough." Beyond the temple is the shrine called Nonomiya, famous for its torii created out of living trees. It receives mention in *The Tale of Genji* as the place where princesses would retire to be purified before going to the shrine for the sun goddess at Ise to take up their duties as priestesses. "Feeling such nostalgia for the past dewed my sleeves completely," Taseko wrote. A path overgrown with grass brought them next to Mt. Ogura, once famous for autumn leaves, but now barren. The contrast between leafless present and leafy past made Taseko pensive, and she devoted her thoughts to "the sacred way in the ancient age of the gods."[52]

Next on the list was Nison-in, a large temple complex built originally in the ninth century, though like so many others, it burned in the Ōnin war of 1467–1477. From Taseko's point of view, it was notable chiefly for the grave of Emperor Sanjō, who reigned for four short years at the beginning of the eleventh century. It also contains a cemetery for three thirteenth-century emperors and other "exalted personages." Taseko carefully offered prayers before each of their graves. Yet deeper in the mountains was a nunnery called Giō-ji, a lovely spot in the midst of a maple grove beyond a bamboo forest. Giō was a dancer beloved of the twelfth-century military leader Taira no Kiyomori, and the temple was dedicated to her memory. The nun who served as the guide was voluble in her explanations. "We watched as she lifted her hands in fervent prayer," but Taseko and Toshisada did not join her. The sun was sinking fast, and it was well over seven miles back to the center of Kyoto. "'We really must hurry,' we said to each other as we went along." They did not reach her lodgings until after nine o'clock.[53]

Late nights, a stream of visitors, no thought of leaving Kyoto after a three-week stay—it was time for Taseko to stop imposing on the Ikemura family. She rented rooms just down the street in a house owned by a calligraphy teacher and tea ceremony master, and there she moved on the second day of the tenth month. Iseya and the tea ceremony master have long since departed Fuyachō. Today the west side of the street displays a small hardware shop, a parking lot, and a large but tasteful Japanese inn. It is one of the most luxurious inns in the city, complete with translucent paper screens, lacquered chests, polished wooden floors, and fragrant tatami mat rooms overlooking private gardens.[54] Taseko's quarters were more spartan. "The mistress at Ikemura and my new landlord really put themselves out for me, preparing everything from the room partition to the bedding. I could not have been more delighted with the warmth of their hospitality."[55] Now she had privacy and no longer did she have to act like a guest.

Few were the days that Taseko spent alone. She had already met a samurai from the Satsuma domain then known by the name Nakamura Hanjirō, a young man of twenty-four who had parlayed his skill as a sword fighter into a position guarding the maternal relatives of the future Emperor Meiji.[56] She spent one day with a commoner from Ōmi, also a poet and disciple of the Hirata school. He professed himself delighted at her visit, and "we spent the entire day together becoming great friends."[57]

The men Taseko met in her guise of patriot and poet treated her well. The same can not be said for the most famous Kyoto poet of the time, the nun Ōtagaki Rengetsu, then seventy-one. Rengetsu was known for the originality of her pottery, especially her teapots, which were much sought by connoisseurs. "I started making teapots because I was so poor that I didn't have any choice," Rengetsu later claimed. "Being extremely clumsy, I couldn't craft ordinary shapes. I decorated the rims with my poetry because I found the effect pleasing."[58] Her entire income came from her sales of pots and poems. Although she knew many of the men who called for expelling the barbarians, her poetry spoke to her desire for a nonviolent solution to Japan's problems, and she was more curious than fearful. "When you get to Nagasaki, try to meet some foreigners," she wrote her disciple, "ask them as many questions as you can, paint some pictures, and bring them all back to me." Reclusive and often rude to strangers, Rengetsu was much more cosmopolitan and sophisticated than Taseko. The two women had, in fact, little in common. Rengetsu gave Taseko an incense burner in the shape of a turtle, said to be an aid for longevity, Taseko gave her one *shu*, and they parted without even an exchange of poems.[59]

Taseko soon made another trip to the western mountains, this time in the company of two young men who worked for Iseya. They took the Shijō Road out of town to the vicinity of what they thought was an imperial tomb at Umetsu. In the long history of Japan's imperial family, the burial mounds for many of the early emperors and their families had disappeared. A number of believers in the ancient way had set themselves the task of reclaiming these sites that they might be shown proper respect. Some had authorization and documentation from the imperial court; others, such as Taseko and her friends, relied on popular memory. In this case it failed them. The only person around, a man they found working in the fields, knew nothing about the tomb. Seeing the ridge poles for two shrines off in the distance, they worshipped them from afar and went on their way.

Taseko's husband brewed sake, making the next shrines they visited of particular interest to her. First was Umenomiya, founded in the early seventh century to the progenitress of the Tachibana clan and moved to its current location by the Empress Danrin, 786–850, consort to Emperor Saga. The buildings Taseko saw and which remain today, all built in the late seventeenth century, include a gate in the Buddhist temple style. The gods enshrined here include Ōyamatsuumi-no-kami, who created sake to celebrate the birth of his grandson, and the goddess Konohananosakuya ("beautiful-as-the-flowers"), who bestowed not only a child on Danrin but an easy child-birth.[60] What Taseko remembered was the large carp pond that reflected the maple leaves overhead. Crossing the Ōi River by boat, she then made a pilgrimage to the sacred shrine of Matsuo. "This being the shrine for the sacred god of my house, I worshiped to my heart's content."[61]

Taseko and her companions walked up the river, crossed the bridge, and admired once again the brocade of autumn colors on Arashiyama.

Kogarashi ni	Colors are supposed to fade
utsurou iro mo	in the cold winds at the end of autumn
Arashiyama	but at Arashiyama
kinōni masaru	the autumn leaves at the peak
mine no momiji	surpass those of yesterday.[62]

From Arashiyama they headed north across a mountain pass beyond the pond called Hirosawa, where they saw mandarin ducks at play. Deep in the gorges of the Kiyotaki River on the other side of the mountains, the group reserved lodgings, then started up Mt. Takao. It was so late in the afternoon that most sightseers were already on their way home, but Taseko was indefatigable. A brief prayer at the shrine for Wake no Kiyomaro, and she was ready to view the magnificent scenery spread before her along the Kiyotaki River from the garden terrace at Jizōin. This retreat, the preserve of an aristocratic monk in the fourteenth century, had already become a tourist sight by the time Taseko arrived. There was even a tea house conveniently in the vicinity.

Taseko's goal was the grave of Wake no Kiyomaro, famous for having prevented the monk Dōkyō from becoming emperor in 772 and planning the city of Kyoto in 794.[63] His shrine being on the mountain gave a clue that the grave must be nearby, but no one she asked knew anything about it. Taseko and her companions went back to the temple. They saw nothing to interest them there. They tried pushing their way through the brush in the gathering dusk, to no avail except the danger of getting lost. They purified themselves at a spring, offered a prayer in what they assumed was the general direction of the grave, and returned to their lodgings.

The next morning Taseko and her companions took a boat trip upriver, refusing the opportunity to stop at one temple, but unable to resist the maple leaves at Togano-o, more often called by its Buddhist name, Kōzanji. Known today for what is said to be the oldest tea leaf nursery in Japan, in Taseko's time it was a flourishing temple complex. As usual she ignored all that, climbing above the nursery to worship the gods Sumiyoshi and Kasuga at a tiny nondescript shrine. That afternoon she returned to Kyoto, stopping at the famous Golden Pavilion, then pausing to worship the god of learning and schol-arship at Kitano Tenjin. "This being the god who had been in my thoughts for a long time, I bowed my head reverently, my heart filled with delight." [64]

Taseko's trip to Takao had not been an unqualified success, for she had failed to find the grave for Wake no Kiyomaro. A few days later when Sera Toshisada from Chōshū happened to be visiting her, she mentioned how she had looked for it in vain.

"I didn't know the grave was on Mt. Takao," he said, looking at me strangely.

"If I hadn't heard it from you some time ago, I wouldn't have known where to look," I replied.

"But this is the first I've heard of it," he protested. How odd. Per-haps I saw it in a dream. When I considered the matter carefully, I was certain someone had definitely told me that the grave for Wake no Kiyomaro was on Mt. Takao.

"I know I told you a while ago that there is a shrine to Wake no Kiyomaro enshrined as the Protector of the Emperor. You must have gotten them confused." We argued back and forth, but I was sure I'd heard of a grave.

"This truly must be something you were privileged to learn from the god. I'll go there tomorrow and look for myself," Toshisada announced. [65]

Naturally enough Taseko insisted that she was going too.

Toshisada and Taseko left her house at dawn, arriving at Mt. Takao about eleven o'clock. Beating through the brush, going this way and that around bamboo groves and clumps of trees, they struggled up the mountain. These merely material obstacles finally parted, rewarding them at last with what they deemed to be the grave. "No words could describe the joy we felt upon reaching this spot so long awaited. We prostrated ourselves countless times in worship, and we offered our petitions to the god with branches taken from the pines at his shrine." Out of sheer delight, Taseko wrote a number of po-ems describing her feelings:

Wake noboru	Having found our way up
Takao no yama mo	Mt. Takao
momiji no ha	the autumn leaves become
mukashi no hito no	the hearts and minds
kokoro narikeri	of people in ancient days. [66]

In poems such as this, Taseko tried to approach the spirit of the past. In the imagined community that she constructed to link then and now, nature pointed the way both to constitute and signify a timeless group identity. Remember that her experience of the landscape itself was always mediated through her literary education; she never provided a straightforward transcription of reality. While drawing on the classical poetic forms she had learned in her youth, she infused them with desires that made sense only within the context of her own time. She laid claim to nostalgia, and as Jennifer Robertson points out, "what occasions it resides in the present, regardless of the sustenance provided by memories of the past." [67]

In the spring of 1994, Kyoto's twelve-hundredth anniversary, I visited the Temple of the Protective Deity, Jingo-ji, that now guards the grave of Wake no Kiyomaro. Founded early in the early ninth century, the temple burned to the ground in the Ōnin war. The gate, the bell tower, and a couple of minor buildings were reconstructed in 1623. In 1851, the emperor raised Kiyomaro to the rank of "Great Shining Deity, Protector of the Emperor" (*go-ōdaimyōjin*).[68] Many of the buildings there today, including the shrine housing Kiyomaro's spirit, were erected between 1898 and 1900. A well-marked path leads through the woods to a tumulus clearly identified with a wooden placard as being the grave of Kiyomaro, who died in 799. On top of the mound is a substantial stone monument giving the posthumous rank bestowed on him by the Meiji Emperor. This monument is dated 1898. If the grave was as ill-marked in Taseko's day as she claims, then what is there now is a modern fabrication.

Taseko's effort to recapture an essential Japan located in antiquity by seeking Kiyomaro's grave has been overlooked by all her biographers. They have spared not a glance for her sightseeing trips, probably because in their eyes these were but a prelude to more significant activities. It is important to remember, however, that Taseko chose what she wanted to see. Her pilgrimages were unusual by the standards of the time, by-passing as she did the most impressive Buddhist monuments in favor of often obscure shrines and imperial tombs. This sacred geography provided the context for her to assert her identity as a poet in recreating literary landscapes and her identity as a Hirata disciple in communing with the divine immanent in nature. It shows another side of her personality and suggests that she found additional motivations for being in Kyoto besides politics.

Taseko has sometimes been maligned for having neglected her familial responsibilities in going to Kyoto to study poetry and participate in the nativist movement. Local historians anxious to counter these charges argue defensively that she must have acted with her husband's full knowledge and

consent.[69] Peasant women having been less likely than samurai women to
wait on a husband's approval, however, she may well have acted on her own.
One postwar historian has suggested that perhaps because she lived life at
such a high energy level, her husband merely looked on "like the master of a
hairdressing salon."[70]

Taseko's cousin Inao offered his own appreciation for what she had done.
He wrote a long poem enviously describing the fun she was having and the
sights she saw. He knew her better than anyone and he admired her extrav-
agantly. He offered no excuses for her having left without informing her family and neighbors, nor did he justify what she had done by claiming that she
had her husband's permission. She simply walked out:

Shikaba are to	Indeed,
tatsu aki kaze ni	with the autumn winds starting to blow
yukuri naku	suddenly
waga ie wo itete	she left home
ie no nari	people gossiped
wasuraetari wo	fast and furiously that
hitogoto no	she had forgotten
shigemi kochitami	her household occupation
imasaka ni	but already it was
omoi tarishi wo	too late
imawashi mo	to think of that.[71]

CHAPTER EIGHT

A Peasant Woman at the Emperor's Court

The scent of the plum
that perfumes the awesome
reaches above the clouds
now clings to the sleeve
of this base-born commoner.[1]
MATSUO TASEKO, 1863

Taseko had a delightful time in Kyoto sightseeing, meeting people, and reciting poetry, but what gave the city special meaning was its sanctity. Rome could have no greater attraction for a Catholic than Kyoto had for her. The emperor was a political symbol, one that had come to be associated with expulsion of the barbarians. He was also and perhaps foremost a religious symbol in that he mediated between the visible and invisible worlds of human beings and gods. Hidden behind thick walls beyond which he never ventured, confined to an elaborate round of rituals and ceremonies, he was increasingly becoming a magnet to people from all walks of life. Following the crop failure and political turmoil of 1787, for example, a crowd of young and old men and women came to circumambulate the palace praying for alms; in the nineteenth century pilgrims were wont to worship his majesty from afar.[2] Taseko too paid him homage. In her eyes, any disturbance of his tranquillity was a mark of disrespect.

While professing to be his loyal servant, the shogun had controlled the emperor financially and politically since the early seventeenth century. He allowed the entire imperial court, emperor and nobles alike, income from lands producing a mere 140,000 *koku*—amounting to .5 percent of the gross national agricultural product. In comparison, some sixteen daimyo had lands officially listed at over 300,000 *koku*. The shogun's portion was 6,820,000 *koku*, or 25.8 percent of the total. The emperor had only 9,000 *koku* for himself and his attendants. The highest ranking court nobles, the Five Houses (*go-sekke*), who were privileged to act as regents to the emperor, outranked even the shogun before the nineteenth century, yet the base for their income came to only 1,500 to 3,000 *koku*.[3] The nobles of lower rank had far less. In some ways they nonetheless managed to live quite well. They had no need for the enormous retinues required of the daimyo nor did they have significant administrative responsibilities. Besides, they could supplement their income by selling their expertise in the traditional Japanese arts, arranging marriage alliances with the daimyo in an exchange of prestige for wealth, and offering their friendship to local merchants.

When Taseko came to Kyoto, the emperor had not yet broken free of the system of controls imposed by the shogun to keep him out of politics. The bakufu insisted that the rank of the nobles it controlled (the regent and the liaison for military affairs) be superior to imperial princes (the emperor's own relatives). In this way it isolated the emperor within the court itself. The regent could and did defy the emperor; with bakufu support he even acted contrary to the emperor's wishes, yet he could always claim to act in the emperor's name.[4] All daimyo and the shogun himself vied for court rank and honorary office, although no daimyo was allowed to accept court rank and office without the shogun's recommendation and approval. This system worked quite well up to the middle of the nineteenth century, but once political activists started flocking to Kyoto, the contrast between the wealthy shogun and poverty-stricken emperor appeared to many to be inappropriate. The regent's manipulation of the emperor's will was deemed nothing less than insubordinate and intolerable.

Rumors making the rounds while Taseko was in Kyoto depicted the emperor's poverty in ever more compelling terms. Once upon a time, for example, the Kyoto Governor had occasion to taste the emperor's sake. Surprised at its lack of body, he sent the emperor some of the ordinary sake that he drank every day. The emperor responded with a fulsome letter of thanks praising its flavor. Another story claimed that when moon-viewing parties were held at the palace, the noble participants could never afford enough strips of the heavy-weight paper needed to record their poems.[5] Paper was expensive. Taseko paid as much as one *shu* fifty *mon* for poem cards, and samurai in the Mito domain counted it so dear that in practicing penmanship, they would use the same page over and over again until it had completely disappeared under layers of black ink.[6] For the court nobility whose chief function was maintaining aristocratic traditions, especially poetry writing, not to have the appropriate paper struck at their very reason for being. In the eyes of those watching the court, how could it mean anything other than disrespect for the emperor by the shogun who held the purse strings.

Whenever Taseko met with her friends, concern for the emperor was never far from their minds. According to one of her admirers, who heard it from his teacher, Taseko was wont to say,

> The bakufu pretends to respect the court, but secretly it whittles away at its teeth and claws, trying to lessen its authority. This is outrageous. Its treachery can be traced back to the Ashikaga shoguns [fourteenth century]. If loyal retainers don't devise plans to remedy this situation, sooner or later we'll see an end to the peace and prosperity our country now enjoys. The opportunity to offer oneself for service on behalf of the nation is not confined to men. Even though I'm a woman, I want to do what I can. How can it be said that the obligation to act is the monopoly of men?

In the heightened atmosphere of the time, this was the kind of speech to bring tears to the eyes of speaker and listener alike.[7] Whether Taseko actually said these words, they are typical of the way rage and frustration were expressed in the circles in which she moved.

Some rumors that came her way had a malevolent cast. In a letter written to her cousin Inao, Taseko exclaimed, "I'm really quite frightened even to say anything, so I'm reporting this to you in secret. It seems that on the fifteenth night of the seventh month, one of the imperial princes was poisoned with something put into his medicine. He almost didn't drink it because the light from a falling star fell across his bowl, but then he did."[8] It appears that she had picked up a slightly garbled version of a rumor that gained more currency the more the talk of assassination filled the city. On the eighth day of the ninth month the Tosa samurai Takechi Zuizan heard that the emperor himself was to be poisoned. That night he went to the emperor's taster who promised to die in service if need be.[9] Five days later the four court nobles and the two ladies-in-waiting implicated in arranging Kazunomiya's marriage were denounced for plotting treason with the Kyoto Governor and accused of planning to poison the emperor or lay a curse on him. If they were willing to show appropriate deference to the court and leave the city, they would be left alone. They prudently decided to make the countryside their place of residence.[10]

As far as Taseko was concerned, getting to know members of the aristocracy was a rewarding experience. She was only too glad to yield to a friend's insistence that she pay a visit to Uratsuji Kin'yoshi, seen at that time as a *sonnōjōi* supporter, and she did not return home until after dark. In a letter to Inao, she praised him to the skies: "Lord Uratsuji is now rallying the loyalists. He is truly a shining example of a man filled with the Japanese spirit."[11] A few days later she visited him once more, this time with the excuse of showing him some drawings done by her children included in a letter from home. There she found a crowd of people much more important than she, including a high-ranking samurai with seven attendants. "Even in the midst of all those people, he graciously inquired after me." He gave her a copy of one of his poems, and she never saw him again.[12] After flirting with the radical expulsionists, Kin'yoshi ended up a firm supporter of alliance between court and bakufu.

Taseko spent a great deal of her time ingratiating herself with the nobles she had met through Fukuba Bisei. She did this in part to further her study of poetry, though it must be said that the poems she wrote in Kyoto showed little of the refined sentiment typical of court anthologies. Using every excuse—a gift of candy that might please their palate, or some persimmons from home—she took advantage of her standing invitation to visit them and carry away material mementos of her encounters. Some of these she kept for herself, but most she distributed to friends both in Kyoto and back home. In another letter to Inao, she told how some of the men she met in Kyoto had asked her for samples of Lord Shirakawa's calligraphy. "I was told that if I asked for two, I should present a gift of about one *ryō* one *bu*, but I had to spend 1000 *hiki* [10,000 *mon*, closer to one *ryō* two *bu*]. I've been thinking about giving him some silk as well. Please let me know if there's anything you desire. I can make whatever requests you like to Lord Ōhara, Lord Shirakawa, or Lord Uratsuji."[13] Through her connections with the court, it would appear that Taseko had developed a thriving trade in souvenirs.

Taseko saw herself as a disciple of Hirata Atsutane as well as a poet. Besides receiving instruction in the arts, she made herself into a conduit for other disciples to gain access to the nobility and spread her mentor's teachings. On the twenty-fifth day of the eleventh month, a samurai from western Japan asked her for an introduction to Lord Ōhara. "Since I was going there on a regular basis, I passed this request along." The two of them went together the next day, and "Lord Ōhara politely deigned to talk to us before we went home." The following day they went to see him again, this time to ask that he help them present Hirata Atsutane's writings to the emperor. On their third visit, he let them know that he had talked to the official in charge of communicating between the nobles and the emperor (the *gisōkata*), and the emperor would be willing to receive the gift in the near future. This called for a poem:

Kototowamu	Through your
kimi no chikara ni	unquestioned power
takaku yuki	the words of my teacher
manabi no oya no	will find their way where they should go
fumi no yukue wo	up to the very top.[14]

The next month Taseko was able to write Inao that Lord Ōhara had been responsible for presenting Atsutane's interpretative history of the age of the gods (*Koshiseibun*) to the emperor. "This should delight all of you."[15] She also played a role in giving "Lectures on Ancient History" (*Koshiden*) to Lord Sanjō. As a proselytizer of the faith, this was, perhaps, her finest hour.

Ōhara Shigetomi was already well informed on Atsutane's work before he met Taseko. The previous year, while he had been in Edo delivering the emperor's orders to the shogun to expel the barbarians, he had written to Kanetane:

> Atsutane's teachings have gradually spread throughout the world [of Japan], and his lessons on the great way of revering what is inside the country and despising what is outside are being understood and taken to heart. In recent years a number of people at court have read his work and many are those who look upon it with favor, even among the lower officials. It is regrettable, however, that so few of his works have been available. Therefore I would like for a complete edition of his writings to be presented to the court college (Gakushūin).

Two months later, Kanetane sent him what he had asked.[16]

In some ways visiting the nobility was easier for Taseko than it was for many of the men she knew. When Shimazu Hisamitsu from Satsuma had arrived in Kyoto to serve as Shigetomi's escort, he received orders to suppress the *shishi*, the men who had absconded from their domains in order to come to Kyoto and demonstrate their loyalty to the emperor. This he did with great gusto, attacking men from his own domain who had planned to assassinate the regent and the Kyoto Governor, then lead troops against the bakufu.

By forcing their opponents such as Iwakura Tomomi into hiding, radicals on the *sonnōjōi* side led Emperor Kōmei to worry that they were getting out of hand, a concern he shared with bakufu officials and the daimyo then in the city. While Shigetomi was in Edo with proposals for bakufu reform in 1862, the regent reminded the court that direct contact between nobles and warriors was forbidden. But who would question the comings and goings of an old peasant woman? "She was intimate with the women officials," one of her friends reported, "so she let us know what was going on at court." It was even said that she spied on traitors to the throne.[17]

Taseko tried to find out as much as she could about court life. To that end she welcomed the men with connections to the nobility who came to visit her. One of them was Kimura Kazuma, a Hirata disciple as well as a servant to Lord Shirakawa. On the eleventh day of the tenth month, he spent almost the entire day telling her about current events, perhaps the assassination of two townspeople whose heads had been pilloried on the riverbank at Nijō street, and explaining to her how the court's internal bureaucracy functioned. Six weeks later he introduced her to the bureau for the maids of honor (*naishi*). In the sacrosanct inner quarters, access to the emperor rested completely in the hands of women officials who in addition to ministering to his personal needs managed his appointment schedule. Many a high-ranking bakufu official and daimyo complained of their high-handed ways and the size of the bribes they demanded in return for arranging meetings with his majesty.[18]

Being in Kyoto allowed Taseko the opportunity to observe ceremonies that featured the emperor. In the eleventh month, he presented the first fruits of the harvest to the gods, then partook of these offerings himself in thanksgiving for a bountiful year. On the day of this festival, the inhabitants of Kyoto were expected to show proper decorum by limiting their excursions and keeping quiet. Taseko had wanted to worship at this festival, but women were not allowed even to enter the palace precincts. "There I was, all alone [her friends having gone inside]. With a bunch of other people outside the eastern gate, I was able to catch no more than a glimpse of the sacred scene before I returned home at dusk. While despising my body, I wrote:"

Iya takaki	No matter how high it is
igaki no uchi mo	my thoughts enter
omoi iri	the sacred precinct
kokoro bakari ni	may the gods allow
kami yurushimase	my heart if nothing else.[19]

Like many other imperial rituals, the first fruits festival constituted part of the yearly round of agriculturally oriented observances. It celebrated the fertility of the soil and, by implication, human fertility as well. How ironic, then, that a peasant woman who had borne ten children would find herself excluded.

Taseko suffered under a double disability. Not only was she base-born, she was also a woman with a body deemed polluted in the Shinto tradition and beyond redemption in the Buddhist. At times she apparently despaired of herself and questioned what she was doing in Kyoto. One of her poems that rails against the constraints placed on her by her position in society hints at the conflicts between the various contexts of her life, the difficulty she had in constructing a loyalist identity as a Hirata disciple, and the obstacles to meaningful action she experienced because of her gender. It is entitled "on regretting being a woman:"

Hisakata no	Morning comes
ama no kawara ni	to the riverbanks in heaven
asa ga shite	high in the sky
hikage mo mizu no	but the sunlight dissipates
shimo ni kuchinan	before it reaches the lower depths.[20]

To represent the self is to constitute the self, as Roland Barthes has said,[21] and in this vision of herself, Taseko admits her innate inferiority to men as a woman and her innate inferiority to the nobility as a peasant. She had struggled against the roles defined for women in her society by insisting on going to Kyoto, but she nevertheless complied with societal assumptions regarding what was essentially female. As with most people, she participated in her own oppression. As long as she saw her world in nativist terms, she supported the system of gendered relations that, in separating her from other less politically conscious women, maintained sexist power. She also supported the status hierarchy that, in allowing her nothing more than a role as the onlooker, buttressed the authority of the ruling class.

On the twelfth day of the tenth month, Taseko rose at dawn, ate her breakfast, then hurried to a friend's house where she borrowed a brazier to warm her while she waited for the emperor's envoy to the shogun to pass by. She waited a very long time. Perhaps she was in the wrong place. She moved to Teramachi. It was almost noon before the envoy appeared, followed shortly thereafter by his companion. "Both lords were beautifully attired," she noted.[22] The escort included samurai from Tosa, Chōshū, and Satsuma. Taseko had friends among the retainers from at least two of these domains, making it possible that she knew why these nobles departed for Edo, and she most probably approved. After all, they carried with them the emperor's unqualified wish that "the unparalleled national dishonor" caused by the barbarian presence on Japanese soil be ended immediately. The foreigners were to be expelled forthwith, not simply forced to withdraw after a period of some years.[23] This demand caused enormous trouble for the bakufu, gave the domains that provided the escort a greater voice in policy debates, and led eventually to the shogun's promise to come to Kyoto the following year to meet with the emperor and fix a date for expulsion. For the nonce, having spent three hours watching the procession, Taseko returned home, worn out by the cold and excitement.

Taseko's diary shows that in the last months of 1862 her mood veered repeatedly from elation to despair as she moved in ever more exalted circles only to be cruelly reminded of her status and the conventional norms of behavior for women. A few days after her interview with Shigetomi in the eleventh month, in which he had promised to present a sample of Hirata's work to the emperor, she went out on the road to see the imperial messenger on his way to the Kamo festival. Then, having just been introduced at the bureau for the maids of honor, in the twelfth month she abruptly left Kyoto for Osaka.

Taseko went to Osaka at the invitation of some men she had met in Kyoto and because "I had something to think over." What that was she never said nor did she mention her trip in any of her extant letters. As soon as she landed in the city after a day's journey by boat, she made arrangements to stay with Nonoguchi Masashiki, the adopted son of Ōkuni Masatane, and paid him one gold *bu*, two *shu* for the privilege. Masatane began his studies of Japanese history and culture under Hirata Atsutane's tutelage and was still seen as one of his followers by the Hirata disciples. He took a conservative approach to current affairs, however, that placed great importance on maintaining the social inequality inherent in the status hierarchy. A trip to Nagasaki in 1862 made him realize that Japan had to become wealthy before it could expel the barbarians. This attitude was seen as entirely too passive by Taseko's friends once they learned of it, and he rejected the possibility of a politically active emperor. Better to delegate the mundane business of governance to a subordinate, he urged, than to sully the emperor's mind with practical matters. It is doubtful that Taseko knew all this when she went to Osaka. She probably carried an introduction to his son Masashiki from Fukuba Bisei, one of Masatane's leading disciples and her first contact in Kyoto.

Was Taseko in Osaka to debate the interpretation of ancient texts, or was she there to inspect its fortifications (crucial for the defense of Kyoto) and have a little fun? The day after her arrival, the fifth day of the twelfth month, she got up before daybreak to view the castle, "having heard that I really ought to see it," and she did not return home until evening. The next day she visited another Hirata disciple who spent the evening showing her Shinmachi by night. This was a famous prostitution district with tea houses for customers interspersed with rows of brothels. In contrast to the high-ranking courtesans who appeared outside only when parading with their entourage from one to the other, ordinary prostitutes had to sit behind wooden lattices that left them visible to passers-by. Taseko made no comment on what she saw. Her only entry for the seventh recorded that she enjoyed herself at a tea house located on a pleasure barge. The party cost 400 *mon*. On the eighth she and a companion went to Osaka's most famous shrine, that for Sumiyoshi, god of the sea and god of poetry. She was delighted to see that it was built in the ancient style, unlike the shrines in Kyoto that could hardly be distinguished from Buddhist temples. "It really brought about a cleansing of the spirit." Despite a fierce wind, they climbed to the top of the tower, where lanterns are hung during festivals. From there they could see all the way from Awaji island to the mountain range behind what is now Kobe, a view that had been lauded in poetry since the tenth century. In need of lunch after this chilling excursion, they stopped in a tea house for food and sake. On their way home, they took a look at the compound owned by the Tosa domain of Shikoku. Snow had fallen the day before, but Taseko never let a little cold weather stand in the way of sightseeing.

The climax to Taseko's stay in Osaka was a poetry meeting held at the Nonoguchi house. Over ten people showed up, none to Taseko's liking. "I saw neither well-known poets nor praiseworthy poems. No one came with whom I could discuss the future. Since things had turned out so differently from what I had expected, I just mumbled my own poem to myself:"

Koto no ba no	All they're concerned about
fushi sae imada	is the rhythm of the poems
Naniwa kata	the people on
yo no ukikoto mo	Osaka Bay know nothing of
hito wa shirazu ya	the terrible things happening in this world.[24]

Taseko was disgusted. Here she was, a woman from the countryside, yet more politically attuned than the men she met in Osaka. Worse, she was visiting a scholar with whom she had expected to share her views on the problems facing Japan, but neither he nor his friends seemed to care. What a waste of time. She decided to return to Kyoto the next day.

Before leaving Osaka, Taseko spent 550 *mon* on souvenirs to take back to her banker, her landlord, and a few friends. Finding fresh river carp said to be particularly delicious in winter, she decided to buy it, and she made up this poem on the spot:

Tsu no kuni no	Living at the Naniwa crossing
Naniwa watari no	in the province of Settsu
hito ni niru	these people are just like
hone naki funa wo	the spineless carp
ie tsuto ni semu	that I'm bringing home as a souvenir.[25]

Taseko began this poem with measured cadences redolent of classical poetry anthologies, then she attacked her Osaka hosts with fine invective. Having put them in their place, at least in her own mind, she still had to wait three days until the Yodo River was free from ice. She spent her time writing poems about what she had seen and did not arrive back in Kyoto until the thirteenth.

Taseko returned to her rooms to discover that her mentor, Hirata Kanetane, son of Atsutane, had arrived in the city during her absence. She spent the rest of the month visiting him, paying her respects to her acquaintances among the court nobles, and calling at the bureau for the maids of honor at the palace. These activities were to pay great dividends in the new year.

By the beginning of 1863, Taseko had been in Kyoto for over three months, and she was not inclined to return home. As far as she was concerned, the capital was the most meaningful place for her to be—so much so that she wanted to share the experience with other members of her family. "I had a letter saying Mitsunaka [her second son] wants to come," she wrote her daughters in Nakatsugawa. "I'll do what I can to entertain him, and if he arrives soon, I'll be able to arrange an interview with our teacher Mr. Hirata. If he puts in a request through me to visit Lord Shirakawa and Lord Ōhara, there shouldn't be any problem at all, so I'd like for him to come without fail. If Makoto [her eldest son] decides to accompany him, the same will be true for him. Please encourage them to come."[26] Taseko invited her sons to join her, not her daughters. As wives, they had too many responsibilities, and as young women they were both sexually vulnerable and sexually threatening to the men Taseko had met in the city. But in the middle of winter, traditionally the slack time for farmers, a man might well take a moment to relax by traveling around to visit friends and relatives.

Taseko's New Year's observances centered on the imperial palace. She worshiped at one of its gates on New Year's Day, before she went to the Gion shrine and paid her respects to Kanetane, her mentor. This was the busiest day of the year for the emperor, beginning at four in the morning when he performed an elaborate ceremony in the eastern garden, calling first on the name of the sun goddess Amaterasu and the three primeval gods, then on the five cardinal directions, including the northwest. This year, however, he had been suffering so much from a cold that he was unable to purify himself, and a number of nobles performed the ceremonies in his place.[27] On the third, Taseko returned to the palace gates, this time to watch five daimyo parade inside to have an audience with the emperor. In her diary Taseko made no distinction between men who were then rulers of domains and those like Mōri Motonori, heir to Chōshū or Date Munenari, officially retired. Their appearance was unprecedented; never before had there been so many daimyo in the city eager to demonstrate their allegiance to the throne. They provided a remarkable spectacle in a city known for its pageantry.

For the next week or so, Taseko went out every day. On the fifth she stationed herself at the intersection of Sanjō and Teramachi to watch the most powerful figure in the bakufu and the shogun's chief advisor, Hitotsubashi Yoshinobu, enter the city surrounded by his troops. A rumor circulated among Tosa and Chōshū samurai that he had brought quantities of gold and silver with which to bribe the nobles to support him in opening the country to trade.[28] Taseko simply noted his arrival and went home. A few days later she made a trip to Mt. Kurama north of the city where the twelfth-century hero Yoshitsune was said to have studied the martial arts as a child. She called at the bureau for the maids of honor where she presented two poems. She took her new year's greetings to Lord Shirakawa, who gave her a dish of unglazed earthenware and rice cakes, then she did the same at the Ōhara compound, where she was bestowed with rice cakes and poem cards. "I can't tell you how grateful I am to have received these," she wrote her daughters.[29] While she was circulating in this fashion, however, she was also preparing herself for one of the highlights of her trip—a chance to get inside the imperial palace.

On the sixteenth Taseko was invited by women in the bureau for the maids of honor to see the banquet and poetry contest, *Sagitsuchō*, traditionally held on this day. First she went to the wardrobe where she was fitted with a figured robe similar to those worn by the court ladies. Dressed in this fashion, she was allowed onto the verandah to view the banquet held in the Shishinden, the palace's main hall. After it was over she received a tour of the emperor's drawing room in the Seikyōden, a rather old-fashioned building (once his living quarters) used only for ceremonies in the nineteenth century, and other buildings deep in the interior accessible only to women. "In a thousand years I could have no greater experience," she wrote, and she composed a poem expressing her pleasure:

Haru no yo no	Is this a dream or the reality
yume ka utsutsu ka	of a spring night?
shizu no me no	Today's finery
kumoi wo kakeru	fit for the imperial palace
kyō no yosoi wa	draped on a base-born woman.[30]

On the nineteenth she was back again, this time to view the dance performed on a stage set up in the garden south of the Shishinden. Like the banquet, it was attended by the emperor. Seated with the ladies behind bamboo blinds, Taseko could see his visage from afar. In some ways the dance was a public spectacle, for the denizens of Kyoto had permission to view the performance by standing outside the south gate. After it was over, Taseko toured the garden noted for its pair of cranes, the small palace where the emperor received messengers from the shogun, and numerous other buildings off-limits to tourists today. Back in the wardrobe she ate the food appropriate for an auspicious occasion, red beans mixed with rice and served with fish and vegetables. That night she wrote an excited letter to her daughters to let them know what she had done. "I don't know how many beautiful and well-dressed ladies I saw. There I was above the clouds observing the customs, and even though I'd like to tell you all about it, mere pen and ink will not suffice." [31] Hearing of her exploits, her friend Sera Toshisada wrote, "I'm delighted that you got to see inside the imperial palace. Thank you for writing down the descriptions I asked for. They'll be handed down to my descendants as family heirlooms." [32]

Two days after Taseko's first visit to the imperial palace, she had allowed Toshisada to talk her into a trip to the famous Inari shrine south of Kyoto in Fushimi. It was an imposing collection of edifices decked out in red paint, the oldest dating from the sixteenth century. Fox statues and stone lanterns were everywhere, and a pathway shaded by thousands of red torii stretched for four kilometers. Up the hill to the southeast was the grave for Kada no Azumamaro, 1669–1736, considered by Hirata Atsutane to be the first great scholar of nativist texts. Today children pray for success in the school entrance exams at the shrine erected for him in 1883. Taseko and Toshisada saw only a small marker erected over his grave. They took a leisurely walk home along the eastern hills, passing by Kiyomizudera with its magnificent verandah built out over the side of a gorge. From Taseko it deserved no more than a glance. The day after this trip saw Taseko's second visit to the imperial court, and then she collapsed. [33]

Worn out from excitement and all her exertions, Taseko rested at home for two days. Fatigue is never mentioned in the biographies that always depict her as tireless in her support of the emperor. Adding to her physical exhaustion was depression unmitigated by a visitor from Shimabara, a domain on the southern side of the island of Kyushu. "In the course of our conversation about this and that, I grew quite weary in spirit." [34]

Taseko quickly recovered from her exhaustion and resumed perambulating the city, visiting her new friends from all walks of life. She carefully recorded her many interactions with men, and she did not neglect women either. At the end of the first month, she spent one evening with her landlord's wife. They ate, drank, and chatted until bedtime. Early in the second month she was invited to the wedding for the son of her banker Ikemura Kuninori. The ceremony lasted all night with an elaboration of ritual that Taseko had never before experienced. "This was indeed a splendid thing to have seen in the capital," she noted in her diary. As a matter of course she composed a long poem to celebrate the nuptials, a poem that began with imagery appropriate to weddings drawn from the teachings of the Hirata school:

Mi musubi no	They are linked through
kami no chihai ni	the blessed protection
musubareshi	of the creator deities.[35]

Taseko went home just before dawn, rested for a few hours, and then went back to the Ikemura house to help arrange the presents they had received. In the afternoon she was called out by her male friends among the Hirata disciples, but she continued to spend moments with women in the neighborhood whenever she had the chance.

Taseko took great pleasure in recording her interactions with all and sundry. She scraped acquaintance with the Hirata disciples or men in the households of court nobles who had joined the Hirata school, and it did not always matter to which faction her newfound friends belonged. At some point, perhaps in the twelfth month, she apparently began to study the *koto*, the Japanese horizontal harp, with Takabatake Shikibu. On the twenty-ninth day of the first month in 1863, she visited Shikibu after having discussed "secrets" with some of her male friends earlier in the day. In her diary that is all Taseko wrote.

What were these secrets? The night before, Kagawa Hajime had been assassinated and dismembered. His crime was being a factotum for Lord Chigusa Arifumi, one of the four nobles charged with promoting Kazunomiya's marriage, usurping imperial authority and plotting to poison the emperor. Instead of pillorying Hajime's head on a riverbank as had become the custom, the assassins set it up in front of the gate to the Buddhist temple where the shogun's chief advisor, Hitotsubashi Yoshinobu, was then staying. The sign posted prominently with it accused Yoshinobu of only pretending to respect the emperor while in reality plotting to open the country to foreign trade. It appealed to him to mend his ways, demonstrate sincere reverence for the emperor, and set a date as early as possible for the expulsion of the barbarians in order to dissolve the doubts harbored by everyone in the realm regarding his conduct. "This head is extremely unsightly, but we offer it for your viewing pleasure as a token of the blood festival for expelling the barbarians."[36] Hajime's arms were thrown into the Chigusa and Iwakura compounds. Having suffered pollution through contact with a corpse, all members of these noble families had to refrain from visiting the court for seven days. Like other widely publicized assassinations, this event became a cause célèbre.[37] For Taseko not to have heard about it appears unlikely, yet all she admitted was talking about things best left unrecorded.

These secrets must have involved Shikibu. Despite her seemingly lofty title, she was not a member of the aristocracy. Instead she was born in 1785 to a candymaker in the coastal town Matsusaka (not far from the shrine to the sun goddess at Ise) and raised by her uncle in Osaka. Takabatake Keiso was her second husband, a blind acupuncturist who enjoyed traditional Japanese music. Among his patrons was the Chigusa family, and after his death Shikibu maintained the connection. She came late to the study of poetry, not registering with any teacher before 1831, then having Chigusa Ariisa, the father of Arifumi who had brought such trouble on the family, correct her poems. Ariisa gave her the sobriquet Shikibu, and Arifumi wrote a preface praising her many talents for her first published collection of poems. Through her poetry, she formed a close friendship with Ōtagaki Rengetsu. "The nun Rengetsu and the woman Shikibu both live on their own," wrote one observer of the Kyoto scene. "They tell wonderful stories."[38] The two women published a joint poetry collection, and it was probably poetry as well as music that attracted Taseko to Shikibu. Shikibu was much the older, being seventy-seven in 1862 when she wrote this poem:

Oiraku mo	Exchanging cups of sake
hana sakura sake	under the cherry trees
kumikawashi	in the ease brought by old age
kokoro niowasu	How the spring while the emperor reigns
miyo no haru kana	causes my heart to glow.[39]

Takabatake Shikibu had a considerable reputation as a poet, but how she spent her days remains a mystery. The scholar of Japanese literature who wrote her biography completely ignored the political implications of her connection with the Chigusa family, even going so far as to put her in Matsusaka at the time of Hajime's assassination.[40] Diaries written by men in Kyoto, however, make it clear that Hajime and Arifumi had visited her a month earlier under dubious circumstances, especially given that Arifumi was supposed to be in exile. "For this she deserves the death penalty," wrote

FIGURE 17.
Takabatake Shikibu,
age 95. From *Takabatake
Shikibu zenkashū*,
frontispiece.

one Aizu domain retainer.[41] Being old and a woman did not make her immune to terror. Muryōin, reputed to be the mistress of one of Ii Naosuke's retainers who had likewise promoted Kazunomiya's marriage, had been assassinated just two months earlier, and she was 55. "Even though what she did was unforgivable, she was not sentenced to die because she was a woman," the placard left with the body had announced. "Her confession of guilt reopened the investigation and led to her being severely punished."[42] One of Taseko's friends then in Kyoto said later that Taseko had lent Shikibu a lantern to help her escape.[43] In any case, she was there on the night when Shikibu decided to leave town.

Shikibu is best remembered for her extraordinarily long and active life. At the age of 96, she was to make a pilgrimage to Futami Bay on the Ise coast to worship the sunrise, and she would go on foot. She died later in that year of 1881, never having had a serious illness. Four years earlier she had published her precepts for good health:

Get up every morning before dawn. Worship the gods, buddhas, and ancestors and place tea before their altars. In a half cup of tea for yourself,
put a small dried plum and drink the water. The brine used for pick-
ling plums should be used as an eye wash. Throughout my life I have
never had any trouble with my eyes, nor have they ever clouded over.
For my food, I fix rice gruel in a small pot, put it in an ordinary bowl,
add a few vegetables and season it with fermented bean paste (*miso*). . . .
Every morning around 8 o'clock I burn moxa on the outside of my leg
just below the knee, and I have never neglected this for over forty-five
years.[44]

In traditional Chinese medicine, burning moxa (a flammable substance obtained from the leaves of the wormwood plant) on the skin is said to relieve
muscular pain and ease the nerves; it is sometimes used on recalcitrant children both to punish them and calm them down.

Shikibu's precepts for a long life had more to do with behavior than diet
and more to do with women than with men.

Because I'm a woman, I take the lead in nothing. . . . Even on a very
long trip I never urinate on the road. When I can't find a good place, I
go to an empty spot with lots of bushes and making noise to scare off
animals and insects, I do it there. . . . When traveling on the highway,
you should stay to the left. When sleeping at night, if you put your pillow to the north, you'll have a long life. If you place it to the west, you'll
get rich. If you put it to the east or south, you'll get sick. Don't line your
pillow up with the ridge pole of the house. Don't sleep over the crack
between two tatami mats. Whenever you go to the toilet, always clear
your throat before you go in. I've done this ever since it was suggested
to me at the age of 26, and for that reason I've never had any trouble
with my nether parts. Most women sleep on their sides, but it's better
to sleep with your face up, your arms and legs stretched out straight,
and breathe gently. . . . It's said that you should eat early, defecate
quickly and walk fast. People who practice this over the long haul will
gain a good reputation and receive many blessings from heaven.[45]

This then was the woman endangered by her friendship with a court noble
and rescued, perhaps, by Taseko.

In simply going to Kyoto, Taseko did what other women of her time did
not, but even that was not sufficient to make her noteworthy in the eyes of
her acquaintances and biographers. Instead they covered the bare bones of her
life recorded in letters and diaries with the flesh of intrigue created out of the

legends about deeds done by the political activists of the time. Everyone was watching everyone else: activists spied on each other and the police, while the police, aided by the bakufu's allies, infiltrated the activists. Surely Taseko must have been a spy, and who knows, perhaps she was. Unfortunately there is no direct evidence, only surmise. One day, for example, she decided to go to Uzumasa, a place she had visited before, and she went alone because "there were some inquiries I had to make in secret." On her way home she stopped by the woods to think things over. There she wrote a poem asking the gods to clear up the confusion that beset the world. That is all she said she was doing.[46] Given this paucity of data, it is all too tempting to fill the irreducible gaps in accounts of her activities with plot fragments drawn from the store of stories common to the time that make her much more significant than she actually was.

Taseko deemed three items to be of special importance in her interactions with the court. The first was that the emperor himself had once asked Lord Ōhara about her. Whether this happened before or after the dance performance she did not say, but simply to have her name pass his lips suggests what a rarity it was for a peasant woman to come to the capital in order to offer her services in national affairs. She also left leaflets at the palace, possibly threats against the regent who obstructed the communication between the emperor and his loyal subjects. Finally, she claimed to have "wandered through the royal flower beds in search of traitors."[47] This list, added to her diary after she had returned safely home, belies the image of the innocent poet crafted in the rest of the text. While it does not represent the totality of her activities in Kyoto, it indicates the two sides of how she saw herself in relation to the emperor.

IT WAS WELL known that Emperor Kōmei vehemently opposed opening Japan to the foreigners. Some historians assume that his xenophobia arose out of sheer ignorance at worst and political inexperience at best; others suggest that he wanted to free himself from the regent's control and used the treaty issue to stir up lower-ranking nobles against the Five Houses.[48] In fact, however, Kōmei and his predecessors had begun to position themselves in national politics much earlier than Perry's arrival in 1853. Acting in full consciousness of his imperial lineage in a line of descent from the sun goddess and his titular position as ruler of Japan, Kōmei's grandfather revived court ceremonies and Shinto rituals designed to enhance his political prestige. After his death in 1840 he was bestowed with the laudatory name Kōkaku (shining standard), in contrast to the place names with which most emperors had been contented since the ninth century. In a further break with tradition, he was called *tennō* (ruler of heaven), not *in* (retired person) with its strongly Buddhist connotations. (Only in 1925 did it become the rule to call all emperors *tennō.*) By acquiring a prestige unthinkable a hundred years earlier, historian Fujita Satoru argues, Kōkaku made it possible for his grandson Kōmei to act politically.[49]

Like his grandfather, Kōmei believed himself responsible to the gods and his ancestors for preserving the purity of Japan's sacred soil. Regardless of whether what he wanted was possible or not, once his wishes became known, they served to focus the fears of many people concerned for Japan's future. Had he not been so adamantly opposed to the treaties forced on Japan by the Western powers in the 1850s, Satoru argues further, there would have been no movement to revere the emperor and expel the barbarians. Instead, given the close ties that had existed for centuries, any attack on the bakufu would have brought the court down as well. Without the emperor to serve as a rallying point for malcontents, nativists, and nationalists, Japan might well have experienced protracted civil war and colonization by one of its enemies.[50] The pragmatic proponents of using the emperor to build a nation state spoke of "seizing the jewel" to describe their instrumentalist view of his role. The office could not have functioned as a symbol, however, if Kōmei had not already distanced himself from the existing political settlement, or if people such as Taseko and her friends had not preached their belief that he was the crucial link between gods and humans.

The decade leading to 1868 marked a watershed in Japanese history. Politically speaking, these years were thick with so many events that no one narrative can encompass them all and still remain coherent. Those who study this period have never been content with "just one plot, just a single 'arc' of narrative reconstruction."[51] Taseko was not the only person to visit Kyoto in 1862, and the chain of events that brought her there was not necessarily congruent with the one that impelled others. Her history is specific and particular to her; its meaning is incommensurate with that of other histories constructed out of likewise fragmentary information around other people who acted at the same time, nor do all of these histories taken together constitute a larger meaning; they cannot be combined into a master narrative of the Meiji Restoration.[52] On the other hand, her history cannot be completely disentangled from that of others; she did not act alone, but rather acted and reacted to the people around her.

Taseko and her friends watched the processions of daimyo and court nobles, scraped acquaintance with anyone they thought might know what was going on, picked over rumors, pooled their information, and debated what to do. They did not have the power to do much, but they were determined to demonstrate their loyalty to the emperor.

Beheading Statues

How do you expect me
to stop now?
my thoughts rise
constantly upward
when I'm crazy with the Japanese spirit.[1]
MATSUO TASEKO, 1862

"As you said, for someone like me to loiter aimlessly about Kyoto is regrettable, and my poetry really isn't all that important," Taseko wrote to her daughters in Nakatsugawa. "I truly do love poetry, though, and I'm not suffering any hardships. I realize that I'm being eccentric, so please just laugh at me. Sometimes I feel like I myself don't know my own feelings, and I act really crazy."[2] Defining herself as crazy locates Taseko in a particular milieu, that of the *shishi,* "the men of high purpose," who had defied the authorities in flocking to Kyoto because the times required acting in ways ordinarily unthinkable.[3] In the eyes of those who did not understand the urgency of uniting Japan against the foreign threat, sacrificing family and career to go to Kyoto made no sense. "The expulsionist argument broke out like bees swarming from a broken beehive," said Itō Hirobumi, later the father of the Meiji Constitution. "If one speaks logically of the things [that happened then], they are impossible to understand, . . . but emotionally, it had to be that way."[4] Taseko teased her daughters, warning them "please be sure to take every precaution against the craziness that's afflicting me." For those who criticized her, she sent the poem given above.

From the first assassinations of men deemed traitors to the throne in the seventh month of 1862 through an abortive coup d'état in the eighth month of 1863, proponents of expelling the barbarians in the name of the emperor dominated the streets of Kyoto. Diaries by activists such as Takechi Zuizan report a constant stream of comings and goings, urgent messages sent here and there, and long serious talks, the contents of which are not divulged. They depict a Kyoto buzzing like a hornet's nest in which samurai and would-be samurai bustled about, always in a hurry, talking to this person, looking for that, filling the city with constant movement from the early morning hours till late at night.[5] From the day Taseko got to the city she would have seen these men striding down the streets, pushing through crowds, swords ostentatiously at their side, ready to fight at the slightest slur. Whenever she went out, and she went out almost daily, she rubbed shoulders with if not the great, at least the violent.

The conflict was between men who promoted a unity of court and bakufu with some degree of input from leading daimyo and their advisors (*kōbu gattai*) versus proponents of "revere the emperor, expel the barbarians" (*sonnō jōi*). Though it was complicated by the disagreement that fissured each faction, at the same time the two sides had much in common. The *sonnō jōi* side argued that the court had existed since antiquity without entropy, the emperor was supposed to delegate responsibility to both courtiers and warriors, and all the people were the emperor's subjects as well as the subjects of the domain where they happened to live.[6] As a strong supporter of *sonnō jōi*, Taseko bitterly criticized the shogun for the way he treated the emperor, but she could conceive of no other way for the barbarians to be expelled than for the shogun to play his traditional role as the commander in chief of Japan's military forces. For her and her friends, the problem was how to make him understand what he had to do, how to rid him of evil advisors whose absorption in their own self-interest had blinded them to the dangers facing Japan, and how loyal men could gain access to decision-making circles. But she had hope. "Truly remarkable things have been happening," she wrote her daughters, "and it seems to me that at this juncture [the authorities] will have to ask people down below for their opinion."[7]

Taseko avidly sought new acquaintances among like-minded men who had come to Kyoto to serve the emperor. The samurai from Chōshū, her friend Sera Toshisada with whom she had gone to Arashiyama, for example, explicitly identified themselves as *sōmō*, grass-roots activists. Yoshida Shōin, the Chōshū teacher martyred in 1859, had used this term to mean anyone without significant bureaucratic responsibilities, that is, ordinary indepen-dent men at liberty to act because they were not bound by the restrictions of office. These men rejected the notion that decisions should flow only one way, from the top down; instead they demanded the opportunity to be heard. Historians have broadened the meaning to include rural entrepreneurs, vil-lage headmen, landlords, town officials, wholesalers and purveyors, shrine priests, and the masters of official inns such as Taseko's cousin Ichioka Shige-masa. These were men of action.[8] From the lofty perspective of the civilian and military aristocracy they might appear infinitesimal, but they were by no means the dregs of society. In their own eyes, their background as leaders in local matters afforded them the experience and knowledge to contribute to national affairs. Taseko never claimed this expertise for herself. Instead she listened to them talk and applauded their commitment to the emperor.

Taseko acted at an extraordinary time, a time of national crisis, when the public space expanded beyond the ability of the ruling authorities to control it and when normative standards of behavior were temporarily in abeyance. Young men defied the political hierarchy that defined their place. Taseko be-came androgynous, an *onna masurao*, (a "manly woman,") as one of her friends called her, "a rare type like nothing in recent history."[9] This was the highest praise he could offer, to allow that she did as well as a man, "that she suc-ceeded in attaining a 'manly' level of achievement."[10] In periods of social confusion, some women have briefly achieved unusually noticeable roles that blur the line between public and private.[11] At such times they take advantage of what Victor Turner has identified as marginality: "people who are simul-taneously members of two or more groups whose social definitions and cul-tural norms are distinct from and often opposed to one another, for example, women in a changed, nontraditional role."[12] This deviation from the norm helped to empower Taseko because while it maintained her distance from the center of authority, it also distanced her from the conventions of female selfhood.

Taseko's presence in Kyoto and her relations with men challenge both the standard histories of the 1860s and the stereotypes of women's place in rev-olution. By appearing in the city at this critical juncture, she usurped the male prerogative to move about and to act on one's own.[13] Unlike the wives and mistresses of male loyalists who participated in events only insofar as they could help their men folk, furthermore, Taseko appeared on the scene without emotional attachments to justify her presence. Like the men around her, she acted on the basis of her beliefs; she came to the city not as a surrogate for a man or out of commitment to a man, but because that was where she wanted to be. Not for her was the role usually assigned women in revolution, that of "giving moral support" to their men folk or undergoing trial, torture, and prison "more out of loyalty than conviction."[14] Once she reached Kyoto, however, she found herself relegated to the role of observer. Her involvement went far beyond that of most women without ever aspiring to the same level as men's. It defies our preconceptions regarding what women might do at the same time that it confirms the reason we hold them.

Taseko spent her days going from one place to another, meeting people, setting up meetings, responding to summons, and talking late into the night. The men she met when she first arrived in the city soon introduced her to others or told their friends about her, and they then came to see her. One morning early in the tenth month, Nagao Ikusaburō, the second son of a Kyoto cloth merchant, appeared on her doorstep. He was one of a number of townsmen who worked in their shops by day, then at night strapped on two swords and sought out fellow xenophobes. He was twenty-five years old, a beautiful youth with refined, delicate features. Despite his effeminate exterior, he was courageous, feared no one, and "his strength approximated the warriors of old."[15] At his first visit to Taseko, he spent the entire day talking earnestly and seriously about his concerns. He fervently believed that having married Kazunomiya, the shogun was duty-bound to expel the barbarians; not to do so offered an insult to the emperor. "I'll always be nearby," he said in an offer of protection when he made his departure.[16]

A typical day for Taseko went something like this: On the seventh day of the eleventh month, she spent the morning with Fukuba Bisei, the samurai from Tsuwano she met when she first arrived in Kyoto. She had earlier sent him some of her poems, and she wanted to know what he thought of them. On her way home she stopped at Iseya, the shop belonging to Ikemura Kuninori who acted as her banker. Kuninori's wife informed her that earlier two men had gone to her house to wait for her. She hurried off to find them, but they had grown impatient and left. Tired from her morning's exertions, she was thinking of taking a nap when two samurai showed up. They admitted that they had inquired after her earlier in the day and they had returned because "they wanted to meet me no matter what." Like Sera Toshisada, they were from Chōshū. One was Fukuhara Otonoshin, born in 1837, so he was twenty-five when he met Taseko. He had absconded from his domain a few months earlier, planning to assassinate the domain elder who had stood by while his teacher and hero Yoshida Shōin went to his death. (In 1863 he was to wind up in Edo where he would be discovered plotting to overthrow the bakufu. Rather than risk capture, he killed himself.[17]) Taseko was impressed with him. "His loyal spirit was unparalleled, and he could also write some poetry. We exchanged poetry cards and talked till at least midnight before he went home."[18]

Taseko met a number of Chōshū men through her allegiance to the Hirata school. Sometime that winter Nagao Ikusaburō wrote her a note saying, "these two men are disciples of the Hirata school. Please meet with them and talk with them. The one called Watanabe Shinzaburō from Tokuyama [a branch of the Chōshū domain] is quite wild and a good friend."[19] Shinzaburō was twenty-nine, still young enough to be audacious. In the tenth month Toshisada told her to be ready for an invitation to meet a Confucian scholar then called Otamura Bunsuke. Taseko later spent an afternoon with him. "He told me things straight from the heart." He had sake and refreshments brought in, and she contributed 248 *mon*. Also present were two "like-minded men" who served the same lord. "We shared our feelings until dark when I returned home."[20] She promised to visit him again, but on the day they were to meet, he sent a message saying he had to return to Chōshū the next day. That evening he came to see her. "No matter how wretched I felt, there was nothing to be done. I asked him why he had to leave, and he replied that his heart was too full to explain. I would have to ask Toshisada for the reason." Toshisada paid her a visit the next day and "told me all sorts of things."[21]

Owing to its daimyo's long-standing marital relations with the imperial court, Chōshū alone of the domains had been allowed to keep a compound in Kyoto throughout the Tokugawa period. What went on inside was off limits to bakufu police, making it an attractive sanctuary for radical retainers. In 1862 the permanent garrison was swelled by men who simply absconded from their domain to be where the action was. Many hoped to find employment in a new army proposed by loyalists from Chōshū and Tosa to protect the court from the barbarians. In the meantime they exacerbated the factional disputes that had already riven Chōshū. It may well be that Bunsuke was ordered back to Chōshū because he did not agree with the tactics proposed by other retainers. He was to find himself in a Chōshū prison in 1864–65, but he would survive to become a powerful figure in the Imperial Household Ministry before dying in 1912 at the age of 83.[22]

Most of the men Taseko met did not have the backing of powerful domains like Chōshū, but had instead come to Kyoto on their own. Late in the tenth month Nagao Ikusaburō reported that a Nishikawa Yoshisuke from Ōmi Hachiman had recently arrived in Kyoto. "He wanted to be sure that he got to meet me." Taseko and Yoshisuke immediately discovered that they had much in common. "Together we lamented the sorry state of this world and wrung out our sleeves [soaked with tears]."[23]

Nishikawa Yoshisuke was of course a Hirata disciple, having joined the school in 1847. Born in 1816, which made him just five years younger than Taseko, his was the sixth generation to head the Nishikawa fertilizer store. For business reasons he had maintained a communications network that extended up the eastern coast to Hokkaidō; the Hirata school brought him correspondents as far west as Chōshū and as far south as Satsuma. These connections got him into trouble in 1858 when a letter he had written to a friend reporting on the debate at the imperial court over the commercial treaty proposed by the United States fell into the wrong hands. After interrogation by bakufu officers, he was ordered into the custody of his local officials and the documents were confiscated. A few weeks later he wrote a pledge promising himself to give up sake for seven years in order to concentrate his energies on praying to the gods for their help in averting the crisis that had befallen Japan. By 1860 he had again fallen under suspicion for collecting information on the bakufu's foreign policy and sending it to his friends at the Chōshū compound in Kyoto. It turned out that he was exposed by a relative who disapproved of his unmerchant-like interest in national politics and hoped that the threat of reprisals would return him to his senses. Forbidden to leave the area, he had thus disobeyed a direct order in going to Kyoto.[24]

Yoshisuke had a wide range of contacts that he used to become remarkably well-informed on foreign initiatives and the domestic response. Living so close to Kyoto, the intrigues in the imperial court were an open book to him, especially since one of his correspondents was Nakayama Tadayasu, maternal grandfather of the future Emperor Meiji. A devoted scholar who filled his house with books, Yoshisuke read everything of importance on coastal defense. He even obtained a secret report regarding gun emplacements on islands that guarded the entrance to the Inland Sea. Through his family doctor, whose elder brother was the official physician for one of the shogun's relatives, he got his hands on the treaties the bakufu had concluded with the various foreign powers, reports on foreigners' visits to Japan, the letters passed between the bakufu and Townsend Harris, the first American Consul to Japan, and other diplomatic correspondence. He copied this information into notebooks, exchanged it for news from other sources, and developed his own proposals for protecting Japan from the foreign threat. He played host to Chōshū retainers such as Kido Takayoshi and Itō Hirobumi, who were later to attain national prominence. It was at their urging that he came to Kyoto where he met Taseko.

In the heady atmosphere of the capital, Yoshisuke and Taseko soon became fast friends. They visited each other whenever they had the chance, to discuss poetry, the role of the emperor in Japanese history, and current affairs. Yoshisuke soon came to look upon Taseko as a trusted confidant and advisor. "Once again I find myself having an urgent request to make of you," he wrote in a note dated the sixth and delivered by messenger. "Please come to my house tomorrow without fail. I have something that must be done right away in order to make a list of all the men of high purpose loyal to the emperor." [25] Yoshisuke neglected to mention the month in his note, but it may well have been the second in 1863. Taseko was busy on the seventh. On the eighth she reported that she was asked to do something in secret. Being a secret, she did not explain what it was.

Yoshisuke shared lodgings with two men from Okayama: Noro Kyūzaemon, a retainer to the domain elder with the generous stipend of 150 *koku*, and his assistant, Oka Mototarō. They had been assigned to Kyoto to collect information on behalf of their domain, and, being Hirata disciples, they longed for an opportunity to offer what service they could to the emperor. All three men entertained such a constant stream of visitors that it made their landlord uncomfortable. Taseko met Kyūzaemon and Mototarō as well, and she found in them the same kindred spirit. Mototarō let her copy his poems written in the loyalist vein. Some months later after they had both left Kyoto, he would send her this:

Wakare tsutsu	Even while we're apart
umi yama tōku	separated a great distance
hedatsu tomo	by seas and mountains
akaki kokoro wa	our red hearts
tsune ni tsujiwan	will always be in touch. [26]

On the twenty-seventh day of the tenth month, Taseko joined Yoshisuke and his fellow boarders on a visit to Nakajima Masutane, then aged thirty-two. He had been placed under house arrest for his part in helping to bring together the samurai from Mito and Satsuma who had assassinated the shogunal advisor Ii Naosuke. One of the conditions of his punishment was that he neither receive visitors nor go out, forcing Taseko and her friends to be discreet. "He was sincere and polite, and we talked about everything that had been happening in the world at large." [27] She visited Masutane again on the ninth day of the eleventh month because she had heard something that bothered her, but "other people were there so I couldn't say what was on my mind." [28] So much for his confinement.

Masutane later described the way Taseko had appeared to him at the time. "She was over fifty, tall and slender, and she had piercing eyes. She was not easily intimidated, and she could assume a great deal of dignity when she chose. If any of the young men did something improper, she never hesitated to correct him. Many lived in fear that she would find out what they had been up to, and they stood in awe of her as though she were their mother. She was no ordinary woman."[29] Taseko wrapped her hair around a comb secured with a long hairpin, tied her simple robe with a black belt, and carried a dagger for protection. She used no cosmetics, nor did she wear jewelry.[30] Like advanced women in Victorian England, her rigid "standards of public decorum in dress, manner and movement" served to mask her unconventional interest in politics.[31]

Taseko met many young men in Kyoto, some less than half her age, and many apt to die before their thirtieth birthday. Their aim was to be not just men (*otoko*) but manly men (*masurao*), that is, brave warriors. Youth and notions of masculinity came together to define a culture in which nonchalance was valued over decorum, impetuosity over planning, and reckless courage above all.[32] On the other hand, Taseko, Ōtagaki Rengetsu, and other women who made themselves the subjects of action in this period of social upheaval were all over fifty. For men, youth has often been seen as the appropriate age at which to launch quests, or to sow wild oats before accepting the burdens of maturity. Women, at least in traditional societies, marry young and raise a family; it is precisely the time of their heaviest responsibilities. According to historian Nagashima Atsuko, for a woman freedom and authority were not compatible.[33] Only after she had turned over the duties of running a household to her daughter-in-law did she have the leeway to do what she wanted.

Having been trapped in an ordinary marriage, Taseko's only chance for adventure came in old age. Life crises occur later for women than for men as Carolyn Heilbrun has pointed out. For them the moratorium before action can last decades until they are old enough to have done with the business of being women expected of them by society.[34] Even over the age of fifty, making that kind of break requires a great deal of courage. According to Ikusaburō's younger sister, "Taseko was considerably different from most women, indeed she was a woman metamorphosed into a man."[35] It might be said, in fact, that being perceived as old so desexed Taseko that it made her interactions with young men possible. Whether they saw her as a mother as Masatane later suggested, they certainly saw her as a comrade. For herself, she found their youth exhilarating:

Kotoshi koso   This year in particular
toshi no wakana wo   with the young greens of spring
miyako-ji ni   beside the road to the capital
oi no kazu sou   I have completely forgotten
koto mo wasurete   to count up how old I am.[36]

Soon more Hirata disciples showed up in Kyoto. On the sixteenth day of the eleventh month, five arrived fresh from their studies with Hirata Kanetane in Edo and full of determination to serve the emperor. "For those of us born in Japan, this was not something that could just be left to warriors," the twenty-two year old Miyawada Tanekage explained. "We knew that every day imperial loyalists from across the country were flocking to Kyoto. We agreed that we should go there too, get to know the other loyalists, and exhaust ourselves in revering the emperor and expelling the barbarians."[37] "They're all straightforward and serious," Taseko reported. "We were able to talk straight from the gut." On the day that they moved into rented quarters at the crossroads of Nijō and Koromonotana, they invited her to a housewarming party. She started visiting them every day, bringing them news of the city, "talking with them about the sorrows and afflictions of this world," and telling court nobles of their arrival.[38] Apparently because the Kyoto Governor had recently reiterated laws against the nobility mixing with samurai, the five men hesitated to approach the nobles themselves. Once Taseko started visiting the women officials at the imperial palace, they formed a rapt audience for her stories of what she saw. "Sometimes we get together and I'm privileged to hear wonderful things," she wrote to her husband back in Tomono. "No matter what the occasion for our meetings, I'm asked to write poetry full of the Japanese spirit."[39]

Taseko filled her letters with the news of whom she met and what they talked about. "I'm living quite comfortably and gradually making new friends," she continued in her report to her husband. "I've had a request from a Chōshū retainer for a long poem about silkworms and for a report giving the details of their purchase and care, so one way or another, I've been kept quite busy."[40] Her friends became quite agitated when fighting threatened to break out between the Fukuyama domain in western Japan and Chōshū. Only intercession by the Chōshū lord prevented civil war. "I was relieved," Taseko wrote. "All the lords are very excitable, and I think something [civil war?] will surely happen within two or three years."[41] Taseko's prediction proved all too accurate, but what else she knew about this relatively minor incident cannot be gleaned from her letter.

Taseko was soon able to report that the man she called teacher, Hirata Kanetane, had arrived in the city. He came on orders from Akita domain to find out what was going on, a task for which he was particularly well situated because he could use the many Hirata disciples as conduits of information. For the northern domains, the situation in Kyoto was worrisome enough to demand attention. Out of deference to the bakufu and to save costs, however, they preferred not to dispatch the same large contingents as the southwestern domains. (The exception was Aizu, but the Aizu lord had been appointed to a new position as Protector of the city.) A boon to historians are the reports and notes prepared by the Sendai domain's man on the scene.[42]

As soon as Taseko learned of Kanetane's arrival upon her return from Osaka, she paid him a visit, the first time they had ever met face-to-face. Thereafter she started seeing him on a regular basis. "Many disciples and loyalists from various domains then in Kyoto flocked to visit him," his attendant Tsunoda Tadayuki wrote. "Taseko came every day and she hosted parties at sake shops."[43] Male disciples, including the Kyoto townsman Nagao Ikusaburō and the fertilizer merchant Nishikawa Yoshisuke, had gone to Edo to study nativist texts with Kanetane, a course of action deemed perfectly appropriate for a man. Taseko had never had that opportunity. Only the extraordinary situation in Kyoto gave her the chance to interact with him just as the men did, "going to visit him almost daily without it being any big deal."[44]

Through her teacher Taseko met many men who "thought as she did," and among them was Kanetane's youngest follower, Noshiro Hirosuke, then just nineteen. A recent convert, he was born the son of a doctor, then adopted by a village headman in Kazusa province just east of Edo. His life as an activist had begun only in the tenth month of 1862 when he apprenticed himself to a doctor of Japanese medicine and a Hirata disciple. In his diary he described how he followed the doctor on his rounds, cleaned the house, and washed the vegetables. Two weeks later he started seriously practicing sword-fighting, then he left for Edo at the beginning of the eleventh month where he met Kanetane. "Listening to his words, I found it hard to pull myself away." Three days later he was back again, and he started showing up with ever-increasing frequency. For the next week he alternated between studying with Kanetane and practicing sword-fighting. When Kanetane was to depart for Kyoto at the end of the eleventh month, Hirosuke was there before sunrise at Shinagawa to see him off. He spent the morning going from one sake shop to another, joining in farewell toasts before Kanetane finally tore himself away in the middle of the afternoon. Hirosuke hurriedly followed him a few days later.[45] Taseko recorded Hirosuke by name three times in her diary, the last being when a group of disciples accompanied Kanetane to Arashiyama. He noted her name only once, in an entry describing a meeting on the following day: she listened while the disciples talked.[46]

Taseko's diary gives an almost daily account of what she and the other Hirata disciples did in the months they were together in Kyoto. It is an excellent source of information about the men she met; their writings are much less forthcoming about her. Even when her diary puts her at the scene of an excursion, she is often omitted from other chronicles that describe the same event. She told Kanetane everything she saw at the imperial palace, but he never mentioned her in his reports. Perhaps he felt it inappropriate to mention her name to his superiors, perhaps he wanted to preserve her modesty, perhaps what she had to say was unimportant in the larger scheme of bakufu and court politics. In any case, her absence from these records demonstrates that relegating her to silence began with her presence in Kyoto.

Hirosuke's fascination with sword-fighting was mirrored by samurai and wealthy peasants. In the confrontation with western military science, learning to use the sword was deemed not only a technique of war but a means to enhance the masculine fighting spirit. For the samurai it dramatized their commitment to the defense of Japan against the outside. For the wealthy peasants it was that and more. Training in this weapon gave them the confidence to deal with unrest ranging from peasant uprisings to banditry and to organize militias for self-defense. Teachers crisscrossed countryside and city, attracting adherents passionate in their devotion to the sword. Many of the Hirata disciples had become devotees of the art. Miyawada Tanekage had become so skilled that he had managed to shake the dust of the village from his feet and make a living as an instructor. To smooth the way for himself and the other four Edo disciples past travel barriers and nosy post station officials, he had acquired documents from a sword-fighting master certifying him as an apprentice and stating that he needed to travel in order to study the techniques of other schools.[47] Taseko always wore a dagger thrust into her belt. She never used it or gave any indication that she practiced with it, but it provided both a modicum of protection and a demonstration of loyalism.

By the beginning of 1863, Taseko could sense that she was in the thick of things. She had seen everything there was to see at the palace, she had helped present her teacher's writings to the emperor, she had met the head of her school, her circle of acquaintances widened almost daily, and she had herself brought in converts. In a letter to her daughters in Nakatsugawa, she wrote: "I have become good friends with at least fifty men who can be called loyalists. When they call at my house we talk everything over without holding anything back, and they tell me all about their troubles." She had a constant stream of visitors, and "really I am so busy every day." When no guests kept her in, she went out. "I've been going almost daily to see our teacher Hirata. He treats me very kindly, and whenever he goes on an excursion, he always asks me to accompany him. Sometimes he asks me to look after the house in his absence while he is away on business, and he has been extremely friendly." To her cousin Inao she wrote, "I have been privileged to talk with our teacher Hirata about all sorts of things because he has taken me into his confidence."[48]

Taseko's growing number of friends kept her delightfully busy. On the fifteenth day of the first month, a poet named Ōhara Chigura from Tsuyama came to invite her to a poetry meeting that afternoon. "He said he absolutely had to have me there, and he refused to take 'no' for an answer. 'Well, in that case, I'll go,' I said, but just at that moment someone else appeared." This was a messenger sent by Kanetane inviting Taseko to accompany him on a survey of buildings that had burned in a fire the night before. "It's a beautiful day, and you really must come," he said.

Futa kata ni	Today, right now
kokoro hikarete	I am being pulled
kyōno kono	in two directions
ika ni shite mashi ya	what on earth shall I do
futatsu naki mi wo	since there aren't two of me?[49]

Confronted by this happy predicament, Taseko decided she would go first to the poetry meeting, then catch up with Kanetane. When she arrived at Seikanji up in the eastern mountains where the meeting was to be held, however, more people were there than she had expected, and Chigura was still waiting for others. Taseko had just learned the topic for the day when another messenger arrived from Kanetane. The poor lad had been looking everywhere for her, he said. Rather than keep him waiting, she allowed herself to be taken away. She spent the rest of the afternoon with Kanetane, ending up at a tea house in Gion. When she finally got to the poetry meeting, it was already more than half over. She was scolded for not having come sooner before being given some sake and encouraged to recite her poem. The one she received in return was titled, "Taseko's manly heart is superior to that of any brave man:"

Tawayame no	Judging from the sign
omo kachikami no	from the god of victory
shirube yori	found in the face of this weak woman
kami yo mayowazu	despite many vicissitudes
waguru hachimata	the age of the gods will most surely come.[50]

Oka Mototarō's poem had praised Taseko's red heart; this one invited her into the loyalist movement. Siân Reynolds has argued that "women are generally welcomed, at least in the early stages of revolution, as proof that 'the people' . . . are involved, thus profoundly legitimizing revolutionary action."[51]

The end of the first month of 1863 found Taseko in constant attendance on Kanetane. On the twenty-second he invited her to join him on an excursion to the upper Kamo shrine, older than Kyoto itself and closely associated with the imperial family ever since Emperor Saga sent his daughter to serve there early in the ninth century. When Emperor Kōmei ordered priests at designated shrines to offer prayers for the expulsion of the barbarians, this shrine was always included. After the visit, the group recovered from its exertions at a tea house that served sake west of the palace in Muromachi. The next day Taseko allowed herself to be enticed to a party in the Gion district at which Kanetane was present. Six geisha made sure that all the guests, including Taseko, had a wonderful time. "Everyone got so boisterous that I found it quite exhilarating:"

Ito take no	Hearing just
sono hito fushi wo	one tune played on
kiki ni sae	samisen and flute
ukiyo no naka no	how easy it is to forget
warurarenu kana	the sorrows of this floating world.[52]

The party lasted till dusk, then on the way home the guests stopped at two tea houses for their evening meal and had more sake. According to Tsunoda Tadayuki, Taseko could drink about two *go* of sake, or about a third of a liter.[53] In a young woman this ability would have marked her as wanton; in an old peasant woman it was barely noticed.

At the end of the month Kanetane decided to move from his quarters near the imperial palace on Nijō to Omuro, just outside the city to the west. Taseko spent two days helping him get ready, then an entire day seeing him off. It was too far to return home that night, so she stayed with the five men from Edo in their rented rooms nearby. Spending the night with men not her husband apparently aroused no comment.

Taseko usually found herself in the company of men. On the twenty-ninth day of the first month she braved a heavy rain to visit the painter and activist Fujimoto Tesseki. He had abandoned a secure if boring position as clerk in the agricultural affairs department of Okayama domain to study military science in Kyoto in 1840. Thereafter he traveled around the country surveying historical sites before returning to the capital to teach history and the martial arts. Taseko liked him a lot and collected a number of his paintings. On this day, she found him with "four brave men who think as I do," but Tesseki was feeling so depressed that he refused to get out of bed. She sat by his pillow and they discussed "secrets."[54]

Taseko's biographers have made much of these secrets. Do they offer proof that Taseko participated in the plots hatched by activists to further the imperial cause? More likely they referred simply to the news of the day deemed too controversial to put in a diary that might be read by unfriendly eyes. The twenty-ninth was the day after the assassination of Kagawa Hajime. Tesseki and Taseko might have been discussing that, or they might have been talking about a series of letters sent by the advocates of expelling the barbarians to the regent and other high-ranking court officials accusing them of being enemies of the nation and threatening their servants with the punishment of heaven for the crimes committed by their masters. Or perhaps they had heard about the meeting of radicals from a number of domains arranged by the Chōshū activist Kusaka Genzui two days earlier. The topic had been how to resist plans by the moderate supporters of a closer relationship between bakufu and court to force the radicals to leave the city.

The Hirata disciples found themselves reminded repeatedly of their position on the sidelines. In the second month Taseko watched three daimyo parade through the streets on their way to an interview with the emperor, then discussed the implications with Miyawada Tanekage. On the night of the tenth, she received the shocking news that four loyalists from Chōshū and Hizen had created a commotion in trying to force their way in to see the regent who gave the emperor so much trouble. The regent refused to see the four; they refused to leave. Finally after the heir to the Chōshū domain had spent several hours calming them down, they agreed to depart. The next day eleven nobles paid a visit to Hitotsubashi Yoshinobu, the shogun's chief advisor. According to rumor, Yoshinobu had resisted setting a definite date for expelling the barbarians, and he hoped to secure an imperial decree to drive the radicals from the city. On the eighteenth she watched as all the daimyo then in Kyoto went to the imperial palace. In an oral statement the emperor insisted that once the shogun had arrived in Kyoto, a date must be set for expelling the barbarians.[55] The next day the daimyo in Kyoto received word that British warships had appeared in Edo Bay, demanding the heads of Shimazu Hisamitsu and other members of his party for the murder of an English merchant the previous year. If the heads were not forthcoming, they would accept an indemnity of 300,000 *ryō* plus an additional 30,000 dollars for the support of the merchant's wife and children.[56] The Hirata disciples were not privy to daimyo councils. They had good sources of information, but no way to make their own views known.

Taseko continued her usual round of visits in the latter half of the second month. She twice saw the mistress of the wardrobe who had earlier gotten her into the palace. She declined the opportunity to join a gathering of loyalists on the thirteenth, though she heard that it had something to do with wooden heads, a cryptic statement whose meaning becomes apparent only later. She ran into Noro Kyūzaemon and Nishikawa Yoshisuke, and she spent several nights at Hirata Kanetane's. On the twenty-second, "I had a good time pick-ing leafy vegetables." The next day she went to Arashiyama with Kanetane, the young Noshiro Hirosuke and other disciples. "We met a number of men from Shimabara and treated ourselves to sake. With the flowers at the height of their glory, it was really quite a party." Scenes so beautiful deserved to be seen again, and Taseko went back the next day with three of the Edo dis-ciples, then spent the night in their rooms. On the twenty-sixth she accepted an invitation to see a Noh performance accompanied by Ikemura Kuninori, Watanabe Shinzaburō, and others. Late that night after she had returned home, Nagao Ikusaburō came to see her. "We had a secret conversation that caused me great pain." [57]

Taseko discretely omitted all mention of what her friends were really up to from her diary. It was only many years later that Tsunoda Tadayuki wrote a secret account of what had happened—an account that places himself at the center.

It all began one day in the second month when Tadayuki, then twenty-nine, went to Tōji-in near Kanetane's lodging in Omuro. Tōji-in was a mor-tuary temple for Ashikaga Takauji, the founder of the Muromachi bakufu and, in the eyes of the Hirata disciples, the greatest traitor in Japanese history. By reading "The Precious Sleeve Cord," Taseko had learned that although an able commander who made it possible for the forces loyal to Emperor Go-daigo to defeat the Kamakura bakufu army in 1333, Takauji later turned on Godaigo and drove him from Kyoto. He had his reasons; Godaigo felt that to the court aristocrats should go the spoils of victory, not Takauji's soldiers. No matter, he was vilified throughout the Tokugawa period for having be-trayed his superiors, first his overlords in the Kamakura bakufu and then, "most monstrous of all," the legitimate emperor.[58] Godaigo and his heirs were forced to remain in the wilds of Yoshino because Yoshiakira seconded his father Takauji in his turncoat endeavors. And then there was Takauji's grandson Yoshimitsu, who through chicanery brought the split between the northern court in Kyoto and the southern court in Yoshino to an end. In ne-gotiating trade relations with Ming dynasty China, he declared Japan a trib-ute state and accepted the title of "King of Japan." Tōji-in possessed statues of these three leaders along with those for ten other Ashikaga shoguns, and Tadayuki wanted to see them. The priest said that the fee for raising the cur-tain was 200 *mon*, but it was already so late in the day that Tadayuki would have to come back another time. Tadayuki stomped out in a rage shouting, "Why should I have to pay to see the statues of traitors?"[59]

Born in 1834, Tadayuki came from a line of hereditary shrine priests who claimed descent from the eighth Emperor Kōgen. He was nineteen when Commodore Perry arrived in Japan, and the event coincided with his first reading of *Taiheiki*, a text that branded the Ashikaga shoguns enemies of the court. Struck by the timeless imperative to revere the emperor and expel the barbarians, he captured this epiphany in a poem:

Mi-yoshino no	The retainers
miya ni tsukushite	rendering service to the emperor
omi tachi wa	at sacred Yoshino
yo no mamebito no	have become a model
kagami narikeri	for faithful people today.[60]

Ten years later, he found himself in close proximity to all that remained of the villains.

Rebuffed in his attempt to view the statues, Tadayuki rounded up the townsman Nagao Ikusaburō and other Hirata disciples. Late in the evening of the twenty-second day of the second month, nine of them attacked the temple. While two stood watch outside, Tadayuki and the others tied up the monks on guard, then invaded the hall where the statues were enshrined. One man suggested that the statues' bodies be destroyed, but the others objected because they were carved in full court dress. Out of respect for the emperor they should remain unscathed, and for that reason the tall hats signifying court rank and office were removed. Having been fashioned from a separate block of wood, the heads were simply yanked out of the bodies. Also at Tōji-in was a statue of Tokugawa Ieyasu. Ikusaburō proposed that the next time, it be decapitated as well. Clasping the heads for Takauji, Yoshiakira, and Yoshimitsu, the nine men departed as noisily as they had come. Once outside the temple, Ikusaburō led them in a chorus of war cries, then they ran back through the city, pausing briefly to bow before a gate to the imperial palace and narrowly avoiding a patrol of Aizu troops.[61]

Their destination was the house rented by Nishikawa Yoshisuke and Noro Kyūzaemon, where Oka Mototarō had promised to build a stand for the heads. Some weeks later, during the interrogation following the incident, Kyūzaemon said he and Yoshisuke knew nothing about what was going on, and in fact they had spent the day in Arashiyama viewing the flowers. They were having a cup of tea when these men, who were mere acquaintances, showed up at their door. Once the deed was done, they had no choice but to bring out the sake to celebrate.[62] While the perpetrators were congratulating each other, Ōba Kyōhei, an Aizu retainer and Hirata disciple, labeled each head and wrote a placard explaining why it was necessary to decapitate statues.

"Now is the time to clarify name and function," the placard began. "To that end, all the disloyal traitors from the Kamakura period down to the present ought to be investigated one by one and punished as they deserve. These three traitors having done the worst evil, their vile statues have been visited with the vengeance of heaven." In mock formal style it ended: "These heads are to remain exposed for three days. Anyone who removes them will most certainly be punished."[63]

Their ranks now swollen with the men they had met at Noro Kyūzaemon's, the perpetrators took the heads, the stand, and the placard to the riverbank at Sanjō bridge. There they left them, at the spot where criminals were traditionally pilloried for the edification of passers-by and where the heads of many men had been exposed as a warning to the emperor's disloyal servants. They could not have found a better place to publicize their vision of the past and their frustration with the present.

To make sure that no one mistook the reason for the pillory of the statues, the would-be sword master Miyawada Tanekage wrote another and longer manifesto that he placed next to the official notice board at the end of the bridge. In it he impeached the entire history of military rule, beginning with the Kamakura bakufu in the late twelfth century "when that traitor Yoritomo distressed the court." The succeeding shoguns continued to betray their responsibilities by allowing disorder to flourish.

It is regrettable that the court was unable to use its punitive power to punish these crimes. Is it not lamentable? Right now we find it impossible to contain our rage at seeing what has been bequeathed to us. Unworthy though we be, had we lived in the ancient world of five hundred years ago, we would have continued to clench our fists and gnash our teeth in rage until we had chopped off the living heads. Now that the tide of fortune is turning, long-standing evils will be swept away, and correct government will be restored (*fukko isshin*), [it has become imperative to] punish these vile traitors for their crimes.

Naturally enough, the object was not simply to rectify the wrongs of the past but to serve as a warning for the present. Too many people

clearly surpass these traitors. . . . If they do not immediately repent and offer loyal service to expunge the evil customs existing since the Kamakura period and offer their assistance to the court, . . . then all the loyalists on earth will rise up together and punish them for their crimes."[64]

The timing was perfect. On the very day that the sight of pilloried statues greeted the Kyoto townspeople, the daimyo for Kaga, the largest domain in all of Japan, entered the city. He would not have needed to cross the river to get to his lodgings at Kenninji on the eastern bank, but surely some of the ten thousand troops he was said to have brought with him would have heard about it and perhaps even visited the site. Besides, there were eighteen other daimyo already in the city, all with large retinues befitting the most powerful men in Japan.[65] The shogun was on his way, and the Hirata disciples planned their deed to serve as an admonition to treat the emperor with respect and to get rid of the barbarians.

Only the youngest and most radical Hirata disciples participated in decapitating the statues. Their school was no more monolithic than any other faction then in Kyoto, and many older men did their best to distance themselves from the deed, fearful that it would be read as a desire to overthrow the shogun. For the perpetrators, however, it demonstrated a commitment to rectify Japanese history and to launch a cultural revolution that in purifying the past of traitors would make possible the remaking of the present.

What did Taseko have to do with all this? According to one disciple, she had complained that although the shogun made a pretense of expelling the foreigners, in fact he did nothing. Decapitating Ashikaga Takauji's statue might serve as a warning that he had better act now. Tadayuki rejected this scenario. "There is no doubt that Tase spied on traitors, but she had not the slightest connection with this incident." Taseko later told her daughter-in-law that on the night when the statues were decapitated, she was home alone. About midnight, several Hirata disciples appeared on her doorstep. Upon lighting the lantern to welcome them, she saw that the hems to their clothes were muddy. "What mischief have you been up to?" she asked. They replied only that it had been raining.[66] Her diary entry nine days earlier suggests that the incident was longer in the planning than Tadayuki's account would indicate, and she refused to have any part of it.

Regardless of how Taseko saw her role in this incident, it is clear that Tadayuki tried to silence her by defining as narrowly as possible her options as a woman. One disciple perhaps subverted her vision of herself by giving her an overly active part. The distance between these two positions is unbridgeable. It points once again to the difficulty of constructing a coherent narrative, especially when a woman is involved. Because "meaning is attributed in interaction," Kathleen Barry argues, it acquires gendered attributes that "subvert, silence or interpret the meaning women attach to their action to be something else," thus creating an unsolvable problem of verification.[67] No matter what Taseko did, she did it as a gendered subject, as a person deemed capable only of certain roles defined by societal expectations, and her deeds have always been interpreted in this light.

Neither Taseko nor her friends expected to suffer any repercussions for this public criticism of the shogun. The rash of assassinations in Kyoto had met with little response from people in positions of power. Since the preceding winter at least thirty men had been killed, a traveling merchant from Ōmi commented. No one knew who was doing these deeds, the authorities never arrested anyone, and they did not even remove the heads and bodies, instead leaving them to rot where they were. It did not make any sense.[68] Matsudaira Katamori, lord of Aizu and only twenty-eight years old, had recently been appointed the new Protector of the city with the responsibility for maintaining order. The disciples believed, however, that Katamori had promised when they talked several days earlier not to interfere with men who sincerely wanted to demonstrate their loyalty to the emperor.[69] This incident changed his mind.

While Katamori had found it easy to overlook the assassinations of low-ranking retainers of the court nobility, criticizing the shogun in this fashion was another matter. Decapitation was a fate reserved for criminals; it was humiliating and dishonoring. More than slander, it threatened to turn the whole social order upside down.[70] "These men swaggered about claiming to respect the emperor. They pretended to be talking about the Ashikaga shoguns, but in reality they attacked the bakufu," Katamori announced. In his view, the pillory of the statues represented less the vengeance of heaven on traitors than an insult to the court itself. Anyone granted court rank and title partook of a "sacred authority which only the emperor and the court could bestow."[71] Katamori again: "To humiliate a high-ranking noble in this way means nothing other than despising the court and disrespecting the bakufu. Such violence is like robbing a grave and flogging the corpse. If [the perpetrators] really wanted to act out of devotion to the emperor, they should have said so, and even though they are base commoners, we would have permitted them to make their proposals. But what sort of people are these to commit such an atrocity without waiting for orders? Having made light of the court's rules, they have forfeited the right to call themselves its subjects. For this they must be punished."[72]

Before dawn on the morning of the twenty-seventh, Taseko received a warning brought by bakufu police in the pay of Ikemura Kuninori that everyone staying in the house rented by the five disciples from Edo had been arrested. "I was dumbfounded." A later report said that some of the men had been wounded. "I realized that the game was up. I gave heed to making sure I'd not act like a woman should I be faced with arrest," she wrote in her diary.[73] Despite her friends' urging to flee, she got out her toiletries and started fixing her hair.

"What are you doing? The situation is so dangerous that you must leave at once."

"No, I can't run far with the legs and feet of a woman. Should the police come, I don't want to look unkempt when I'm arrested. If anything goes wrong, it's only a matter of ending a life, so please don't worry about me. You go ahead and escape if you think you can get away with it." [74]

This conversation is one recalled by Inoue Yorikuni in 1911, who said that he had heard it from one of the men trying to convince Taseko to flee. It probably did not happen just the way he reconstructed it, yet it is clear that Taseko and the men around her felt that she was in danger. Even the Chōshū elder Ura Yukie saw fit to mention her predicament in his diary, the highest ranking official ever to do so: "Perhaps because she had a hand in this incident, we heard that the bakufu police were going to Fuyachō as well, so she hid herself in our compound." [75]

One of her acquaintances among the Hirata disciples from Chōshū, Watanabe Shinzaburō, took it upon himself to get her to safety. As Taseko related in her diary, she bundled up all her papers, then "I snuck stealthily out and made my way to the Chōshū compound in Kawaramachi. In the compound were Kusaka Genzui, and Shinagawa Yajiro [among others]. They all looked after my every need and put my mind at ease." Kusaka Genzui, a young firebrand with countless connections among the various factions that thronged the streets of Kyoto, had read Atsutane's works even though he was not a Hirata disciple and shared their frustration at the shogun's vacillating approach to the foreigners. In 1864 he was to join an attack on the Aizu forces that had earlier allied themselves with Satsuma in driving the Chōshū contingent out of the city. Wounded in the battle and fearing capture, he would take his life at the age of twenty-four. Taseko wrote the following poem while watching the cherry blossoms fall in the garden of the Chōshū compound. At the time she was thinking about her friends arrested so unexpectedly in the predawn raid, but all too soon it would apply to him:

Kinōkyō	The cherry blossoms fall
tsuraki arashi ni	in the cruel storms
chiru sakura	of yesterday and today
nagarete no na wa	What will happen
ika ni naruran	to those that have been swept away.[76]

CHAPTER TEN

Going Home

How I regret
returning home
the sight of my traveling clothes
keeps pulling me back
to the Imperial Court.
MATSUO TASEKO, 1863[1]

Before dawn on the twenty-seventh day of the second month, 1863, Kyoto city police reinforced by Aizu troops marched on the rooms rented at Nijō and Koromonotana by five Hirata disciples. They surrounded the house, put ladders against the walls, beat down the door, and burst in with their spears. The sword master Miyawada Tanekage was severely wounded. Sengoku Satao, then twenty-one, a samurai from a branch of the Tottori domain and not one of the men who had pilloried the statues of the Ashikaga shoguns, fought back with his dagger. He wounded several soldiers, then leaped up the stairs to the roof where he killed himself. The policemen cut off his head, thrust it on a pike and carried it off in a show of triumph. Several others were captured alive.[2]

Having wiped out one nest of Hirata disciples, the police-men and soldiers moved to the rented house shared by Nishikawa Yoshisuke and Noro Kyūzaemon. There they wreaked havoc, breaking down the door to the main entrance, then smashing screens, furniture, utensils, everything. The servants thought they had been attacked by bandits. Unable to find the men they wanted, the police tied up four hapless souls who happened to be there, beating them and reviling them before they realized that they had captured not nameless malcontents but Okayama domain retainers. "The destruction was beyond description," reported the Sendai observer in Kyoto. "No officials would have shown so little restraint in causing such damage so close to the palace. They must have been ruffians who borrowed the Tokugawa crest."[3]

Taseko knew both places well. Ever since the disciples from Edo had arrived the previous winter, she had exchanged visits with them, joined their discussions, and occasionally spent the night with them, most recently just three days earlier following a trip to Arashiyama. Her friendship with Yoshisuke and Kyūzaemon had ripened quickly in the months they were together. She learned the details of the attacks when six other disciples showed up at the Chōshū compound, also in search of sanctuary.

The Hirata disciples had dribbled into Kyoto from all over Japan. They did not have the kind of domanial affiliation that would have provided them with safe houses off-limits to the bakufu.[4] They welcomed anyone who expressed allegiance to the teachings of Hirata Atsutane, and among them was an Aizu man, Ōba Kyōhei, an amusing fellow who had penned the placard for the statues' heads. Ōba was also a spy; he held a junior position in the Kyoto Protector's public affairs office with the assignment of infiltrating groups of unattached warriors (*rōnin*). Once he had fingered his friends, and implicated himself, he then tried to warn them of what was coming.[5] Several men, including the ringleader Tsunoda Tadayuki, prudently left the capital. Nagao Ikusaburō apparently passed the word to Taseko, while himself refusing to flee lest he bring trouble to his family.

For reasons of his own and perhaps because he suspected that there might be reprisals, Yoshisuke had left for Ōmi Hachiman soon after the incident. Kyūzaemon learned that the Hirata disciples had been summoned to see the Kyoto Protector, the lord of Aizu, but "as far as I was concerned, I was not really in on the plot. Besides, I was an Okayama retainer with nothing to do with Aizu. The only way I'd respond to a summons would be if it came through the Okayama liaison office."[6] Instead he walked all night on the twenty-sixth, the same night that Ikusaburō had visited Taseko, to catch up with Yoshisuke. An Aizu patrol quickly picked up the trail. On the second day of the third month the patrol summoned Hikone domain troops to help attack the Nishikawa house in Hachiman. The troops smashed up the furnishings and did as much egregious damage as they could, sticking their spears into every cranny that might possibly hold a human body. They intimidated the family, grabbed papers and correspondence, and filled two carts with materials to haul away. They did the same at Yoshisuke's brother-in-law's house and threatened a relative with torture. Yoshisuke and Kyūzaemon were arrested in a village near Lake Biwa and bundled ignominiously back to Kyoto. "Yoshisuke and Kyūzaemon have been captured," Taseko wrote in her diary. "Just hearing that made me feel my heart would break."[7]

In the meantime, Chōshū samurai had taken it upon themselves to act on behalf of the Hirata disciples. As soon as he learned that the Kyoto Protector was threatening to execute the men who had decapitated the statues, Yamagata Aritomo, later the father of Japan's modern army, wrote a memorial excoriating him for punishing loyalists who had acted with the best of intentions. He was joined by two other men, one from Chōshū and the other from Tosa. They could not present their memorial to the Protector directly. After all, as low-ranking retainers of different domains they were in no position to tell him what to do. In terms of bakufu protocol they had no business interfering where Chōshū and Tosa interests were not directly at stake. Instead they presented the memorial to Gakushūin, a school for court nobles. It had been granted formal permission to receive statements of opinion and memorials from grass-roots activists and commoners only ten days earlier. This made possible a public alliance between the men in the streets and the radicals among the nobility who supported immediate expulsion of the barbarians. It also meant that debate within the court could no longer be controlled by the regent and chief ministers; instead low-ranking nobles acquired new ammunition to push their own agenda.[8]

Taseko's diary shows that she knew about this memorial. She got the date wrong, but she may have confused when it was written with when it was presented. She probably knew what was in it because "one by one patriotic men come to see me, and they tell me all sorts of interesting things about what is going on in the world."[9] Before she sought sanctuary with the men from Chōshū, she had met only those who were Hirata disciples. (Nine men from that domain had joined the Hirata school before 1868. Sera Toshisada was one of the few samurai; most were rich peasants, and none played a significant role in national politics.[10]) Now she was in a position to meet the men who were to have a lasting impact on Japan's future. While she might not have thought that decapitating statues would do much to further the debate over how to rid Japan of the foreigners, she understood all too well the motives for the deed. She and the other fugitives were well positioned to make sure that Aritomo did too. He perhaps wrote his memorial out of sympathy with the disciples. More likely he saw an opening to embarrass bakufu supporters and demonstrate Chōshū's commitment to the emperor.

"These men came to Kyoto to do their utmost in loyal service to the nation," the memorial began. "Unable to snatch a moment's rest or wait for the barbarians to be expelled, they acted out of an excess of valiant rage and hatred for the Ashikaga traitors." The bakufu had recently issued a general amnesty for the assassins of Ii Naosuke, showing that it recognized the sincerity of their motives, even though Naosuke held appointment to court office. If they could be pardoned, why not the men who simply decapitated statues?

> The masterless samurai involved in this incident did what they did trying to rectify the great treason committed by the Ashikaga, and we think that is just like assassinating Naosuke. In our humble opinion, when it comes to rectifying name and position, no matter what rank a person holds, he should be denounced if he does evil deeds and a person, even a commoner, who exhausts himself in loyal service should be rewarded. Otherwise, people holding court rank can do evil deeds whenever they please." [11]

Never one to let pass the opportunity to lecture his betters, Aritomo proposed that the court itself posthumously punish Ashikaga Yoshimitsu. He had usurped imperial authority by calling himself king in paying tribute to China, and this claim was still evident on the memorial tablet enshrined in his mortuary temple of Kaenji.

> This is completely illegal and the deed of a traitor that ought not to be permitted in the realm even for a day. You should remove it at once and erase the inscription. By thus admonishing traitorous retainers and unfilial children, you will encourage loyal subjects and filial children and promote the highest teachings of the sages. The men of high purpose would then be unable to stifle the fervor of their thanks. Indeed, the emperor's authority over this sacred land would shine beyond the seas.

Rectifying the past had consequences for the present. "Already the barbarian ships are raiding Yokohama and who knows when they will invade the Inland Sea." Given this danger, it did not make sense to imprison brave men who simply wanted to serve the nation. [12]

Of all the memorials addressed to the court nobles on this subject, Taseko was most likely to have seen the one written by Aritomo. The young Noshiro Hirosuke had proposed that Hirata Kanetane appeal for the pardon of his disciples, but all too conscious of the delicacy of his own position, Kanetane refused. The memorials provoked heated debate, the upshot of which was to ask the most powerful bakufu officials then in Kyoto, Hitotsubashi Yoshinobu (the shogun's chief advisor) and Matsudaira Shungaku (the shogun's guardian) if they thought imprisoning men of proven sincerity was a good idea. Shungaku said yes. "People who are truly sincere would never cause disorder." Besides, it was not the business of poetry-writing nobles to question the military. "We would appreciate it if you would leave dealing with such matters to us." The nobles disagreed. The only disorder they had heard about was committed by Aizu troops in smashing up houses and killing people in the vicinity of the palace. Besides, "the more sincere the man, the more likely he is to explode when confronted with wickedness and you will never be able to suppress such people simply by trying to overawe them. . . . We think that the people who are in charge of ruling the country ought to realize that in trying to intimidate those who do not tamely submit, they may end up punishing over half the population." [13]

By using the court to put pressure on bakufu authorities, the memorialists who pleaded for the Hirata disciples managed to get a compromise. The Kyoto Protector agreed not to execute men who had decapitated statues, but the charge stood of insulting the emperor by assassinating the character of shoguns who had held court rank and office. Most of the men incriminated in this incident, including the spy Kyōhei, were put in the custody of various domains a good distance from Kyoto, where they spent the next five years in relative isolation. They were permitted to write to each other, and they often did. They even wrote to Taseko. "I am enclosing a letter for Takemura Taseko," stated one note kept by Tsunoda Tadayuki. "Please send it on to her." [14] Unfortunately it and the other letters that she exchanged with the men trapped in this incident have disappeared.

Not all Hirata disciples were so fortunate as to sit out subsequent events in the tedium of domanial custody. A few court nobles who had received financial assistance from Nagao Ikusaburō tried to do something for him. In the view of the Aizu samurai, this simply showed their ignorance of bakufu regulations that mandated class differences in the punishments for samurai and commoners. Ikusaburō remained in the Rokkaku prison in Kyoto. There he wrote many poems that drew on his extensive knowledge of Japanese poetry. One repeated lines from the long poem in the *Man'yōshū* particularly prized by Atsutane that became the popular World War Two song, "If I go to sea" (*Umi yukaba*).[15] In another he likened himself to a falcon:

Hashitaka no	For the valiant-hearted
takeki kokoro mo	falcon
komenarete	to be vainly caged
aware hakanaku	day after night after day
okuru tsukihi no	is more than he can stand.[16]

The falcon is smaller than the hawk but equally fierce. Even though Ikusa-burō's thoughts soared above the clouds, he had no opportunity to display his courage. Worst of all would be to grow old in prison while opportunities for great deeds passed him by. He need not have worried: During the battle for the city between Chōshū and the combined Aizu-Satsuma forces in 1864, his jailers were to kill him. He was twenty-seven.

The Ashikaga incident ended in a severe setback for the Hirata school. More than twenty of the radical faction had been driven from the city, placed in the custody of various domains, or forced into hiding. Having attracted unwelcome attention from the authorities, those left behind kept to their original task of collecting information for their superiors, as in the case of Hirata Kanetane, or lecturing on ancient texts, as was done by Fukuba Bisei. Exiled to a remote village and guarded by unsympathetic relatives, Nishikawa Yoshisuke fumed, "Shut up as I am, the world is passing me by. Whenever I think about how difficult it is to tell whether I'll ever be able to do anything in the realm of national affairs, I weep so much that my family thinks I'm crazy."[17]

Taseko and her friends had been pushed off the streets, but those lucky enough to end up in the Chōshū sanctuary still had access to news. On the same day that Yamagata Aritomo was preparing his petition for clemency, Taseko learned that the heir to the daimyo of Chōshū, Mōri Motonori, had received orders to fortify the port of Hyōgo, now Kobe. Under the terms of the 1858 commercial treaty with the United States, the foreigners were to have gained access there in 1863. Because it lay so close to the sacred center of Kyoto, however, a protocol had been negotiated in 1862 to delay its opening until 1868.[18] Motonori set out on the first day of the third month. "In great secrecy I humbly bade him farewell," Taseko reported. She probably saw him off only at a distance while she remained concealed with the rest of her friends in a room at the back of the compound.[19]

Great expectations greeted the arrival of Shogun Iemochi on the fourth day of the third month. This was the first time a shogun had bothered to visit Kyoto since 1634, and at that time he had come to overawe the emperor with an army of 307,000 men.[20] Iemochi came to consult with the emperor and to make yet one more attempt to unify court and bakufu. The moderates among the daimyo and the court nobility hoped his visit would restore order and place the decision-making process firmly where it belonged—in their hands. The imperial loyalists hoped that he would finally stop vacillating over when to expel the foreigners. Taseko reported only that "tumult" marked his entrance into the city. This was also the day that she learned of the danger facing Yoshisuke and Kyūzaemon.[21]

Two days later, on the sixth, Taseko learned that Hitotsubashi Yoshinobu had paid a visit to the emperor. "He said one thing and another," she reported, but nothing about the barbarians that found favor with Taseko's informants or with she herself. "He is really hateful."[22] It was during this meeting that the emperor publicly confirmed the shogun's responsibility for governance and the bakufu promised to consult the court. This was the first time the shogun had ever sought or been granted confirmation of his authority; before he never needed it. On the other hand, Yoshinobu made no promises regarding the foreigners, nor was there any indication that either side would listen to people lower down in the social hierarchy as Taseko and her friends had hoped.

The shogun paid his first visit to the palace on the following day. He offered the emperor "a sword of finest temper, a horse, a hundred pieces of gold, a thousand pieces of silver, a picture, a pair of standing screens, an incense burner of blue earthenware, paper and a writing box, a writing table, a pair of folding screens, fifty pieces of blue silk and a thousand pieces of brocade." He also had presents for the imperial princes and princesses and the maids of honor.[23] Taseko never mentioned this visit. Instead she composed poetry that contrasted her anxieties with the balmy spring weather:

Ōzora wa	Even though the entire sky
hare watasu tomo	may be completely clear
hare yaranu	what can be done about
yo no ukigumo wo	the floating clouds, the wretched clouds
ika ni shite mashi	that refuse to clear up in this world of ours.[24]

Four days later the emperor left the palace to pray for the expulsion of the barbarians at the Kamo shrine. This was the first time in 250 years that an emperor had ventured beyond the palace walls without getting the shogun's permission first. It was not even his own idea, but one thought up by the young Chōshū radical and Taseko's new friend, Kusaka Genzui. The emperor and his ministers rode in palanquins befitting their high status; the shogun followed on horseback. Only the emperor entered the shrine's inner recesses. The shogun and daimyo had to wait for him, either standing out in the rain or sitting in a drafty wooden building usually given over to poetry meetings.

Hiding in the Chōshū mansion as she was, Taseko missed the opportunity to gaze upon the emperor's palanquin on his way to the Kamo shrine. Instead she enviously saw off her friends among the Chōshū samurai who went to see it, and they gave her a full report upon their return. "Even though I remained in the shadows, I respectfully bowed down to the ground in gratitude and awe." She then titled a poem "hearing about how the Matsudaira shogun attended his majesty on horseback." By calling the shogun by the surname he shared with most of the daimyo in Japan instead of the Tokugawa name restricted to his immediate family, Taseko apparently alluded to the argument that he was no more than first among equals.[25] It was therefore unreasonable for him to decide foreign affairs without consulting his peers and without taking into account the wishes of the one individual whose opinion mattered the most. In the poem itself, Taseko reminded the shogun that he should function in accordance with his office:

Kimi to omi no	At the sacred fence around the shrine
michi wo tadasu no	that rectifies the way
kami gaki ni	of lord and retainer
idemashi no yo to	In awe I respectfully greet
nari zo kashikoki	the dawning of the imperial age.[26]

Like most of her friends among the imperial loyalists, Taseko could not conceive of a Japan without the shogun. He simply had to remember that he was the emperor's servant and obey the emperor's wishes. His place in the emperor's entourage at the Kamo shrine thus served as a fitting gesture toward the power relations that ought to obtain in the new Japan.

The young Chōshū samurai brought Taseko news of the outside world and tried to keep her entertained. She lauded their efforts to ease the emperor's mind, she urged them to expel the barbarians as soon as possible, and she reassured them by her presence that they acted on behalf of the people, not just for themselves or their domain. One day she received ten poem cards with requests that she inscribe her poems on them. On the ninth day of the third month she watched respectfully the Chōshū heir's return from Osaka. He presented her with a dagger in admiration for her spirit and integrity. She later had the handle decorated with a design of falling cherry blossoms and a poem by Motoori Norinaga cited in "The Precious Sleeve Cord:"

Shikishima no	If people ask
Yamato kokoro wo	about the essence of Japan
hito towaba	and the Japanese
asahi ni niou	it's there in the flowers of the mountain cherry
yamazakura hana	fragrant in the dawn.[27]

FIGURE 18.
Hazama Hidenori
following his retirement.
Courtesy of Hazama Jōji.

Taseko treasured the dagger for the rest of her life, and it became one of her family's heirlooms.[28] With great satisfaction she noted that she was being treated graciously and hospitably. In short, she was having a wonderful time.

ON THE EIGHTH day of the third month, Taseko heard a rumor that some people claiming to be her sons were in Kyoto looking for her. The Chōshū samurai were suspicious of strangers, however, and put them off. Finally one of the men who had come with them, Hazama Hidenori from Nakatsugawa, found someone he knew who could vouch for him with Kusaka Genzui. On the evening of the tenth Taseko saw her two older sons for the first time in over six months.

Hidenori was eleven years younger than Taseko but much closer to her in temperament than her cousin Shigemasa. In her letters to her daughters in Nakatsugawa, she often mentioned that she had written him. He had a thin face dominated by hooded eyes and a determined chin. He was well educated, having begun his study of Chinese at age six. He later studied Chinese poetry with Shigemasa. He also enjoyed writing classical Japanese poetry and haiku at the moon-viewing parties he organized for his friends and relatives along the Nakasendō. He justified this interest by claiming descent from the *Man'yōshū* poet and court bureaucrat Ōtomo no Tabito, who died in 731. He was wealthy. In addition to the salary he received for managing packhorse consignments, he was a sake brewer with a hand in rice marketing, and he acted as a middleman in putting out cocoons to be spun into silk. He was one of the most influential men in Nakatsugawa with permission to use a surname and wear swords. Whenever important officials stayed the night at the *honjin* run by Shigemasa, Hidenori would be summoned to chat with them and exchange poems.[29]

Hidenori had the connections and experience to become well-versed in national affairs. He was in Kyoto in 1853 when the emperor ordered prayers offered to the gods to protect the country against the barbarians from the United States. In 1859 he went to Yokohama to sell silk thread to the foreigners, and he did not like what he saw of the way they behaved. As soon as he returned home, he joined the Hirata school. He was one of the first commoners in the region to make this commitment, and he eventually recruited more disciples than anyone else in Nakatsugawa. Among them were his elder sister and Shigemasa as well as Shimazaki Masaki, father of the modern novelist Tōson. Also in 1859 he contributed twenty *ryō* to the Owari domain coffers (the Owari daimyo was one of the shogun's most important relatives) and received in return a lacquered cup embossed with the wisteria crest. Enraged by the bakufu's purge of imperial loyalists that same year, he took the cup out to his garden and smashed it against a rock.[30]

Hidenori's most intense tutelage in national affairs came in the sixth month of 1862. That was when Kido Takayoshi from Chōshū spent ten days at Nakatsugawa, hiding out in a tea house under the protection of Shigemasa and Hidenori, while he waited to report on conditions in Kyoto to his lord. Mōri Takachika had been delayed by measles that felled over four hundred men at Suwa. Once he arrived on the twentieth, he and his advisors closeted themselves for almost five days, an unusually long time for a daimyo to spend at a post station. Takayoshi argued heatedly for Chōshū to demonstrate its loyalty to the court by taking an aggressive stance on expelling the barbarians. Only by reflecting the emperor's wishes could it replace Satsuma as the court's favorite negotiator in wringing concessions from the bakufu. Takayoshi spent another week arguing this position after he returned to Kyoto with Takachika, but the groundwork had been laid in Nakatsugawa where Hidenori was a witness.[31] When he and Taseko's sons arrived in Kyoto the following year, it was Hidenori who had the connections to convince the Chōshū samurai that they were who they said they were.

Hidenori and his party had not originally planned to spend time in Kyoto. They left Nakatsugawa on the twenty-third of the second month, the night after the attack on the Ashikaga shoguns' statues. They were eight: Hidenori and his daughter Mitsuko, Shigemasa, his wife Teruko and Teruko's sister Kame, Taseko's two older sons and a servant. In complete contrast to Taseko's determined and solitary departure, they went at a leisurely pace. "Despite the rain which made no one anxious to depart, we finally left about noon, planning to go to the Arima hot springs [now part of Kobe]," Shigemasa noted in his diary.[32] He composed poems at every occasion and strove for a literary effect to his prose. "Surely this is my lucky day," Hidenori wrote. "On this day last year I left to view the great shrine at Ise with my daughter. This year she is going with me to see the gates to the imperial palace. In my heart I count the blessings I have received from the gods who guard the visible and invisible worlds."[33]

The party took the same road traveled by Taseko and saw many of the same sights. They suffered delays, however, because so many important officials were crowding the way. Just past the Aichi River, they unexpectedly ran into Tsunoda Tadayuki. "We went to a tea house with him and drank some sake," Shigemasa wrote. "He reported that something strange was going on in Kyoto."[34] Taseko's sons decided that they had better hurry, so they hired palanquins to speed them on their journey through the rain. They missed the famous views at Seta and Ishiyama that Taseko had praised in her poetry and had themselves carried over the pass between Ōtsu and Kyoto.

Upon entering Kyoto, the whole group went straight to Ikemura Kuninori, Taseko's banker. Taseko was nowhere to be found. Kuninori said there had been some problems. They ran into Iwasaki Nagayo, who had first proselytized for the Hirata school in the Ina Valley. He offered to try to find out where she was. Once it became clear that they would have to remain longer in Kyoto than they had intended, they needed a place to stay. Why not take over the rooms so recently vacated by Taseko, Kuninori suggested. That night Hidenori wrote a poem praising her for having gone inside the imperial palace:

Kasunaranu	Even someone unworthy of being counted
mi mo ōkimi no	has managed to approach
he ni koso to	the emperor.
omoi noborishi	My thoughts fly high
miyako e no sora	through the sky to the capital.[35]

Remember that according to Atsutane, the gods had rushed production of the countless multitudes. Taseko was to refer to herself in similar terms to the end of her life.

Over the next few days Hidenori and his friends managed to find out where Taseko had gone. With so much happening in the city, getting to see her was another matter. On the first day of the third month, the young Noshiro Hirosuke came to tell them all about how the Hirata disciples had been arrested. In the afternoon they paid a visit to the court noble Shirakawa Sukenori. Two days later they visited Hirata Kanetane. At each occasion they exchanged many cups of sake. They had planned to watch the shogun enter the city, but he took a different route. The next day they saw the lord of Mito arrive and were gratified to learn that he had put on a much more impressive spectacle. For the shogun's first visit to the emperor they got up before dawn to wait and watch. "Noble and base, men and women were squeezed together," Hidenori wrote. "Everyone tried to push his way forward, making even the broad boulevards of the capital seem narrow. . . . The vanguard of fifty or sixty men wearing formal robes [*kamishimo*, not armor] did nothing to clear the way. Hitotsubashi Yoshinobu too went past almost furtively and with no substance to him at all. 'What is the world coming to,' people muttered." [36]

Two days later Hidenori found a way to get past the guards at the Chōshū compound. He and Taseko's sons stayed only a short time with Taseko because they wanted to find a good place to watch the emperor's procession to the Kamo shrine, and that meant sitting out all night in the damp. This spectacle was done properly, with attendants carrying bows and arrows to clear the way. "When I respectfully viewed the phoenix carriage, my tears fell harder than the rain," Hidenori wrote.[37] The next day he stayed home with a cold while his companions went to Gion for a party. Taseko's sons then left to see the sights of Osaka. Hidenori continued to cultivate the Chōshū samurai. On his next visit, he took a letter for Taseko written by Shigemasa that included this poem:

Ie mo mi mo	May the gods of heaven and earth
wasurete tsukusu	take pity on and protect
magokoro wo	that pure heart
aware to mamore	which has done its best
ama tsuchi no kami	forgetting self and family.[38]

Whatever Shigemasa's earlier objections to Taseko's trip to Kyoto, they had vanished once he got to the city and talked to the people who knew her only

in her guise of a poet-activist. Being firm supporters of the emperor themselves, both he and Hidenori had to be impressed with how far she had penetrated into the loyalist movement.

While Taseko remained in hiding, her friends went sightseeing. On the
fourteenth Shigemasa, Hidenori, and the women in their party stopped by
the Golden Pavilion where they expected to see a statue of Ashikaga Yoshimitsu. Ever since the pillory of the statues from Tōji-in, it had been kept out
of sight. "Strange." They went to Arashiyama, watched a performance of sacred dance at the Matsuo shrine, and viewed most of the places Taseko had
seen earlier. On the seventeenth they learned that the Chōshū heir had gone
to Hyōgo and Shimazu Hisamitsu was returning to Kagoshima where British ships were massing to punish Satsuma for the murder of a British merchant. They met with a shrine priest from Iyo to read the petition he had
written demanding that the men who had decapitated the statues be freed.
They gaped at the heads of two Buddhist priests, executed because they had
"committed deeds inappropriate to their status." [39]

On the eighteenth and nineteenth Shigemasa and Hidenori talked to
Genzui and others about releasing Taseko into their custody in order to take
her home. "How are you going to do this, given so many watchful eyes on
the Tōkaidō?" the samurai asked. "We were planning to shelter her ourselves
until we could send her back." They were in no hurry to give her up, she was
in no hurry to go, and with all the commotion in the city, who knew what
might happen next. Better to wait until the end of the month. [40]

Not until Taseko's friends and relatives had been in Kyoto for four weeks
did she finally and reluctantly leave the Chōshū compound. When her sons
had returned from Osaka on the twenty-third, Shigemasa wrote, "We've already been a month on the road and we've accomplished nothing. I'm shocked
at how vainly time has passed." Taseko spent the night of the twenty-seventh
with Kuninori, then the next day she went back to thank all the warriors who
had been so hospitable, especially Kido Takayoshi and Kusaka Genzui. "How
could I express my gratitude for the money they gave me to pay our expenses
on the road, the allowance I received while I was in hiding, and all the other
presents," Taseko wrote. "When the time came to say farewell, we kept talking back and forth about what the future might hold and wrung out our
sleeves at the thought of parting." [41]

Even more painful was leaving the environs of the imperial palace. In the
darkness before dawn Taseko and her companions stopped on the bridge at
Gojō to bow deeply in its direction. She grieved for her friends arrested for
decapitating statues whose fate was still unknown. Hidenori pondered "the
way back to the past while we plod through the real world of the present."

Their route took them to a series of shrines and temples between Kyoto and Uji, including Manpukuji founded in 1661 by a Zen sect from China and the graceful Byōdō-in. They had to take a slippery and difficult side road to worship at the Iwashimizu shrine because the main staircase was under repair in preparation for a visit by the emperor. The next morning they took a boat down the river to Osaka. Taseko spent the trip longing for the capital and thinking herself into the spirit of classical courtiers forced into exile:

Miyako e ni	While my heart is being pulled back
kokoro hikarete	to the capital
Yodo gawa no	the waves rise around me
nami tachi soete	on the Yodo River
sode wo shiboritsu	where I wring out my sleeves.[42]

Shigemasa, in contrast, thoroughly enjoyed himself. "The willows on the riverbanks were green. The violets, dandelions and other wild flowers competed to perfume the air."[43]

Taseko and her companions spent five days in Osaka. On the first day of the fourth month most of the party went off to see a play, but she was too depressed to accompany them. Instead she visited Nonoguchi Masashiki, the man with whom she had stayed some months before. There she learned to her delight that two men implicated in the affair of the decapitated statues and "who felt as I did" had escaped to Hiroshima. For the next few days she stayed with her group, going to a play and visiting the famous sights of the city. Hidenori whiled away the time in prayer. Shigemasa continued to enjoy himself, admiring the scenery and drinking at every opportunity. Finally on the fourth he, Taseko and Hidenori exchanged farewell poems with Masashiki. In recognition of Taseko's commitment to the imperial cause, Masashiki wrote the following:

Nagara gawa	I will be waiting for you
nagaraete ware	while the Nagara River
kimi matan	flows on and on through time itself
Yamato damashii wo	cleansing and purifying
arai araite	your Japanese spirit.[44]

As they had promised the Chōshū samurai, Taseko and her companions stayed off the busy Tōkaidō. From Osaka they went to Nara, site of the capital more ancient than Kyoto. Hidenori carefully described the imperial tombs that had been identified a year or so earlier. In front of the tomb for Emperor

Yūryaku from the fifth century they prostrated themselves in worship, then went on their way, their "hearts filled with joy." Of all their party, he and Taseko were clearly the most committed to the nativist message. On the outskirts of Nara they left the group to visit the Tatsuta shrine described at some length in "The Precious Sleeve Cord." "I was deeply moved to see the shape of ancient days," Hidenori wrote, "but it was also painful to see how dilapidated it had become. A certain Tarao from Shigaraki had been put in charge of this place, and I must say that he was really heartless. He had made repairs to the temple to attract passers-by, and it was gorgeous. Contrasting that with his neglect of the shrine brought a tightness to my chest." Taseko found little to recommend in Nara. The great Buddha she called a "detestable inanimate object."[45]

Taseko showed slight enthusiasm for the trip home. She merely listed the places where they stopped and wrote a few poems. Near the town of Yagi she and the others went to worship at the tomb for Emperor Jimmu refurbished the preceding winter.[46] Jimmu is now considered the mythical ancestor of the imperial house, but to Hidenori and Taseko, he was real indeed. No matter what she saw, however, her thoughts remained in Kyoto, and her prayers were for an imperial reign undisturbed by intrusive barbarians.

From the Yamato Plain the travelers climbed through mountains where the villages were so squeezed in the gorges that it was rare to see more than a single house at a time. Along the way they enjoyed the beautiful scenery, the clean air and the streams full of trout. At a town called Ōishi, "we had someone catch fish for us and we ate a great quantity" (Taseko). "Soon we saw the moon reflected clearly on the river waters. Clusters of fireflies swarmed around us and the temperature was just right" (Shigemasa).[47]

While Taseko and her companions were on the road they heard that the emperor had completed his visit to Iwashimizu shrine. Fearing he would be forced to make a sacred pledge before the gods to expel the barbarians, the shogun had excused himself owing to a sudden illness. Hitotsubashi Yoshinobu accompanied the emperor in the shogun's place, but before he could receive the sword of justice for the expulsion of the barbarians, he too took sick and left the shrine.[48] This slight did not go unnoticed by the men already critical of the way the shogun treated the emperor. In her poetry, however, Taseko simply celebrated the emperor's visit as evidence of his growing visibility in the world outside the palace.[49]

Taseko and her companions spent the fourteenth day of the fourth month at the great shrine to the sun goddess in Ise. For her it was such an awe-inspiring experience that she said only, "we went around the shrines, our hearts filled with prayer." The next day they went to the river where the trees for rebuilding the shrine were being hauled on shore in carts decorated with red and white flags. The sight moved Taseko to produce a poem:

Azusa yumi	Even though I can't take up
te ni wa toranedo	a catalpa bow in my hand
omoi iru	my resolute heart
yatake kokoro wa	is braver
iwaku mo takan	than words can express.[50]

In ancient Japan, bows made from catalpa wood believed to have magical powers were used for hunting as well as Shinto ceremonies. Strumming the bow string was thought to summon spirits. While Taseko was neither a shamaness nor a hunter, worshipping at Ise, the shrine for the emperor's divine ancestress, gave her the courage to withstand visible and invisible dangers.

Having come so far, the travelers spent the next three days sightseeing along the Ise coast in the vicinity of Futami, still a popular resort for people on holiday. They found men known to Hidenori and Shigemasa from their previous trips to the area, and naturally they had to have a party. Off in the distance they could see the fortifications recently built to defend the coast against the foreigners. On the night of the eighteenth they viewed the moon over the mountains, then they got up before dawn to watch the sun rise out of the sea. Banks of clouds lying low on the horizon turned crimson in the morning light while the moon was still sinking in the west. Everyone composed poems. They hired a boat to take them out to the salt pans, and for lunch they ate rice cakes that were a specialty of the region. Had any bakufu officials been looking for Taseko, surely they would not have expected to find her in a bunch of tourists.

Taseko and her companions split up temporarily on the outskirts of Matsusaka. Shigemasa and Taseko's sons went into town, where they stayed comfortably in an inn. In the course of their next day's journey they remarked at the sight of a criminal being beaten at Anoura. Taseko, Hidenori, and Hidenori's daughter Mitsuko turned inland and spent the night at a temple. They copied a long poem Hidenori had written the year before, then created new ones to celebrate their visit to the grave of Japan's great nativist scholar, Motoori Norinaga.

Norinaga chose the site for his grave himself, and Atsutane had applauded his choice in "The Precious Sleeve Cord." Located five miles southwest of Matsusaka just below the summit of Mt. Yamamuro with a fine view toward Ise, it is seldom visited. Near the bottom of the mountain is the Yamamuro shrine where today's school children pray to the spirit of Norinaga for help

on their entrance examinations. Above and beyond, up a steep, slippery and
washed-out path is a man-made plateau. To the left are two modern steles
that identify the grave. Beside them is a smaller stone erected by Hirata disciples in 1867 to commemorate Atsutane's visit to the site. When Taseko and
her friends arrived, they found only a single monument on a dais surrounded
by a stone wall. Taseko made an offering of some lilies she had found bloom-
ing along the road and recited her poem:

Ashibiki no	Mt. Yamamuro
Yamamuro yama wo	drew my feet
natsukashimi	to his eternal dwelling
natsuno wake irite	making my way through the summer fields
sayuri hana	I have plucked the lilies
orite zo temuku	to make an offering
mata sara ni	awaiting the time
sayurite mo komu	when once again
toki wo koso mate	I will come on bended knee.[51]

Unlike Hidenori, Taseko made but one trip to Ise and Mt. Yamamuro.

The twentieth found Taseko, Hidenori, and Mitsuko in Matsusaka, looking for the house where Norinaga had lived. "Even though we asked its owner
all sorts of questions, we couldn't ascertain a thing." At lunch in a tea house
they tried some of the local sake and met other travelers. "I listened as carefully as I could to their news from the capital, and it really put me in anguish." [52] This was the same day that the shogun promised the emperor to
expel the barbarians on the tenth day of the fifth month, a promise he knew he
could not keep. Rumors that this announcement was coming were in the air,
but Taseko was more likely worried about what was going to happen to her
friends, then being cruelly interrogated for having decapitated the statues.

Taseko, Hidenori, and Mitsuko caught up with Shigemasa and her sons
two days before they all arrived together at the thriving metropolis of Nagoya.
There they spent three nights. First they visited the Atsuta shrine, said to
contain the sacred sword, one of the three imperial regalia. When Taseko's
fellow disciple Tsunoda Tadayuki later became its chief priest, he decided that
the shrine looked entirely too much like a Buddhist temple. He was to write
numerous petitions to the central authorities before getting permission to
rebuild it. Today it sits in a grove of evergreens, its series of roofs accented
with long cross pieces perched above plain wooden boxes in the unadorned
style of the Ise shrines. After Taseko paid it careful obeisance, she went discreetly back to the inn because everyone felt that she had better remain hid-

den while her companions went sightseeing. The next day she was allowed
out to shop for souvenirs. On the twenty-fifth day of the fourth month, she
and her companions headed for home. At the Kachi River she wrote:

Kachikawa wo	While wading across
kachi watari tsutsu	the Kachi River
furusato ni	I really begrudge
kaeru mo oshiki	returning home
yume ka utsutsu ka	Was it all a dream or not?[53]

Two days later Taseko and her companions arrived safely in Nakatsugawa. She was in no hurry to go farther. While they were gone her grandson
had changed his hairstyle from that sported by children, and Shigemasa reported that he looked quite grown-up. On the second day of the fifth month
Taseko sent a message back to the Chōshū samurai in Kyoto to let them know
that she had gotten safely back to her relatives. "I shall be thankful for the
rest of my life for all the blessings you showered upon me. There is no way I
can ever adequately express my gratitude."[54] On the fourth she finally went
home. She had departed a poet with a yearning to be part of events larger
than herself; she returned a committed imperial loyalist, her identity recognized by the men who knew her.

One local booster has argued that Taseko went to Kyoto because Shigemasa, Hidenori, and the Ina Valley nativists had talked her into it.[55] Without
their influence and example, she would never have studied poetry, entered
the Hirata school, and later risked going to Kyoto alone. It is easy to deni-
grate this kind of rhetoric that presumes only men to be capable of action, but
that begs the question of influence versus agency. According to the tenets of
postmodernism, no one, man or woman, can be said to conform to the heroic
mode of rugged individualism because there is no such thing as a unitary self.
Everyone changes as they go through life; they craft different identities depending on the contexts in which they find themselves. From this perspective, the person we call Taseko is little more than a subject position trapped
in an infinite web of power, sex, family, religion, and poetry relations.[56] It is
clear that Taseko's cultural, social, and intellectual environment powerfully
ordered her experiences and self-representation. Room must be left, however, for accident and opportunity.

Before World War Two, the women portrayed in Japanese textbooks or
educational tracts were either wise mothers who bravely sent their sons off to
war, or good wives who worked hard, usually while enduring extreme poverty.
Rather than being women who lived as individuals, they were praised for hav-

ing sacrificed themselves for husband, family and country. Only in the last twenty years have critical biographies treated women as other than subordinate to men or mere sex objects. For writers and biographers today, the notion that a woman has her own wants, desires, ego and self-expression apart from her husband and family is still too recent and too important to be discarded.[57] Juxtaposing their approach with that of postmodernist critics suggests that it is worthwhile to construct context and actor in terms of each other without denying the vagaries of history.

By going to Kyoto to act on her own, Taseko transformed her life. The opportunities she found to interact with "brave men who think as I do" heightened her dedication to the loyalist movement and made her conscious that she too was an imperial loyalist. Her deeds suggest that there are singularities beyond the reach of social history; there are individual idiosyncrasies beyond the reach of the postmodern critiques. In the end, Taseko surprised even herself:

Arashiyama	In the shadows of the flowers
hana no kikage ni	on Arashiyama
omou yori	I have passed a spring
omoi no hoka no	that was more extraordinary
haru wo he ni keri	than anything I ever expected.[58]

PART THREE   *Taseko and the Meiji Restoration*

CHAPTER ELEVEN

On The Sidelines

I go on my way regretting
that like the leech child
I cannot stand alone
sick of deploring
my weak woman's body.
MATSUO TASEKO, 1863[1]

Taseko must have found it boring to be back home. One month
she was at the center of things; the next she was in a rural backwater dependent on the kindness of friends and relatives for
news of the outside world. Six days after she returned to
Tomono, on the tenth day of the fifth month, the day the emperor had ordered the foreigners driven out of Japan, Chōshū
batteries fired on foreign ships in the straits of Shimonoseki.
Two months later Satsuma troops tried unsuccessfully to re-
pel British invaders who shelled and burned the castle town
of Kagoshima in retaliation for the murder of a British citizen
the year before. In the eighth month the same Kyoto Protector who had rounded up the Hirata disciples for the pillory of
the heads from the Ashikaga shoguns' statues staged a coup
with the help of Satsuma troops to drive the Chōshū loyalists
from the city. The emperor and his advisors then purged seven
court nobles accused of having falsely claimed to be acting in

the emperor's name in demanding the immediate expulsion of the barbarians. The radical seven fled to Chōshū. Loyalists professing the "revere the emperor, expel the barbarian" line were no longer welcome in Kyoto.

The League of Heavenly Vengeance (*tenchūgumi*) had attacked the bakufu outpost at Gojō, deep in the countryside east of Nara, just days before the Aizu-Satsuma coup. The loyalists planned to take it over in the emperor's name and called on other samurai and daimyo in the area to put themselves under imperial rule as well.[2] Among those who lost their lives to the domanial troops sent against them under bakufu orders was Taseko's acquaintance from Kyoto, the painter and poet Fujimoto Tesseki. While admiring one of the paintings he had given her, Taseko wrote the following poem dedicated to his memory:

> Totsu kawa no   Had you not disappeared
> nami to kiezu ba   into the waves of the Totsu River
> itazura ni   right now you would be
> nagarete imashi wo   idly tracing strokes
> mizuguki no ato   with your writing brush.[3]

Taseko apparently approved of Tesseki's self-sacrifice. Better to have died for the emperor than lead a leftover life doing nothing.

Taseko was not the only person to feel sidelined. Her comrades and fellow disciples in the Hirata school had been imprisoned, put in domiciliary confinement, forced into hiding, or killed. The fertilizer merchant from Ōmi, Nishikawa Yoshisuke, spent his days in house confinement collecting information and entering it into his record of current events. "Who knows how things will end up, whether for better or worse," he wrote to a friend. "I take no interest in life's simple pleasures. Sometimes I hate the world, sometimes I hate people, and I've even been so foolish as to hate the gods. I spend days asserting violent arguments or railing at fate. Few here think as I do, and there is no one with whom I can be perfectly frank. I neglect my reading, I'm unable to write poetry, and I wait for the days to pass making a friend of the wind in the pines."[4]

At the end of 1864 Yoshisuke mentioned that he had received a letter from Taseko. He did not bother to repeat what it said; all he did was copy the poem she had sent, one that bemoaned her fate at being born a weak woman when the times called for strong men.[5] It was a long poem, the form used for eulogies and complaints even as late as the fifteenth century, and Taseko had much to lament. It is an important poem, I think, for it shows her relating her "reading and living, construing texts and making sense of life."[6] In it Taseko speaks specifically about herself.

Taseko begins her poem in typically nativist fashion by positioning herself in a direct line of communication with the gods and emperor. In this setting the political and administrative structures established by the bakufu are unremarkable:

Sumeragi no	What use am I
kami no shirimasu	as a person appearing
utsushi yo no	in the visible world
hito to aredashi	governed by the gods
kai ya nani	through the emperor.

The vocabulary for this section comes straight out of "The Precious Sleeve Cord." The term used for emperor, *sumeragi* or *sumerogi*, applies not only to the current monarch but to all the men (*gi* is a male suffix) who came before him in a line of descent unbroken since the sun goddess sent her grandson to govern the land. Taseko's assertion that this lineage rules the visible world also links it with the invisible world inhabited by the gods and ancestors which, according to the teachings of Hirata Atsutane, is also always present. The emperor acts in both. While performing rituals he moves in the hidden world of the deities; as a physical presence he rules over the land and its people. Taseko thus establishes her identity as a Hirata disciple at the same time that she questions whether she has any role to play at all.

The next line doubles the usual number of syllables to signify that it is an emphatic statement. It also contains a direct statement of the self in the word "ware," meaning "I." It was unusual for anyone, male or female, to make explicit a subject position most often left unspoken, but Taseko defies convention in stating:[7]

Ware mo otoko ni araba	If I were a man

In poems from the *Man'yōshū*, the preferred term was *waga*, used often in a form akin to a possessive—"my" or "our" beloved lord, for example.[8] In her poem expressing her envy of male privileges, Nomura Bōtō, another woman famous for her dedication to the imperial cause, used the term *waga mi* to stand for herself: "Would I arrive / even a step after you / if I were / numbered among those / who carry the catalpa bow?"[9] *Ware* occasionally appears in classical poetry; for example, the *Tales of Ise* includes a poem by a young women who calls out, "I am here."[10] In most poems, however, the subject of action remains implicit. Furthermore, although men used *ware* to refer to themselves from the medieval age on, women seldom if ever did the same.[11] In Atsutane's "Lectures on Ancient History," for example, the god

Ōkuninushi uses *ware* to refer to himself when giving orders to other gods.[12] Taseko thus picks precisely that term which jars most sharply against the culturally defined character of women and uses it to reinforce the masculine subject at the center of her desire.

Taseko wrote a variation on this topic of regretting being a woman in which she again takes the masculine pronoun for herself. Titled, "a long poem expressing my thoughts," it begins:

Chihayaburu	Born in the country
kami no megumi ni	of the rising sun
hi no moto no	blessed by
kuni ni umarete	the awesome gods
taoyame no	weak woman that I am
ware zo kai naki	I am useless.[13]

Instead of the Japanese syllabary always considered more appropriate for women, here the effect of employing a masculine term is heightened by the use of a Chinese character, which itself casts a masculine shadow, followed by the emphatic *zo*. Does *ware* really point to a contradiction lying at the heart of the poem? Perhaps it could be read as ironic self-deprecation or rhetorical posturing for public consumption. I think, however, that Taseko took herself far too seriously to be consciously ironic and valued too highly the sincerity of the true loyalist to lapse into hypocrisy.

This use of *ware* links Taseko to the female founders of new religions such as Nakayama Miki, 1798-1887, and others who continue to appropriate the accouterments of male identity to give themselves the authority to speak in public.[14] *Ware* was also used by Kishida Toshiko, 1863–1901, who just as Taseko had done took advantage of an encounter with a significant political event to talk politics, in her case the Popular Rights Movement of the early 1880s.[15] Higuchi Ichiyo, 1872–96, the Meiji period essayist and short story writer, used it in a statement regretting not being woman enough to have children. As historian Nishikawa Yūko points out, women of the nineteenth century—Miki, Taseko, Toshiko, and Ichiyo—lived betwixt and between the certainties of the early modern political order and the completion of the centralized modern state, a time when language like so much else was up for grabs.[16]

Having postulated a sex-change, Taseko then describes what she would do were she a man. She begins with the polysyllabic pillow word for Shinano, a favorite phrase of the nativist proselytizer Iwasaki Nagayo, found in the *Man'yōshū* which derives from and testifies to the spirit of ancient Japan. The lines describing the sword appear in a long poem from the same anthol-

ogy written by an old man mourning the loss of his youthful vigor.[17] She had
used the last two lines before in praising the assassins of Ii Naosuke in 1860:

Misuzukaru	In my left hand
Shinano no mayumi	I would grasp
hidarite ni	a straight bow from Shinano
tanigiri mochite	where the fine bamboo is cut
tsurugi tachi	I would carry a straight sword
koshi ni torihaki	at my hips
ie wasure	I would forget my family
mi mo tanashirazu	and consider my life to be less than nothing.

In her life of the imagination, Taseko envisions herself not only a man but a
warrior. Like many commoners who joined the Hirata school, she refuses to
be bound by status distinctions that limit weapons and the opportunity for
self-sacrifice to the samurai. Another way of reading these lines is to see them
as an admonition to her readers. If they truly profess the same beliefs she
does, they will cast aside all self-interest and act, even if it means following
Fujimoto Tesseki's example.

Despite her dreams, Taseko cannot long forget that she is not a warrior.
Even were she a man, in fact, she is still nothing more than a commoner.
With that realization, she encourages other men to act in her place:

Sono michi ni	Even though I am not worthy to be counted
idete tsukauru	among the mighty warriors
mononofu no	who go out to serve
kasunarazu tomo	on that way
o-nakata no	graced with
kami no mitama wo	the departed souls
tamawarite	of the imperial ancestors
Yamato kokoro wo	I shout bravely
furi okoshi	to enflame
isami takebite	true Japanese hearts.

In these lines as in the poems written by so many of her contemporaries, we
can see the veneration paid military men in this society. Here she is perhaps
remembering that darling of the nativists, Kusunoki Masashige, who had
died defending Emperor Godaigo against the perfidious Ashikaga shoguns.

Taseko next castigates not only the barbarians who flock to Yokohama in
search of trade, but her compatriots who fawn on them. She probably has in
mind men such as her neighbor Majima Toshinari, who despite his commit-

ment to the Hirata school had sought profit in foreign trade, or the merchants in Iida threatened with pillage if they did not stop marketing local products abroad:

Michi shiranu	People who know not the way
hito no kokoro wo	the warriors from the boondocks
Yokohama ni	who incline their hearts
iyori tsudoeru	to dwell
inaka bushi	on Yokohama
shiko no emishira	I say drive them all out
hitori naku	down to the last
yaraite mashi to	despicable savage.

The term for barbarian, *emishi,* originally referred to tribes deemed aborigines by the civilizing Yamato court that in ancient history had tried repeatedly to suppress them and conquer northeastern Japan. Nagayo too used the phrase "despicable savages" (*shiko no emishira*) in a long poem upon hearing that Chōshū forces had fired on foreign ships in 1863. Yokohama was a neologism in terms of the poetic tradition, but an important site in the intercourse between Japan and the West.

All that prevents Taseko from acting on her beliefs is her body. The second to the last line in the poem sent to Yoshisuke draws on a *Man'yōshū* poem, this one found in Yamanoue Okura's "Lament on the Instability of Human Life" from the early eighth century. He grieves that he cannot afford to clothe his children; Taseko's grief is for not being able to serve the emperor. She also figures in the leech child highlighted in the chapter that she had helped publish from "Lectures on Ancient History" (perhaps partially as an advertisement of her contribution to this project). When the creator gods Izanagi and Izanami circle the heavenly pillar, Izanami, the woman, speaks first. Her indiscretion causes the first child born of their union to be so ill-formed that they repudiate it. They call it the leech child and cast it adrift in a boat made of reeds.[18] Taseko here compares herself to this unfortunate creature, neither human nor animal, male nor female, but an ineffectual hybrid:

Murakimo no	From the bottom of my heart
kokorobayare do	I am filled with ardor, but
ka ni kaku ni	as you can see
koshi sae tatanu	I grieve not knowing what to do
hiru no ko no	like the leech child
semu sube wo nami	unable to stand on its own
wabi tsutsu zo oru	and I am here to apologize.

The leech child has a complicated history. Some accounts say that after it was cast out of heaven, it was discovered and raised by the deity Emishi Saburō Daimyōjin, whose first name suggests his connection to the barbarians of the northeast. He has another name, however, that of Kotoshironushi-no-mikoto, the eldest son of Ōkuninushi, ruler of the invisible world. Eventually the leech child became worshipped as the deity Ebisu, one of the "Seven Lucky Gods." On the other hand, in his work on the *Kojiki,* Motoori Norinaga "read the leech child as a metaphor for a crippled or deformed child." [19] That would appear to be the meaning Taseko attached to herself. The leech is also a pest, especially for those who must wade in mud up to their knees to plant rice seedlings.

Having filled the main section with language evocative of ancient texts, Taseko then follows with an envoy that sums up her emotions. For the poem she sent to Yoshisuke, the envoy contains a cry of frustration at her helplessness:

Taoyame no	I air my regrets at having
mi wo kui akashi	the weak body of a woman
namayomi no	and I enumerate
kai naki koto wo	all the ways
kakikasou naru	in which I am useless.

Namayomi is a pillow word found in the *Man'yōshū* for the province of Kai, a homonym for "utility." In the envoy for her second long poem on re-gretting a woman's body, Taseko drops the euphemisms altogether:

Masurao no	How awful
kokorobayare to	to have the ardent heart
taoyame no	of a manly man
kai naki mi koso	and the useless body
kanashi kari keri	of a weak woman.[20]

The bifurcation between men's and women's roles implied in the mas-culinity of *masurao,* not just a man but a brave man, versus the femininity of *taoyame,* not just a woman but a frail woman, allowed many poets to struc-ture a seemingly natural contrast between the two. In the following poem found in "The Precious Sleeve Cord," Atsutane asserts that prose and his-torical research are the province of men; the classical poetry venerated by so many nativists—including his great predecessor Motoori Norinaga—as the wellspring of the Japanese tradition is of considerably lesser import:

Masurao no	Don't they know
nasubeki waza wo	what real men
shirade are ya	should be about?
taoyame mo suru	What are they doing
uta yomi wa nazo	writing the same poetry as weak women? [21]

Taseko's poems can be read as a direct statement about the process of constructing a life story, revealing as they do her profound ambivalence about her position as an interloper in androcentric space and suggesting that like all women who have led unconventional lives, she teetered uncertainly between two destinies, masculine and feminine, "clearly the rightful possessor of neither." [22] Her vulnerability to the cultural fictions about appropriate female behavior appears in the writing of other Tokugawa period women as well, notably the poet-painter Ema Saikō, 1787–1861, who despite her fame felt that she had failed as a woman because she never married. [23] Both of these women became the subjects of their own lives, but in so doing they had to go so far beyond the conventional female plot of their day that they could not always deal with the consequences. Perhaps for that reason they retreated into a denial of their achievements. Taseko's poems mirror cultural expectations about appropriate feminine behavior and offer reassurance that she fundamentally accepts her identity as the silent and passive woman demanded by the patriarchal culture of her time.

Reading this poem in another way would emphasize that to the extent Taseko defined worthwhile action in male terms and acknowledged the male-centered ideology of selfhood, she gained "the cultural recognition that flowed to her as a person who embodied male-identified ideals, but she also perpetuated the political, social, and textual disempowerment of mother and daughter." [24] She needed disclaimers as a measure of self-defense lest others attack her for being unwomanly. On the backs of two portraits that she gave her relatives in the Ina Valley, she wrote short poems. "I am completely fed up with my useless body" begins the one in the Kitahara collection. For Higuchi Mitsunobu, Inao's younger brother, she wrote, "realizing I cannot take up the catalpa bow, my heart breaks like a stone smashed to bits." [25]

In the end it was simply not possible for Taseko to integrate her multiple identities as a woman and an activist. Her adventure in Kyoto failed to lead her to the self-illumination that might render it truly subversive according to contemporary standards, but it is hardly fair to judge a woman of the past by the most advanced feminist standards of the present. As Dea Birkett and Julie Wheelwright remind us, "rather than raiding the past to find satisfactory models for today, we should look to the difficulties, contradictions, and triumphs of women within the larger context of their own times."[26] In regretting the weak body of a useless woman, Taseko speaks directly to the contradictions that result from her crafting of a loyalist identity. In reflecting on this critical moment in her life, she is unable to maintain the fiction of a unified self.

Other women who like Taseko found themselves involved in loyalist activities in support of the emperor expressed feelings more akin to envy toward men rather than anger at themselves. Ōtagaki Rengetsu, with whom Taseko had spent a few brief hours in Kyoto, wrote a poem entitled, "envious of people who are male, in jest," and she gave no hint that she despised her body: "Oh, had I been born / as one who could take up / bow and arrow / gird on a sword and serve / our sovereign in this world!"[27] It was thus not all that unusual for women at this time to realize the disabilities they faced as women. Taseko went farther, however, in castigating herself for failing to measure up to male standards of behavior. Of all the women among the loyalists who yearned toward male-identified selfhood, she would have best understood Mary Wollstonecraft, participant-observer of the French Revolution, who likewise strained against the constraints of her sex and cried out in frustration, "Why was I not born a man, or why was I born at all?"[28]

Perhaps I have made too much of Taseko's poems bewailing the fragility of her woman's body. They are always quoted in her biographies. Of all the letters and poems that she sent to Yoshisuke, this is the only one found in his records. Poems that appear to give the most insight into her psyche probably also provide the most satisfaction to the men who have written about her. Most of her biographers grew up and wrote before World War Two, when the slogan "men are superior, women are inferior" (*danson johi*) was taken for granted, as it still is in many parts of Japan today. Accordingly it would not do for Taseko to act too independently of men, and the underlying message of these poems is she knew she could not. Just as other women (and Eva Peron comes to mind), she had to prove that despite her defiance of social conventions, she was not an anomaly, she was "still a woman in the most conventional sense."[29] The rhetoric of self-abnegation not only obscures the transgression of female roles that her going to Kyoto had represented, it constitutes an implicit response to her neighbors who had maligned her for having gone at all.

FOR THE NEXT four years, Taseko stayed close to Tomono, and little is known of what she did. Fragmentary glimpses in letters, reports, and poems suggest that she never ventured farther than Nakatsugawa, where she could always claim to be visiting her daughters and where she sometimes stayed for months on end. She raised silkworms. She watched her grandchildren grow up. She hosted study meetings and encouraged men from her village to attend.[30] She corresponded with friends and relatives, begging them for news, and she talked to travelers to find out as much as she could about what was going on outside her valley. "I recently got a summary of conditions in the east explaining just how dangerous the road has become. This was from a man who was on his way home to Ajima [a nearby village]," she wrote to her cousin Inao, then in Edo, early in the fifth month of 1864. "For the most part I've concentrated on news that concerns the capital."

Taseko also read a letter that Inao had sent his son in which he described how a faction of radical samurai from Mito had fortified Mt. Tsukuba while they sent a memorial to the bakufu calling for it to expel the barbarians immediately. "The events going on in the east are truly terrifying," she commented.[31] What happened next proved to be the most momentous incident to shake the Ina Valley before 1868.

Under the leadership of Tokugawa Nariaki, Mito had been the first domain to urge the bakufu to strengthen the country's defenses against the foreign threat. Its scholars had developed their own brand of heterodox Confucianism that stressed Japan's unique historical heritage, which was predicated on the imperial line, unbroken for ages eternal. The way to demonstrate loyalty to the emperor, however, was to fulfill the functions of one's position in the status hierarchy. Since the emperor had delegated administrative authority to the shogun, and he had commissioned the daimyo to rule their domains, a good samurai had to do what his lord told him. As a branch of the Tokugawa family, moreover, Mito had a particular obligation to support the bakufu. But when it appeared that the shogun was ignoring the emperor's wishes in allowing more and more ports to be opened to foreign trade, then the samurai found themselves torn between duty to their lord and loyalty to the emperor. Out of this conflict arose a three-way power struggle between factions of the conservative upper-ranking samurai, reformist middle-ranking samurai, and radical lower-ranking samurai.[32]

The Mito samurai who were encamped on Mt. Tsukuba under the banner of "Revere the emperor and expel the barbarians" defied their superiors' orders to disband and submit to authority. The conservative faction retaliated by using regular troops from the bakufu and other domains to attack them. Some members of the Tsukuba faction at first tried to surrender, protesting that they had not intended to rebel against the shogun. When their leaders were ordered to commit suicide, they changed their minds, deciding to make their way to Kyoto and appeal to the court through Nariaki's son, Hitotsubashi Yoshinobu, the shogun's chief advisor. They started off over a thousand men strong, marching under banners that proclaimed "The Japanese Spirit," "Service to the nation," "Reverence and Expulsion," and "Execute the Imperial Decree." As they marched along in full armor they chanted Chinese poetry and shouted, "for the sake of the country." [33]

The Mito warriors took the Nakasendō through the mountains in the winter of 1864. They fought their way past Takasaki, then on the fifteenth day of the eleventh month they found themselves confronted by troops from three domains at Wada Pass. Seven men were killed. Yokota Tōsaburō, a youth of seventeen and a townsman, was grievously wounded. Realizing that he could not keep up, he asked his father to kill him and take his head lest his enemies capture it. Weakened by the cold and the battle, the Mito forces decided not to try to force the barrier at Kiso-Fukushima. Instead they took the Ina Road.

Iida was the only domain of any size to stand in the way of the Mito warriors. Zakōji was on the first line of defense because it straddled the Ina Road. Ordered to barricade their villages and arm themselves as best they could against the intruders, the peasants thought mainly of escape and spent their energies hiding the old people with the children and valuables in the mountains. The nativists sympathized with the Mito warriors, and they knew that among them were several Hirata disciples. To protect his village and save the lives of fellow believers, Taseko's cousin Inao came up with a plan to avoid a confrontation by guiding the Mito warriors along backroads around the castle town. Too ill to travel himself, he had his younger brother Imamura Toyosaburō go to the Mito camp to propose this plan, then Toyosaburō went to Iida, where he negotiated with officials there. He was given to understand that while the Iida authorities could not publicly accede to his proposal out of deference to the bakufu, they would be delighted if the Mito warriors kept out of sight. Toyosaburō then met with town officials who, in return for saving the town from fire and destruction, agreed to serve lunch to the Mito warriors and give them 3,000 *ryō*. Toyosaburō made the mistake of not collecting this money in advance or getting the promise in writing. Trying to cover this commitment once the danger was past drove him nearly to bankruptcy.

On the morning of the twenty-fourth day of the eleventh month, Inao took a palanquin to guide the Mito warriors along the roads through the foothills behind Iida. They stopped at a shrine for lunch, then went on south through Yamamoto to Komaba where they spent the night. One of the Hirata disciples left his diary of the trip with Taseko's son Mitsunaka.[34] Her eldest son Makoto also had an interview with the Mito leaders. His purpose was to dissuade them from continuing past the well-fortified barrier at Namiai and thence to the heavily guarded Owari domain. Instead they should double back to Yamamoto and go over the Seinaiji pass because the guards at its barrier had already received orders to let them through and the Hirata disciples on the other side would give them aid.

Makoto spent the night with the Mito warriors in Komaba. There he wrote a letter to his brothers-in-law, Ichioka Shigemasa and Hida Kurōbei, and to Hazama Hidenori.

> Tonight I was able to have a conversation with Fujita Kōshiro [one of the two leaders]. He filled my heart with joy by telling me everything that has happened since the righteous forces rose up. . . . They've suddenly decided to take the Kiso Road. Circumstances might change tomorrow, however, so it's difficult to predict what they'll do. In any case, they'll probably spend the night in your area on the twenty-sixth. I'm telling you this so you won't be surprised. Fujita was going to give me some of his poetry, but regrettably there's no decent paper to be had here. Once he arrives where you are, please make sure you get two or three poems for me. They're planning to go to Kyoto, and you must have your own sources of information regarding what's going on there so please help in that way as well.

In a postscript written the next morning Makoto added, "Rather than go to Kyoto, they'll probably take the army to Hida. . . . Please send someone along to guide them. This morning they gave me a spear as a parting gift. I was overwhelmed."[35]

"The announcement that the Mito warriors would spend the night here came without any warning," the sake brewer and post station official for Magome wrote in his diary. "Everyone rushed about in great confusion, and some fled to the countryside. They put their possessions in their storehouses and set guards over everything out to the back gates." No one could rest easy. All negotiations involving money and the revolving credit associations came to a complete stop.[36] The next day the Mito troops moved on to Nakatsugawa. Yokota Tōshiro asked Shigemasa and Hidenori to bury the head of his son that he had been carrying since the battle at Wada pass. They did so in the Hazama family graveyard in the middle of the night. Only after many years did they dare erect a gravestone for it. Other warriors gave them pieces of armor. Later the two men proudly had their portraits done showing them dressed in these items. Taseko's son-in-law Kurōbei joined them in scraping together 650 *ryō* and trying to issue a promissory note for an additional 350 *ryō* redeemable in Kyoto.[37]

The promissory note was never delivered. Just as Toyosaburō had been stopped when he tried to follow the Mito warriors with the money that he had promised them, so too did the nativists in Nakatsugawa find post station barriers closed against them once they finished drafting their note on the twenty-ninth.[38] On the thirtieth, Hitotsubashi Yoshinobu received permission from the court to suppress the Mito warriors. Twelve days later they learned that the man on whom they had pinned their hopes had raised an army against them. Exhausted and cold, they surrendered to Kaga domain on the sixteenth day of the twelfth month. After two miserable months, they were turned over to bakufu representatives, who promptly executed 352 of them, exiled another 100 and returned 130 to Mito. Once the pickled head of the leader had arrived home, his wife, daughter, son, and maid were executed, along with the family of his eldest son. The relatives of the other men suffered humiliation, ostracism, and poverty in revenge for having crippled Mito militarily and politically.[39]

For the Hirata disciples, this denouement was tragic indeed. Living scattered across the countryside without access to the level of military organization that would have allowed them to realize their own agenda, they had followed the flight of the Mito warriors as closely as their news sources would allow. In Ōmi Hachiman, Nishikawa Yoshisuke described their order of battle and drew pictures showing their banners. He copied the letter Inao wrote to the Iida domanial officials asking that the warriors be allowed safe passage, and he noted that Taseko's son from Tomono had a face-to-face interview with the leaders.[40] Kanetane wrote a letter to Inao, Makoto, and the men in Nakatsugawa praising them for their righteous handling of the situation.[41] Although some say that Taseko had urged Makoto to talk the Mito warriors into going over the pass into the Kiso Valley rather than run the risk of confronting Owari troops, she herself remained discreetly at home.

EVEN THOUGH she had to stay home, Taseko found ways to contribute to the loyalist cause. While she was in Kyoto, Yoshisuke had promised to shelter her in Ōmi Hachiman should fighting break out; now she offered a refuge to men who claimed to think as she did. In the social flux of the 1860s, young men from across Japan took advantage of the political turmoil to travel around the country observing local conditions. They talked of restoring the emperor to direct rule (*ōsei fukko*) in hopes of unifying the country against the foreign threat and rectifying the evils that plagued it internally. In going back and forth from Edo to Kyoto and beyond, they preferred to avoid trouble by taking unofficial roads such as the one that bisected the Ina Valley. For Hirata disciples the area had an additional advantage in that they could find food and lodging in the houses of their compatriots. Taseko's hospitality soon turned the Matsuo family into a link on an underground network stretching from western Japan to Edo.

The first man to take advantage of the welcome offered by the nativists of the Ina Valley was Tsunoda Tadayuki, Taseko's friend from Kyoto who took the credit for having thought up the plan to behead the Ashikaga shogun's statues.[42] Having fled to avoid arrest, he spent several days in Nakatsugawa. As an important post station on the Nakasendō, it frequently welcomed official guests, and it would not do to have a single man skulking about too long. On over the mountains in the Ina Valley Tadayuki hid out with the Kitahara, Katagiri and Matsuo families. By the time Taseko had returned from Kyoto, he was already familiar with her neighborhood.

Tadayuki spent close to two years in the Ina Valley, proselytizing, lecturing, and fanning the flames of antiforeign sentiment. Among his many manuscripts expounding Hirata Atsutane's teachings is one compiled at this time entitled "One hundred poems telling of the age of the gods."[43] On the night of the thirteenth day of the eighth month of 1863, a poster appeared at the end of a bridge in Iida: "It is utterly outrageous that Ōharaya Gonzō is selling silk to the barbarians. If he stops these transactions, he will be forgiven; if he does not, he will be punished with the vengeance of heaven."[44] This threat could have been crafted only by someone who had spent enough time in Kyoto to have become familiar with the rhetoric of assassination proclaimed on placards left with severed heads and decapitated statues. Iida domain immediately set spies to find out who was responsible, but to no avail. Tadayuki was safely beyond domanial boundaries across the river in Tomono.

Tadayuki spent many months living with the Matsuo family and became a lifelong friend. Hating to remain idle, he helped Taseko's son Makoto draw up a record of his sake-brewing transactions, though because of his short temper, the two often fought. He taught Taseko's youngest son Tameyoshi to read Chinese. Once he had Taseko shave the top of his head. She was standing behind him shaving away when he felt a tear fall on his cheek. His hair was so hard to cut that she was crying at the thought of how it must hurt to have the razor dragged through it, or so he once told his daughter. Years later Taseko was to make a pilgrimage to the Atsuta shrine near Nagoya, where Tadayuki was then the chief priest. Struck with nostalgia at seeing him again, she flung her arms around him crying, "Tsunoda-sama, you're looking well." Tadayuki turned bright red with embarrassment. "That was really in bad form," he complained. Impetuous as a youth, he had turned dignified with age. In 1914 he would be forced to resign his position because an underling had embezzled money. Thereafter the Matsuo family sent him a barrel of sake every other month to ensure that he always had his nightcap.[45]

Tadayuki was a big man with bright eyes who spoke impatiently in a loud voice. He habitually awoke extremely early, and except on the very coldest winter days he would immediately fling open the doors on the verandah to let in the fresh air. He was also a man of strong likes and dislikes. He hated Buddhism and he hated all things western. He never let the meat of a four-legged creature pass his lips, but he was extremely fond of whale meat. To the end of his life he refused to wear western dress except for one occasion when he had an audience with the emperor. For the most part he got along extremely well with the Matsuo family. He developed a strong antipathy to Nishikawa Yoshisuke, however, whom he accused of having revealed his Kyoto address to the authorities in 1863 despite having pretended to have undergone torture rather than betray his comrades.[46]

Tadayuki was still staying with Taseko when another loyalist arrived who needed a place to hide for a few months. This was Hara Yūsai, a low-ranking samurai from the neighboring province of Mikawa. Having joined Fujimoto Tesseki and others in their attack on the bakufu outpost at Gojō, he fled as soon as he realized the game was up, taking some of the money collected for military expenses with him. Armed with the information that the Matsuo family was willing to provide righteous men with food and shelter, he went to Tomono. There he changed his name and made a pretense of practicing medicine. He did quite well until Taseko's daughter Masa from Nakatsu-gawa came to be with her mother at the birth of her child. Her pregnancy was a hard one. "If it's all right with you, would you please look after my daughter?" Taseko asked. Her request forced Yūsai to admit that he lacked the medical knowledge he had claimed. Tadayuki started singing the praises of another man Taseko had met in Kyoto, the nativist doctor Gonda Naosuke. Yūsai decided he would like to study with him. He had Taseko write him a letter of introduction and off he went. "When he left, he said that he'd write us as soon as he got to Kawagoe," Taseko reported to her cousin Inao. "As yet we've heard not one word."[47] According to Inoue Yorikuni, Naosuke's disciple and the man later responsible for much of Taseko's fame, Yūsai did indeed end up with Naosuke in Edo. "When I went to my teacher's house in the eleventh month of 1864, I met Yūsai. He was extremely learned in Chinese studies, he had read the ancient books on medicine, and he was also well informed on current affairs, telling us all about everything that was going on in the domains."[48]

Yūsai visited Taseko at least once more. When he joined the Hirata school in 1866, he was sponsored by her son Makoto. That same year Nishikawa Yoshisuke reported in his record of correspondence that Yūsai had visited him bearing a letter of introduction from Takemura Taseko. The gist of their conversation was that several more loyalists had found it necessary to hide out in the Ina Valley.[49]

Owing to Taseko's reputation among the loyalists, the Matsuo family found itself greeting a steady stream of visitors. Taseko took them in, hiding them on the second floor of her house where she raised silkworms or boarding them in a nearby house that happened to be vacant. They were said to be completely unsuitable for farm work and they despised commerce. According to her daughter, Taseko begrudged them nothing. She gave them food and firewood, clothes and traveling expenses, wrote them letters of introduction, and did everything she could to sustain her sector of the underground railway. Among them were some samurai who had escaped from Mito following the civil war. They stayed next door and visited the Matsuo compound every morning asking for a light in their odd Mito accents.[50]

Taseko venerated the men who came seeking her help while they continued their struggle to rectify the government and expel the barbarians. One in particular was Muramatsu Bunzō. He was born the second son of a shrine official in Ise and later adopted into a peasant family. He escaped from village life in 1858 by going to Kyoto and devoting himself to the imperial cause. He fled the city when loyalists were being rounded up later that year, spent some time learning sword fighting in Edo, visited Mito, and then went back to Kyoto. There he met Fujimoto Tesseki but failed to join him for the rebellion at Gojō. He briefly joined the Mito forces encamped at Mt. Tsukuba. After they were dispersed, he landed in Edo where he narrowly evaded capture by bakufu spies. He went on the road again, this time in the disguise of a chanter for the puppet theater. He spent some months in Tomono before Taseko helped him get to Sanuki on the island of Shikoku. At his departure she wrote a poem in his honor:

Haritsumeshi	When a stout heart that like a bow
yatakegokoro no	has been pulled taut
kuni no tame	and then releases its arrow
ihanatsu toki wa	for the sake of the country
kokoro shitemashi	my heart vibrates too.[51]

To a jaundiced eye, some of the men whom Taseko helped appear distinctly unsavory. Hasegawa Tetsunojin, for example, was born the third son of a village headman in Echigo. Like Bunzō his birth order relieved him of the responsibility of succeeding his father but left him without a predetermined position in society. Taseko may have met him in Kyoto as they had friends there in common. He joined the Chōshū forces when they were ex-

pelled from the city then served as a messenger during their attempted coup
d'état in 1864. His travels following their defeat brought him to the Ina Valley
and the Matsuo house. He was black as iron, tall, with a broad face. He smoked
a huge pipe and drank sake by the gallon. When he got drunk, as he frequently did, he would whip out his long sword, wave it around, and sing at
the top of his lungs. He also liked vulgar poetry:

Hitoya naka	The only things that escape
dezuru mono	from prison
namida no hoka wa	besides tears
tada onara nomi	are farts.[52]

Despite his faults, Tetsunojin could claim to have fought on the loyalist side,
and he brought news of what was happening in the wider world to the Ina
Valley. Taseko's cousin Inao carefully copied his account of his experiences in
Chōshū, where he had briefly joined the peasant-samurai army being trained
in western-style arms.

Taseko's willingness to harbor anyone who pretended to be a loyalist
finally got the Matsuo family in trouble. In 1866 she received a man named
Hori Kenkichi introduced through a letter from the nativist doctor Gonda
Naosuke. He whiled away his time copying reports Taseko had received
from her banker Kuninori in Kyoto regarding the attempted coup d'état by
Chōshū forces in 1864. He then announced that he was going on to Kyoto to
work on Chōshū's behalf, at that time proclaimed an enemy of the court and
the object of a punitive expedition organized by the bakufu. Needing money
for his expenses, he proposed pawning his sword. Taseko's son Makoto found
a pawnbroker in Tomono willing to give him 13 *ryō* for it. Kenkichi cut off
his topknot, dressed himself as a peasant, collected a letter of introduction
from Makoto to Kuninori and set out for Iida. He spent several days in the
castle town's red light district having a wonderful time and spending every
mon he had. Instead of going to Kyoto, he went in the opposite direction to
Kōfu, where he hung around the brothels. There he caught the eye of bakufu
officials who arrested him for behaving suspiciously. In his baggage they
found the letter of introduction and the reports on Chōshū.

Thanks to the diary Makoto kept of his interrogation by bakufu officials
at the end of the sixth month of 1866, we can see how he tried to avoid im-
plicating himself or his mother in Kenkichi's activities:

"Did you know him before [he arrived on your doorstep]?"
"I'd never met him before."
"What made you decide to put him up?"

"We let him stay because he was carrying a letter of introduction from Gonda Naosuke." . . .

"Why are you friendly with this Gonda person?"

"I received medical treatment from him once when I was ill." [Makoto had met Naosuke at the Chōshū compound in Kyoto where Naosuke was hiding along with Taseko.]

"This man had a document that he'd copied from you concerning conditions in Chōshū. How did it come into your hands?"

"I'm embarrassed to admit this, but I really don't remember. Please take into consideration that it wasn't an official record."

"True, but there's no reason for someone of peasant status to come by such a thing, and yet you had it anyway."

"As I recall, it was just a bunch of rumors collected on the road."[53]

Thanks to the intercession by Tayasu domain officials, Makoto was allowed to go home after he had presented a written confession and apology. In this document he denied all knowledge of any report on conditions in Chōshū. "I have a number of sidelines in addition to farming. Many merchants come and go; perhaps one of them brought it. We've not been able to find it anywhere in the house, and I've certainly never owned such a thing."[54] This statement was disingenuous at best. For the rural entrepreneurs like Makoto, collecting information on domestic affairs had become an obsession in the 1860s. Given a bakufu policy that officially forbade publicizing current events and no newspapers, commoners who wanted to know what was going on had to rely on their own informal communications networks and compile reports culled from the rumors and letters that came their way. Makoto might well have collected news on what was happening in Chōshū anyway, but his mother's contacts had brought him the item that got him in trouble.

Having spent six weeks in the Chōshū compound, Taseko would have paid particular attention when the bakufu ordered two punitive expeditions against that domain. The first, which followed the attempted coup d'état of 1864, involved little fighting because Chōshū backed down and purged the men who had allowed the coup to take place. When Chōshū continued to build up its peasant army trained in western-style arms and to criticize the way the shogun handled the foreigners, the bakufu launched a second attack in 1866. It justified its action by having the emperor brand Chōshū an enemy of the court. Given her experiences in Kyoto, Taseko would surely have found this decree hard to believe. The expedition bogged down when Shogun Iemochi died in Osaka. The end of the year saw the sudden death of Emperor Kōmei.

Kōmei had moved farther and farther from the men who claimed to be acting out of loyalty to him in trying to expel the barbarians. In 1865 he issued a decree approving the foreign treaties in an effort to restore unity between court and bakufu. He urged the shogun to pursue its attack on Chōshū even after the daimyo from western domains wanted war to stop. To the end of his life he believed that the shogun had the responsibility to govern Japan, making him an obstacle to the men who had decided that the shogun must go. A large and vigorous man, Kōmei was only thirty-six when he died. His death was concealed even from the court for four days, leading to rumors that he had been poisoned, and his angry spirit was said to appear day and night near the new Emperor Meiji.[55] Taseko mourned his passing:

Yamagatsu mo	Even the very least of his subjects
nageki wabi keri	cried out in grief
sumeragi no	hearing that the emperor
kami no mikado	has departed for
miyuki aru to wa	the dwelling place of the gods.[56]

CHAPTER TWELVE

Kyoto, 1868

At Mt. Kagami
the clouds on my mind
have been dispelled
seeing the visage of
a world restored.[1]
MATSUO TASEKO, 1868

At the end of 1867 Chōshū and Satsuma, now allies instead of
enemies, gratefully acknowledged the decree they had received from the imperial court to attack the bakufu. Behind
their newfound amity lay months of negotiation and frustration on the part of samurai such as Sakamoto Ryōma, who tried
to cajole their daimyo into uniting against the very institution
that had guaranteed their rule. The shogun, the former Hitotsubashi Yoshinobu, promptly returned his patents of office
to the throne in a moving scene at Nijō Castle. Shortly thereafter he prevailed upon his troops to withdraw to Osaka. He
had, however, no intention of relinquishing his lands or his
court rank. Given the support he still enjoyed among bakufu allies, he could expect to dominate any new body established to advise the emperor on domestic and foreign affairs,
as his opponents well knew. Despite its appearance of being

ready to dissolve at any moment, the coalition arrayed against him managed to get an announcement issued on the ninth day of the twelfth month that in order to "restore the country's prestige," Emperor Meiji, then a boy of fifteen, was to head the Japanese government. The restoration of imperial rule was at hand.[2]

Where was Taseko while these momentous events were taking place? In a diary entry for the third day of 1868, Ichioka Shigemasa, her cousin from Nakatsugawa, noted that Matsuo Sajiemon Makoto, Takemura Taseko, and others had gone to Kyoto together, "promising to act as a shield for the emperor."[3] According to her youngest son Tameyoshi, her Kyoto banker Ikemura Kuninori wrote her a letter early in 1868 telling her how the combined Satsuma-Chōshū forces, using the new peasant-samurai army trained in western gunnery, had engaged the shogun's main army in battle outside Kyoto, also on the third. The news filled her with delight. Just three days after the battle began, she completed the new year's round of ceremonies with a purifying bath and set out with her eldest son for Kyoto. Her life's ambition had been achieved.[4]

There is also a letter from Iwasaki Nagayo in Iida written on the twenty-third day of 1868 to Taseko in Kyoto. It implies that she was already in the city before the battle outside Kyoto ended in defeat for the shogun's army and raises the possibility that she left the safety of her valley as soon as she received word that the shogun had resigned. If she saw him as a foe dangerous to her personally, it would make sense that she felt free to return to the imperial capital only after he was no longer in a position to do her harm. "Truly it's a matter for great rejoicing that as soon as the shogun renounced his office, the battleships sailed for the capital to enhance his majesty's prestige," Nagayo wrote. "I'm really envious that you were so fortunate as to see all this having chosen the right moment for your departure. My only regret is that when you left last year, I tried to stop you."[5]

Given these conflicting accounts, it is impossible to say when Taseko left for Kyoto. Perhaps in later years Tameyoshi confused a letter describing the battle with one announcing the restoration of imperial rule. Only a segment remains of the diary Taseko kept during this trip, and it begins six months after she arrived in the capital. For that reason, a narrative of what she did has to be gleaned from the recollections of people she knew and a sampling of her letters. These are both fascinating for the glimpses they allow of her and her times and frustrating because they always remain fragmentary. They survive only by accident. Taseko did not even keep track of her diaries, and she had to depend on her recipients to preserve what she sent to them. That even a few friends and relatives found it worthwhile to keep a woman's writings says more about the extraordinary times than whether they valued her as a person. Loss salts what is known of what she did.[6]

One of Taseko's letters further clouds the issue. Written on the eleventh day of the second month of 1868, it is addressed to Matsuo Sajiemon in Tomono and signed "mother."

> It turns out that Haida from Satsuma and two or three other people are leaving on the twelfth to go to Yamabuki for a meeting, and I'm sending just a word of warning now. It seems that the army's departure for the east is already imminent, and I've received word that Prince Arisugawa will be leaving on the fifteenth. Should Mr. Haida put in an appearance where you are, you, Sajiemon should go as far as Yamabuki to hear everything he has to say. He's really a good person and I've been able to talk to him freely. When I met him on the tenth, he said he wanted me to let you know as quickly as possible that on his trip to Yamabuki he would also like to stop by Tomono. He was really delighted when I said I'd forward his request in my next letter, so you must treat him very cordially. I hope you'll meet with him as soon as possible. I'm afraid he'll have time on his hands before Lord Zakōji returns so I'd like for you to return with him to Tomono. Besides, I think you'll enjoy his company if you speak to him freely so please take that into consideration as well.

In a postscript, she added: "You should know that I'm extremely busy on all sorts of matters."[7]

From this letter it appears that Makoto had left his mother in Kyoto while he made a brief trip back to Tomono. Shigemasa noted on the thirteenth day of the second month that "Matsuo of Tomono" stayed with him on his return from Takasu. On the fourteenth "Matsuo went to Kyoto."[8] If that is the case, Makoto probably left Tomono before the letter arrived. The person identified as Haida may be Hatta Tomonori, 1799–1873, a samurai from Satsuma who had studied poetry with Kagawa Kageki and numbered Atsutane and Kanetane among his correspondents.[9] Yamabuki was the home of Katagiri Harukazu, founder of the Hongaku shrine, and headquarters for the Zakōji family of bakufu bannermen, then trying desperately to distance themselves as quickly as possible from the shogun, their erstwhile lord. Prince Arisugawa had been made commander-in-chief of the imperial armies on the ninth. The man who carried this letter for Taseko, Ochiai Naoaki, was a friend of Gonda Naosuke, the nativist doctor whose letter of introduction had gotten Makoto into trouble in 1866. Naoaki and Naosuke had received orders from the court noble Iwakura Tomomi to prepare the way for the imperial army marching on Edo.[10]

This letter places Taseko in the thick of things. A gleam of self-importance can be glimpsed in the way she appraises her son of what she knows and who she knows. In contrast to 1862–63, she and her friends could openly walk the streets of Kyoto and meet anyone willing to receive them without running afoul of bakufu police. But while she was renewing her acquaintance with her friends among the Hirata disciples and through them meeting men important to Japan's future, the stage was being set for yet another tragedy.

The victory over the shogun's forces at the battle outside Kyoto followed by the capture of Osaka Castle left the troops under the imperial banner in control of western Japan while the former shogun retreated to Edo. The men who spoke in the emperor's name tried to maintain their coalition against the bakufu and convince foreign diplomats to recognize the new government. Getting an army ready to fight was expensive, the fledgling government required its own funds, and the various factions competed among themselves to find the money they needed. The Kyoto pawnbroker Kagiya Chōjirō reported on the ninth day of the first month that Satsuma troops were already asking the townspeople of Kyoto to donate 20,000 *ryō* to the war effort. The emperor's maternal grandfather, Nakayama Tadayasu, appointed the Ōmi fertilizer merchant Nishikawa Yoshisuke to be the fundraiser for the region around Kyoto on behalf of the imperial court.[11] Not until early in the third month did the vanguard of the new imperial army actually leave the Kyoto area. In the meantime, court nobles anxious to prove themselves worthy of the emperor's favor had joined militia commanders who promised them the honor of being first to pacify the east. Among them was a man known to Taseko as Sagara Sōzō.

Sōzō had already tried fomenting disorder in Edo at the end of 1867 at the behest of Saigō Takamori, the Satsuma military commander.[12] Sōzō had no long-standing connection with Takamori; in fact he was not a samurai at all. As with so many of Taseko's friends, he came from a wealthy rural family with samurai pretensions. By the time Sōzō was twenty in 1858, his leadership qualities had already attracted almost a hundred men to accept his instruction in nativism and the martial arts. For a time he joined the Mito radicals fortified on Mt. Tsukuba, though he left before they had begun their doomed journey westward through the mountains. He ended up in Kyoto in 1866 where he managed to meet a number of prominent Satsuma samurai, including Takamori and Ōkubo Toshimichi.[13] At some point he also met Taseko.

When and where Sōzō got to know Taseko is unknown. It may have been in Kyoto in 1862, though she makes no mention of him in her diary. It may have been later. Sōzō traveled a great deal in the 1860s, often using an assumed name, and he might well have hidden out in the Ina Valley. While Makoto was in Edo in 1866 trying to get Tomono's post horse levy reduced and evading the consequences of having sheltered a miscreant, he happened to meet Sōzō and later received a letter from him. "Should you have occasion to send tidings back home, please report to your respected mother that for various reasons I returned to the capital without visiting your area. I had been quite concerned that she might be suspicious of me, but since I spoke to you the other day, I feel that the matter has resolved itself." [14] Sōzō also knew the nativists in Nakatsugawa and the Ina Valley through travel and connections to the Hirata school. His familiarity with this terrain may well have affected his course of action in 1868.

From the end of 1867 through the early months of 1868, a number of would-be samurai organized militia in support of the court or the bakufu. [15] Takamori sent Sōzō to Ōmi for that purpose with 100 *ryō* and a quantity of small arms. The men whom Sōzō recruited called themselves the *Sekihōtai*, "the brigade that offers the red heart of patriotism in service to the emperor." Just as the main body of the imperial army was placed under the nominal command of an imperial prince, so too was the brigade commanded by two minor court nobles. On the ninth day of the first month, Sōzō returned to Kyoto to ask the court for formal recognition as a vanguard unit of the imperial army. The court authorized the creation of the brigade after the fact, but refused to give Sōzō the brocade banner that would have bestowed official sanction. That would have to wait until the regular army marched east. Sōzō was further instructed to attach his brigade to the army taking the coastal road, the Tōkaidō.

The first month of 1868 was a period of transition and instability for the new government. Lines of command remained vague, irregular appointments were made, and political opportunism was the order of the day. While Sōzō was negotiating for official recognition in Kyoto, he may have well heard rumors that the court had decided to lower taxes in order to gain popular support. In the meantime, his brigade and the two court nobles convinced the domains lying in their path to give them arms. Flushed with success, they started moving up the Nakasendō, which is where Sōzō caught up with them. That first night and at every stop thereafter he erected a signboard announcing that the emperor had been restored to power, the land tax would be halved, and anyone who needed assistance would receive help from the court. This was to apply not only in bakufu lands but in domanial lands as well. Naturally enough, this announcement met with considerable dismay on the part of administrators (who considered the current tax rate far from adequate) and great rejoicing on the part of the peasants. The brigade's ranks swelled with each passing day.

Still concerned that he had not received public authorization, Sōzō sent a messenger to Kyoto at the end of the first month asking that he be allowed to take the brigade up the Nakasendō where he knew the people and the land. His answer was an order to return to Kyoto. He and his followers feared that if they obeyed, the brigade would be disbanded and the leaders imprisoned. The two court nobles fled, and many members of the troop deserted. Determined to win the honor of being the first to enter the Kanto plain at the head of the imperial army, Sōzō pushed forward. He believed that if he could capture the important pass at Usui, his disobedience would be forgiven and forgotten in the flush of victory.

Sōzō spent his first night in the Ina Valley at a temple in Yamamoto.[16] There he sent letters to the local notables and village officials asking for supplies and men. "We already know to what extent you have devoted your red hearts in loyal service to the emperor," he wrote in a letter addressed to Makoto. "At this great opportunity to restore the ancient imperial system of rule we ask for you to exhaust your strength once more in bringing this matter to a speedy conclusion. The two court nobles Ayanokōji and Shiganoi make this their sincere request as well, so please help us in raising troops."[17] Makoto was in Kyoto, but his younger brother Mitsunaka in Yamamoto found some men later discovered to be gamblers and vagrants who were willing to join the brigade. Most of the men who provided provisions were Hirata disciples.[18]

Sōzō set up camp at Lake Suwa on the sixth day of the second month. He sent messengers to nearby domains ordering them to submit to imperial authority, a command they cravenly obeyed. He reorganized and disciplined his troops, and he sent frequent reports on his activities to the headquarters of the regular imperial army. During this time, his friends in Kyoto wrote letters urging him to return. At one point he rushed frantically back down the Nakasendō, hoping to find someone to whom he could explain himself, but without success. In the meantime the troops encamped at Suwa learned that they had been branded a false imperial army. Other men whom Sōzō had sent to recruit soldiers knew nothing of this. They led their new troops against the guards at Usui pass and captured it in the name of the emperor. In a counterattack launched by the same domains that had earlier submitted to Sōzō but which were now embarrassed at having been duped, most of the new troops were killed or captured. When Sōzō returned to Suwa on the twenty-third, he appealed to Saigō Takamori to clarify his position. An exchange of letters settled nothing.

The end came swiftly. On the evening of first day of the third month Sōzō

was summoned to meet with Iwakura Tomisada, the commander of the imperial army for the Nakasendō. Thinking he was to join the regular army, he
went gladly with one attendant, only to be arrested as soon as he entered the
compound. The sixty men who had stood by him were likewise summoned
by Tomisada in groups of two or three, stripped of their arms, and tied to the
trees in the Suwa shrine precincts in a freezing rain to await the dawn. On
the evening of the third, Sōzō and seven of his closest followers were beheaded without ever seeing or being seen by Tomisada and his staff, without
any investigation or interrogation. In the announcement of the executions,
Sōzō's crimes were defined as having disobeyed orders and allowed men
under his command to steal. The promise to halve taxes was carefully left
unmentioned.[19] The day after his execution, the military high command
put Owari domain in charge of administering bakufu lands in Shinano and
ordered it to collect the land tax in full.[20] Taseko was shocked. In a letter to
her daughter-in-law she wrote, "worse things have happened than I ever
expected." [21]

Like the Mito warriors or the Hirata disciples who had beheaded the statues of the Ashikaga shoguns, Sōzō assumed that zeal on behalf of the imperial court justified itself. Haga Noboru points out that the popular hero Saigō
Takamori used Sōzō to rally popular support, then when the brigade made
inconvenient promises and got in the way of the regular army, he betrayed
and abandoned him. Samurai egoism may have come into play as well, in
the form of jealousy over who was to be the vanguard, traditionally the most
prestigious position.[22] On the other hand, an old 1600 law had warned that
if in battle any individual advanced in secret to put himself in the lead, he
was to be executed.[23] Sōzō's former comrades-in-arms Gonda Naosuke and
Ochiai Naoaki blamed Iwakura Tomomi for his death. They planned to assassinate him, but he talked them out of it.[24] Later, when Naoaki was chief
secretary for Ina prefecture in 1870, he, Makoto, Taseko's cousin Inao, and
other local men petitioned the government for permission to raise a monument over Sōzō's grave and solicited contributions from nearby nativists.
Among those who responded was Taseko.[25]

Sōzō's fate constituted a warning to all grass-roots activists. Historians
have long decried the lack of national consciousness among the commoners
who remained largely apathetic to the conflict between court and bakufu
that decided the future of their country. The imperial cause in particular apparently attracted little popular allegiance. For the most part, however, the
samurai commanders from the southwestern domains who led the troops that
overthrew the bakufu disdained commoners' offers of anything but money.
Kido Takayoshi even accused the militias of harming the state.[26] Given their
vulnerability to use and abuse by samurai strategists, the only option for

dedicated loyalists was to play a subordinate role to the new imperial armies. This was the path taken by Taseko's son Makoto.

MAKOTO USED connections developed by his mother in gaining new opportunities for himself. The crucial figure was Tsunoda Tadayuki, who had changed his name and returned to Kyoto in 1866. There he managed to attach himself to the Sawa family of court nobles. Their stipend was a mere thirty *koku*. Upon receiving the announcement that imperial rule had been restored, Ina Valley nativists sent Tadayuki 300 *ryō* as thanks for his efforts on behalf of the imperial cause. Tadayuki offered some of this money to the Sawa house and used the rest to help samurai who had absconded from their domains. Before he left at the end of the first month with Sawa Nobuyoshi, commander of the punitive expedition against bakufu supporters in Kyushu, he introduced Taseko to the Sawa compound. When Sawa Tamekazu was appointed vice-general for the imperial army sent to pacify the northeast, Taseko found positions for Makoto and Inao's son Kitahara Nobutsuna on his staff.

The army sent to pacify northeastern Japan was to fight the bakufu's staunchest supporters. On the second day of the third month it left Kyoto for Osaka; on the eleventh it set sail for Matsushima near Sendai. Taseko wrote numerous poems celebrating its departure and encouraging Makoto and Nobutsuna to excel:

Michinoku no	Purge the north of
uwara shikogusa	thorns and weeds
uchiharai	dress yourselves
hana no nishiki wo	in a rainbow of flowers
mi ni matoite yo	load yourselves with honors.[27]

Taseko wrote her first letter to her son just four days later. "I opened and read your two letters from Osaka the other day as quickly as possible. . . . Please do your best now that you have been so highly favored with the opportunity to serve close to where the most exalted men above the clouds may be seen, in the company of the great warriors of today." Most of the letter contained news of what other people were doing, but she also talked about herself: "After you left, all sorts of people came to tell me things, and I've been very busy living my life from day to day. . . . I hear rumors that there's a lot of turmoil in the east. I fervently hope that you're taking every precaution to stay on your guard. . . . I get envious when I think about how well you've been treated by everyone and how you've been to nothing but really interesting places."[28]

Taseko decided that she had to stay in Kyoto so long as her son and young cousin remained with the army. In contrast to the rest of Japan where daimyo either rushed to proclaim their newfound loyalty to the emperor or like Iida remained neutral, the daimyo in the northeast and in Echigo along the Japan Sea had a long-standing antipathy to the southwestern domains that now claimed to speak in the emperor's name.[29] When the apology and surrender offered by Matsudaira Katamori of Aizu, the bakufu's chief mainstay and former Kyoto Protector, was rejected, he and his supporters had decided that the only honorable course remaining to them was to fight. With no battlefield correspondents to report on the war, the rumors that reached the countryside tended to exaggerate the severity of the fighting and the number of the dead. Through her friends and connections in Kyoto, Taseko had access to much more reliable sources. The news garnered from them she passed on to the Kitahara house in Zakōji and her own family in Tomono.

"It's difficult to know what's going on given all the rumors," she wrote to her daughter-in-law who had been left in charge of the house. "I'm extremely grateful that I'm informed every time there's news from the Sawa camp." She noted that despite a constant stream of reinforcements being sent to the northeast, the political situation remained unsettled. She also discussed the currency inflation that plagued both Kyoto and the Ina Valley, showing a grasp of the political situation rare in letters written by the women of this period.[30] Her lack of discretion can be explained in part by her concern for her son and the Matsuo family economy, but with advancing age, she was also becoming much more forthright in writing down her thoughts.

During the nine months that Makoto served the imperial army sent to pacify the northeast, he called himself Shōshi, an ancient term meaning "estate manager." By changing his name, he changed his identity from that of the ordinary village official represented in the name Sajiemon to the imperial subject of antiquity. Taseko proudly recognized his achievement by using his new name in her correspondence. "A number of people have borrowed the letters you sent," she wrote at the end of the seventh month. "Even though I'd wanted to forward them home, I'm in a bind because other people have them all." Two months later she mentioned that Iwakura Tomomi, a central figure in the new government, had asked for proof of Makoto's commission. She had been unable to get confirmation from the Sawa household because the officials in charge of personnel were all in the field. "'In that case,'" Tomomi replied, "'once you've returned to your home, you and Shōshi should search everywhere you can and then send it straight to me. Please keep in mind that it has to be in the name of 'the estate manager of Tomono in the Takasu domain.'" She signed her letters, "your mother Takemura."[31]

Taseko did her own bit to contribute to the success of the imperial armies.

When detachments of men from Owari domain went to occupy Shinano in the intercalary fourth month, the leader of the troop dispatched to Iida used intermediaries from the Takasu domain to ask Taseko to recommend trustworthy guides. (The daimyo of Owari was the eldest son of the Takasu daimyo.) Taseko proposed her son Mitsunaka and sent a note asking Kurazawa Kiyonari, the most important Hirata disciple in the upper Ina Valley, to consult with her regarding others: "I'd like to discuss this matter with you since you're also from my home district in order to figure out how to deal with this request. Please come see me right away. I'm impatiently awaiting you."[32] It is remarkable that a solicitation for guides went through a woman, especially when a local notable like Kiyonari was right there in Kyoto. Perhaps he was overlooked because he came from a domain with no connection to Owari, or in the particular circumstances of Kyoto at that time, Taseko had more visibility. A few months later she received a commendation for her efforts: "When Tamiya Joun [from Owari] set out on horseback, you exerted yourself to have Takemura Taemon [Mitsunaka] and others submit to his command. For this you are to be given a roll of cotton by the emperor's attendants."[33] At the end of the year, Owari gave her a thirty-man stipend, that is, the amount officially required to support thirty men for one year, in recognition that "you have devoted yourself to serving the emperor for many years, and you have provided various services for this house as well."[34]

Taseko used her nativist connections to meet new and important people. The nativist doctor Gonda Naosuke, with whom she had been concealed in the Chōshū compound, introduced her to Gojō Tameshige, a court noble who took advantage of the restoration of imperial rule to gain a position of power that his rank would normally never have allowed him. Hara Yūsai, whom Taseko had befriended when he needed a place to stay but who had been unable to doctor her daughter, is probably the person who introduced her to Iwakura Tomomi. Tomomi had emerged as the chief liaison between the court and the warriors from Satsuma and Chōshū who led the armies in the emperor's name, and he had drafted the edict summoning loyal daimyo to overthrow the bakufu.[35] For a man such as him to agree to meet an old peasant woman suggests just how extraordinary the times really were. In 1862 Taseko's interest in poetry had provided her with the excuse for introductions to court nobles; in 1868, she met them in her guise as an imperial loyalist.

Taseko used her newfound acquaintances to help some samurai establish their credentials as the emperor's loyal subjects. This was a particularly necessary and delicate task for the bakufu bannermen. Zakōji Tametomo from Yamabuki, site of the Hongaku shrine, had Taseko introduce him to all the im-

portant people she knew.[36] His hereditary obligations to the shogun notwith-
standing, Kondō Masatoshi, whose fief included Yamamoto, had fled Edo
on the tenth of the second month. This was two days before Yoshinobu had
moved out of Edo Castle and a month before his representative surrendered
the city to Saigō Takamori. As soon as Masatoshi reached Yamamoto, he sent
his retainers to volunteer his services to the imperial armies. At the end of
the third month, accompanied by his chief retainers and Taseko's grandson
who served as his page, he appeared in Kyoto to demonstrate his desire to
serve the emperor. Taseko complained in a long letter to her daughter-in-
law that she had to go far out of her way to answer his summons for an audience. Another bannerman, a Mr. Tsubouchi, also asked Taseko for help. "To
have people I never expected make such requests has really kept me busy."
Through introductions by Taseko and others, Masatoshi managed to meet
Tomomi and various court nobles. They put him to work procuring money
and supplies as well as raising troops. After he had donated 1,000 *ryō* to the
war effort, he received confirmation of his domain. He made a second donation of an equal amount at the end of the seventh month. Having proven his
sincerity, he was allowed to return to Yamamoto.[37]

At the end of the tenth month, Taseko found herself invited to a banquet
by the lord of Iwamurada, Naitō Masakoto. Also in attendance was Gojō
Tameshige. Masakoto had been a *fudai* daimyo, one of the shogun's trusted
allies with a small domain worth just over 15,000 *koku*. Like Kondō Masatoshi, he had been in Edo at the announcement of the imperial restoration.
His delay in offering his services to the new government had led to his being
ordered into house confinement. Tsunoda Tadayuki, originally from Iwamurada, had worked to get him released, and Taseko had lent her efforts to
his. The banquet, which lasted from two in the afternoon until ten in the
evening, was his way of celebrating his freedom and thanking his supporters.
"There was nothing to complain of in the entertainment they provided for
me," Taseko noted in her diary. To her daughter-in-law she wrote, "truly, really, I'm amazed at all I've received."[38] She was there not as an entertainer or
even a poet but because she had achieved a position of influence far beyond
her wildest dreams.

Taseko helped a number of men who had little experience in dealing with
Kyoto. No one knew what the new government would do next or what its attitude would be toward former bakufu allies. For that reason, many daimyo
felt that it behooved them to have men on hand to gather information and
protect their interests. Most spent their time drinking and carousing; indeed
it was only through these activities that they could pry news out of government officials or help their domains. Taseko's stay in Kyoto in 1862–63 had
provided her with the credentials of a proven loyalist and given her access to

men who could get things done. Because Tomono was in the Takasu domain, its officials quickly moved to appoint her its agent. Part of her stay in Kyoto was subsidized by Takasu, and she lived for a few months with a Takasu samurai, Matsuoka Toshinori. When her grandson arrived with Kondō Masatoshi, he too boarded with Toshinori while he studied reading and swordfighting. "I'm busy every morning with my daily chores and seeing Mr. Matsuoka off to his office. I'm finding much more to occupy my time than when I was here before."[39]

In a government dominated by Chōshū and Satsuma, men from other domains had to struggle to find position. "You'll be delighted to hear and relieved to know that Takasu domain has been ordered to patrol the streets of Kyoto," Taseko wrote her son in the third month. "Mr. Matsuoka says that things are so busy at the office that he's been working into the night every night." Four months later he received an official appointment to the central government, "just like a Chōshū samurai. This has given me a great deal of unexpected pleasure." He joined another of Taseko's old friends from 1863 in the police department, positions for which Taseko had recommended them. Kakehi Mototada, also from Takasu, used her name to get a position in the bureaucracy, then later became a superintendent in the Greater Nippon Beer Company.[40] All of these men remained friends with Taseko for many years afterwards. Toshinori's younger brother would later marry one of Taseko's Kitahara cousins, and Taseko continued to exchange greetings with the Kakehi family until shortly before she died.[41]

Taseko managed to place seven men in the new central government, and many more asked for her help. "It really puts me on the spot when people come and I can't do anything for them," she wrote her daughter-in-law.

> People like Mr. Kawase [perhaps her former tea master] have come to see me with all sorts of requests, and I'm at my wits' end. I can have well-known men with a reputation for righteousness talk to someone and somehow or other they can quickly be found employment. People with no reputation are the ones who really cause me trouble. I can definitely guarantee acceptance into the Hirata school, but that's all. . . . He needs to realize that it's in his best interests to give up his plans. I really don't know what to do about all the men who come here from the countryside thinking that if only they get to Kyoto, they'll be able to do something.[42]

A handful of Hirata disciples from the Ina Valley appeared in Kyoto around the same time, hoping to offer their services to the emperor. Little came of their efforts.[43] Their failure suggests that at least in some cases, the dearth of commoner participation in the new government can be blamed less on their passivity than on elite indifference.

It probably required more than just a word from Taseko for an aspirant to find a position. Usually job seekers would pull every string they could, hoping that one would land them the crucial introduction to the men with patronage. Taseko's chief biographer, Ichimura Minato, complained in 1915 that some of the people Taseko had recommended in 1868 and 1869 preferred to forget all about her. "Over the past three or four years I've been visiting people who knew her, and I've met a number like that. There are even a few who say, 'the very idea that I might have received help from a peasant woman is ridiculous.'"[44]

Some of Taseko's friends among the Hirata disciples sought not employment with the new government but a change in customary practice. As far as they were concerned, the end of bakufu rule meant release from its tiresome religious restrictions, particularly the law that everyone had to be registered at a Buddhist temple at birth and receive a Buddhist funeral at death. In 1865 Taseko's acquaintance from the northern Ina Valley, Kurazawa Kiyonari, had gotten himself made a retainer of the Shirakawa family in charge of Shinto ceremonies in order to take his family's name off the Buddhist census records. His local temple refused to comply, insisting that Kiyonari had to be registered where he lived. The next year Kiyonari appealed to the bakufu magistrate in charge of temples and shrines for permission to be registered at a Shinto shrine and receive a Shinto funeral. The magistrate agreed, but his temple, backed by four hundred others, launched a fierce countersuit. The conflict dragged on until 1868, costing the Kurazawa family a great deal of its assets. Kiyonari's reason for coming to Kyoto was thus to petition the authorities to allow Shinto funerals as a demonstration that the state was committed to the return to ancient ways.[45] Hazama Hidenori from Nakatsugawa presented a similar petition four days after Kiyonari's was accepted. During the months that Kiyonari and Hidenori worked on their case, they met frequently with Taseko, sometimes on visits to their teacher Hirata Kanetane, sometimes exchanging cups of sake while viewing the moon, sometimes going to poetry meetings. An excerpt from Hidenori's diary: "Ninth day of the ninth month. Yonegawa [Tsunoda Tadayuki], Matsuoka, Tase and Morooka came to see me. They went home that night completely drunk."[46]

The daimyo of Tsuwano had ordered all funerals performed in his domain to be done at Shinto shrines as early as 1844. He was encouraged in this by Taseko's acquaintance from 1862, Fukuba Bisei. In 1868, when this daimyo got himself appointed to the new Office of Rites, he had his decree adopted as a nationwide policy. Historians have seen it as one example of how the ruling authorities, determined to promote an emperor-centered ideology, attacked the Buddhist institutions and their social organization.[47] In the Ina Valley and Nakatsugawa, this top-down directive was preceded by a grassroots initiative. A Buddhist priest from Magome went to Kiso-Fukushima to perform a Shinto funeral in 1862, a deed that got him into trouble the following year.[48] Katagiri Harukazu who planned the Hongaku shrine had a Shinto funeral in 1866 as did Taseko's friend Hara Sugako in 1867.[49] Although a number of Taseko's friends petitioned for permission to perform Shinto funerals, she did not. It was not a woman's place to make public decisions that would have lasting consequences not just for the individual but for the entire family. By the time Makoto, the Matsuo family head, had returned to Kyoto at the end of 1868, the change in government policy had taken away the necessity to appeal. That same year the Matsuo family left its local Buddhist temple.[50] Even today the Matsuo and Kitahara families continue to remember their dead not with Buddhist memorial tablets (*ihai*), but with Shinto spirit markers (*rei-i*).[51]

The ceremonial observances surrounding the emperor were largely created anew following his restoration to direct rule, and Taseko's diary shows that she was there at their birth. In the eighth month she went to the lower Kamo shrine to await the imperial procession, now routinized since Emperor Kōmei had overturned two centuries of precedent by his visit in 1863. She happened upon two of Lord Shirakawa's children who to her great delight invited her to sit with them and fed her delicacies and sake. She noted the emperor's coming of age ceremony on the twenty-seventh, his visit to the imperial mausoleums the next day, and his observation of army field exercises at the end of the month, actions unthinkable just a year earlier.[52] Performed primarily for a domestic audience, these occasions marked the beginning of efforts on the part of government leaders to "utilize public ritual as a means of effecting or exercising power."[53] Taseko was suitably impressed.

During these months in Kyoto, Taseko spent much time with old friends. The Hirata disciples continued to meet together, sometimes with a representative of the Hirata house, but more often by themselves. As they had in the past, they held poetry meetings where they discussed contemporary events. Taseko's diary begins with an entry for the first day of the sixth month when she and Hazama Hidenori sang, drank, and jested at a restaurant overlooking the Kamo River. On her way home she stopped to see the Chōshū samurai Shinagawa Yajirō, one of the men she had met at the Chōshū compound in 1863. "We chatted for awhile, and I asked about what was going on in the northeast."[54] According to Hidenori's diary, they had first paid a visit to the lower Kamo shrine. There one of Taseko's protégés had joined the guards organized to protect the grounds should the imperial family ever have to flee the palace.[55] While she was living with Matsuoka Toshinori, she invited the court noble Gojō Tameshige to a moon-viewing party along with the nativist doctor Gonda Naosuke and his disciple Inoue Yorikuni. At the height of the party Tameshige began to recite Song dynasty poetry at the top of his lungs. For Yorikuni it was a truly memorable occasion.

Taseko also played the tourist, though she did much less sightseeing than she had six years earlier. Late in the sixth month she went to the festival for Kusunoki Masashige, the great loyalist hero who died fighting the Ashikaga shoguns on behalf of Emperor Godaigo. Her only diary entry for the seventh month describes horse racing at the Kamo shrine. "We borrowed straw mats, ate some pickles and had a drop or two of sake. The gentlemen who rode the horses were extremely elegant. It caused me great pain to see among them a horse forced to carry a foreign saddle." [56]

A month later Hidenori reported that Taseko had been summoned to the Justice Department and questioned regarding the "Nagasawa affair." [57] Nagasawa is not a prominent name in this period of Japanese history. Hidenori gave no further details, nor did Taseko ever mention anything of the kind in her diary or letters. It was highly unusual for a woman to be summoned by government officials unless she had done something wrong, and Taseko's role in this case remains completely obscure. Perhaps it has never been investigated because it reflects ill on her, but more likely it has never occurred to any of her biographers that as a woman she would have been summoned by so public a tribunal.

Taseko had been in Kyoto for over eight months before she found a position for herself in the household of Lord Iwakura Tomomi, 1825–83, one of the leading architects of the Meiji Restoration. As the court gained in importance during the 1860s, nobles who took a positive attitude toward enhancing the emperor's prominence expanded the size of their households by incorporating the grass-roots loyalists. Tsunoda Tadayuki served the Sawa family. Hazama Hidenori likewise found a place for himself in the Shirakawa household. In this way men with no family history of court connections were able to satisfy their longing to serve the emperor, and the nobles had retinues that reflected their newfound status. For Taseko as well, serving the Iwakura family afforded her the opportunity to demonstrate her loyalty to the emperor.

Taseko stayed in the Iwakura household for six months while Tomomi accompanied the emperor to the eastern capital of Tokyo. That procession included 3,300 attendants and distributed 3,500 barrels of sake to the spectators en route.[58] Taseko assured Tami, her daughter-in-law, that she had really not planned to stay so long, and she apologized profusely for the inconvenience she had caused by her decision. "I realize that it's indeed too bad that I've been absent for such a long time, but please put up with me for just a little while longer. . . . I'm sure you'd have a lot for me to do with all your comings and goings. Since I'm thankfully being put to work here, however, please bear with the situation." She also asked Tami to send her more clothing. Soon after she first arrived in the city, Tami had sent baggage for her; after all, it would have been difficult for Taseko to carry everything she needed on her back. Now that she had a regular position, she needed more formal attire. "I'm waiting for you to send me my jacket done in wrinkled cotton with the stripes like you'd said you would." A month later she reciprocated by sending some fabric remnants for Tami and her daughters to use in decorating their collars and sleeve openings, and she promised once again to return home sooner or later.[59]

While serving in the Iwakura mansion, Taseko kept an eye on her grandsons, then in the city to gain education and experience. When the westernizing proponent Yokoi Shōnan was assassinated early in 1869, the authorities rounded up everyone who might have been implicated. For fear she might be arrested, one of Taseko's friends from her earlier days in Kyoto talked her into hiding in Osaka with her grandsons, or at least so Ichioka Masaka recalled years later.[60] Being less burdened than his grandmother by obligations to the nobility, he, Taseko's other grandson Chiburu, and their cousin Kitahara Nobutsuna stayed through the end of the first month of 1869, then took a leisurely trip home, repeating the route Taseko and his grandfather Shigemasa had taken in 1863.

Nobutsuna had earlier come safely back to Kyoto with Makoto and the rest of the imperial army. Makoto returned to Tomono as soon as he was discharged. As a reward for his services, he received 50 *ryō* from the Military Affairs Ministry and a ceremonial court robe from Sawa Tamekazu, his commanding officer. Taseko continued to live in the Iwakura compound, however, because Tomomi had remained in Tokyo to prepare for moving the central administration there.

Taseko joined the crowds of Kyoto townspeople who flocked to watch the emperor return to his city at the end of the 1868. She was still there to witness the mighty procession surrounding the enclosed palanquin as tall as a room topped by a phoenix that marked his final departure in the third month of 1869.[61] He and his court had lived in Kyoto for over a thousand years; their ancestors were buried in the graveyards that ringed the city, and their poetry had bestowed meaning on its landscape. If Osaka had been Japan's chief trading city and Edo its government headquarters for over 260 years,

Kyoto had been known for scholarship, high culture, and taste because it housed the court, a function it would perform no longer. Having witnessed the end of an era, Taseko like so many loyalists left for home.

When Taseko reached Nakatsugawa, she discovered that her oldest daughter, Masa, was ill. She died at the end of the fourth month at the age thirty-six, and Taseko was there to the last.

TASEKO TOOK a much more public role in 1868 than she ever had before. The Meiji Restoration enabled her to remake her identity several times over, from peasant wife, to poet, to woman of influence. This process links her to men such as Tsunoda Tadayuki who went from shrine priest to sword fighter to government bureaucrat. For a brief moment even her son had the chance to become a servant to the emperor. Festivals were recast; shrines were rebuilt to conform to the holy and anachronistic style deemed appropriate for a return to imperial rule. In all cases a reaction later set in and the pendulum swung back, for Tadayuki as well as for Taseko. Before it did, however, the new age brought new opportunities.

Historians have long debated what the Meiji Restoration really meant. Some have so far rejected its revolutionary implications as to deem it nothing more than a "transition." [62] I disagree. Its beginnings were already present in the 1850s when young men started to leave their domains and their fathers' way of life in search of a means to have an impact on bakufu policy decisions regarding the foreigners. Its transformative connotations can be seen in Taseko's decision to abscond from her family in going to Kyoto in 1862. By 1868 it contained the potential for everyone and everything that came in contact with the center to become something other than what had been before. It took time for the waves of change to spread across Japan, but ultimately universal education, new venues for work, and new modes of transportation meant that even peasant women led lives different from their mothers.

CHAPTER THIRTEEN

Famous Friends

On the last blade of grass
unworthy of being counted
the grace of words
fallen from on high
fills me with joy.
MATSUO TASEKO, 1882[1]

Taseko took full advantage of her trips to the center, first to Kyoto and then later to the new capital at Tokyo (formerly Edo), to expand her range of acquaintances beyond her own valley and even beyond the network of Hirata disciples. They proved useful connections in gaining her political influence. Such people also introduced her to a more rarefied lifestyle than she had ever before experienced and provide the best evidence we have of her friendships with other women. Among the many people she met, three in particular were to have a lasting impact on her life and reputation: Iwakura Tomomi, Miwada Masako, and Shinagawa Yajirō. Aside from Masako's biographical essays, these friendships attracted scant public attention, and none receive mention in the biographies written about Tomomi and Yajirō or in their published papers.[2] Were it not for the evidence of Taseko's own letters and a few of her poems, it would be hard to credit that they ever existed at all.

The largest claims for Taseko's connection with Iwakura Tomomi, the court noble and central figure in the early Meiji government, come from Inoue Yorikuni, the man chiefly responsible for having her receive posthumous court rank in 1903. His mentor, the nativist doctor and student of Japanese folk medicine, Gonda Naosuke, had met Taseko in Kyoto in 1863. Together they hid in the Chōshū mansion following the arrest of men deemed responsible for decapitating the Ashikaga shoguns' statues. Sharing the same quarters, indeed the same room, they had plenty of time to trade stories about what they had done. In the years that followed, Taseko's name became familiar to Yorikuni. It is through him that we have the story of how Hara Yūsai was forced to admit ignorance when Taseko asked him to treat her pregnant daughter. Yorikuni did not meet Taseko himself until he accompanied Naosuke to Kyoto in 1868. Yet he confidently asserted that she met Tomomi in 1862 and saved his life.

Tomomi figures prominently in all histories of the Meiji Restoration, primarily because he played a key role in bringing together various factions to overthrow the bakufu and support the new government. In 1862, however, he held one of the lowest ranks allowed to appear in the emperor's presence. He did not come from one of the five houses traditionally allowed to fill the position of regent and advisor to the emperor, nor was he eligible to serve in any of the ministerial positions in the court bureaucracy. His family had an income base of only 150 *koku*.[3] Its chief residence near the southeastern corner of the palace district backed directly onto the street called Marutamachi, making it an easy target for his opponents outside the nobility. Like many low-ranking samurai, he used the conflict surrounding the foreigners' demands on Japan to meddle more in politics than his ancestors had ever dared to do.

Despite his low rank, Tomomi's political acuity made him a man with whom to be reckoned. He had encouraged Kazunomiya's marriage to the shogun because he thought it would promote the unity of court and bakufu that Emperor Kōmei so desperately wanted. In return for the marriage, he hoped to make the shogun "return in private to the Court the substance of political power" and have his decisions take account of "the views of the country at large."[4] By "the country at large," Tomomi meant the daimyo and court nobles, not ordinary samurai and most certainly not Taseko's friends among the Hirata disciples. Once his part in arranging the marriage became known, however, it brought down the enmity of imperial loyalists who accused him of selling the court's prestige for a vague promise that the barbarians would some day be expelled.

The most ardent proponents of expelling the barbarians were hardly mollified when at the end of the eighth month of 1862, shortly before Taseko arrived in Kyoto, Tomomi was ordered to place himself under house arrest. The grounds offered were: he had meddled in policy decisions, trying to manipulate relations between the court and bakufu in a way unseemly for one of his rank, and "his deeds had fouled the emperor's judgment."[5] In response, he agreed to resign from office and take the tonsure. Samurai from Tosa thought this punishment too lenient. Two weeks later they threw an unsigned statement into the Iwakura compound accusing him of having been swayed by corrupt bakufu officials to damage imperial authority by promoting Kazunomiya's marriage, a humiliation unheard of since ancient times. He ought to have been punished by the vengeance of heaven, but out of respect for the court, he had been spared. Nevertheless, it was difficult to wait any longer. Should he leave the capital within two days, nothing would happen to him. Should he linger, his head would be exposed beside the Shijō bridge.[6]

"I have no idea what I could have done that would be construed as disloyal," Tomomi complained, but he prudently found shelter in a temple outside the city.[7] Even after he had rusticated, he found himself forced to move from one hovel or another to escape the threat of assassination. Early in the tenth month he moved to Iwakura village north of the city. Except for brief periods when rumors of approaching assassins forced him to flee, he remained there until 1867.

According to Inoue Yorikuni, imperial loyalists set Taseko to watch Tomomi because she could move through the streets of Kyoto undetected by bakufu police. Through the connections she developed at poetry writing parties, she wrangled an introduction to the Iwakura house and finally managed to meet Tomomi himself. Although she came as a spy, she was able to gain his trust, and he convinced her that he was indeed devoted to the emperor. Her avowal of his sincerity convinced the loyalists to spare him. "This was Taseko's greatest achievement."[8]

There is not the slightest shred of evidence that Taseko met Tomomi in 1862, and the anecdote about how she saved his life sounds much like other stories from the same era. Her diary mentions him not at all, though admittedly it leaves out much of what she did. Nor does his diary mention her. "Those who tried to serve the emperor didn't do so to leave a name for future generations," Tsunoda Tadayuki later wrote to one of her Kitahara cousins, "and they didn't write anything down. Even if I once had some documents, everything connected with your query [regarding what Taseko did] has long since been lost." Most of the letters that she exchanged with imperial loyalists or her friends and relatives back home were burned if they made any mention of national affairs.[9] In 1868 Gonda Naosuke himself had resolved to kill

Tomomi in revenge for Sagara Sōzō's execution, and Tomomi had to do some fast talking to change his mind. Either Naosuke or his disciple could have easily doubled this incident, inserting it into Taseko's story as well as his own. In this way it served to fill in a gap, for how else would an old peasant woman have come to the attention of a soon-to-be powerful court noble.

When Taseko had her first meeting with Tomomi remains essentially unknowable. At some point early in 1868 she had been granted an audience with him, and she apparently received a standing invitation to visit his compound just as earlier in 1862 she had developed the habit of calling on Lords Shirakawa and Ōhara. A noble house without a throng of guests and hangers-on would have presented a desolate sight indeed. Hazama Hidenori noted that she was present when Nishikawa Yoshisuke introduced him to Tomomi in the middle of the eighth month. "Taseko felt no scruples in speaking her mind to high ranking nobles," said Kakehi Mototada, a Takasu domain retainer who used her to get a position in the new government. "She was outspoken and eloquent, there was nothing she did not know about the internal workings of the administration, and she also knew many secrets related to foreign affairs." Her biographer Ichimura Minato asserts that she helped Tomomi develop his positions on policy issues, a dubious assumption.[10] For one thing, she was still extremely xenophobic at a time when the new government was reaching an accommodation with the West. For another, simply because Taseko had achieved an influence in personnel matters, it is all too easy to exaggerate her impact on larger areas of state. It appears that Taseko indeed gained Tomomi's trust, but purely in the most domestic of realms.

On the fifteenth day of the ninth month, right before the emperor left for his first trip to Tokyo, Taseko received a summons from Tomomi. "I've been ordered to look after his house while he's in personal attendance on the emperor," she wrote her son. "There was no way that I could refuse so I feel compelled to render this service. He'll leave on the twentieth and return without fail in the middle of winter. This means that I'll not be able to go home before the cold weather begins. Such being the case, should you be able to return now that the Aizu forces have been defeated, I think it would be a good idea for you to stop back home before you come to Kyoto."[11]

And so Taseko, an old peasant woman from the boondocks, moved into the Iwakura mansion. She entered not as a servant but as a *kyakubun*, an "honorary guest," or regular if temporary member of the retinue, and *rusuban*, the person left behind to look after the house. Her duties were various, from being at the entrance to receive visitors, to helping younger daughters with their poetry, to supervising the maids. They do not appear to have been onerous. "The lord's wife and daughters treat me with great kindness, and I'm greatly honored with their regard," she noted in her diary. "I spend everyday in attendance on Lord Iwakura's wife and his daughters," she wrote her family back in Tomono. "With all the trifling gratuities and fewer constraints than if I were at home, I'm really being treated quite well. It's true that I was anxious [about my reception], but I'm really much obliged for the opportunity which I never dreamed I'd have of living above the clouds." Five days after she arrived, she said she would like to make a pilgrimage to the Kitano shrine. "I was graciously told that whenever I had something I felt like doing, I should let them know, and I was given a small piece of change to take with me." [12]

Taseko developed a lasting friendship with Maki, the woman who ran the Iwakura household. The daughter of a low-ranking samurai from the Zeze domain in Ōmi, she had started out a maid-in-waiting in the Iwakura mansion where her sister was Tomomi's chief concubine. By the time she was twenty, she and her sister were sharing his affections. She bore two sons and five daughters and eventually became his chief confidante, visiting him while he was in exile and watching over her children's careers. After Tomomi's consort Nobu died in 1874, she became his second wife. [13] "As we have become more intimate, she has been saying to me, 'Tase, what about spending three years here,' and that has really put me in a bind," Taseko reported to her daughter-in-law. "I proposed that I go home just once and then come back to Kyoto. She replied with such statements as, 'I'd love to go to a place like Shinano, but I'll never be able to,' or 'I know that even though you may promise to return, it's all lies once you get home.' . . . She is so overwhelmingly gracious that it quite puts me on the spot." [14]

While she was staying at the Iwakura mansion, Taseko also became friends with Tomomi's aunt Suga. Rather than marry and bear children, Suga had spent her life as an official in the empress's court living independently on a seven-person stipend and fifty *koku* of rice. [15] She began by serving Emperor Ninkō's consort Heimon-in. When Heimon-in died in 1847, she cut her hair and took the Buddhist name Chikō-in though she remained at court in the retinue of Emperor Kōmei's empress. Her visits to the Iwakura household on her days off were always the occasion for a formal banquet. At such events the hostess and her chief guest as well as the other family members would seat themselves on cushions before low-legged trays covered with small dishes containing tiny morsels of food. In this situation it is always more polite to pick up a dish and bring it close to one's lips rather than bend over it or risk spilling food on a expensive kimono. Taseko was allowed to sit opposite the guest. She did not have a tray of her own, rather she would nibble at whatever Chikō-in did not want, exchange cups of sake, and engage her in conversation.

Taseko kept Chikō-in company at a number of banquets and outings. In the fall she received an invitation to go on an expedition to view the maple leaves in the eastern hills. There she composed a poem that said less about the beauty of the scenery than the honor bestowed on her:

Iya no me ga	How should this base-born
nani to kotaemu	woman respond?
kōyō no	Your poetry
iro yori fukaki	has left a deeper impression
kimi ga koto no ba	than the color of the autumn leaves.[16]

The only reason we know that Taseko went on this outing is because she put this poem in two of her anthologies with a heading describing the circumstances of its composition. Most probably she accompanied a group of women, members of the Iwakura household perhaps, but Chikō-in may have invited members of the court as well. We can assume that the younger women paraded their most beautiful fall kimonos; the older women, and Chikō-in was ten years older than Taseko, would have worn darker hues. They must have had a wonderful time, admiring the autumn color and either having servants bring along a picnic or reserving rooms in a tea house with a view of the mountains. It was the perfect opportunity for Taseko to practice the style of living she had glimpsed in her study of classical poetry.

Six months later the peach blossoms were in bloom. On the third day of the third month when she was invited to a celebration marking the day when the household set out dolls representing the emperor and his court, Taseko summed up her feelings in the following poem:

Michitose no	Even at the end of three thousand years
sue mo wasureji	I will not have forgotten
kyō mo kono	the sake cup under the peach blossoms
kimi yori tamau	that I received from you
momo no sakazuki	this very day.[17]

Taseko may have based her poem on one from a late medieval collection, the *Shinsenwaka rokuchō:* "Blessed by the numbers / of three thousand years, / sake cups under the flowers / of the third month that never cease [to bloom] / throughout the spring."[18] Both poems draw on legends of the peach tree that flowers and produces fruit once every three thousand years in the enchanted land ruled, according to Chinese legend, by the Queen Mother of the West.

In the Noh version of her story, she presents the emperor with a jeweled drinking cup containing the fruit because his virtue is known throughout the universe. One sip sends him into ecstasy. She then performs a dance to wish him a long and prosperous reign.[19] Taseko wrote her poem shortly before she left Kyoto to return to Tomono. Chikō-in responded with a poem suggesting that they grow old together in a mountain village.[20]

Taseko's chief duty appears to have been to keep Tomomi's women company during his absence. In addition to Maki and Chikō-in, these included three daughters. Masu, the eldest, described her thus: "At first glance she resembled a man in looks and body movement, but once you got to know her, you realized that she was actually gentle and kind. . . . She always thought it a shame that my handwriting was so clumsy." Taseko shared Masu's food and bed, it being unheard-of for a noble woman to sleep alone, and the two became quite close.[21] Taseko herself was highly cognizant of the special privileges she had received and took delight in becoming "the humble recipient of her talk."

Oguruma no	Let the moon and sun
tsuki hi mo hayaku	revolve quickly
kaere yo to	once it becomes night
kimi machikanete	I can't bear to wait for you
kimi ōsuramu	to hear what you have to say.[22]

For the six months that Taseko spent with the Iwakura women, nothing in her writings suggests that she ever identified with them as one woman to another. Her encounter with them took on meaning precisely because the vertical hierarchy kept them so far apart. Social inequality was in the very air she breathed, and she consciously did her part to maintain status distinctions. "Late one night the princess did me the honor of paying me a visit. I was so overwhelmed with awe that I wrote this to present to her:"

Kumo no ma ni	How could I have expected
mishi tsuki kage no	that the light from the moon
neya no to ni	glimpsed between the clouds
sasu to wa sasu ka	might strike
omoikakeki ya	the door of my sleeping chamber?[23]

Taseko often played the poet while she was in the company of Maki and her daughters, repaying their hospitality with poems crafted to suit every occasion. One night they saw white cats caught outside during a snow storm. The cats were crying and the young women asked Taseko to compose poems on that topic. She obliged with two, one that depicted the cats in the throes of sexual passion, another that expressed pity for creatures left outside on a wintry night. She apparently proselytized for the Hirata school because Masu wrote her a poem indicating that she had glanced at "The Precious Sleeve Cord," Taseko's favorite text. Taseko responded with her own poem in which she expressed her hope that while the words of an old woman were meaningless, Masu would treasure what she had read.[24]

Taseko later incorporated numerous poems in her anthologies that had first been written during the evenings whiled away with the Iwakura women. She composed on set topics—the charm of the moon on a spring night, for example. She also wrote poetry designed to amuse and entertain. For one poem she explained that "my superiors had given me the topic of a man who has his gold stolen. It received a big laugh:"

Kintama wo	Cinch your jock strap
otosanu yō ni	tightly lest
fundoshi wo	your golden balls
kataku shime yo no	fall out.
ue no koto no ba	That is only common sense.[25]

Fundoshi is usually translated simply as "loin cloth," but as a garment it is little more than a g-string. It was not a word that would normally pass the lips of a well-brought up young lady or be spoken in her company. Taseko must have had enough knowledge of polite society to realize that the most sophisticated circles had a long tradition of taking delight in the juxtaposition of the elevated and the vulgar. In his introduction to "The Precious Sleeve Cord," Kanetane had reminded his readers that true *miyabi*, that demonstrated by the goddess Miyabi in her lewd dance, lay in making people laugh.[26] Besides, the topic had given her the perfect opportunity to create the literary equivalent of a dirty joke.

Taseko often wrote admonitory poetry for the junior and subordinate members of the Iwakura household. At one point she got so angry at the way the maids did nothing but gossip that she wrote a poem castigating their behavior:

Mitsu kuri no	Don't say bad things
nakagoto iwanu	about everyone around you.
ono ga mi no	You should simply always try
yogore wo tsune ni	to cleanse yourselves of
uchi harae tada	the stains on your own souls.[27]

She even wrote poems containing instructions for Tomomi's sons. His eldest, Tomosada, was already of an age to have been made the nominal commander of the imperial army advancing up the Nakasendō. A number of younger sons had remained in Kyoto, and to them Taseko felt it incumbent upon herself to write the following:

Kimi to omi no	Once committed to the way
michi ni musubite	of lord and retainer,
kimi ga yo no	I ask you please to become
kimi taru hito to	the kind of lords suitable
narase tamae ya	for this imperial reign.[28]

Taseko saw new things in the Iwakura household, not all of which she approved. According to her diary, on the evening of the second day of the tenth month, "we were talking about sundry things when they brought out something to show me made by the barbarians and called an organ. For awhile they let me try it. It was such a novelty that it entranced everyone." Seeing the pleasure that the family took in this foreign toy, Taseko composed a poem to express her displeasure:

Hi no moto ni	In Japan
hayama koto narazu	the koto cannot be quick
sakashira no	but I ask you not to listen gladly
kara koto yoshi to	to this barbarian harp
kikina tamai zo	no matter how clever it is.[29]

One daughter responded with her own poem expressing her agreement with Taseko's sentiments. They did indeed treat her graciously.

Taseko humbly accepted a number of gifts while she was staying at the Iwakura mansion. These she noted in her letters and diary as examples of the kind condescension with which she was treated. "Since it's gotten so cold, I've been given a kimono, a padded vest and a heavy jacket. I've also received a hair pin as a hand-me-down from princess Toki, and when I get home, I think it will delight the children to see it," she wrote her daughter-in-law. "Chiburu is well; he sometimes visits the Iwakura compound, and he is always delighted with the various presents he is given." These were gifts to be treasured, less for what they were than for whom they were from. "Words cannot express the consideration they have shown me both day and night."[30]

The gifts that Taseko received from the Iwakura family had great symbolic value. Some were goods that Chikō-in herself had once used—a sta-

FIGURE 19. The Meiji emperor's toys now in the possession of the Matsuo family. From *Matsuo Taseko*, frontispiece.

tionery box, a tobacco pouch and pipe, a hairpin, and a doll. Taseko's children took these items with them when they married. Chikō-in also gave Taseko poems on strips of dyed paper crafted by the empress plus a poem in the hand-writing of Prince Arisugawa, commander in chief of the imperial armies. Even today the Matsuo family proudly displays toys enjoyed by the Meiji emperor: a tiny drum, two wooden sparrows on wheels, a lion dog, and a collection of small dolls. They both added luster to the family's reputation and engaged it more closely in imperial affairs. Government bureaucrats deliberately tried to construct a sense of national identity by enhancing the people's commitment to the new emperor-centered state, to turn commoners into citizens.[31] In this effort they were inadvertently aided by women like Chikō-in and her willing accomplice, Taseko.

Gifts received had to be reciprocated, not with goods of the same monetary or symbolic value, but of equal rarity. At the end of the tenth month she thanked her daughter-in-law for having sent clothes for herself and Chiburu. In addition she had received buckwheat flour and paper strings for tying up the hair, both regional specialties, and chestnuts. "I presented one bag of the flour to Mrs. Iwakura. She professed herself delighted to have received it and will keep it against Lord Iwakura's return." Taseko gave another bag to one of the Takasu domain agents and saved the rest for the people she knew who had accompanied the emperor. "The chestnuts are really a rare treat. When they appeared in Kyoto recently they cost about 1,200 *mon* for two quarts, and they were so expensive that I didn't eat even one. Rather than me eating the ones you sent, I would like to give some to the three princesses, reserve plenty for Chiburu, and save the rest for my superiors."[32]

Taseko was to maintain her connection with the Iwakura family for many years. During the months that she spent in Tokyo in 1869, she stayed a number of nights at the Iwakura estate right in front of the imperial palace and became a regular caller on Maki and her daughters.[33] In one letter to her father and Mitsunaka, she reported that the Iwakura daughter serving the imperial family had returned home with "secret information": the emperor was to return to Kyoto at the end of the year.[34] (It turned out to be a false rumor.) Early in the eighth month she recorded in her diary that her visit to the Iwakura mansion had found the women studying the first imperial poetry anthology, the *Kokinshū*.

A week later the Iwakura daughters announced that they had received permission to visit the Hama palace on the edge of Tokyo Bay, and they wanted Taseko to accompany them. They spent the morning admiring the grounds. In the afternoon they went boating to watch the cormorants catch fish. Once again inside the palace walls they joined a great company of men. "Everyone became quite drunk while watching the setting sun. The moon extended its light over the sea, and somehow or other my heart was filled with melancholy. Recalling the palaces in the capital to the west [Kyoto], I recited:"

Hama dono no	While watching the moonlight
nami ni teru sou	glitter on the waves
tsuki mi tsutsu	at the Hama palace
miyako no kage no	how nostalgic I have become
natsukashiki kamo	for the shadows of the capital.[35]

Taseko noted that the emperor himself had visited the Hama palace just three days before she did, but she neglected to mentioned that the British crown prince had stayed there a month earlier. She was indeed in illustrious company. Built by the Tokugawa shoguns as one of several detached residences, the Hama palace was taken over by the Meiji government and turned into a guest house for important foreign guests. Former President Ulysses S. Grant stayed there in 1879. Today it is a public park with a cormorant sanctuary that will quickly drive away anyone with even the faintest sense of smell.

In the years following Taseko's trip to Tokyo, she continued to correspond with Maki. "I'm living where I always have, isolated from the world that passes me by, my only pleasure recalling the times long gone," she wrote in a draft for a new year's greeting in 1875 that was both a reflection of her circumstances and conventional in expression. She had heard the news that Tomomi had been attacked and seriously wounded by samurai disgruntled at his refusal to countenance war with Korea. "The age we live in seems to be changing so much in so many different ways that just thinking about it makes me anxious. Reflecting that this happened to someone dedicated to serving the emperor, I live my life as purely as possible, thinking that if only I had the opportunity, I'd like to serve you in whatever capacity you require."[36] Taseko probably did not mean for her offer to be taken seriously. She felt she had to make it, however, because she was but a peasant woman presuming to correspond with her betters.

Taseko would be seventy when she made her last trip to Tokyo in 1881 at the behest of the Iwakura family. What she did there remains largely unknown because if she kept a diary it has been lost; nor did she write poems and letters that people bothered to preserve. All that remain are episodes and anecdotes. She stayed at first with a former tenant farmer for the Kitahara family who went to Tokyo in the early 1870s to make his fortune. After she had settled in, she summoned her grandson Chiburu, and he joined her in May, just four days after the death of his wife to whom he had been married for eighteen months. They soon arranged to rent an single eight-mat room (approximately 135 square feet) with an attached kitchen. Tomomi got Chiburu a position in the Ministry of Justice, and Taseko spent her days at the Iwakura mansion, though she also visited her friends about the city and participated in poetry writing circles. "Chiburu came here from Tomono on the twentieth," she wrote her cousin Kitahara Hata then in Tokyo. "Depending on his circumstances, I'll let you know when I leave. It now appears that we may stay here for some time."[37]

Taseko attended the Iwakura ladies and ran errands for them. She accompanied Tomomi's aunt Chikō-in as part of the empress's entourage for a Noh performance in Shiba Park at which the empress-dowager was also present. She was invited to a party held at the Iwakura estate for the wives of government ministers. She helped Maki distribute charity to the aged and indigent. When the emperor went to view the dogs used as target practice for horseback archers in the old Satsuma domain compound, Taseko was sent to convey the Iwakura family's greetings along with some western-style cakes.[38]

Taseko was herself apparently a figure of some renown. Inao's daughter Hata, then employed by Ishiyama Teruko, one of the attendants for the crown prince in the Akasaka palace, made it be known that she was related to her famous cousin. "Just once I'd like to be introduced to that hero Taseko," was Teruko's response. She had her chance at the Noh performance in Shiba Park.

On her way home Teruko told Hata, "now that I've seen Taseko, I've achieved my heart's desire."[39]

Among the letters from Taseko to Hata is one that gives some insight into their relations with noble women. "From what you say, it appears that things are getting easier for you day by day. I'd like to offer my hearty congratulations that you've managed to fit so smoothly with your mistress and everyone else. I've been pondering the invitation I received some days ago to become a lady-in-waiting myself, but it seems to me that this might make problems for you. In any case, my first inclination is to refuse because I don't think I'd be a good person for the position."[40] In 1868 Iwakura Maki had suggested that Taseko accept a three year contract to be a member of her retinue. Taseko had rejected it then as she did now. Perhaps she truly thought herself to be unworthy. It is possible, however, that she made excuses because she did not want to commit to living away from home for so long a time or to restrict her freedom of movement.

Taseko took great pleasure in hobnobbing with the nobility. She made several visits to the house of her former daimyo, the Matsudaira of Takasu who lived in Yotsuya. In October, when the chrysanthemums were at their peak, she and Matsuoka Toshinori, a former Takasu retainer, were invited to a private party to see them. The chief guests were the former daimyo of Owari, Aizu, Kuwana, and Hitotsubashi. "It was extremely rare for me to be in such an illustrious gathering, and I felt just like one of the flowers when I received an official jacket from Lord Hitotsubashi. I wrote this poem for my humble reply:"

Kasunaranu	Even I who am unworthy of being counted
mi ni mo megumi no	have received this blessing
atsu fusuma	of heavy curtains
kasanete chiyo no	let us hope they will become a jewel
tama mono ni sumu	that piles up for a thousand years.[41]

According to Toshinori, Lord Hitotsubashi had gotten so extremely drunk that he threatened to spoil the party. When he saw Taseko, he called out, "so the old woman came, how about that," and insisted on taking off his crested jacket to give to her.[42] There is no record that it remained in the Matsuo household. Perhaps she realized it was an unsuitable gift and returned it discreetly at a later date.

Chiburu gradually discovered that serving the emperor in the new bureaucracy was not to his liking. "I hated listening to lawsuits that polluted the emperor's reign, not knowing what to do about them," he later recounted. "I'd rather continue the occupation of my ancestors and put my efforts into being productive."[43] Taseko told her acquaintances that with the approach of the hundredth anniversary of the 1783 eruption of Mt. Asama, she wanted to go home to help prepare memorial services for the victims. Another reason might have been a consequence of the government's deflationary policy that had depressed silk prices, to the distress of the producers. Their response was to produce more, and they needed every helping hand. Makoto having come to Tokyo on business around that time, she and Chiburu returned with him. Out of consideration for her age, Chiburu suggested that she ride in a rickshaw, which had been invented in Tokyo in 1869. She would feel better if she walked, she told him, and so walk they did.[44] Before their departure, she received many presents more valuable for their association with a former owner than as objects. Among them was a needle once in the possession of Emperor Meiji.[45]

Taseko continued to correspond with the Iwakura women and her other friends in Tokyo into the 1880s. In 1884 she received word that Tomomi's aunt Chikō-in had died. "She was considerate of me in the past, and I was shocked to receive word that she had gone to the invisible world. I would humbly like to proffer my condolences to you and the rest of the family in your grief. Even though my gift is but a trifle, please offer it to her spirit." In the same letter Taseko enclosed a note to Masu, the eldest of Tomomi's daughters and the one with whom she had shared a bed in 1868.[46] When Taseko had left Tokyo, Masu wrote her a poem in farewell:

Wakareji no	Until the gods take away
namida ni kami wa	my tears
kuchinu made	at our parting
akaki kokoro no	I will never forget
wasurarenu kana	your red patriotic heart.[47]

Taseko's meeting with Iwakura Tomomi made her reputation as a woman of influence. It may have helped her place the samurai from the Takasu domain and others in the new government bureaucracy, and it was the reason for her going to Tokyo in 1869 and later in 1881. From reading her diaries and poems, however, it is clear that she mostly interacted with women. Regardless of what her biographers say about her influence on Tomomi, the friendships that had meaning for her at the time were with Maki, Chikō-in, and Masu.

WHEN TASEKO had moved into the Iwakura mansion in 1868, she met a woman with whom she was to remain friends to the end of her life. This was

Miwada Masako, thirty years her junior. Masako's responsibilities were to read the materials that came for Tomomi and mark in red the places that she thought were important for him to see. She also taught his daughters Chinese. She was herself exceptionally talented, having learned to read the Chinese classics as a child at the private school for boys run by her father on the outskirts of Kyoto. (The study of Chinese had traditionally been a male bastion. Beginning in the early nineteenth century, a few women began to invade it, partly because the increasing supply of instructors needed students.[48]) From the age of twelve, she occasionally substituted for him in giving lectures to boys not much younger and certainly much bigger than she was. "I resolved that so long as I studied there was no reason why I should not become a superior scholar even though I was a woman," Masako later wrote. She was an only child, and throughout her youth her parents reminded her of how they regretted her not being a boy. Perhaps because she never felt close to her mother, she formed strong attachments to women much older than herself, the first to the scholar of Chinese and painter Yanagawa Kōran and the second to Taseko.[49]

"I loved and respected Taseko as a elder sister," Masako recalled. "She had an openhearted and cheerful disposition. When she laughed, it was in a high voice, 'kyakkya, kyakkya.' She never held a grudge and she was never vexed by little things, nor was she ever rude or haughty. When she told people what she thought of them, her presence was so commanding and she had so much more dignity than one would expect of a woman that even though the maids might smart from the lash of her tongue, they willingly submitted to her."[50]

Depictions of Taseko as "frank and openhearted," or "never vexed by little things," sound less like individual traits than the qualities most admired in Japanese heroes. No one is ever described as devious, craven, and given to fretting. According to Kakehi Mototada, "when Taseko was drinking, her ears would burn with passion while she debated national affairs and agonized over the conditions of the times. She had a majesty to her that one would not expect to find in a woman. . . . She was an extremely good talker and a fiery debater. She was sincere in everything she said, and everyone was willing to give his all for her."[51] These statements employ vocabulary usually used to describe men, and as Masako and Mototada inadvertently suggest, they represent qualities unanticipated in women. Given the paucity of suitably heroic attributes, Taseko's admirers had no choice but to define her in male terms, to recreate her character according to male values. It might also be said that to some extent these attributes structured Taseko herself, for they provided models of behavior for her to emulate when she accepted the challenge of a more public life than she would have lived had she remained in the Ina Valley.

Masako later told a number of anecdotes about the life she led with Taseko in the Iwakura mansion. After a major winter storm, the maids divided into two teams, the Taira and the Minamoto, the classic antagonists in the old war tales, for a snowball fight. "I disliked that sort of rumpus, and I kept out of the way in my room reading a book. Taseko came looking for me and said, 'Miss Umeno, it's all right if you choose to be different from the maids in preferring to read books, but your body needs exercise. Besides, given that people are the way they are and you're not living under your own roof, just once you need to join the others. If you aren't willing to do at least that much, you'll find it hard to get along. Please, come on out with me now.'" In other words, you should sacrifice your own inclinations for the sake of harmony in the group. Another time Masako thought to make herself look older by blackening her teeth. She ended up a filthy mess covered in black powder. "I was horrified for fear that people would say the maids in the Iwakura house lacked decorum. It really bothered me so I talked it over with Taseko. As usual she laughed cheerfully and said, 'Things that embarrass you the world will soon let pass, and there's nothing to be done about your having gotten flustered. I think it'll be all right so long as you're more prudent in the future.'" [52]

Taseko was also responsible for finding Masako a husband. "'It's not good for women to remain single,' Taseko told me. 'You should get married if a suitable connection can be found . . . then you can help each other work for the good of the nation.'" Taseko's candidate was Miwada Mototsuna, the younger son of a shrine priest from Shikoku and fifteen years Masako's senior. Having devoted his life to the imperial cause and spent five years in domanial custody following the beheading of the Ashikaga shoguns' statues, he had no prospects before the creation of a new centralized government gave him a chance for steady employment. At first Masako was doubtful because she assumed he would not want a bookish wife, and Mototsuna himself questioned whether it was a good idea. The marriage came about only because Tomomi took an interest in the matter and urged Masako to do it. Her parents were not pleased at her choice of a man who would take her away from court circles, but she ignored their objections. [53]

Masako was a strong-willed woman. A month after the marriage, Mototsuna left her behind in Kyoto while he accompanied the emperor to Tokyo. He neglected to let her know he had arrived safely; all she received was a brief message some weeks later saying that at Tomomi's instructions, he would be staying in the city for a while. "Even though my heart had gone to the eastern skies, without wings I couldn't fly," Masako wrote. "How I re-

FIGURE 20. Miwada Masako in old age. Courtesy of Miwada Yoshiko.

gretted what I couldn't do because I am a woman." Learning that Tomomi's
daughters were being sent to join their father, Masako got approval to join
them. In saying farewell, her first mentor Yanagawa Kōran reminded her
that sewing is a woman's true vocation; study was only for when she had extra time. This from a woman who had made her reputation as a poet and
painter! Masako arrived in Tokyo four months after Mototsuna had left
Kyoto. At Shinagawa she received a message from him telling her to go on
to the Iwakura mansion with her charges. He would meet her there the next
day, and he graciously promised not to scold her for having come to Tokyo
without his permission.[54]

In her later admonitions to women, Masako insisted that a wife should try
to understand and respect her husband's personality. No matter how much
trouble he caused, she should never let him know it. Instead she should take

pride and joy in overcoming the hardships imposed by married life. Mototsuna was seldom home. When he was not working late at his position in the
Ministry of Foreign Affairs, he was out carousing with his friends and fellow
workers. They all loved to drink no matter what the time of day. Occasionally they came home with him for an informal party, never giving Masako
any advance warning. In the third year of their marriage, Masako wrote a
poem in Chinese in which she pleaded with her husband to drink less and to
switch to tea before he passed out. It had no effect. He loved to exchange sake
cups with his friends, wax nostalgic about the old days, and rail against the
present.[55]

Masako and Mototsuna spent over three years in Tokyo, living for a time
in the hilly area north of the imperial palace. Taseko included them in her
round of visits while she was there in 1869 just as she did the Iwakura family, and sometimes she spent the night. "One day I happened to be looking
out the window when I saw Taseko approaching," Masako later remembered.
"She called out at the gate in her cheerful voice and entered the garden, laughing as she came. I flew down to the entry way. She was dressed elegantly in
a crepe jacket over her kimono, and she was dragging a large black object
wrapped in straw. At first I thought it was a dog. 'Miss Umeno,' Taseko said.
'It's been a long time since we last saw each other, but I'd just heard that you'd
arrived in town. As I was going past Nihonbashi this morning, I saw lots of
beautiful tuna fish on the bank. You'd never see a sight like that in Shinano.
They were so pretty that I simply had to buy one for you as a present, but
not knowing the address or a reliable messenger service, I brought it along
myself.'"[56]

The tuna is a large fish that weighs sixty pounds or more. Not many people
would think to take one as a housewarming gift. At that time there was still
a fish market next to the bridge called Nihonbashi that marked the center of
the commercial district east of the imperial palace. It was a little over a mile
to where Masako lived at Surugadai Kannonzaka, and the last part was all
uphill. Taseko was then fifty-eight years old, still high-spirited and unconventional enough to do what she wanted.

When Taseko left Tokyo at the end of the twelfth month, she and Masako
exchanged farewell poems just as they had when she left Kyoto earlier in the
year. They promised never to forget each other, and they never did:

Wakarete wa	Now that we're parting
oi sushinanu ni	throughout the years
toshi wo hete	as I grow ever older
yo no uruwashiki	I will be awaiting
tayori wo zo matsu	your intimate letters of friendship.[57]

Among its many meanings, *uruwashii* refers the beauty of friendship among equals, a reference to the fifth of the five human relationships and one more often applied to men than women.

In 1872 Mototsuna had a falling out with Tomomi that forced him to resign his position. He and Masako left Tokyo for Matsuyama, where his brother still ran the shrine that had been in the family for generations. There he opened a private school. Masako had four children, three of whom died in infancy before Mototsuna died in 1879 at the age of 49, leaving her with a large number of debts. She borrowed money from her parents for a new school to which she accepted every boy who applied, regardless of his age or previous learning, and gave each individual instruction using whatever books he happened to bring with him. By 1880, she had repaid her parents and moved to better quarters. She went back to Tokyo in 1887 where she opened a private school in Kanda. After it failed, she founded the Miwada Higher Girls' School in 1902 at the age of fifty-eight. The school's reputation derives in part from its founder's erudition, and it still exists today.

Masako is considered to be conservative because she believed that the purpose of education for women should be moral development; she also believed it could be best be inculcated through a study of the Chinese classics, and its goal was to make women into good wives.[58] On the other hand, she blamed Western education for leading to the denigration of women and fiercely opposed the contemporary trend that elevated men and despised women. Men and women were equal, but they were not the same. Whereas westernizers like Fukuzawa Yukichi and Nishimura Shigeki believed that women should confine their work to the home, Masako argued that women should function outside in medicine, education and the arts. She herself continued to teach until shortly before her death at the age of 83 in 1927.[59] In 1893 she wrote a biographical sketch of Taseko and recalled their friendship: "Let us remember the past when we talked intimately morning and night, viewing together both the flowers and the moon."[60]

TASEKO'S CONNECTION with Iwakura Tomomi brought her the lasting friendship of urban and urbane women. Her relationship with Shinagawa Yajirō was neither so intense nor so intimate. At the age of twenty he had welcomed her into the Chōshū compound in 1863. He had participated in all the major events involving his domain, including planning an attack on the foreign legations in Edo in 1862 and the attempted coup d'état in Kyoto in 1864. He was one of the men responsible for cementing the Satsuma-Chōshū alliance against the bakufu in 1867. In some accounts he is credited with scheming to incite public unrest by dropping talismans inscribed with the names of the gods on the houses of wealthy merchants in Kyoto and elsewhere. Families so blessed had to reciprocate by ladling out food and drink to passers-by. This initiated the orgiastic festival of dancing and singing known as "Ee ja nai ka" (anything goes) that in sweeping Japan's towns and cities seemingly portended the fall of the bakufu.[61]

Yajirō had been hunting down the last remnants of bakufu supporters in Echigo for most of the time that Taseko was in Kyoto in 1868. They saw each other occasionally in Tokyo in 1869, and they corresponded thereafter. His letters to her have disappeared, although it is said that he sometimes wrote several times a year; her letters to him remain only in the form of a single draft. It says very little, beginning with a poetic fragment, "the clouds are continually passing overhead." She had received his letter, and she has found a man going to the capital willing to carry a response for her with a gift. "Even though the white silk that I humbly present as a token of my regard from years gone by is nothing but a rough thing made by an old woman's hands, I earnestly prithee to take it from me."[62] Additional evidence of their ongoing relationship is a copy of a poem written by Yajirō celebrating the 1880 imperial excursion through Nagano prefecture that ended up in the Matsuo house.[63]

Taseko's last chance for a meeting with Yajirō came in 1880 at the behest of local boosters who tried to use her influence to get national recognition for a grave. Prince Tadanaga, the reputed grandson of Emperor Godaigo, was said to be buried in Namiai, a village south of Yamamoto. In the 1380s Tadanaga tried to raise troops for the imperial cause, only to be defeated in battle, or at least so the legend goes. Chiku Yorihisa, the bakufu bannerman whose fief included Namiai, erected the first monument to Tadanaga's memory in the precincts of the local shrine in 1742. The Chiku family claimed to have fought for his father, Prince Munenaga, claimed that a Chiku daughter was Tadanaga's wet nurse, and proudly displayed his brocade flag. (Shrines erected in Tadanaga's name may be found as far away as Nakatsugawa.[64]) In the 1830s Namiai villagers proposed to erect a new monument. As part of the plan to make the site better known, they published a brief biography that a Confucian scholar in Nagoya said that he had extracted from a 1488 text. Scholars soon challenged its authenticity. Most damning of all, the death poem attributed to Tadanaga was actually written by Minamoto no Arimasa before his execution in 1221. The monument was never erected.[65]

The following story is told by Matsushita Shōzō, the clerk in the Ina District Office. In 1880, the emperor was to travel the Nakasendō, then go to Ise and on to Kyoto. This was the fourth of six excursions that he made between 1872 and 1885 to survey his dominions and attract popular support.[66] Rather than visit the Ina Valley himself, he sent Yajirō, then an important official in the Home Ministry, as his personal representative to meet with local dignitaries in Iida and report back to him at Kiso-Fukushima. As soon as he learned of the intended visit, Shōzō sent word to Masuda Heihachirō, who had spent a lifetime trying fruitlessly to win recognition for Prince Tadanaga's grave. Heihachirō prepared fresh copies of his documents and wrote a petition asking for official validation. It was not Yajirō's place to concern himself with matters better left to the Imperial Household Ministry, however, and he refused to look at them. "We had a long discussion on what to do, and I remember that it was Higuchi Mitsunobu's suggestion to ask Taseko for help." (Mitsunobu was Kitahara Inao's younger brother.) The men sent a palanquin for her. She willingly agreed to be their tool.

At the entrance to the district office, Taseko swept past the guard who tried to bar her way. Calling out, "hey Mr. Yaji, it's been a long time," she entered the room where he was ensconced with the local officials. Yajirō was delighted to see her. They had an excellent time talking and laughing about the days of yore, so much so that the Namiai contingent feared that she had forgotten why she was there. Gradually Taseko brought the conversation around to the story of the prince and the battle in which he died. Food and drink were made available. In a fortuitous coincidence, a Chinese poem about the incident had been hung in the alcove for the room where Yajirō and Taseko were seated. Being slightly drunk by the time he caught sight of it, Yajirō took a fancy to it and started reciting it over and over. Taseko's words had already made him favorably inclined toward Namiai, and the poem so moved him that he impulsively agreed to meet with the supporters and examine their documents.

Yajirō left the next morning to meet the imperial party at Fukushima. Within two days, on June 27th, a messenger arrived in Iida warning that a party of officials from the Imperial Home Ministry was on its way to view Tadanaga's shrine and grave. Three years later, in 1883, the reputed grave of this reputed prince was officially designated an imperial tomb and put under the supervision and protection of the Imperial Household Ministry. It is still the only site so designated in Nagano prefecture.[67] People living throughout the lower Ina Valley could now stake a claim to being a part of the national history embodied in the emperor and his ancestors.

In 1892, when Taseko was already eighty-one, Yajirō became Home Minister. Either she or someone using her name wrote to congratulate him on his appointment and take advantage of the opportunity to raise an issue that had long vexed shrine priests. Although written in the epistolary style, it reads more like a petition. The concepts and the language come straight out of nativist texts. At this stage in her life Taseko could not see well enough to know whether her brush had hit the paper. She must have had someone write the letter for her, or perhaps she simply agreed to associate herself with what she deemed a worthy cause.[68]

In making her appeal, Taseko set forth her philosophy of the relationship that ought to obtain between people, ruler, and gods in the light of her training as a Hirata disciple.

> It is my humble understanding that in both words and practice there is to be no distinction between official and subject in our country and all are to repay their debt of gratitude to the ancestors. This being the basis of our national essence (*kokutai*), ever since the ancient age of the gods, both the awe-inspiring deities and the especially meritorious heroes are worshipped for the sake of our emperor and country at the shrines for heaven and earth. Having these rites performed correctly is the foundation for governing the country.[69]

She goes on to emphasize the unity of rites and rule, claiming that in ancient times, rulers made worship of the gods the fundamental principle of governance. The nub of the problem is that whereas the government officially acknowledges the men serving the national and prefectural shrines, priests at local shrines receive nothing. "They do not have an official position and their selection is left up to the community. . . . For them to be cast off and abandoned is simply dreadful. While weeping bitter tears, this old woman becomes more and more overwhelmed with grief."[70]

Now that Yajirō is Home Minister, Taseko or someone close to her hopes that she has enough influence with him to rectify the situation. "Ignoring the scorn of people around me, I have taken up my brush because of our connection in the past. Please take pity on the longwinded ramblings of an old woman, and to the extent that you have the power to do so, if you would reverse the decline in our country's path, solidify our country's foundations, and clarify the direction that citizens ought to take, it will make this old woman happier than she has ever been in her life."[71]

There is no indication that Yajirō ever received Taseko's letter or responded to it directly. Eighteen months later, in February 1894, the national government announced that local shrine priests were to be given official appointments. Taseko was by no means the only person to petition the government on their behalf, and she must not be given the credit for this change in policy. The letter should rather be read as evidence that her continuing concern for the proper approach to politics suffered no diminution with age, and she continued to structure her thought according to the categories she had learned in reading texts such as "The Precious Sleeve Cord."

These written remains are all that survive of interactions that were once ongoing and satisfying. They attest to the opportunities opened to Taseko by her commitment to the imperial cause and suggest that hers was a personality with the right combination of deference and charm to attract the lasting goodwill of busy people who played important public roles as statesmen and educators. These friendships have been ignored by mainstream historians. They speak not to the issues that engaged the builders of the new Japan and their biographers, but to the private web of personal exchanges that bridged the gap between town and country.

CHAPTER FOURTEEN

Political Intrigues and Conflicting Visions

Forgetting how old
my body has become
I spend my life praying
for the day when the emperor's reign
is not buffeted by change.
MATSUO TASEKO, the 1870s[1]

Following her trip to Kyoto in 1868, Taseko had hardly settled back into daily life when she was summoned to Tokyo, once again to play a minor role on the national stage. She did not want to go. "Please, I beg of you, come up with some excuse so I don't have to," she wrote Makoto, himself then in Tokyo. "It's just as hot as it can be, and I really don't want to move. Please help me out. I made the excuse that your father is sick, but I'm still being asked for my assistance and I'm really in a bind. I've also pointed out that you're now in Tokyo so please, with this in mind, I'm asking you to find out what you can even though it's such a bother."[2]

The men asking Taseko to lobby on their behalf were desperate. They represented bakufu bannermen, or at least families who called themselves bannermen, and therein lay the rub. The Chimura had received a fief of 4,400 *koku* from Tokugawa

Ieyasu for exploits at the battle of Sekigahara in 1600 that gave him control of Japan. In 1603, the head of the family was made the intendant for the lands ruled by the bakufu in the Ina Valley. Eventually the land in eleven villages was given over to the family in trust (*azukarichi*), meaning that the Chimura administered it and collected taxes from it just as though it was part of their own domain, with the proviso that the bakufu could always take it back. The Chimura maintained a headquarters at Kuguri in Mino, an office in Iida, and an official residence in Edo. Like the daimyo, the family alternated each year in Mino with a year in Edo in attendance on the shogun. The Yamamura had likewise served the Tokugawa cause by holding the Kiso gorges in 1600. By 1838 they administered land with a nominal tax base of 7,500 *koku*. Their headquarters was at Kiso-Fukushima, up the road from Nakatsugawa, and they too maintained a residence in Edo. Because they also held large tracts of forest land in trust for the Owari domain, they had a residence in its castle town of Nagoya.

The Yamamura and Chimura pointed to the services they had performed in 1600, their autonomous and hereditary administrative responsibilities, and their residences in Edo as evidence that they were indeed bakufu bannermen. In 1868, however, the new Meiji government gave Owari jurisdiction over bakufu lands in Shinano while allowing the various daimyo to continue administering their domains as before. Owari moved immediately to establish a claim over the lands that the Chimura had held in trust. Worse, it claimed that the Yamamura and Chimura were not direct shogunal vassals, but vassals of the Owari daimyo. It justified this assertion by presenting records showing that in 1619 the two families had indeed been transferred to the Owari rolls.[3] For the Yamamura this made particular sense because the bakufu had delegated responsibility for security on the Kiso gorge section of the Nakasendō to Owari. It was not difficult to serve two masters so long as both wanted the same thing.

The ambiguity in status enjoyed by the Chimura and Yamamura for 250 years could no longer be tolerated once the Meiji government demanded clarification. Even though the Owari branch of the Tokugawa family had moved quickly to position itself as a loyal supporter of the emperor, betraying the very institution that it had been created to protect, the Chimura and Yamamura still had more prestige as the defeated shogun's bannermen than they would have had as the retainers of a daimyo. They argued that while their families had been transferred to Owari, their lands had not and the size of their fiefs put them in a category far above that of the Owari retainers. The Chimura, moreover, derived over half of its income from the lands it held in trust from the bakufu. If those were to be turned over to Owari, many of the retainers would be out of a job. Among them was the Ichioka family of Iida, and Ichioka Tami had married Taseko's son Makoto. Onari, Tami's younger brother and the man who had escorted Taseko to Nakatsugawa in 1862, was in Kyoto in 1868, staying with her banker Ichimura Kuninori. He was the conduit through which she became involved in Chimura affairs.

Taseko's role in this imbroglio is not one that has been emphasized by her biographers. Most, in fact, prefer to ignore the incident because it makes everyone involved look petty. It exposes all too nakedly the jockeying for position that marked the creation of the new central government, but whereas the leaders cloaked their ambition with principle, the Chimura and Yamamura did not. They deserved rank and status less because they had served the emperor than because it was their hereditary right. For Taseko to use her influence for them casts her in the part of a political lobbyist acting on behalf of special interests. This is not an identity that jibes well with being a poet, nativist scholar, or imperial loyalist. Acting in this way, however, inadvertently put her on the scene in Tokyo for that brief moment when the Hirata disciples believed their school to be in ascendance.

THE CHIMURA family started trying to confirm its claim to the lands it held in trust in the middle of 1868. The man responsible for the negotiations was Kushida Denbei, until then the chief Chimura retainer resident in Edo. Like other agents for the daimyo and bannermen, he had moved to Kyoto as quickly as he could following the fall of the bakufu. He first had Onari approach Taseko to ask her to mediate with Iwakura Tomomi. Through an Iwakura retainer, Denbei then petitioned the Executive Council (Dajōkan), only to be told that his request should have come from Chimura Nakayasu himself, then seriously ill in Kuguri. Denbei sent a fast messenger to get Nakayasu's seal stamped on the request, with orders that it be wrapped in oil paper and attached to a board lest it get soiled or creased. At the end of the letter giving these instructions, Denbei wrote:

> I've been wining and dining people to hear the talk of Kyoto. I asked O-Tase how long she plans to stay. She said she'd go home soon. Plus Onari has to get home by the middle of next month so he'll leave by the twentieth at the latest. If we don't know by then, I'll have to remain behind. If the two of them were planning to stay past the middle of the tenth month, I'd have time to distinguish between black and white. Ever since the fourth month of this year we've been sending soldiers to far away provinces and excelled in battle. Besides, we've been donating lots of money for military expenses so what we've actually done in serving the emperor will most probably be recognized. It would really be

too bad if it weren't. It would be even worse if the lands that we hold in trust were to be taken away from us, so I'm doing all I can.[4]

When Denbei wrote this letter, Taseko was still planning to leave Kyoto early in the tenth month, at least according to a letter she wrote her son from the Iwakura compound. At that point she optimistically predicted that having presented a copy of the grant from the bakufu showing the land held in trust, Denbei would soon have it confirmed. Such was not to be the case. Six days after she had planned to depart, she mentioned to Tami that she had been meeting almost daily with Onari and Denbei for "secret talks. I've been kept quite busy by the concerns of these bannermen unaccustomed to life above the clouds. Even though I'm supposed to be living in the Iwakura compound, I'm asked to go out a lot."[5] Now that she had become a woman of influence, she found herself involved willy-nilly in the affairs of other people.

While Denbei was trying to get recognition by the imperial government, local administrators were facing their own problems. Ina prefecture had been established in the eighth month to replace the Owari jurisdiction over the old bakufu holdings. The new governor was Kitakōji Toshimasa, a low-ranking court noble who had previously enjoyed a paltry income base of thirty *koku*. Upon his arrival at the prefectural headquarters early in the tenth month of 1868, he promptly summoned the bakufu bannermen to meet him. At this critical juncture Nakayasu was still sick in bed, and he had to send a representative in his place. His lapse was particularly unfortunate given that even the daimyo of Iida had put in a personal appearance at the prefectural office to protect his claim to his domain by prostrating himself before the new governor. The Chimura representative feared that not only would the family lose the lands it held in trust, it would have to ruin itself by donating large sums of money to the new regime. To forestall that eventuality, he bribed everyone on the governor's staff and proposed making Toshimasa the present of the best horse available, since he was known to fancy himself a connoisseur of horseflesh. His efforts proved in vain when Owari moved to have the Executive Council declare the Chimura to be its retainers.[6]

While Taseko was on her way home from Kyoto in the third month of 1869, she spent the night at Mitake on the Nakasendō close to Kuguri. "I think it was still before dawn when one of the men serving at Kuguri came to tell me all about the troubles afflicting the Chimura family," she wrote in a letter to Miwada Masako.

In the course of his conversation he expressed his delight at the extraordinary warmth with which I had been treated by you and the Iwakura family. When he came to talk about his anxieties regarding the future of the arrangements being made in Tokyo, I couldn't help but sympathize with him. He's been offering his prayers for a successful outcome to the Tokyo situation, but he has no one to rely on besides the Iwakura family and you. He wants you to look at the presents he's prepared for the lord, but I'm not sure they'll do any good since it's a question of what's already been done in the past. I really felt very sorry that he'd to come to stay at such a lonely place. He told me everything, withholding nothing. Once I agreed to appeal to you regarding how the Chimura feel about this matter, he was delighted. He said he'd tell Lord Chimura, and he also wants to send along a few gifts as soon as possible. I think I'll have to help out because this matter has already caused the Chimura family so much concern. I most sincerely appeal to you for help as well.[7]

Taseko prefaced this letter with a poem that gave her message a decidedly noble cast:

Ura mo naki	With straightforward hearts
kokoro tadashiku	keeping nothing back
yoki kimi ni	the good people of our nation
yoku tsukaeru zo	can really serve
kuni no yoki bito	a good ruler well.[8]

Now that the emperor had become the ruler of Japan, all the people who had been oppressed by the former system of social inequality that confined them to narrowly defined roles had the opportunity to act on his behalf. At the same time, the new government had the obligation to take advantage of their zeal. As a woman Taseko knew that she herself could do very little beyond promoting men of talent and ability as she had done in finding positions for Miwada Mototsuna and various Takasu domain retainers. In other words, she claimed that she was trying to help the Chimura not simply because family ties demanded it, but because she believed that the bannerman and his retainers could perform valuable services for king and country.

Soon after Taseko returned to Tomono, she wrote another letter, this one to Sonoda Ichibei, son-in-law to her good friend Hazama Hidenori from Nakatsugawa. Ichibei was then in Tokyo at the behest of the Yamamura family, and Taseko wanted him to meet Nakajima Masutane. Masutane was a former samurai from Tokushima and a Hirata disciple who had fled Kyoto following the decapitation of the Ashikaga shoguns' statues. He had a position in the new government as a judge in the Justice Ministry. When Taseko ended up in Tokyo, he spent many days in discussion with her and Hidenori. "You know, he really fooled me," Taseko noted later. "That a man like him would become a slave to things Western."[9] When she wrote her letter, however, she had no way of knowing what his leanings would turn out to be.

"I'd like to find out how things appear for a decision on this matter regarding the Yamamura family," she asked Ichibei,

> so please give it your attention. In any case, before too long we need to know which way the wind's going to be blowing from Owari. Please keep in mind that both the Chimura and the Yamamura are worried sick. It's of the utmost importance so please be extremely careful how you handle it. I have a letter from me along these lines to be presented to Mr. Nakajima, and I'd like for you to deliver it. I touch a little on the affairs of these two families, but I think you'll find it superficial and the brush strokes are pretty poorly done, so please explain everything to him orally. Owari has said nothing but lies about the status of these two families. I really think it would be better for you to talk everything over with Mr. Nakajima down to the smallest detail, and that's the reason why I'm writing you.[10]

It is quite possible that Taseko wrote other letters to friends in Tokyo on behalf of the Chimura and Yamamura families, but these are the only ones that remain. They provide glimpses of how she tried to work behind the scenes, pulling strings from a distance in the months before she finally ended up going to Tokyo herself. From the point of view of the men at the center of government, the question of what to do about two bannermen whose status was in dispute was a minor matter. For Taseko and her connections, however, it was of crucial concern.

Governmental institutions were changing fast in the early years of the Meiji Restoration, and no one could be sure how she would be affected. At the end of the second month of 1869, the four southwestern domains whose military support had been decisive in securing all of Japan for the emperor returned their land registers to him with the understanding that he would confirm their holdings. For them it was a purely symbolic gesture that both guaranteed their position in the new order and emphasized his standing as the fount of authority. Over the next few months, the other daimyo followed suit. The Chimura and Yamamura turned over their land registers and at the same time petitioned the Executive Council for a formal separation from Owari.[11] This brought to a head the power struggle between the former bannermen on the one hand and a powerful domain on the other. To have any chance of winning, the bannermen's retainers knew that they needed all the help they could find.

For the Chimura and Yamamura families, the question of status involved not simply their relations with Owari, but their rank in the new order. On the seventeenth day of the sixth month in 1869, the Executive Council announced that court nobles and daimyo were to be combined into a single order of nobility, called *kazoku*. With the exception of a few samurai who were also to be included by virtue of their outstanding contribution to overthrowing the bakufu, the vast majority were to become "former samurai" (*shizoku*) and "foot soldiers" (*sotsu*). Everyone else would be commoners. In Aizu, rural entrepreneurs who had bought samurai privileges shortly before the Restoration tried desperately to get themselves included in the *shizoku* status.[12] There was every possibility that the bannermen might end up ranked no higher than samurai from domains all across Japan whose stipends had not equaled one-tenth of theirs and whose status had been concomitantly lower. This was unfair, at least in their eyes. Their stipends as bannermen might fall in the 5,000 *koku* range, but they had managed lands held in trust worth much more than that for the bakufu and Owari. If these lands were included in their accounts, it would make them equal to the daimyo, defined as lords of land worth over 10,000 *koku*. They would thus both escape Owari control and become part of the new aristocracy.

Taseko had arranged introductions for the Chimura retainers while she was in Kyoto, she had given them advice on how to approach those in authority, and she had even written letters on their behalf. Now she was called on to do still more—to go to Tokyo and use her influence. "I refused," she wrote her son early in the fifth month. "I stated in several different ways that this is something to be decided by men high in the government. Even if I were to go to Tokyo, there'd be nothing I could do."[13] The Chimura retainers continued to press her, however, until she allowed herself to be talked into going. She was not the only local person so importuned. Among the men rallied to support the bannermen's cause was Hazama Hidenori from Nakatsugawa.

Hidenori had been in the capital for a month before his diary reports that Taseko had arrived on the sixth day of the sixth month, 1869. He spent his time consulting with the Chimura and Yamamura retainers, visiting government offices, reestablishing his connections with the court nobles who might be able to make a difference, and doing a lot of heavy drinking. Hirata Kanetane and many of the Hirata disciples who had gone to Kyoto in 1862 and 1868 were also in the city. Hidenori met with them for discussions on Atsutane's texts and their relevance to the present. He made a list of his doubts; whether he shared them with Kanetane is unknown, but they suggest that considerable debate was going on in nativist circles. In particular Hidenori questioned whether foreigners could be expected to believe that Izanagi and Izanami had indeed created Japan. If not, then how could he believe it either?[14]

Taseko and Hidenori spent considerable time together plotting strategy and allowing themselves to be entertained by the bannermen's retainers. Taseko visited the Iwakura compound the day after she arrived in the city, partly to pay her respects to the women she had come to know in Kyoto, partly to mention the reason for her presence in the city to Tomomi. Two days later, on the ninth day of the sixth month, she and Hidenori met at the Chimura mansion, and on the twelfth they had a liquid lunch. On the eighteenth she introduced him to Miwada Masako's husband Mototsuna, and they went to the central government offices to see other Hirata disciples known to Taseko since 1862 who had managed to find positions in the new bureaucracy. This building was not a place that old peasant women normally visited.[15] Hidenori's diary lists the people they importuned on the bannermen's behalf; ever discreet, hers reads more like a pleasure trip, and only occasionally does she reveal her true purpose.

Toward the end of the sixth month the Chimura retainers invited Hidenori and Taseko on a boating trip up the Sumida River, a pastime celebrated in novels and woodblock prints for two hundred years. Taseko was pleased at seeing such famous sites, even though they brought home to her the strangeness of this city now to be the emperor's chief residence. She and Hidenori exchanged poems about the birds they saw; his called on the river to run clear in reflecting the glory of the imperial reign (he should see it now!), hers lamented that the capital had been moved. On the way home she remarked on the presence of foreign ships in the bay:

Kage takami	How sad it is
kumoi no tsuki no	for the moon that casts its shadows
Sumida gawa	from high above the clouds
oyobanu kata wo	to see things unsuitable
miru zo kanashiki	in the Sumida River.[16]

Remember that above the clouds means the imperial court. It was bad enough that the barbarians continued to pollute Japan's sacred soil, but for them to appear in the vicinity of the imperial presence made it all the worse. Despite the fun of the outing, Hidenori noted that "for some reason I've lately been strangely depressed."[17]

Once Taseko and Hidenori had introduced the Chimura and Yamamura retainers to their connections in the city, they found time hanging on their hands while they waited for the outcome of the appeal to the Executive Council. Taseko sometimes spent nights with her friends at the Iwakura mansion or with Miwada Masako even though she was ostensibly lodged in the Yamamura compound at Shinbori. Hidenori watched the opening ceremonies for Yasukuni, the shrine built to house the spirits of those who had died for the emperor, and enjoyed the sumo tournament. The next night Yamamura Ryōjun invited his retainers plus Hidenori and Taseko on a boat trip to watch the fireworks welcoming the spirits to the shrine. The outing was capped with a supper liberally washed down with sake. When they tried to return, "an evil wind blew so fiercely that it damaged the roof of the boat and we barely made it home." [18]

While Taseko and Hidenori were filling their hours with sightseeing, trouble was brewing in the Ina Valley. The first years of the Meiji Era saw considerable peasant dissatisfaction with the new regime, expressed all too frequently in violent uprisings. In 1869 they broke out more frequently than in any single year in the entire history of Tokugawa rule. Many were local conflicts between tenants and landlords, moneylenders, and rural entrepreneurs over fees, foreclosure of loans, and rice-hoarding. In others, Sagara Sōzō came back to haunt the government when peasants demanded to know what had happened to early promises of tax relief.[19] Peasants in the Ina Valley had a specific grievance against unscrupulous merchants who brought in debased currency to buy not only silk but paper and other goods as well. It was virtually worthless by the time the government outlawed its use, and in the meantime over 100,000 *ryō* had ended up in peasant hands. For three days in the seventh month of 1869, the hapless victims attacked merchants in Iida and demanded that the government redeem the old currency for new at face value. According to Kären Wigen, "the counterfeit riots grew into the most massive eruption of popular protest of the nineteenth century" for the lower Ina Valley.[20] In letters to her cousin Inao and her son Mitsunaka, Taseko reported that news of disorder had spread to Tokyo. "What an unpleasant surprise," she wrote to Inao. "Given how conditions in the world are changing, you must be very, very careful. To be involved in such business right at the start of a new era is truly regrettable." [21] She sent the following advice to Mitsunaka: "Please take every precaution in your daily lives. Those who indulge themselves too much in amassing gold and silver will naturally receive the punishment of heaven." [22]

At the end of the seventh month Miwada Masako's husband Mototsuna proposed a pilgrimage to Kamakura-gu. This was a recently refurbished shrine marking the spot where Emperor Godaigo's eldest son Morinaga had been confined in a cramped and damp cave before his murder at the hands of the Ashikaga forces in 1335, an episode recounted in "The Precious Sleeve Cord." Being young and recently married, Masako was expected to stay home, making Taseko the only woman to join Hidenori and six other men for the trip. First they rested at a tea house in Shinagawa at the outskirts of Tokyo. "It had an extremely fine view of the road along the coast," Taseko noted in her diary, "but there were entirely too many foreign ships in the offing." The first night they spent at Kanagawa, the next at Enoshima, still today a popular spot for vacationers. They got up before dawn to visit the shrine for Benten, actually a Buddhist deity known as a god of good fortune, who had recently been purified of his Buddhist elements and given the name Iwajima no kami. They worshipped joyfully at the shrine erected for Prince Morinaga before going back to the beach to see a blow hole. "The spray shot up at least two hundred yards high," Taseko noted, "and my heart was filled with awe at the thought that the god was truly there." [23]

At the end of the eighth month Taseko allowed herself to be drawn into a trip to Yokohama, site of the foreign concession and already distinctly different from the rest of Japan with its brick buildings, glass windows, and gas lights. The streets were thronged with people from all over the world: "English, Americans, Dutch, French, Prussians, Swiss, Portuguese, and nondescript," according to Francis Hall as early as 1866.[24] He ignored the Chinese, over half of the foreigners resident in the city, who had come as household servants or trading assistants to the Europeans and Americans.[25] They lived in a Chinese quarter that still remains today. The British Crown Prince had paid Japan its first formal state visit the month before, but Taseko was not impressed. As she reported to her son Mitsunaka, "everything I saw was disagreeable." [26]

Despite the efforts of Taseko and her friends, preserving the Chimura and Yamamura's rank and status proved difficult. Taseko pulled every string she could, visiting officials who might be in a position to help and writing letters. To Iwakura Maki on the eleventh day of the eighth month, she wrote, "when will we know about the matter of the Chimura family? Please don't let the lord see this letter. I want it to look as though the query is coming from you." [27] Two days later she noted that everyone in the Yamamura compound appeared to be extremely worried. "When I asked what was going on, I learned that they had received a message from Owari summoning them to the government office on the morrow." On the twentieth the Chimura retainers were told to present documents attesting to their fief's origins in 1600 and records showing its size and the number of villages it contained. This had to be done as quickly as possible. In the middle of the eleventh month Taseko and Hidenori spent several days meeting with the Chimura contingent to decide which documents to produce, how to explain them, and whether they could get by with copies.

Taseko continued to meet with the Chimura retainers intermittently throughout the twelfth month, but she found her presence to be increasingly pointless. In the meantime her son Makoto had come to Tokyo on business. When he had finished, she and Onari took advantage of his departure to return to Ina. In recompense for her efforts she received a halberd, a barrel of shellfish, and a long outer robe (*uchikake*) from the Yamamura family and a set of lunchboxes, a pocket watch, and a short sword from the Chimura.[28] A few months after she left, in the third month of 1870, the two families were informed that they were to be *shizoku,* former samurai.

WORKING ON behalf of the Chimura and Yamamura families brought Taseko to Tokyo within months of its becoming the new capital. There she once again found herself with her mentor Kanetane and her fellow Hirata disciples. These were heady days. The new government at first appeared to promise a "Unity of Rites and Rule" (*saisei itchi*) that harkened back to the early imperial state when political policy, foreign affairs, and agricultural production were said to have been conducted through rituals of worship that linked them directly to the gods. The fertilizer merchant from Ōmi, Nishikawa Yoshisuke, had already been summoned to give lectures on Hirata Atsutane's perception of the nativist way to the women of the court in 1868. He was appointed an official lecturer in 1869, a position which necessitated a move to Tokyo.[29] Hirata Kanetane had a position in the new Office of Rites, soon to be the Ministry of Rites based ostensibly on the seventh and eighth century model. On the first day of the eighth month of 1869, the National University, Daigakkō, was established for the study of Japan as well as Chinese and Western studies. Kanetane became its titular head although at seventy he left most business to his son. The chief disciples served on its faculty. Their long desired return to ancient practices appeared to be becoming a reality.

Taseko had not wanted to leave her home and family for Tokyo, but once she arrived, she was delighted at the ascendancy of her fellow disciples and the promise of governmental reform. To celebrate the new age she composed a poem titled "Spring in Chiyoda," Chiyoda being the name of the former shogun's castle where the emperor now lived in temporary quarters in the heart of the city.[30] The introduction contains four lines from *Man'yōshū* poems written at the death of rulers in which the speaker expresses his, or in Taseko's case, her hesitation to speak on august and awesome affairs of state.[31] She then goes on to celebrate the founding of the imperial regime:

Sumeragi no kami	The exalted grandson
miko no tōtoyu	of the imperial god
tori ga naku	in the eastern province
azuma no kuni ni	where the cock cries
yachida no	in the dwelling of Chiyoda
Chiyoda no sato ni	among eight-thousand fields
miya hashira	is building the foundations
futoshiku tate	for the pillars of his palace / of his administration.

The last two lines are from another *Man'yōshū* poem written by the greatest of Japan's early poets, Kakinomoto no Hitomaro, when Empress Jitō made an excursion to the palace at Yoshino in the late seventh century: "Many are the lands under heaven / and the sway of our Lord, / sovereign of the earth's eight corners."[32] Taseko thus transforms a dirge into a song of celebration.

Taseko next fills in a few lines describing Japan with the verdant images found so frequently in the *Man'yōshū* and early historical texts, phrases such as "the land of reed plains," or "luxuriant rice fields." She foresees that with the coming of the new age, the emperor's writ will become known throughout the land and the divine authority which he receives from the gods will envelop the people:

Takachiho no	Should his great authority
kami nagara naru	in accordance with the way of the gods
ōmiitsu	from on high
terashi tamau to	shine down on us
ame no shita	everywhere under heaven
shio no yaoe no	as far as the distant islands
harukanaru	so far away
toitsu shima made	where the tidal currents meet
taniguku no	as far as the toad can leap
sawataru kagiri	to the very ends of the earth,
ki mo kusa mo	then the trees and grasses, officials and people
yorite tsukauru	will come to serve
kimi ga yo no	and the imperial reign
tōtoku mo aru ga	which is exalted
tōtoki zo kamo	will become indeed exalted.[33]

Atsutane's texts had taught Taseko that the emperor rules the entire earth. By invoking the leaping toad, she alludes to a *Man'yōshū* poem that describes how the emperor reigns "Here beneath the gleaming sun and moon /

as far as the ends of the earth / where the clouds trail from the heaven."[34] In Taseko's political philosophy, the relationship between ruler and people is a natural one. In the unity of rites and rule which her study of nativist texts had shown her is the correct way of governance, obeying the emperor's decrees and worshipping the gods is one and the same. Even natural phenomena such as trees and grass have a consciousness of imperial grace when it is allowed to manifest itself without obstruction into every nook and cranny of the land. The word for grass (*kusa*) is a metaphor for "the people," the commoners, the countless masses. Previously there had been no place for them to be the subjects of their own actions. Now that they were enveloped by imperial authority, they could work in harmony with the emperor and the gods as a matter of course.

For many of Taseko's friends, working in harmony with the emperor meant scrambling to make their voices heard in the new government. The nativists who had thought the imperial restoration would be carried out on their terms quarreled among themselves; the samurai from the southwestern domains of Satsuma and Chōshū who had conquered Japan in the emperor's name had their own ideas. They wanted not a divine order but, in the words of James Ketelaar, a rational one.[35] If, as Miyachi Masato has argued, the nativists conceived of the state in social terms, constructed in layers from the bottom up while most samurai saw it as a political and military machine, the domain writ large, then men at the center of the new government had yet a different vision, one that envisioned the state to be complete in itself. Having the highest value, it could reconstitute existing society in accordance with its own needs.[36] While they shared the nativists' fears of foreign domination, they differed dramatically in their plans for resisting it.

One of Taseko's fellow Hirata disciples had a brief opportunity to put his views into practice. This was Maruyama Sakura, born in 1840 to a low-ranking retainer from the Shimabara domain who had been based in Edo.[37] The family was so poor that as a boy Sakura was apprenticed to the domain tea master in hopes of learning a trade that would distinguish him from his peers. Perry's arrival in Japan when he was thirteen led him and his friends to pledge their lives in defense of the nation. Five years later he enrolled as a disciple of Hirata Atsutane. He won praise for his diligence as a scholar, so much so that he was given a sample of Atsutane's calligraphy. He treated it as a lucky charm, carefully keeping it always with him and attributing to it the power to protect him from harm. He was one of the men Taseko had met in Kyoto in 1862, and like her he hid in the Chōshū compound following the decapitation of the Ashikaga shogun's statues. After numerous adventures he was imprisoned by his domain for his effrontery in complaining to the daimyo that an Englishman had been allowed to climb one of Japan's sacred moun-

tains. He improved his stay by teaching nativism to his jailers, criticizing domanial policies, and reciting poetry at the top of his lungs. He was not released until Sawa Nobuyoshi, with Taseko's old friend Tsunoda Tadayuki in
his train, came to claim the bakufu outpost in Nagasaki for the imperial
forces. He received his first appointment in the new Meiji government as
Nobuyoshi's assistant.

When Taseko arrived in Tokyo, Sakura was headed for a diplomatic career. At the announcement that the British crown prince was coming to
Japan, he had been put in charge of investigating historical precedents for his
reception. There was not much to go on since the emperor had never before
granted an interview to a foreign ruler. In the ninth month of 1869, Sakura
received court rank, a generous stipend of 420 *koku,* and a position in the foreign service. Taseko visited him the next day to offer her congratulations.
Five days later on the ninth, she took a farewell present to him. He was off to
Sakhalin, also called Karafuto, to deal with the Russian encroachment on what
he considered Japanese territory. The Russian presence in the chilly northern climes had been a sporadic issue since before Taseko was born. In 1869
Russians advanced on the southern half of the peninsula and destroyed Japanese fishing camps. Sakura's orders were to protect the Japanese inhabitants
without disrupting the relations between the two nations and to avoid war.

Sakura and Taseko saw his mission a little differently. They thought it was
an opportunity to expand Japan's national boundaries. When Sakura was
first given the commission, he proposed building a fortress staffed with soldiers and asked for authorization to take whatever measures necessary in
dealing with the Russians. Taseko expressed her understanding of what he
was to do in a poem:

Utsusegai	When you pay your respects
Karafuto shima ni	on Karafuto
iyabu toku	of the empty sea shells,
mikuni no hashira	don't come back before establishing
tate kaera na	the pillars for the sacred country.[38]

Here Taseko is creating her own pillow word for a place that did not appear
in the classical poetry anthologies. "Empty shell" is a metaphor for "without
substance," but she is more probably using it to refer to the occupation of the
people who inhabited the area. "The pillars for the country " is a nativist expression that like "the pillars of the palace" in her long poem refers obliquely
to the establishment of imperial rule.

Sakura's tenure in Sakhalin was not a happy one. He found the Russians
busy digging roads, right through the natives' graveyards in some cases, and

setting up their own fisheries. He tried to negotiate with them, at the same time sending out his own survey crews and urging the government back in Tokyo to agree to a military solution. The situation was complicated when six of his underlings destroyed the fortifications being built by the Russians around one of their bases. The men were arrested, causing a diplomatic incident for which Sakura received the blame. Summoned back to Tokyo, he found himself criticized for opposing the government's wishes, yet many of Taseko's friends among the Hirata disciples looked to him for what they saw as a correct solution to the problem. Three of his henchmen even threatened to go to Ōkubo Toshimichi's mansion and once there, to commit suicide if the Satsuma statesman refused to accept Sakura's proposals. Sakura spent fruitless weeks petitioning Iwakura and other leading figures while also meeting with scholars to search the ancient histories for mention of Karafuto. He managed to arouse considerable controversy, and when in 1871 he advocated an invasion of Korea, he was arrested and put in domanial custody. A few months later he was sentenced on extremely flimsy grounds to ten years in prison for having incited grass-roots activists and samurai to plot against the state.

Sakura was single-minded in his determination to restore the ancient way. He founded a *Kana* society to promote the use of the Japanese syllabary in place of Chinese characters. He made an enemy of the post office because he insisted on using nothing but the syllabary in writing addresses, even on the hundreds of New Year's cards that he mailed every year. Naturally he arose early enough to greet the sun, and no matter how chill the dawn he would pour cold water over himself in a ritual of purification before praying to the gods. Like his friend Tsunoda Tadayuki, he always wore Japanese dress. He celebrated the body's natural functions, and he delighted in producing loud manly farts.

After his years in prison, Sakura was to become increasingly conservative. He worked with Tadayuki to raise the status of the Atsuta shrine near Nagoya. He founded a patriotic society in 1881 to promote gradualism in politics in opposition to the Popular Rights Movement, at the same time that he supported instituting a bicameral legislature with a limited franchise. He participated in the movement to purify Shinto of Buddhist elements but also to rectify what he saw as degenerate practices, the lascivious dances that had characterized the Bon festival, for example. In 1886 he was invited back into the government and his court rank was restored. The next year he would travel to Europe to assess the merits of the various governments, some years after Itō Hirobumi's more famous trip to study constitutional theory. On his return he was appointed to the office that studied imperial systems, and he helped sort out the imperial genealogies. In 1890 he became a member of the House of Peers.

As a man and a former samurai, Sakura was able to expand his horizons considerably beyond anything Taseko ever experienced. She watched from the sidelines while he led one adventure after another, and she supported his efforts through her poetry and letters. At the first anniversary of her death, he wrote a poem titled, "Longing, pining for the old days:"

Sono na sae	Even her name
yo ni Takasago no	summons the old pine
oimatsu no	at Takasago
kage wo tanomi shi	that died long ago
mukashi shinu hoyu	where I once sought shade.[39]

Matsu as in Matsuo means pine. Sakura may well have been drawing on a famous *Kokinshū* poem that uses the pines at Takasago as a metaphor for friendship: "Who then shall become / my dear companions even / the many pines that / stand at Takasago are / not those friends of long ago."[40]

Sakura was not the only Hirata disciple whose career in government service was cut short in the early 1870s. Taseko's friends who had eagerly joined the government either as teachers in the National University under Kanetane or as bureaucrats soon found its direction not to their liking. Nakajima Masutane in the Justice Ministry adapted to the new ways; others were vocal in their disapproval of what they saw as rampant westernizaton. The National University became a hotbed of controversy where the nativist scholars quarreled bitterly with each other. Fukuba Bisei had been one of the first Hirata disciples to befriend Taseko in Kyoto in 1862, but by 1870, he had less and less patience with Kanetane's faction. Having the more influence, he was instrumental in getting the government to close down the National University.[41] Kanetane's supporters tried to get Nishikawa Yoshisuke, the erstwhile fertilizer merchant, to join them in reprimanding Bisei. Yoshisuke put them off, feigning illness so as not to get embroiled in a fight that might hurt his career. Tsunoda Tadayuki was furious. In his eyes, Yoshisuke was "a despicable little man."[42]

Bisei and his supporters had a notion of the "Unity of Rites and Rule" that effectively sidelined the Hirata disciples. In its basic formulation it apparently meant what Taseko's poetry described, the harmonious interaction of gods, emperor, and people in the creation of a new state where religious practices structured political space.[43] It brought the emperor into the public limelight; hereafter no government initiative could be taken without his ratification and his announcing it to his ancestors among the gods. "His political function was inseparable from his priestly function."[44] But at the same time, Bisei emphasized hierarchy. Rather than allowing the people spontaneously to offer their services to the emperor, they should act by aligning their thoughts and feelings with those of their superiors.[45] At the most concrete level, the Hirata disciples wanted the formal notice of restoration of imperial rule to go not only to the Ise shrine of the sun goddess, but to major shrines all over Japan, to the gods of the earth as well as to the heavenly deities. Bisei disagreed.[46] Haga Noboru is just one historian who blames Bisei and the Ōkuni school for opening a wedge between the people on the one hand and government ministers and the emperor on the other, a gap that the Hirata disciples had tried to close.[47] Yet the Hirata disciples still clung to the hope of expelling the barbarians, and their position had become increasingly anachronistic.

For many Hirata disciples, the commitment to restoring the emperor to direct rule was compromised at its source by their attachment to their hereditary status. The men who had cut all ties to their domains and their families tended to be younger sons like Miwada Mototsuna or professional men such as Gonda Naosuke and his disciples. Nishikawa Yoshisuke was an exception. By the time he became politically active, however, his family had already forced him to choose a successor. In hotbeds of nativist sentiment such as the Ina Valley, the leading figures — Taseko's cousin Inao for example — seldom ventured beyond hearth and home. In an oblique nod to their interests, Yano Harumichi, who became the leading spokesman for the Hirata side, argued that the restoration of imperial rule should be based on the creative principles articulated by the ancestral deities. This was not a recipe for social equality or representative government.[48] In other words, the rural entrepreneurs who joined the Hirata school wanted to give power to the emperor and change the world, but not their own place in it.

By the autumn of 1870, the conflict between the Hirata disciples and Bisei, who supported the hard-headed pragmatists in the government such as Ōkubo Toshimichi, had come to a head. When Harumichi insisted that the emperor's enthronement ceremonies be performed in Kyoto, Bisei accused him of standing in the way of progress and enlightenment.[49] At the same time a more radical faction of disgruntled grass-roots activists started scheming to take the emperor back to Kyoto by force. The discovery of their plot gave the government a convenient excuse to round up all dissidents in the "Offense against National Affairs Incident (*Kokuji ihan jiken*)." In 1871, 257 people were punished and nine were executed, plus two nobles who were allowed to commit suicide.[50] Among those caught in the net along with Sakura were Harumichi, Gonda Naosuke, and Tsunoda Tadayuki, all Taseko's friends. With these arrests and the closing of the National University, the nativists' hopes for making a lasting impact on the new state came to an end. Harumichi wrote a bitter poem expressing his disappointment:

Kashiwara no	My assumption
miyo ni kaeru to	that we were returning
omoishi wa	to the divine age of Kashiwara
aranu yume nite	has become nothing more than
arikeru mono wo	the impossible dream.[51]

Kashiwara in the hills of Nara prefecture is said to be the site of Emperor Jinmu's enthronement ceremony, marking the origin of the Japanese state. For Harumichi as for Taseko herself, the return to the ancient system of imperial rule was supposed to have been literal.

Despite her early optimism, Taseko gradually became less enamored of the new government. "I do think that before long the time will come when the country is suitably reformed," she wrote in a letter to her cousin Inao early in the sixth month of 1869. Two months later in a letter to Mitsunaka she was more cautious. "Concerning the way politics has been handled up to now, some things I am pleased with; others I am not." In another letter that she wrote him from Tomono after a year or so had passed, she complained of the changes that had come to Japan, changes most definitely not to her liking.

This reign has only just begun, and I've been having a hard time because every day I do nothing but worry about government affairs. Even though I know I can't do anything, that's just the way I am. I have no idea when a truly auspicious era will be inaugurated. As for the old, it's farther away than the invisible world. It appears that more and more of those lousy foreigners are strutting their stuff in our country. Recently I sent the following poem to someone I know in Tokyo:

Habikoreru	When will it be possible
emishi shiko gusa	to purify this realm
kariharai	by cutting down and expelling
miyo kiyomareru	these noxious barbarian weeds
toki wa itsu kamo	that have grown so rampant?

This is what I sent them. The people who think as I do read it and sigh.[52]

THE "OFFENSE against National Affairs Incident" had seen the demise of the Hirata school as a political force in national politics. For Taseko, how-

ever, the categories of thought that she had imbibed through reading Atsutane's texts continued to structure the way she saw the world. While she and
Chiburu were still in Tokyo at the beginning of 1882, she wrote a long poem
exclaiming at how quickly the first fifteen years of the Meiji Era had passed.
As with all her nativist poetry, she emphasized the direct connection between the august ruler and the common people:

Ōmi-kokoro wa	The emperor's heart
aya ni aya	is awesomely
tōtokiko mo ya	precious
sono kiyoki	and the common people
nagare wo kumeru	from the country of luxuriant rice ears
ashihara no	and reed plains
mizuho no kuni no	can imbibe
hito kusa no	its clear flowing purity.
Miyo wa nigosaji	As long as the imperial reign is neither
kegasaji to	muddied nor polluted,
aukane mono no	and there is nothing
arame ya mo	with which we cannot cope
tsutomenu hito wa	then I think that there will be
araji to zo omou	no one who does not exert himself.[53]

This poem is as usual layered with lines drawn from the *Man'yōshū* that celebrate imperial rule. Despite all the administrative changes that have taken
place, Taseko still hopes that so long as the people feel that they have a direct
connection to the emperor, both will flourish. She is, however, considerably
less than sanguine that this will be achieved. Despite her protestations to the
contrary, she is forced to admit, if only by implication, that the restoration of
imperial rule has not turned out as she had expected.

As she grew older Taseko managed to accept the changes that transformed
the Japanese political landscape by explaining them in terms that had long
since fallen out of fashion. On February 21, 1889, the emperor promulgated
the Meiji Constitution, a gift from him to his subjects. Taseko cared not a
whit that it had been written by a small group of oligarchs based largely on
German models or that while sovereignty resided in the emperor, actual governance was to be by ministers and bureaucrats. Instead she wrote a series of
poems to celebrate the auspicious occasion. One proclaimed that Tokyo had
become the imperial capital for all time; another argued that by bestowing a
constitution on the people, the emperor proved that he had the interests of
the commoners at heart. A third asserted that the constitution represented
what the nativists had most desired, a return to antiquity:

Ki mo kusa mo	The trees and grasses, officials and people
koto yamete kiki	stop their business to listen
sumeragi miyo wa	in today's ceremony
mukashi wasurenu	the emperor's reign
kyōno mi-matsuri	has not forgotten ancient days.[54]

Historians know that Taseko's poems expressed pious hopes largely left un-realized. Japan developed a well-trained civil service proud of its elite status and disdainful of the people, for it served not them but the emperor. On the other hand, by performing public functions in public ceremonies, the emperor became much more closely identified with the Japanese nation than the nativists had scarcely dared hope some twenty years before.

Taseko remained a xenophobic observer of national politics to the end of her days.[55] In a set of poems dated 1890, she once again urged her compatriots to "hunt down and expel the noxious weeds" that obstructed the ancient way. She consoled herself with the thought that even though patterns of speech and behavior are mutable, the underlying cultural essence of the Japanese, the *kokutai*, would always remain the same. The bicameral National Diet, with its House of Peers and House of Representatives, began deliberations for the first time in that same year. This was innovation indeed, and Taseko marveled at the growing complexity of the political universe:

Yachimata ni	Cataloging and describing
kakaru yachi kuma	the myriad crannies
kaki wakete	caused by the branching road
michi hirori yuki	in this imperial age
kimi ga miyo kana	how broad the way has become.[56]

PART FOUR *Taseko in Modern Japan*

CHAPTER FIFTEEN

Taseko in Old Age

A single cry
rings out and is lost
in the depths of Shinano
hidden in the clouds
is the mountain cuckoo.
SHINAGAWA YAJIRŌ, 1894[1]

Taseko held an enviable position as matriarch of the Matsuo family. The latter half of the nineteenth century was still a time when women gained respect as they grew older, when experience earned them wisdom valued by family and neighbors. Taseko complained about her aches and pains and used the decrepitude of age as an excuse for not answering letters. She greeted visitors with delight and gladly handed out samples of her poetry. She engrossed herself in the life of her family, raising silkworms, marrying off her children and grandchildren, and in some cases mourning their deaths. She took great satisfaction in recollecting her adventures, and she died surrounded by her progeny.

While Taseko enjoyed the rewards of a long and varied life, the Japanese political landscape went through a whole series of transformations. Iida domain was abolished in 1871. The castle was demolished, its walls torn down, and the moat filled in. The multiplicity of old administrations disappeared. Ina prefecture, which had been created out of bakufu lands, was absorbed into Chikuma prefecture with its headquarters at Matsumoto. When the number of prefectures was reduced in 1877, the Ina Valley found itself in Nagano prefecture. In a letter to her son's wife in Yamamoto, Taseko complained, "since the government office at Takesa [for the Takasu domain] closed, we've really been completely out of touch."[2] It is easy to discount the significance of the domanial boundaries in a region so politically fragmented as this valley had been, but the old administrative channels had served a useful purpose as communication routes, even for women. In 1875 the number of villages had been dramatically reduced by combining the already existing villages, hereafter called hamlets, into new amalgamated units to be run by mayors and vice-mayors. Tomono joined three other villages in becoming Kumashiro.[3]

Other changes came more slowly. For so long as Taseko lived, Tomono was connected to the west side of the Tenryū River only by a hand-poled ferry boat. The roads remained narrow, rutted, and unpaved: dusty in summer, muddy in spring and autumn, and completely unsuitable for wheeled vehicles. The postal service began in 1872, but the nearest post office was in Iida. For communications within the valley, people continued to hire messengers or rely on friends and strangers. Kumashiro did not receive a post office until 1909. The telegraph and telephone offices arrived in 1911.[4] The railroad, the biggest generator of economic development, by-passed the Ina Valley completely until a private line was built in 1923. Living in Tomono, Taseko need have little contact with the new-fangled Western devices that transformed city life.[5]

Taseko's later years were comfortable. She lived in her garden cottage where first the plum and then the cherry blossomed in spring, the green leaves of trees and grasses deepened in color throughout the summer, the chrysanthemum heralded the arrival of autumn crowned by the red of the maple, and then drifted snow ended the year, at least according to her poetry. The cottage was a two-story structure connected to the main house by a passageway with communications served by a bell. The ground floor had three rooms and a water closet, and the second floor had two smaller rooms used for storage. The room closest to the main house was Taseko's sitting room; the middle and larger room with its alcove and shelves was for reading and entertaining guests.[6] There she enjoyed her grandchildren and wrote poetry with her friends. She even had her own students, men such as Yuasa Masanobu who practiced medicine in Ajima and Chiku Fumimizu, a former samurai. She took pride in Makoto, whose career in local politics culminated in his 1878 election to the first Nagano prefectural assembly.

Domestic life is always so much less documented than public life that it quickly escapes from the record altogether. Taseko's letters attest to her ongoing connections to her relatives, in particular the Takemura and Kitahara families. Interviews with her descendants and friends in the early twentieth century reveal anecdotes that often say as much about the conventions of old age as about her personality. She continued writing poetry, and in the headings for her poems can be glimpsed the family-sized events that punctuated her last twenty years. Pieced together these resemble nothing so much as a patchwork of different jigsaw puzzles, none of them complete.

Setsuko had a fund of stories about her famous great-grandmother. After Taseko's husband died, she shared her quarters with her granddaughter Kiyo. According to Setsuko, Taseko was kind enough to make up the bed for Kiyo rather than the other way around. Setsuko was only nine when Taseko died, and in her recollections, Taseko was always full of energy. When one of her neighbors built a new bath, she rushed over to try it out. She continued to raise silkworms, wielding a sickle to chop off the mulberry branches. "Her diligence in preparing the leaves was an inspiration to the younger workers." Whenever a visitor asked for tea, she would respond with "yes, yes, right away." All crouched over she would scurry along the passageway to the main house to fetch it. She always had a smile for her great-grandchildren. "We called her, 'oii-sama' (respected elder). At the New Year she would give us a ball and five *zeni* [one hundred *zeni* equaled one yen]. That is one of my happiest memories." [7]

Taseko had the reputation for being strict with young people, especially her children and grandchildren, but she indulged Setsuko. "Once when my aunt from Nakatsugawa came for a visit, she was wearing a new style of kimono. I was about six or seven at the time, and I liked it a lot. 'All right, I'll sew one for you,' great-grandmother said. She immediately found some scraps of cloth and made me a little one with red cuffs. I can still remember how delighted I was." The aunt would have been Taseko's daughter Tsuga, who had married the headman for the post station thirty years earlier. Taseko and Setsuko shared a passion for parched beans. "In the autumn a frame for drying beans would be set up north of the house. Grandmother would take me there to pick up those that had fallen off and then roast them for me on a little grill. She always said, 'Setsuko likes beans so much that she should marry into a family where she can eat lots of them.'" Setsuko later married a man in Ōkawara, a village famous for its beans. [8]

The heir to the Matsuo house, Taseko's great-grandson Haruomi, remembered her with respect. He was a man; not for him was the indulgence reserved for Setsuko. When he was five, he received a notebook with a rubber band attached, very popular at the time, from his aunt in the Maijima family. "I took

FIGURE 21. Front row left to right: Matsuo Isa, née Kitahara, wife of Taseko's youngest son Tameyoshi; Maijima Setsuo, née Matsuo, Taseko's great-granddaughter; Matsuo Tami, née Ichioka, wife of Taseko's eldest son Makoto; Matsuo Suzu, née Onda, wife of Taseko's grandson Chiburu; Kitahara Yaso, née Matsuo, Taseko's youngest daughter. Back row: Matsuo Torashirō, Tameyoshi's adopted son; Matsuo Haruomi, Taseko's older great-grandson; Matsuo Tameyoshi, Taseko's youngest son; Matsuo Samashi, Taseko's younger great-grandson. From *Matsuo Taseko ihō chō*, p. 8.

it to show great-grandmother and asked her to write something in it. She wrote the following poem to encourage me in my studies:"

Yoki hito no	Listen carefully to the teachings
oshie yoku kiki	of good people
yoku oboe	and remember them well
yo ni yoki hito to	let it be said of you
hito ni iware yo	that you are a good person.[9]

This injunction served Haruomi as her last testament. It reminded him that he had inherited the responsibility to manage the Matsuo house and work for the common weal.

Taseko's fame as a participant in the events leading to the Restoration and her reputation as a poet brought a steady trickle of visitors to her cottage. They came to exchange poems or simply beg a sample of her calligraphy. She was always happy to oblige. As her eyes weakened, she had difficulty seeing the tip of her brush. Asking, "is it on the paper?" she would happily scratch away at a poem.

When she was eighty-two, three men who wrote poetry with her came for an unexpected New Year's visit. "We came today to see the poems you received from the empress," they announced. "That's easy to do," Taseko replied, and led them into the formal drawing room at the center of her cottage where a selection of poems was on display. She showed them the one written by Prince Arisugawa, and they read it reverently. Somehow she could not find the poems she thought had been written by the empress. She pulled out her boxes and while she was searching, the men noticed a beautiful strip of gold paper with a poem in a woman's hand. "That's not a very good poem. Who does that woman think she is to be using such fine paper? Come on, show us the empress's poems." "That poem is the empress's," Taseko finally admitted, laughing out loud. The three men could not have been more embarrassed. "When you look at a poem as poets," Taseko asked, "do you think you should be concerned with matters of status?" [10]

Most of Taseko's visitors lived in her vicinity or claimed a connection through marriage or blood. One of the most noteworthy was Andō Kikuko, like Taseko a descendant of Sakurai Chie (see the Sakurai genealogy in chapter two). Kikuko was born in Iida Castle to a high-ranking samurai official in 1827. She had started to learn poetry from her cousin Sakurai Haruki before her formal education was cut short by her father, who put her to learning weaving, sewing, and sericulture. And a good thing, too. Her husband died after they had been married for only nine years, leaving her pregnant, a son by his first wife, and three children of her own. When her father-in-law died the next year, the family's stipend was cut, and Kikuko had to use all her skill to make ends meet. Not until 1873 did she manage to get her children married off or adopted, and caring for them kept her close to home during the years before the Meiji Restoration. [11]

Following her release from child care, Kikuko promptly began her lifelong avocation: writing poetry and meeting poets. In Kyoto she exchanged poems with Takabatake Shikibu and Ōtagaki Rengetsu, women Taseko had met in 1862. She also heard Iwasaki Nagayo lecture on nativist texts. In 1874 she was called back to Iida to hear her father's dying words. He told her to enjoy herself with her beloved poetry. She should go to the city, make new friends, find good teachers and relish old age. That she did, moving to Tokyo in 1875 where through poetry-writing circles she met members of the nobility such as Mōri Motonori, once heir to the Chōshū domain, and Konoe Tadahiro, the former Regent. In 1891 Kikuko returned to Iida for the first time since her father's death. While she was there, she arranged an introduction to her cousin Taseko. "Long ago she was known for her loyalty to the emperor, and she liked to read poetry so we soon became intimate friends," Kikuko wrote in her autobiography. "I enjoyed myself staying with her for two or three days, and she sometimes wrote to me after I returned to Tokyo." The two women exchanged many poems of friendship. "Please come again across the Tenryū River," Taseko penned when they parted.[12]

Kikuko and Taseko talked at length about poetry, the poets they knew, and Taseko's experiences in Kyoto. When Kikuko was getting ready to leave, Taseko told her about Miwada Masako. "She's living in Tokyo now. I think if you make friends with her, you'll both enjoy each other very much. You should visit her, saying I told you to do so." Kikuko did as requested, taking Masako a poem Taseko had once written about how the dazzling light reflected on the snow at the top of Mt. Fuji paled in comparison to the glorious great plain of heaven. A common love for poetry brought these women together, and it was through poetry that they expressed their friendship. "Your fine Japanese spirit means more to me than the perfume from the flowers," was Masako's response. Kikuko added her own that alluded to both:

Yuki wo yome	Reciting poems about the snow
hana ni utaishi	singing songs of flowers
omokage wa	every time I see the moon,
tsuki miru tabi ni	I am reminded with longing
shinowaruru kana	of your visage.[13]

Kikuko maintained her connection to Taseko and the Ina Valley despite living in Tokyo. In 1905 she made a pilgrimage to Taseko's grave where she recalled the poems they had exchanged and talked about the past with the women in the Matsuo family. Her stepson who had remained in Iida married his daughter Isa to Inao's youngest son Achinosuke. Through his interest in poetry, Achinosuke too became friends with Kikuko, and he wrote poems in celebration of her eightieth birthday in 1907.

When Kikuko's eldest son (who had been adopted by the Yanagita family) found himself with no son to succeed him, she recommended that he adopt a young man from Hyōgo named Matsuoka Kunio. In his "Tales of old-fashioned poetry" (*Kyūha uta monogatari*) Kunio wrote, "There were some old people in their fifties and sixties who used to attend the poetry meetings, and among them was a woman of about seventy with pure white hair wearing glasses. She loved to talk and she talked a lot about everything. . . . She was a cheerful old soul who laughed loudly. Her poetry was pretty bad, but she liked the meetings and came frequently." This was Kikuko, as seen by the pioneer in Japanese ethnology.[14]

Taseko received visitors on several occasions not because she was a poet or a hero of the Restoration but because she had influence. One letter to her son-in-law Kitahara Nobutsuna described how a merchant from Nakatsu-gawa had asked her to intercede for him. The merchant could pay back only a portion of a large sum owed Nobutsuna even though it was the end of the year when debts were traditionally paid in full. He had brought Taseko 50 *ryō* in gold certificates, asking her to hand them to Nobutsuna because he was ashamed to show his face at the Kitahara house. "I tried to refuse and urged him repeatedly to see you. He said that if he had all the money in hand, he'd be happy to do that, but right now he really and truly could do no more than 50 *ryō*. He earnestly begged me to explain the circumstances to you, and he promises that he'll definitely bring you the remainder by the end of the first or second month, leaving me no choice but to accept the money."[15] This merchant, whom Taseko identifies only by the first characters of his family and personal names, went well out of his way to ask for her help. Rather than rely on any of the Kitahara's friends and relatives living in his own town, he went to the other side of the Tenryū River in search of an effective ally. Taseko also found herself asked to be a go-between in marriages and to help young men get out of trouble.[16] There is no knowing how frequently these demands were made on her time. That they occurred at all and involved people from outside her valley is one indication of how far her reputation had spread, and in village society, reputation can be an important form of capital.[17]

One of the pleasures of old age is visiting friends and relatives. Taseko walked all over the lower Ina Valley and as far as Nakatsugawa to see the people she knew. She made sure to visit the Takemura family in Yamamoto at least once a year to offer her prayers before the graves of her ancestors. She would also visit her uncles, Hōbei who had been allowed to establish a branch of the Takemura family, and Chokuji who had been adopted into the Shio-zawa family. Everywhere she went, she wrote poetry and talked to all and sundry.

Taseko loved to talk, according to her fellow Hirata disciple Higuchi Misuko, the wife of her cousin Inao's younger brother, and she had a lively, engaging manner. "Without bragging about what she'd done or getting in a rage, she'd speak frankly and openheartedly with a womanly warmth and sympathy in a way that was quite attractive." Despite her lachrymose poetry, she herself was a cheerful old soul. "She always had lots to say and she could converse with people of any class or status on an appropriate topic. It was her skill at conversation that made it possible for her to become friends with the loyalists in Kyoto." [18] Her cousin on the Takemura side, Shiozawa Heigo, said that he enjoyed talking to her because she spoke well without being verbose or facile. She never boasted about herself, she was never presumptuous, but she was never servile either. He saw her as more of a man's woman who preferred to talk with learned males rather than giddy females.[19]

Yuasa Masanobu, her student in poetry, remembered her to be openhearted and no stickler for details.

> When her best friends came to visit, her greetings were extremely brief. She'd make just one remark about the weather with a slight bow, and in that way she was very like a man. She wasn't at all like most women who harp on one point and bow a thousand times. She'd invite her guests to sit around the *kotatsu* [a low table placed over a hole in the floor in which a brazier is placed to warm the feet in winter], and she herself would sit at her ease with her legs stretched out in front of her. She wanted her guests to tell her everything, good and bad.[20]

Few Japanese women of any age feel comfortable sitting in front of a man except with their heels tucked under them. For Taseko to have sat as she did suggests that she enjoyed being unconventional. No one really remembered her as a young woman. They tended instead to assume that she had always been the way they remembered her best, and their recollections were always tinged with the knowledge that they were talking about a woman who had become famous.

Taseko could be quite critical of other women. She once stopped by the Higuchi house after a meeting in Iida. Misuko encouraged her to stay, but she insisted that she had to get to the Kitahara house that very night. Before she left, however, she described what she had seen and commented sarcastically on the showy costumes and heavy makeup worn by the women. "They looked really great, just as though they were clothed for battle." She herself always dressed plainly, all in black with straw sandals on her feet. On another occasion when Taseko and a group of women were talking around the fire one winter night, Misuko sighed and said, "I've never taken even the shortest trip. Just once I'd like to try going on the road the way you did." "That wouldn't do at all," Taseko replied coldly. "You're right in the middle of raising children, and it has to be the most important time of your life." [21]

Even though Taseko scolded Misuko, the two women were fond of each other. They corresponded regularly and exchanged poems in a comity of rural companionship. When Taseko was already in her final year of life, Misuko paid her a visit. After she had gone home, Taseko wrote to thank her for coming. "In days gone by the unrelenting heat has really been unbearable, and I'm extremely grateful to you for elbowing your way to the hut where the mole lives in seclusion. Many are the things I ought to have said to you, and I've read and re-read your newsy letter." Taseko included some poems of her own in the missive. Most precious of all, she gave Misuko two poems written by the Meiji empress that she had received in 1881.[22] Taseko had acquired many gifts from noble families that she handed down to her children and grandchildren; these poems she gave to the woman whom she thought would treasure them the most.

Taseko's adventures in Kyoto colored her life to the end of her days. She continued to correspond with Hirata Kanetane and then with his successors after his death.[23] Whenever she visited her relatives or had friends come to see her and the sake bottles came out, she would reminisce about her experiences and the people she had met. One of her favorite stories was of how she had borrowed an elegant robe from one of the ladies-in-waiting in order to see the court dances. Her description of how peculiar she looked in that garb was enough to make her younger visitors burst out laughing.[24]

One autumn, Taseko made a last trip to Yamamoto. Saying she knew she would never come again, she stayed longer than usual. Her great-granddaughter Koseki recalled that the visit came right when the maple foliage was especially beautiful. "One day we decided that we'd all enjoy a day in the mountains, and we took a trip to the tutelary shrine about half a mile away. Taseko came with us, leaning on a staff, and we spent the whole day having a wonderful time. This is the poem that she wrote at the time:"

Sumu bito no	The color of the hearts
kokoro no iro mo	of the people who live here
niouran	must be glowing
nishiki orikaku	with such a sweep of rich brocade
Yamamoto no sato	in the village of Yamamoto.[25]

To write this poem Taseko drew on her classical training that celebrated the changing of the seasons. At the same time, by comparing the heart to the red of the maple leaf, she was making a plea for patriotism and looking back, perhaps, on the scenery she had enjoyed in the company of young men in 1862. Her patterns of thought always remained tinged with the commitment she had made to revere the emperor, or at least that is the way she is remembered.

TASEKO SPENT a great deal of time and effort arranging marriages for her progeny. Marriage meant alliances with potential political and economic benefits. There was also the question of status to be considered. It would have been unseemly for the palanquin that carried the Matsuo daughters to be set down anywhere except inside a gated compound. And then there were younger sons and grandsons who faced an uncertain future if they wanted to stay in the valley unless they could find adoptive parents willing to make them the family heir. That Taseko's descendants fared well in this regard is further testimony to the family's standing and her reputation.

Taseko's youngest daughter Yaso married the eldest son of Kitahara Inao, Taseko's cousin and lifelong friend in 1870. Yaso and her husband Nobutsuna were second cousins once removed in an age that considered marriages of first cousins to be entirely appropriate.[26] It was a match made by their parents to reestablish a connection already several generations in the past, and it testified to the affection that Inao and Taseko had long felt for each other. Planning for the wedding began in the few months that Taseko was at home between her 1868 Kyoto trip and her 1869 Tokyo trip. In a letter to Inao, then stationed in Iijima as a member of the Ina prefectural staff, she wrote, "You have given me great pleasure in having agreed to accept my clumsy daughter into your family."[27]

As with his father before him, Nobutsuna played an active role in public affairs, leaving the management of his household and its enterprises to his wife. He had been in his early teens when he joined the Hirata school, and he had begged his father repeatedly to allow him to go to Kyoto to serve the emperor. Refused permission, he had run away from home. By the end of 1864 he had found a position on the staff of the court noble Sawa Yoshitane. In 1868 he and Makoto had joined the army sent to subjugate the northeast. Following his marriage, he became the village headman at the tender age of twenty-one. In 1873 he became one of six township heads, four of whom were Hirata disciples, as well as superintendent of schools. He later took a position at the judicial court in Nagoya, being transferred to Yamanashi prefecture in 1880. He resigned when his father died, to return to his village where he served as the head of the village assembly, opened a development company, and in 1884 became a prefectural assemblyman. Despite encouragement to run for the National Diet in 1892, he declined because he disliked political debates by partisan politicians and feared his voice would not be heard above so many others struggling for their own self-interest. Two years later he allowed his scruples to be overcome.[28]

While Nobutsuna was making a name for himself at the prefectural level, Yaso followed the conventional pattern for women by staying home. She bore two sons, both of whom died before their parents. To carry on the family name, the couple adopted a young man from a nearby village and married him to Taseko's great-granddaughter Koseki, thus reincorporating the Takemura family into the Kitahara lineage. Yaso maintained close ties to her mother. Taseko's letters to Inao concern issues of poetry and politics; others are addressed to "the wife in the Kitahara house" and point to exchanges of gifts and services.

"Recently you most kindly sent me Hachijū," Taseko wrote a year or two after Yaso's marriage. "I want to thank you for responding to my earnest plea for his assistance and for the other things as well, including the goods to offer to the visible symbol of the gods. [Taseko was apparently planning a memorial service for the Matsuo family ancestors, but given her opposition to Buddhist practice, it had to be done Shinto style.] I'm grateful to you for telling us that we may use Hachijū as we please until it rains." [29] "You're so busy this year and then right when you're all in the midst of upheaval to get your news today!" Taseko wrote later. "I was so thankful and so delighted to receive not just the letter but all the other things you sent with it. In return for your kindness, I'd like to have offered you some buckwheat flour as a token of my appreciation, but we don't have any that would be suitable. It'll have to wait until I get another letter from you." [30]

Taseko also continued her ongoing connection with the Takemura family. One letter to her son's wife Machi and her granddaughter Hisa acknowledged their having sent two women servants to help feed the silkworms. "In particular I want to thank you most fervently for allowing O-Kinsa to be such a help to us for such a long time. O-Tami wants me to convey her appreciation as well. . . . She also wants me to tell you that with so many people here, there's no need for you to worry about whether the laundry gets done and she wants you to realize that you need not keep sending us such expensive goods as a token of your concern." Hisa had come for a rare visit, but it was too short. "I find myself living a delightful life in my retirement with all my family around me, and I do nothing but entertain myself all day. When spring comes, I think I'd like to come see you again." [31]

These family letters deal with truly trivial subjects: the ongoing exchange of gifts worth little in terms of monetary value, or the loan of a servant to help prepare for a memorial service or feed the silkworms. Compared to the major transformations Japan was undergoing or the struggle over what kind of government the country was to have, Taseko's concerns appear petty indeed. It is these issues, however, that make up the fabric of life for women. They constitute the kin work that sustains the households and the connections between them without which public life would be impossible. [32]

Underlying public life was the web of interlocking marriage connections that wove men of similar status into a pattern of kinship and common interests. Barely two years after Yaso's marriage, her niece, Taseko's granddaughter Tazu, married Maijima Chokutarō. Tazu was just sixteen. Chokutarō's grandmother, Kitahara Mino, had taught his father Masami poetry. Together they had decided on eight views in the area around their village that could be modeled on the eight views of Ōmi made famous in classical literature, composed poems describing the hour at which each was most beautiful, and painted pictures to accompany them.[33] Masami having joined the Hirata school in the early 1860s, Tazu was moving to a family that had the same traditions and intellectual background as her own. Politically and economically, however, the marriage represented a step up. In an excess of poetic hyperbole, Taseko claimed in one of her poems that the Maijima had occupied their land for a thousand years. They had in fact dominated their neighbors for several centuries from their hilltop compound. With its walls and massive gate, it was almost a miniature fortress. The Maijima ruled as village headmen and kept their tenant farmers tied to them through rites of subordination that continued well into the nineteenth century. The Matsuo family apparently met their standards; Tazu's niece Setsuko later married her son.

In her delight at the match Taseko wrote an extremely long poem in the *Man'yō* style that traced the Maijima lineage back to the age of the gods, exclaimed at its prosperity and praised it for its devotion to the nativist tradition. Not for the Maijima was the pollution of superficial Chinese teachings, instead:

Yūdasuki	With sleeves tied back by cotton cords
kakemaku kami no	they make an offering of sake
hami someshi	for the repast
miki sasage mochi	of the manifest gods.
asa ni ge ni	From morning till night
utage utaite	they recite poetry at poetry meetings
kotohokai	and should they get drunk
hokihoki areba	in celebration,
niki mitama	it might happen that the two gods
kushiki mitama no	of the jeweled comb box
tama kushige	the god of harmony
futa mikami no	and the god of the nine senses
kami gakari	would appear at the gathering
mikuni no miitsu	to raise up the authority
furi tatemu kamo	of our great country.[34]

"The jeweled comb box" is both a pillow word for the word that comes after it, *futa* meaning both "two" and "lid," and an allusion to a text written by

Motoori Norinaga. These are precious gods whom Taseko summoned to the marriage feast. The purpose of drink was not simply intoxication but to enter into communion with the gods, to experience a personal encounter with the numinous.

Taseko's final triumph in the marriage market came in 1886. That year she wrote the Takemura family a letter right in the middle of the silkworm season when she was at her busiest chopping mulberry leaves. She had tidings, however, that could not wait.

> Recently Chokutarō came to see us about Saburō [Taseko's grandson], bringing us the news that all of a sudden the Fukuzawa family wants to adopt him. We said no way could we guarantee that everything would work out. He kept urging us to accept, so we've given a preliminary approval. We should have talked this over with you first, but he came just when the rice was being transplanted on the new fields. There were so many other things going on as well that we just didn't have time. I've been told that I should send you a letter announcing this good news so that's what I'm doing. It's really too good to be true, and I'm really hoping it'll work out.[35]

The Fukuzawa was a wealthy and prominent family from what is now Komagane city in the upper Ina Valley. In the early nineteenth century the head of the family had married a woman from Kyoto skilled in the poetic tradition of the imperial court, and he had traveled to Kyoto several times to hone his skill in that medium. Naturally he had exchanged poems with Taseko's cousin Sakurai Haruki and other local notables before his death in 1847. He had been a district magistrate for the lands ruled by the Kondō bannermen of Yamamoto, and the two families were said to be related by marriage.[36] This was an illustrious connection for the Matsuo family, and Taseko had every reason to be excited. This letter is interesting because in apologizing to her daughter-in-law and granddaughter, Taseko reveals the assumption that she continued to expect her natal family to be involved in decisions involving her grandchild over fifty years after she had left Yamamoto.

During the last twenty years of her life, Taseko celebrated many marriages. Her granddaughters and Saburō left the house as her own children had done before. They carried off samples of her poetry in their dowries because their in-laws all appreciated a memento from a noted poet. As the oldest grandson, Chiburu introduced a bride into the family, first Horikoshi Kiyo from Iijima in the upper Ina Valley, then when she died, he married Onda Suzu. Suzu bore Taseko three great-grandchildren, including Haruomi, the heir to the house. Taseko could thus take satisfaction in knowing that while individual family members might come and go, their places would always be taken by the next generation.

Taseko celebrated marriages; she also grieved at funerals. Living to an advanced age herself, she saw a number of younger men die. The first was Hazama Hidenori from Nakatsugawa, who had been her friend for many years. They had written poetry together, discussed Hirata Atsutane's teachings, and spent many evenings over sake lamenting the condition of the times. Hidenori had rescued Taseko from the Chōshū compound in 1863 and accompanied her to visit Motoori Norinaga's grave. He had been in Kyoto petitioning for a Shinto burial in 1868 while she was collecting news and connections. They had both tried to help the Chimura and Yamamura families stay out of the clutches of the Owari domain in 1869. Hidenori had been sick with palsy ever since. He wrote bitter poems bewailing his fate not to have died fighting for his country before he passed away in 1876. Twelve years later a poetry anthology was published in his honor with poems collected from 190 people, eighteen of them women. Some probably knew him by reputation only; the former Regent Konoe Tadahiro, for example, or Matsudaira Shungaku.[37] Others were fellow disciples of Hirata Atsutane. Among this illustrious company was Taseko:

Omou koto	Without my realizing it,
narade kienishi	it has disappeared
tama no o no	that thread of life, that jewel of a soul
hikari wa nagaku	whose light had so long
yo ni todomekeri	remained in this world.[38]

Born eleven years after Taseko, Hidenori was just fifty-four when he died.

Taseko's husband died in 1879. He has been so completely overshadowed by his wife that little is known about him. He was evidently an astute businessman and a conscientious village official despite the ailments that required therapeutic trips to hot springs. He preferred Chinese to Japanese poetry, and he never joined the Hirata school. In terms of intellectual interests, it would appear that Taseko had a much more direct impact on her sons than he did. At the same time, however, he was not above producing a Japanese poem when the occasion warranted it:

Taezu nomi	I just can't stop myself
kayou kokoro wa	My heart keeps yearning for you
shiranami no	like the white topped waves
omou kata ni wa	that come
nado ya yori konu	from out of nowhere.[39]

Written on the theme of love as inexplicable desire, its object is as intangible as the lovers whom Taseko had addressed in her poetry. The couple shared a life; none of their writings allows us to glimpse the kind of passion they felt for each other.

Two years after her husband died, Taseko lost her cousin and intellectual companion, Kitahara Inao. After the Restoration he had tried to use the economies of scale introduced by government rationalization to promote agriculture and manufacturing. In 1871 he started managing a fund comprised partly of money collected from villages for poor relief plus mandatory contributions collected from every family in the lower Ina district. In 1876 he moved to Matsumoto in order to give it his full attention. He lent money to those who wished to plant mulberry, tea, tobacco, and fruit on waste lands, raise silkworms, cows, pigs, chickens, and ducks, build new irrigation ponds, dig for coal, cultivate the sweet potato, and improve silk spinning equipment. He charged an interest rate of 12 percent a year, higher than Taseko's husband had charged in the 1830s and 1840s. The conditions for receiving loans were so strict that only families with substantial holdings were able to benefit, and the fund aroused considerable resentment.[40]

Inao took an extremely paternalistic perspective on the development of his valley, and he continued to put his family first. When he had let his son succeed him in 1869 and gone to the Ina prefectural office to offer assistance to the new governor, he did so out of a commitment to the emperor, the country, and his descendants.[41] Surely it was no accident that one of the largest loans made by the development fund was for a steam-powered filature in his own village of Zakōji. Yet at the same time, he was personally abstemious. Out of his monthly income of forty yen, he gave his wife seven for household expenses and used the rest for charity, public works projects, and disaster relief. He encouraged the mechanization of silk spinning and actively pursued opportunities to trade with foreigners at the same time that he wrote three memorials to the national government disparaging that exemplary proponent of westernization, Fukuzawa Yukichi: "He knows nothing of respecting domestic affairs and despising the foreign, he is a degenerate who misunderstands the great way unique to our sacred country, and he acts counter to its customs."[42] In 1877 Inao wrote a set of precepts for the Kitahara house that lauded the usual virtues of harmony, frugality, and diligence and recalled Atsutane's admonition in "The Precious Sleeve Cord:" "A house doesn't have to be a palace so long as it doesn't leak. Clothes don't have to be brocade so long as they are warm. Food doesn't have to be fancy so long as it's nourishing. A wife need have no color in her face so long as she's smart."[43]

Inao stayed much closer to the Ina Valley than did Taseko. Even in 1868 he went no farther than Lake Suwa in offering his services to the imperial armies while she was in Kyoto and their sons joined the forces fighting in the northeast. The two nevertheless shared intellectual interests and a common concern for Japan's future. They had been close friends ever since childhood, and they exchanged many poems attesting to their abiding fondness for one another. Thirteen years Taseko's junior, Inao died at the age of fifty-seven in 1881. His loss left her bereft. In a poem expressing her grief, she compared herself to a grasshopper abandoned to cry all night alone in the desolate winter fields.[44]

Most women can expect their husbands to die first. Taseko's tragedy lay in seeing her sons die as well. Mitsunaka fell sick in the autumn of 1884, and it quickly became apparent that this was no ordinary illness. "I'd like to receive a daily report, just a note regarding the condition of your patient," Taseko wrote his wife Machi and her granddaughter Hisa, and she recommended that he be fed rice gruel as frequently as possible. "Please be sure to do everything you can to take good care of the patient and the children." A few weeks later she wrote again. "I have just one thing to tell you through my tears. I really don't know what to say about the news that Mitsunaka's condition is getting worse. It's really unbearable. The care that you've given him for so long has been to no avail, and I don't think there's anything I can say that will do any good. If I lived nearby, we'd be able to talk together in our sorrow, but because we live so far apart, you'll have to imagine everything that I've kept to myself. . . . I too have come to look like a corpse in my grief."[45] She was also worried that Machi would wear herself out with her nursing duties, and Hisa was pregnant. She herself was tortured with such bad abdominal pains that she had been unable to eat. Makoto's wife Tami, who always took Taseko's anxieties upon herself, had been unable to go in her place because her husband was frail and Chiburu was away. There was nothing to do but wait and worry.

Taseko's next letter shows her trying to reconcile herself to her son's death. She notes approvingly that Machi and Hisa have remained in good health throughout the mourning period, and they are performing the appropriate purification ceremonies that mark its end. "My grandchildren have been coming to see me from here and there, every day has been quite lively, and little by little they've assuaged my grief." This almost cheerful note is immediately contradicted by what follows. "I've been thinking that I'd like to make a pilgrimage to his grave, but it pains me so much to be seen by others that I've remained in seclusion." She ends with a poem titled, "Even viewing the cherry blossoms doesn't stop me from remembering:"

> Chiru hana no   If mourning for the
> oshimu ni tomaru   falling flowers

mono naraba	could keep them on the branch
nani yo no naka ni	what would matter the sorrows
uki wa arashi na	and storms of this world?[46]

In a typical displacement of emotion onto the changing seasons, Taseko draws on a poem from the spring chapter of the *Kokinshū* to express her grief: "If weeping for the / falling flowers could keep them / securely on the / branches my cries would rival / the song of the mountain thrush."[47] The cherry blossoms falling at the height of their glory constitute a hackneyed metaphor for young men killed in the full bloom of youth. Mitsunaka was forty-seven, but to have died before his mother made his death especially poignant.

Taseko lost her eldest son when Makoto died in 1888. He had joined the Hirata school just two years after she did, and he had accompanied her to Kyoto in 1868 to offer his services to the emperor. Like her he was deeply suspicious of westernizing trends that seemed to pose a threat to the Japanese cultural identity:

Kani moji mo	It may be all right to study
yoshi manabu tomo	horizontal crab-walking writing
kōkoku no	but not if you get confused
makoto no michi wa	traveling the true way
fumi na madoi zo	of imperial Japan.[48]

Makoto had his wife Tami run the household while he spent much of his adult life in public service, including a protest against high taxes in 1873 that left him incarcerated in Iida for twenty days.[49] He was to have been the support of Taseko's old age, and he acted always with her encouragement and approval. She wrote numerous poems in which she urged him to serve the emperor, to dye his heart red with patriotism.[50] She wrote no poems at his death, or at least none that have survived. Perhaps it was too painful to express even in poetry, but more likely what she wrote has simply disappeared.

In 1899 the Kumashiro villagers erected a stele in Makoto's honor. Similar commemorative monuments may be found all over Japan, marking the spot where a poem was composed, a battle was fought, or a nursemaid sacrificed herself to a rabid dog to save her young charge. According to anthropologist Jennifer Robertson, "they function by locating the remembered past in the present landscape, they reclaim and revivify that past."[51] The one erected for Makoto recapitulated the family's connection to the heroes of the Meiji Restoration. Iwakura Tomosada, who had led the imperial army up the Nakasendō and executed Sagara Sōzō, graciously provided the calligraphy for Makoto's name. A local notable composed the Chinese text inscribed by

Tsunoda Tadayuki, by then the chief priest at Atsuta shrine.[52] The inscription stated that Makoto had resolved long-standing disputes as village headman, devoted himself to the imperial cause, met the Mito warriors on their flight through the Ina Valley, and served as an official of the Meiji government. In his later years he tried to spread enlightenment, though always in accord with the national essence, and he had promoted agriculture and sericulture to nurture the foundation of the state.

Not everyone was equally impressed with Makoto. As early as 1861 his overbearing ways had made him the target of a drunken outburst by one of the villagers.[53] Like his mother, Makoto had become a fervent supporter of Hirata Atsutane and a deadly foe of Buddhism. One man who turned against him was the priest Shinjō who had helped get the Mito warriors past Iida. Shinjō had attracted widespread respect among the ordinary peasants for his support in their conflicts with the authorities—support that eventually forced him to flee the district. Before he did, he wrote a poem satirizing Makoto's self-importance when he had accompanied three officials from Ina prefecture on a tour of inspection:

San chō no kago no	There's Matsuo Sajiemon
Matsuo Sajiemon	with his three palanquins
saji saji to	little by little
machigaisō na	he might be mistaken
on-yakunin	for a real official.[54]

Like many Hirata disciples, Taseko and Makoto vehemently opposed the reforms launched by the centralizing state to introduce Western technology and Western goods. In his novel of the Meiji Restoration, *Before the Dawn,* Tōson brilliantly portrays how his father's commitment to an idealized and purely Japanese past leads him to abandon first his family in becoming a shrine priest and then his senses. He was the exception. A few disciples tried to remain true to the vision of a unity of rites and rule, such as Iwasaki Nagayo and Tsunoda Tadayuki, for example, but those who had a house to maintain continued in the tradition of public service bequeathed by their ancestors. Inao filled prefectural offices; his son, Taseko's son-in-law, eventually served in the National Diet. Taseko's sons and grandson likewise dedicated themselves both to their family enterprises and local affairs, and Taseko applauded their endeavors.

Taseko's grandson Chiburu launched the most significant public works project Tomono had ever seen. This was to build a levee along the Tenryū River, then turn the fields behind into rice paddies. The problem had begun in 1750 when a stone levee went up along the opposite bank. When the current hit with full force, it was thrown back on itself. The backwash chewed up the earthen Tomono levee whenever the river rose higher than normal. In 1860, the levee and the fields behind it were swept away following heavy rains. Rebuilding took four years, only to be destroyed in 1865. Construction started again in 1866; the results were lost in 1868. Over thirty hectares of land had gone to waste by 1877.[55]

In 1883 Chiburu announced a massive new project for a new embankment to all the property holders in Tomono. He proposed forming a development company to be funded by collecting rents for twenty-five years on the new fields to be opened behind the levee, then the land would revert to its original owners. He raised the capital by selling shares in the company, and the shareholders agreed to cover any deficits. In 1889, for example, income was 754.55 yen on expenses of 789.81 yen. Since the company had issued fifteen shares, each shareholder had to pay 2.35 yen. Chiburu held 8.3 shares, making his contribution 19.5 yen. The other thirty-two members of the development company owned between .5 and .1 shares. In 1886 the previous years' work was swept away by a flood, and Chiburu had to start over. Using his connections to the governor, he arranged for a 750 yen prefectural grant with another 450 yen to be contributed by the local government. The development company kicked in 150 yen and Chiburu paid an extra 83 yen out of his own pocket. Not until 1895 did the income from the new fields generate a return for the shareholders, and the company was dissolved as promised in 1909. Today a modern levee follows the course of the old stone embankment for over a mile, protecting 35 hectares of good rice fields. At one end is a small park and a monument to Chiburu.[56]

The current head of the Matsuo house calls this levee the family's most enduring legacy. It is not that he values the deeds done by men over those by women; rather, it produced lasting benefits for the village whereas in the postwar period Taseko has become something of an embarrassment with her outmoded xenophobia and emperor worship. Taseko too approved of Chiburu's project. In 1891 she wrote a poem to celebrate it and to spur him to complete what he had set out to do. She began by calling on the protection of the creator deities and summoning omens of good fortune. Then she launched into a series of admonitions:

Take takaku	Learn well
manabu no michi mo	the lofty august
yoku oboe	way of scholarship.
kimi to oya to ni	Serve well

yoku tsukae   your parents and ruler.
ie no nari wo mo   Do not neglect
okotarasu   the customs of the house.

. . . . . .

yo ni mo koitaki   Just like the brave men
masurao no   beloved by all
chiyo yorozuyo mo   do not weaken for as long as
nagaku yoware na   a thousand years, ten thousand years.[57]

The envoy for this poem praises Chiburu for placing a barrier in the water
that will rebound to the greater glory of the Matsuo house.

Chiburu's efforts to build the levee represented the culmination of a dedication to public service to which he had been trained since he had joined the
Hirata school in 1866 at the age of twelve. He had the knowledge of local conditions based on years of observation and study, and he had financial resources and a leadership position inherited from his ancestors. He also had
the means to mobilize resources made available through a centralizing government. He was elected to the prefectural assembly six times and even
served as its president. He was defeated twice in his efforts to be elected to
the National Diet, the second time because he was too ill to campaign.[58] He
died in 1892 at the age of thirty-eight, leaving behind his mother, his wife,
three children, and his grandmother. On the first anniversary of his death,
the villagers held a memorial service. In the title for the poem that Taseko
wrote marking this event she stated simply, "it was painful for me when
Chiburu passed away." The poem itself thanked the villagers for their efforts
which had surely gladdened the soul of the dearly departed.[59]

Chiburu was the instrument by which Taseko began to be recognized for
her exploits. While he was a prefectural assemblyman, he met Sekiguchi Tomoai from Matsumoto, who had connections to a local literary magazine.
Through Chiburu, Tomoai prevailed upon Taseko to allow him to publish a
copy of her 1862 and 1863 diaries. "I'm really embarrassed to show people
this old diary in which I recorded things from the past just as I thought of
them without exercising any care at all," she wrote. "Please accept it in the
spirit meant. I'd wanted to prepare a more finished copy for you, but everyone is so busy with the silkworms that this is all I have." The diaries were serialized in the *Seirai shinshi* (The Pure rustling of the wind new magazine)
between July 20, 1885 and October 5, 1886. Tomoai wrote a preface in which
he praised her devotion to the emperor and bemoaned her lack of fame. He
hoped that by making the diaries public, he would make her better known.

He admitted, however, that at certain crucial points all she wrote was, "this is something secret." "At these places one feels grief and frustration. The author was born in 1811 and her name is Tase. Even today she is in good health." [60]

Taseko received imperial recognition for her achievements not long before she died. At the end of 1892, the Meiji empress sent her a roll of white crepe to reward her for her efforts on behalf of the emperor during the Meiji Restoration. The idea probably came from Shinagawa Yajirō, then Home Minister, who had the gift delivered. He closed his letter that accompanied the announcement with "I'm so delighted I can't write any more." In a postscript he added, "Please take care of your old self during this cold weather, and I pray that you will offer up your love and protection to repay the obligation you owe the court." Masako sent two poems to congratulate her, saying, "I'm so happy that the dew of the emperor's blessings has come to rest on the sleeve of a commoner living in Tomono." Kikuko sent similar verses. Taseko carefully composed a poem of thanks by positioning herself among the countless masses. (Remember that the chapter of "Lectures on Ancient History" that she had helped publish described how they were produced by the gods):

Kasunaranu	Even the last blades of grass
kusa no sueba mo	that are unworthy of being counted
iro ya sou	take on color
ama yori tamau	upon receiving the gift
tsuyu no tamamono	of dew from heaven. [61]

Taseko wanted to have the crepe hung as curtains in the tutelary shrines for Tomono and Yamamoto as a reminder of the imperial family's love for the people. [62] For this she needed the help of Hisa's husband Daisuke because her son Tameyoshi was unwell and there were no other adult males in her immediate family. "I really ought not be asking you to take on this kind of role when you are so busy with so many other things. Please understand that there is absolutely no one else on whom I can rely." She promised to pay all the expenses involved in hanging the curtains, and she assured Daisuke that she did not want him to displace the treasures already displayed in the shrines. To Hisa she apologized at length for all the trouble she was causing. "I am really and truly delighted that he is going to accomplish my long-cherished desire." The Tomono villagers had decided to erect a new stone torii to mark the occasion. "Everyone is rushing about in mad confusion. Despite the disorder, my heart is at ease because nothing could make me happier." [63]

Taseko had hoped to go back to Yamamoto to see the curtain and worship at the shrine. By the time all the preparations had been completed, however, she was ill. The young men of the village asked her for a poem to decorate the float for the annual village festival. She rallied enough to write:

Moro hito no	Everyone
kokoro mo kiyoku	having pure hearts
yūdasuki	let us worship in high spirits
kakemaku kami wo	our beloved gods
isame matsuramu	with sleeves tied back by cotton cords.[64]

A doctor was called in, to no avail. For the first time in her life, she spent weeks unable to rise from her bed. Cancer made movement painful. Despite the daily prayers offered by members of the household, she died on June 10, 1894, at the age of eighty-three.[65]

CHAPTER SIXTEEN

Remembering Taseko

How beautiful the red hearts
filled with reverence for the emperor
the men of high purpose gathered
like the clouds and mist
and then there was one brave woman
who mingled with them
her name will remain famous for eternity.
HASHIZUME USON, 1903[1]

One November afternoon in 1903, the sixteen-year-old Matsuo Haruomi was sitting in his English language class in Iida.
His hair was cut short, and he wore the uniform of a second-
year middle school student. Suddenly a teacher appeared at
the door with instructions for Haruomi to go immediately
to the Lower Ina District Office. There he found his uncle
Tameyoshi and the village mayor. They frowned at his clothing. He should be wearing his formal attire, but there was no
time to send to Tomono for it. Fortunately one of his cousins
who happened to be at the entrance lent him a *hakama* (pleated
trousers) to pull over his pants and a black crested kimono to
cover his jacket. They were both much too large, and in his
own estimation, he looked ridiculous.

Haruomi and the other men lined up in a solemn row while the District Chief read aloud from a certificate received that morning from the Imperial Household Ministry. It announced simply that Matsuo Tase had been granted posthumous court rank, the fifth grade. Haruomi bowed, accepted the certificate, and the ceremony was over before he had time to react. The three men bought a notebook at a nearby store to protect the certificate, then with Haruomi still clutching it, they hired three rickshaws to take them back to Tomono. This was the first time that Haruomi had ever ridden in a rickshaw.[2] A few days later a formal ceremony was performed at Taseko's grave to tell her and the assembled villagers of the honor that had been bestowed upon her. It featured the song composed for the occasion by Hashizume Uson and an address written originally in Chinese:

> Heroes are rare, but they appear when the times require it. I had never heard of a woman hero before, but lo, one has appeared. . . . Our Matsuo Taseko was well versed in politics, she was skilled in national literature and national poetry, and she early decided to devote herself to the imperial cause. Expressing her resolve in her poems, she went to Kyoto where she mingled with the men of high purpose, called on the court nobles, busied herself with national affairs, grieved at the death of the loyalists, worked to bring them in harmony with each other, and despite the surveillance of bakufu spies managed to visit Iwakura in his hideout. She helped bring about the restoration of imperial rule. . . . This bestowal of court rank contributes to her glory and the whole world's prosperity. We give thanks to our sagacious emperor that he in his infinite wisdom has made it possible for her to be known forever.[3]

With this public recognition, Taseko jumped from local notable to national hero, and she joined in spirit the nobility she had so long admired.[4] In Tajiri Tasaku's biographical sketches of people who had received posthumous rank, she was one of twelve women and 2,360 men.[5] The occasion for the award was Emperor Meiji's trip to Hyōgo to oversee special field exercises held by the army. The site was close to Minatogawa where Kusunoki Masashige had led his troops in a futile battle against Ashikaga Takauji in 1336, making it an appropriate place to honor people of proven loyalty. Fifty-three people were honored that day. Many had supported Emperor Godaigo and his descendants in the fourteenth century; the rest had contributed to the Meiji Restoration. In recognition of Taseko's achievement, the Matsuo family erected a new and larger gravestone, one that completely overshadows her husband's.

松尾淳齋及び多勢子墓

FIGURE 22. Left: Taseko's gravestone emblazoned with her posthumous court rank. Right: The grave of her husband Motoharu enscribed with his retirement name of Jun. From *Matsuo Taseko*, frontispiece.

Taseko had not been completely forgotten in the years between her death and her receipt of posthumous court rank. Following the first Sino-Japanese war of 1894–95, Shinagawa Yajirō wrote her son-in-law Kitahara Nobutsuna saying, "I truly regret that old lady Tase did not live to see the day of our great victory."[6] In 1899 two men from Tokyo, one of them Inoue Yorikuni, had business in Iida and having come so far, they made a pilgrimage to Taseko's grave. Yorikuni wrote a poem in which he related how he had recalled the past and shed tears in her memory.[7]

Yorikuni is the man chiefly responsible for Taseko's having received posthumous court rank and for propagating the legends of her exploits. Born in 1839, he went from a sickly child to a well-upholstered, balding man by 1900. His father had been a doctor and geomancer; Yorikuni's interest in divination led him to the Hirata school in 1861 and he later studied Japanese medicine with Gonda Naosuke. He loved books. "Books are the weapons of a scholar," he said, and "someone who tries to write history without them is like a man who starts a war without weapons or a business without capital."[8] By the time he died in 1914 he had managed to acquire over 34,000 volumes. They are now housed in a ramshackle wooden building overshadowed by a damp and gloomy forest on the outskirts of Tokyo where they are guarded by an ultra-nationalistic society dedicated to the preservation of the Japanese territory and spirit. Yorikuni had an amazing memory for things heard and read. In comparing manuscript versions of the *Kojiki* (Record of Ancient Matters), for example, he could tell immediately which characters differed from one text to another. He taught at the first women's college founded in Tokyo in 1901 by Naruse Jinzō, whose goal was to produce virtuous, accomplished, and strong women. When Ogino Ginko asked to receive a license to practice medicine before a system for women doctors had been established, the licensing board said her request was unheard-of and impossible. Yorikuni then brought documents to the board's attention showing instances of women doctors in Japanese history. Ginko got the license.[9]

Yorikuni proposed Taseko for posthumous court rank not because he was an early feminist but because she was a member of the Hirata school. Early in the 1870s he had petitioned the court repeatedly to award court rank to the four nativist teachers worshipped at Hongaku shrine in the Ina Valley, and he put on his own festival for them every year. He had Kamo Mabuchi's grave at Tokaiji near Shinagawa moved when it was threatened by a new railroad, and he refurbished Hirata Atsutane's grave. He helped raise money to publish the collected works of Kamo Mabuchi, Motoori Norinaga, and Hirata Atsutane. He often invited the Hirata disciples to his house to discuss the events leading to the Meiji Restoration and the disciples' role in it. It was important to teach the way of the gods, he believed, lest the westernizing trends sweeping the country destroy its indigenous cultural essence. The Hirata message had been slighted by the government and was in danger of being forgotten by the people. As a reminder to both, he took the initiative in petitioning the Imperial Household Ministry to confer court rank on Taseko and eight other disciples.

For the first twenty years after the Meiji Restoration, its heroes were the samurai from the southwestern domains who through their teaching and example had demonstrated a patriotic spirit and loyalty to the emperor. Vilified as traitors were the shoguns and bakufu allies, especially those who had continued to fight against the new government even after the last shogun had surrendered. With the promulgation of the Meiji Constitution in 1889, designed to provide a firm foundation for the state, continuing to discriminate against former enemies was not only no longer necessary but counter to the goal of national unity. Apologists for the bakufu began their own redress of history, beginning with Fukuchi Gen'ichirō's monumental essay on the fall of the bakufu in 1892.[10] At the same time, while the 1890s brought victory in battle over China, it also saw political conflict in the Diet and the first flowering of the pursuit of individualism. Ever since Aizawa Seishisai had written his influential *New Theses* in 1825, Japan's ruling class had worried that foolish and misguided commoners would be attracted to evil foreign ways.[11] Bestowing court rank on loyal commoners was seen as countering that threat in that it forged a personal link between them, their descendants, their locality, and the emperor, thus contributing to national spiritual solidarity.[12] Although the Hirata brand of religiosity had fallen out of favor with Meiji leaders, the school's commitment and devotion to the emperor could be used as a prophylactic against Western liberalism. This deployment of Taseko's memory captured her for the conservative side; not until well after World War Two would historians and pundits of a more progressive slant show her even the slightest interest.

In addition to bringing Taseko national recognition, Inoue Yorikuni tried to define the role she should play in public memory by confining her deeds to the narrow bounds of conventional behavior for women. Just a few months before she died, he wrote to tell her that he had seen Miwada Masako's memoir published in the journal she edited called *Jokan* (Mirror for women). "I hope the places that are in error may be pointed out to Mrs. Miwada because it is my aspiration that the truth be handed down to later generations."[13]

What were the errors that Yorikuni had in mind? Surely not that Taseko met central figures in the Restoration such as Iwakura Tomomi and Sakamoto Ryōma in 1862 or that she had forced two spies in the Chōshū compound to disembowel themselves, since these were stories he told himself. Masako did not always get her dates right, and her knowledge of Ina Valley place names was uncertain. Nevertheless, it was most likely her depiction of what happened after the Ashikaga statues had been decapitated that bothered Yorikuni. "Taseko changed to male clothing. With everything hanging by a hair, this was no time to make mistakes. Now appearing, now disappearing, she worked diligently to save her comrades. She hid by day, walked by night and concealed herself wherever she could."[14] The notion that a respectable woman had practiced cross-dressing was anathema to the men who wished to hold Taseko up as an example to their wives and daughters, and just the suggestion that she might have become androgenous was enough to send many of them into paroxysms of denial. For all her reputed conservatism, Masako resisted confining women to narrowly feminine roles. "If perchance all the women of the realm were to use her words correctly, who would scold them for being hens who crow like roosters?" [15]

With the proliferation of high schools and colleges for women in 1880s, Japanese history was ransacked for appropriate models of femininity. Masako had just begun teaching at the model high school for women, the Tokyo Kōtō Jogakkō,[16] and her article was aimed at her pupils. "A person who does deeds out of the ordinary and achieves her mission ought to become a model of worldly activity," she claimed. Taseko was a "woman worthy of respect." She had demonstrated her loyalty to the emperor, and in addition "she served her husband submissively, managed her household, helped her neighbors, worked at agriculture and sericulture and nurtured her family above all else." In short she functioned appropriately as a wife plus she "studied books, wrote poetry and while promoting the basis for a happy home life created an elegant and elevated environment." In contrast, "today's girls either never clean the dust from their desks because they are too busy with their chores, or they so aspire to scholarship that they know nothing about running a household." In describing Taseko's interactions with the men she met in Kyoto, Masako asserted that Taseko had prevented fights. "To make up quarrels is characteristic of women, something for which their harmonious nature is well suited. But today's women are the cause of disharmony among people and create enmity instead." [17]

The first florescence of stories about Taseko appeared between 1900 and 1913, although never in the number that celebrated the deeds of samurai such as Saigō Takamori. Many were written by men who had known her or been alive during the Restoration years. They wanted to remind readers of the glorious deeds that had culminated in the emperor's return to direct rule before the passage of time obliterated their traces. Books of poetry written by Restoration heroes, including Taseko, recalled the men who died in service to the emperor and women who supported and praised their deeds.[18] This was an optimistic time for Japan; following the Sino-Japanese war and the abolition of the unequal treaties, it emerged victorious in war with Russia and annexed Korea. After a lull of about twenty years, the second Taseko boom erupted between 1936 and 1943 during the dark years of the Pacific war. It too was part of a larger wave of hagiographic accounts about the glorious and idealistic Restoration heroes and the poetry that stirred men to action.[19] Even then few commoners and fewer Hirata disciples enjoyed anywhere near the attention Taseko received. The first period saw considerable disagreement over the way she should be portrayed; in the second she conformed to much more rigid standards of behavior.

The first memoirs by male pundits recalled the deeds of the Hirata disciples while insisting that Taseko had played only a supporting role in 1862–63. Watanabe Shinzaburō, who had guided Taseko to the Chōshū mansion in 1863, and Nakajima Masutane, who had earned her secret scorn for his attachment to things Western, described her deeds in an interview at the *Shidankai* (Oral history society) in 1899. (Founded with support by the Imperial Household Ministry in 1891, the organization's first goal was to compile accounts of the Restoration by the former daimyo of the principal domains.) "In some of the things that have been written about her, she appears to have gone beyond a woman's portion (*onna no bun*) and become a woman warrior (*onna sōshi*) which she was not," Masutane insisted. "She was a womanly woman with a fearless spirit, but she was not a woman warrior." Shinzaburō denied categorically that she had ever dressed in men's clothing, she had never sworn to commit suicide rather than be captured by bakufu police, nor had she exposed spies in the Chōshū compound. Instead she had cheered the loyalists from the sidelines, giving them money and writing poetry, urging them to devote body and soul to the emperor.[20]

Shinzaburō and Masutane want their readers to understand that while Taseko was an extraordinary women, she had never acted contrary to their standards of femininity. Like other biographers, they draw a clear line between appropriate and inappropriate behavior, a difficult task because Taseko did not conform to conventional models of action for women. They remember that when they knew her in Kyoto, nothing about her struck them as outrageous, forgetting that normal standards of conduct, even for themselves, were then temporarily in abeyance. Looking back forty years later, when the nineteenth century ideal of womanhood has come to mean "women who could extend the domestic sphere to necessary dealings with the outside world but who played no active independent role in that world,"[21] they fear that Taseko might indeed appear to have acted in the mode of a hero, not a heroine.

Even within the conservative camp, disagreement over appropriate roles for women had an impact on the way Taseko was remembered. While unwilling to grant her the opportunity to dress like a man, Yorikuni was still willing to grant her more leeway for action than Shinzaburō and Masatane. Claiming to have been a close friend, he published his own memoir in 1911. He had her go to Edo to enter the Hirata school, meet Iwakura Tomomi in 1862, and force two spies in the Chōshū mansion to commit suicide. "She was intelligent and quick-witted, her deportment was austere, and she had a thorough knowledge of poetry and the classics." He then balances this assessment with empty platitudes that conform more closely to conventional standards of feminine behavior. "She managed her household well, she was able to get the best out of her servants, and her family prospered because she devoted herself to agriculture and sericulture. She was a model for brides in her neighborhood and helped improve its morals."[22] With no direct experience of her early life, how did Yorikuni know that?

In their desire to carve a space for local stories in the national narrative, early Ina Valley boosters worried less about whether Taseko had made herself unfeminine. When she received court rank, the pioneer in local history, Hanyū Eimei, wrote an article published on the first page of an Iida newspaper.[23] "Her courage and bravery in the face of danger are a model for today's women," he asserts. "Some people might criticize her, saying that a woman who was so passionately devoted to poetry and busied herself in national affairs could not possibly be a good wife." Eimei disagrees: "Her dedication to poetry and her enthusiasm for national affairs did not harm her virtue, and to criticize her for exerting herself on behalf of the emperor is a vulgar opinion showing too much haste to censure." Eimei himself is less interested in confining women to the household than in taking potshots at officials. "When one considers the arbitrary acts of today's corrupt and debauched bureaucrats who not even in a dream have ever attained the deeds of the loyalists, one must say that they are degenerate in spirit compared to Taseko."[24]

Eimei admits that his vision of women is more progressive than that of his neighbors. "Dedication to the family and subservience are the great female virtues, but I cannot agree that being cooped up indoors knowing nothing of the great affairs of state is all there is to a woman's life." This is a remarkable statement given that in the world in which he had been raised, samurai women were kept out of politics and in the late nineteenth century, the Meiji government had extended this prohibition to all women. Eimei never questions that a woman like Taseko would have subordinated herself to her husband and his family's needs on an ordinary basis. To applaud her for her public achievements, however, undercuts the division of household responsibilities so recently defined in the New Civil Code of 1898.[25]

As the crucial set of events that launched modern Japan, the Meiji Restoration has been subjected to considerable historiographical analysis;[26] its representations in the popular press have been largely ignored. This is not the place to trace the twists and turns of how the Restoration and its leaders have been remembered; rather, my focus is on what happens to Taseko and what that implies for notions of womanhood. The disputes between popular writers, local historians, and national pundits over her deeds took place within a context of increasing urbanization that allowed new opportunities for women and considerable disagreement over what it meant to be Japanese. The ways in which authors addressed these issues, usually by implication, say a great deal about what they hoped their respective audiences would retain.

In the early years of the twentieth century, the popular press emphasized a number of themes in stories about Taseko's life. First, she sold her cosmetics, some say her entire dowry, to buy books.[27] Second, her personality and deeds derived from the influence of her father and husband, becoming in a sense the social site where these male forces converged. One local publication from 1915, for example, traced her character to growing up surrounded by the natural beauty of the Shinano mountains and to her father. "Her dignified bearing, her frankheartedness and her fidelity were all owing to his example."[28] Third, since she was famous for having mingled with men from all over Japan, she must have met or spied on the heroes already closely associated with the Meiji Restoration (Sakamoto Ryōma, for example) or the brigade of masterless samurai organized into a bakufu police force called the *Shinsengumi*. She is depicted discussing the plans for the 1863 Ikuno uprising with Hirano Kuniomi and mediating his quarrels because, as Masako had said, she was a woman and naturally good at restoring harmony.[29] (While Taseko was in Kyoto, Kuniomi was in prison in Fukuoka.[30]) Finally, she herself acted in the guise of a warrior. Following the arrest of her friends for beheading the Ashikaga shoguns' statues, she dressed like a man and strapped on the two swords of the samurai to confound the police. Fearing that it would put her husband to shame were she arrested and imprisoned, she had resolved to commit suicide before her rescue by Chōshū. Back in the Ina Valley, she hoped to join the Mito warriors. Some say she accompanied them as far as Nakatsugawa, others say illness prevented her meeting them, but she proposed the plan whereby they passed safely through Iida.[31] These accounts both deny her the agency to make up her own mind and define her exploits according to male models.

One author let his imagination run away with him. In 1911 Watanabe Mokuzen serialized a "true historical story" of her life in *Fujin sekai* (Women's world) that scandalized her family and neighbors.[32] On the one hand it depicts her as the passive recipient of influences by her father, cousin, and husband; on the other it transforms her into a woman warrior. Her husband is a good match for her because he is a Confucian scholar and his wide circle of acquaintances broadens her horizons. When she asks him for a five-year leave of absence, he points out that going to Kyoto might be dangerous. Has she given any thought to how she will protect herself? She replies that she has learned swordfighting and unarmed combat from the samurai who used their house as a refuge. "If I end up in a situation that's beyond me, I've resolved to cut myself beautifully rather than meet an ugly end."

Mokuzen's "true story" reads more like "The Perils of Pauline." Taseko leaves home dressed as a samurai. While praying at the village tutelary shrine, she is seen by a drunken porter named Benkichi who, on his occasional visits to the Matsuo house, has fallen in love with her. As a demonstration of his affection, he tries to rape her. She uses her knowledge of martial arts to throw him to the ground and tie him up. He escapes and gathers two cronies from Iida to help him pursue her up the steep, rocky Ōdaira pass on the other side of Iida. Taseko kills one with her sword, seriously wounds the other, and Benkichi runs away. He then lodges a complaint against her with the Nakatsugawa authorities. They take her into custody. At first she tries bluffing, fearing that if she confesses to being a woman, she will have to explain why she has dressed as a man and her reason for going to Kyoto would be enough for her to be turned over to the bakufu "to die like a dog." Her interrogator will have none of this. "If you still claim you're a man, how about showing us your tits," he growls. Taseko admits to being a woman. She is wearing men's clothing lest evil men try to take advantage of her on the road, she says, and her destination is Hikone to take care of a sick aunt. No one believes her. She is kept in prison for over a month, frantic to be on her way. "Finally the gods go over to her side," a good official's suspicions are aroused by the miserable Benkichi, and his investigation leads to her release.

Taseko's titillating adventures continue in Kyoto. Never one to let mundane accuracy dilute a good story, Mokuzen has her roam around the city with her hair tied like a man's, wearing a crested kimono with pleated pants and carrying two swords. Only her comrades know her secret. In the course of conspiratorial meetings in the pleasure district of Gion, she attracts the amorous attention of Shirotae, a famous entertainer. The loyalists were notorious for their liaisons with the Kyoto geisha; if Taseko refuses to take advantage of her opportunity, she will become the object of suspicion. She takes pity on the woman's passion and writes her a poem, at the same time letting her know that she too is a woman. Shirotae responds by saying, "if you are a woman, I will go with you as a man. I am resolved never to renounce my love for you." On a more serious note, Taseko originates the plan for decapitating the Ashikaga shoguns' statues. On the night the deed is done, she keeps watch outside the temple. When some priests challenge her, she fights them off. They later identify her to the bakufu. She flees to friends in Osaka where she hides beneath the floorboards of their house, coming out only for meals. With the police on her trail, she returns to Kyoto, resolved to commit suicide lest her capture bring shame on her husband. "She was just bringing her dagger to her throat when heaven took pity on this brave woman. Quite by chance Watanabe Shinzaburō appeared. 'It's not yet your turn to die,' he says, grabbing her hand. 'You still have too many things to do.'"

People in the Ina Valley were outraged at the wanton woman depicted in this account. "These errors have caused the Matsuo family a great deal of

grief," Ichimura Minato fumed.[33] Not only did he object to the suggestion of
an illicit love affair with a porter, she had never dressed as a man. Despite his
protestations, just a year later, the same journal published another account
of her life that while removing any suggestion of sexuality left her in male
disguise hiding beneath floorboards.[34] By drawing on the all too pervasive assumption that love justifies rape and writing what would have passed at the
time for softcore pornography, Mokuzen warned women of the perils of
traveling and acting on their own. He praised Taseko for the purity of her devotion to the emperor, but he also demonstrated that acting politically required becoming unwomanly. Having risked her virtue, she became anything
but a role model for his readers.

Following the end of the Meiji period in 1912, stories about Taseko took
on new seriousness. More attention was paid to what she might actually have
done, but at the same time, her actions came increasingly to be viewed through
the lens of what was considered appropriate behavior for respectable women.
Ichimura Minato was the first to correct factual errors by relying more on
documents and interviews with family members than on hearsay, and he eschewed dramatic dialogue. Minato had been born in Yamamoto village in
1878. By the time he died in 1963, he had published over seventy volumes
on the Ina Valley and its residents.[35] He became the premier local historian
for the region, and it all began in 1911 when the Ina District Office appointed
him to compose Taseko's biography. He went on to write several versions of
this work, including a popular edition. In 1940 he revised his original 1913
biography to celebrate the 2600th anniversary of the founding of the Japanese nation.[36] His research had a tremendous impact on all subsequent work
done by historians, most of whom took his assumptions for granted. In trying to make Taseko into an exemplar of womanly virtues, he vehemently denied that she had ever worn men's clothing, or that "she had to pretend to be
visiting relatives in order to escape from her husband in going to Kyoto."[37]
She must have asked for her husband's permission to join the loyalists because in addition to being a firm supporter of the emperor system, she was a
"good wife and wise mother."[38]

Dress was important. In the late nineteenth century, Western clothes for
men quickly became the norm, at least in public. For women, however, the
kimono was not just something to wear. According to Murakami Nobuhiko,
it symbolized the restrictions imposed on women by the feudal family system that remained rooted in society throughout the prewar era and offered
living proof that the wearer was a good wife and wise mother.[39] By practicing cross-dressing, Taseko would have liberated herself from these constraints and challenged the norms of ideal womanhood. Taseko's portraits

FIGURE 23.
Retouched photograph of
Matsuo Taseko. Courtesy
of Matsuo Yūzō.

depict her in the loose robes of a grandmother. Her photograph on display at
the Matsuo house, on the other hand, shows her sitting stiffly with a formal
kimono pulled tightly around her neck. The present head of the household
told me that before the war, his mother had decided that the original photograph did not represent Taseko properly. To recast Taseko in a suitably dignified position, she cut out the head and had it stuck on the appropriate
attire.

Even biographers who continued to dress Taseko in men's clothing began
to insist that she acted always in accordance with her husband's wishes. She
asked his permission not only to go to Kyoto, but to write poetry, and she never
wasted her time reading trashy novels.[40] Hanyū Eimei argues that while
everyone has praised Taseko's achievements, one should not forget her husband's benevolence in trusting his wife and letting her do what she wanted.
Had he not allowed her the freedom to go to Kyoto, she would have disrupted

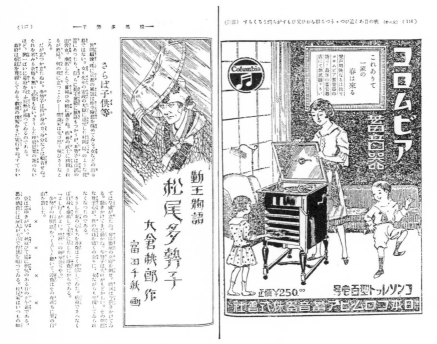

FIGURE 24. Taseko braving the elements opposite an advertisement for Columbia phonographs. From "Kinnō monogatari: Matsuo Taseko," *Fujokai* 41.5 (May 1929): 116–17.

the family or run the risk of being suspected of infidelity. Furthermore, Taseko's expenses in Kyoto must have been enormous. If her husband had been narrow-minded and mistrustful, he would have begrudged paying for them, and she would not have been able to do what she did. "Their relationship must have been based on the mutual love and respect that enabled them to live their lives in harmony."[41]

As a good wife and wise mother, Taseko represented the polar opposite of the "new woman." By the early twentieth century, the national press regularly reported on women in the urban centers of Tokyo and Osaka who questioned men's authority in the home and sought to redefine women's roles. Hiratsuka Raichō demanded state protection of and special privileges for mothers while attacking the patriarchal marriage system enshrined in the Civil Code that gave husbands power over their wives. Yosano Akiko argued that women must have the opportunity to make a living regardless of their marital circumstances.[42] In reaction to this threat to the family system and the state, stories about Taseko praised her devotion to both. "Taseko was a woman with the determination of a man. In today's world, the new women bewitched by vainglory who make such mischief by putting themselves forward would do well to learn from Taseko's indomitable spirit of diligence, loyalty and fidelity."[43]

Few stories about Taseko appeared in the national women's journals of the 1920s, and those that did must have seemed increasingly anachronistic to urban readers. In a serialized version of her life that appeared in *Fujokai* (Ladies' world), one episode illustrated with a picture of Taseko braving the rain in straw hat and raincoat appeared opposite to an advertisement for Columbia phonographs showing a housewife and two children dressed in modern clothes dancing in a Western-style living room.[44] Taseko herself was a progressive woman, however, because she had learned to read despite her parents' opposition. When her father caught her in his library sobbing over the story of how Ashikaga Takauji forced Emperor Godaigo to hide in the mountains (a story that as a student of things Chinese he knew nothing about), she taught him a lesson in loyalty. Later at the visit she and her husband made to the Takasu domain lord in Edo, she talked him around to supporting the emperor. When she was not winning political arguments with men, she diligently worked in the fields or collected leaves to feed silkworms.

Taseko's biography serialized in *Fujokai* made her sterling devotion to duty part of her persona as a rural woman. In proposing her trip to Kyoto to her husband, she points out that, "there is no difference between men and women when it comes to loyalty to the emperor and feelings for the country." Learning that the Hirata disciples believe Iwakura Tomomi to stand in the way of restoring the emperor to direct rule, she argues that it would be easier for her as a woman to ascertain his true intentions than it would be for a man. During a spring trip to Arashiyama, she falls behind her male companions. One man who turns around to see why catches sight of her urinating standing up. "Hey, Tase's doing it again," he shouts boisterously. "It happened in the countryside all the time. Taseko may have read her poems before highborn nobles and discussed national affairs, but she was still someone who cut grass with a sickle. Her companions were young enough to be her sons, and she was certainly not going to worry about children laughing at her."[45] It is unlikely that urban women would have acted with such nonchalance. How could they, lacking as they did Taseko's strength of character?

In the period between the wars, urban life in Japan changed dramatically. Trains carried salaried workers dressed in starched shirts and neat suits from their offices in the center of the city to their houses in the suburbs. Women bought Western-style dresses in department stores, learned to play the piano, and cooked on kerosene stoves. The brief appearance of the "Modern Girl" in the late 1920s symbolized the very essence of westernized decadence in the eyes of conservative supporters of the emperor system.[46] This first wave of consumer culture seemingly attacked not only the tried and true virtues of diligence, thrift, and fortitude, but the very notion of patriotism. In the 1920s the contrast between urban frivolity and rural sincerity was lightly drawn; in the 1930s, it became increasingly humorless.

In the militaristic atmosphere of the 1930s, the heroes of the Restoration came to epitomize the pure Japanese spirit (*Yamato damashii*), and stories about Taseko appeared with considerable frequency in journals and books aimed at women. She became not merely an imperial loyalist (*kinnō ka*), but a patriot (*aikokusha*) and a woman who nurtured patriots. Even her xeno-phobia had merit. "Japanese women did not simply run and hide with the coming of the red-nosed foreigners. Hating the barbarians' oppressive and impolite behavior, some burned with anger toward the enemy and took posi-tive steps to resist."[47] The popular writer of historical novels, Yoshikawa Eiji, included Taseko in a series of short sketches he did on patriotic women for the longest running of the women's journals, *Shufu no tomo* (The housewife's companion), in 1938.[48] "While cutting the mulberry leaves, she thought deeply about the obligations she owed the emperor. Without the nation, how could old mothers and fathers live their lives in peace? What about her beloved husband and children?" In Kyoto the Hirata disciples treated her as a near and dear relative. "Aunty, please sew on my collar," "Aunty, please give me a little change." "You're the mother of imperial loyalism," they said. "No, I'm just working to repay the obligation I owe the soil," was her response.[49]

Dedicated to "all women in Japan," a 1938 book-length popular biogra-phy likewise calls Taseko "the mother of reverence for the emperor" who mingled with the samurai and raised seven children as well.[50] This author gives Taseko an understanding father who recognizes her talent and tries to provide her with the best possible education. His passionate loyalty to the emperor deeply influences his daughter, and she is trained in the code often associated with the samurai, that of raising her children to serve the state. As a good wife and wise mother, she works from before dawn to after dark. In Kyoto she looks after the young loyalists as though they were her own chil-dren and gratefully accepts condescending praise from the Chōshū lord: "Even though you're the wife of a country bumpkin, your spirit is equal to the finest warrior." After she returns to Kyoto in 1868 at the restoration of imperial rule, she dedicates her sons to the emperor's service, saying, "you must realize that to throw your life away for the sake of your country is the sacred duty of all people born in the land of Japan."[51]

This book provides an excellent example of how the cloth of Taseko's life was cut to fit the fashion of the time. In an increasingly jingoistic age, she is naturally enraged at Commodore Perry's threats, the harsh commercial treaty Townsend Harris forces the shogun to sign, and the arrogance of the British that leads a merchant to be killed at Namamugi village. Japan had been unable to withstand foreign pressure in 1858; eighty years later the humiliation rankled anew. The author evidently had access to Taseko's diaries from 1862–63, but he read them extremely selectively. Nowhere does he allude to her anti-Confucian or anti-Buddhist sentiments; in fact he has her stop at Kōryūji and worship at a famous statue of the Buddha carved by Prince Shōtoku, who had built the ancient Japanese state along Chinese lines. On her way back to Tomono she makes a point of visiting the Buddhist temples at Nara. By the time this book was written, Buddhism had regained its position as a pillar of the state. No one accused it of being a foreign religion, and in most areas of Japan it remained an integral part of people's lives. Taseko's views on this subject detracted from the construction of patriotism in the 1930s; better simply to ignore them.

Articles written about Taseko in the war years were confined to women's journals and local publications. They all tame her audacity in going to Kyoto by putting her trip in the context of self-sacrifice for the family and the state.[52] In a magazine aimed at teenage girls, Mizushima Ayame, the first woman to essay Taseko's biography since her friend Miwada Masako, depicts "the mother of imperial loyalism" who obeys her father, serves her in-laws with greater devotion than she had her own parents, and never neglects her studies. "The more she reads, the more her heart is filled with respect and thanksgiving for the immutable national essence of our Japan." Into her mouth is put a statement that must have brought joy to Japan's leaders: "Even though I am a woman, as long as I have a sincere heart, there must be something I can do for my country." Her real contribution to the cause comes in pursuing the appropriately feminine task of nurturing the men of high purpose, both in Kyoto and the Ina Valley.[53]

Of all the wartime biographies, only one stands out for its fresh approach. This is the sketch published in *Fujin kōron* (Women's Review) in 1939 written by a nationalist poet, Kawada Jun. (He was to instruct the Crown Prince in poetry after the war until a sex scandal forced his retirement in 1949. He died in 1966 at the age of 84.) Jun argues so vehemently against any meeting between Taseko and Iwakura Tomomi in 1862 that he even convinced Minato to question whether it had in fact taken place. He disparages her education and her poetry, pointing out that none of the Ina Valley poets was particularly notable and her teachers knew little more than she did. Her diary has value as a historical document; despite her efforts to craft it in the mode of a literary journal, it is not literature. Her study of poetry had nothing to do with her becoming a heroic loyalist. Instead she owes everything to the Hirata school, which both offered her the opportunity to write better poetry in the pure style of the ancients and taught her politics. Jun is also the first writer to make an issue of her age, though he subsumed agency to fate. "Had she been young and fresh looking, no matter how virtuous she was, she would have become the subject of gossip. It would have been difficult for her to share rooms with young men or go out late at night on secret business. It must have been divine providence that put her to work in her old age." [54]

OVER TWENTY years separate the last wartime publication on Taseko and her appearance in postwar print. Not only had patriotism fallen out of vogue, so had the ideological constructs that had supported what was known as the emperor system. For a few decades even the slogan "good wife and wise mother," with its emphasis on self-sacrifice for the sake of the family and obedience to the patriarch, lost ground. Historians eschewed the study of heroic individuals and studied the economic rather than the spiritual foundations for the Meiji Restoration and modern Japan. Not until the postwar recovery was well underway did stories about Taseko begin to pop up in women's journals and restoration histories. Once again she was more likely to be the subject of attention than commoner men unable to compete with the male models of valor represented by the samurai. The Hirata disciples in particular are now seen as so anachronistic as to find scant favor with authors and readers. Many stories treat her as yet one more figure in the endlessly fascinating Restoration saga. Others use her to talk about issues relevant to contemporary women. They have continued to appear every year or so down to the present.

In the intellectual freedom of the postwar period, Taseko's life has become illustrative of a much greater variety of arguments than before. Historian Hayashida Tatsusaburō uses her to exemplify the local notables and their families who had a nationwide vision and came close to seeing themselves as citizens, in contrast to the lower classes who did not have enough education to comprehend the fate of Japan as a nation or the economic wherewithal to engage in political activity.[55] According to Akagi Shizuko, Taseko exhibits the Ina Valley's "intellectually progressive spirit." [56] For the pacifist and local historian Morosawa Yōko, Taseko's untamed spirit represents a successful struggle against "Confucian household morality" with its requirements of absolute submission and service to superiors. "Her action in ignoring her husband to go to Kyoto was remarkable and unprecedented." [57] Suzuki Yukiko too attacks gender inequality. In a reversal of prewar conventions, she argues that Taseko's husband and sons were completely dependent on her. They probably had no idea of what she planned to do in Kyoto. Women like Taseko from wealthy farm households had much more freedom than samurai women. Life became worse for them after the Meiji Restoration because the men who seized power came from a region of Japan with a strong tradition of respecting men and despising women.[58]

The women of postwar Japan have also fastened on Taseko's story to talk about personal concerns and problems. In complete contrast to prewar historians who gloried in the blood shed in the name of the emperor, Yōko argues that only the centuries of peace preceding the Restoration made the appearance of outstanding women possible.[59] A notably intimate approach to Taseko's life appears in a dialogue between Yoshimi Kaneko and the television scriptwriter, Hashida Sugako, famous for stories such as "O-Shin" which depict women buffeted by the impossible demands placed on them by their families.[60] Unlike prewar writers who defined Taseko as the recipient of influences emanating from others, they posit volition. "It is wonderful that some women actually managed to have their own ideas during this period." Taseko achieved a reputation for having done deeds that no man could have done, probably because she had a round face with a dark complexion. It is more often the ugly women who get involved in social movements or pursue careers. How else to explain why Taseko acted apart from her family for the sake of her ideals, not for love or lust.

HASHIDA: "She must have really hated being at home if she made so many trips to Kyoto and Tokyo. But what was her husband doing? Given an age in which men dominated women, for a wife to become famous rather than her husband suggests a peculiar couple."

YOSHIMI: "We don't know what made Taseko do what she did. Maybe it's because she was finished with childbearing, or perhaps she was not satisfied with her husband."

HASHIDA: "She's like today's women searching for a reason for living."[61]

No other writers ever suggest that Taseko and Motoharu were less that perfectly suited to each other. In talking about the past, this dialogue says a great deal about current preconceptions regarding the kind of women who take an active part in public issues. Behind its light-hearted banter lies the reality of postwar married life and the issues confronting women who may find little meaning in their lives once their children are on their own.[62]

A few women writers have retold Taseko's story in such a way as to help women look beyond their roles as housewives and mothers. As early as 1973,

Anzai Atsuko points out that like the poets Ōtagaki Regentsu and Nomura Bōtō, Taseko had spent her middle years as a housewife. "Once they had graduated from housework, they were able to do as they pleased. Men have this freedom when they are young, but women get it only after they have completed their social obligations."[63] Sixteen years later, Japan's graying population has become an issue. Takahara Sumiko uses Taseko's life to urge people approaching eighty not to feel their age but to live their last years to the full.[64] In her essay on women who work in farm villages, Yanagi Miyoko celebrates the pleasures of retirement from household responsibilities. Because Taseko came from a wealthy family, in her later years "she was able to enjoy a free, cultivated and active life."[65] Taseko has thus become a role model for the older woman.

Articles written about Taseko appear primarily in women's publications or in special features devoted to women in the Meiji Restoration. Just as the Civil War maintains an enduring fascination in the United States, the Japanese demand for stories about this period is seemingly inexhaustible. No details, no matter how fanciful, have been left undiscovered by the insatiable maw by the mass media, and the category of women has become a recognized part of its diet fed even by men who consider themselves professional specialists. Doing so allows them to keep their other work untainted by the female presence. The only exceptions are one or two historians who study the Hirata school, perhaps because it too seldom figures in either popular or academic accounts. Taseko is thus doubly marginalized, first as a woman and then as a member of a movement that went nowhere.

Many biographical sketches that appear in postwar publications simply summarize Taseko's achievements in the Restoration years. None of them includes her poetry, either her love poems or her patriotic doggerel. A few carefully avoid anecdotes for which there is no documentary foundation, in particular Taseko's saving Iwakura Tomomi from the hands of assassins or her forcing a spy to commit suicide in the Chōshū mansion, nor has there been much talk of how diligently she worked in the fields and served her in-laws.[66] On the other hand, some writers, including respected historians, tend to uncritically regurgitate the legends current before the war.[67] They may allow a note of condescension to creep into their accounts: women like Taseko did little to further the Restoration, but it is noteworthy that they acted at all.[68]

Not all Japanese pundits approve of the new Japan with its emphasis on consumerism and material goods. In their eyes, too much has been abandoned with the old emperor system and they look back to the heroes of the Restoration for models of sincerity and self-sacrifice. In calling for a revival of traditional Japanese virtues, they once again turn Taseko into a good wife and wise mother who raised her children to serve their country.[69] Some have gone so far as to call her "the mother of imperial loyalism."[70] One points out that Taseko never asked anything for herself. She went to Kyoto not out of political ambition or a lust for glory but out of a sincere sense of patriotism and a desire to serve the emperor. "She is called a hero, but the way she expressed herself was truly womanly."[71]

This conservative trend characterizes the sole postwar historical novel that features Taseko. Furukawa Chieko depicts the woman behind the patriot by focusing on Taseko's maternal side.[72] The crux of the plot is Taseko's relationship with the young Kyoto townsman Nagao Ikusaburō. They quarrel at their first meeting because Taseko tries to caution him against being too reckless. "He is as single-minded as a child," and refuses to listen.[73] At their next meeting he proposes to assassinate Iwakura Tomomi; Taseko says he should be given a fair hearing first and she will be the one to provide it. Ikusaburō calls her a spy. When she tries to win him over by bringing food to a meeting of the Hirata disciples, he rudely refuses to eat it. She scolds and even slaps him, demonstrating "tough love" that he has never known, his mother having died when he was young. Later she saves his life when he is captured by bakufu supporters, and the two become close friends. Upon learning that he is to be executed following the plot to pillory the statues of the Ashikaga shoguns, she grieves for him as though he were her own son. In the meantime she uncovers a plot to poison the emperor, suffers a shoulder wound in a fight with bakufu samurai, and meets Sakamoto Ryōma at his water closet. She accompanies the disciples who decapitate the statues even though she disapproves of the plan because "any mother would go to hell and back to watch over her children."[74] A television network expressed interest in televising the novel, but to my knowledge it has not happened yet.[75]

That Taseko was first and foremost a mother has a great deal of appeal in contemporary Japan where motherhood is still considered to be a woman's reason for living and her chief justification for bridging the public and private spheres.[76] Unasked is the question of whether casting her in such terms is really so different from wartime and prewar publications that deemed her "the mother of imperial loyalism." Granted, much has changed. Taseko's role in the Meiji Restoration may be the reason why she has found a place in the public memory, but she has also become a symbol of the potential latent in all Japanese women. Taseko would have doubtless approved of these stories. Her approbation of my project is less certain.

Epilogue

This old person
who has lived through the years
still feels young at heart
in greeting the new year
that has just begun
MATSUO TASEKO, 1873[1]

When I first visited the Ina Valley in search of Taseko in
June 1989, I quickly discovered that she is well remembered.
No sooner had I arrived at the Lower Ina Educational Society
than I was told of an exhibition of her portrait in the lobby of
a bank in Yamamoto. There I found copies of two photographs,
her most famous poems, and gifts received from famous men.
Given pride of place was her portrait inscribed with a poem
by Shinagawa Yajirō. Recently discovered among the possessions of an old family in Uji-Yamada near Ise, it had been returned to Yamamoto to validate the claims of local historians
that she had indeed known this famous Restoration hero and
high-ranking government official. The bank passed out scrolls
as souvenirs that contained a brief biographical sketch and a
selection of her most famous poems: her celebration of the assassination of Ii Naosuke, her prayers to gods for protection

during her trip to Kyoto in 1862, her delight at rising above the clouds to meet the court nobility plus other poems written in an appropriately patriotic spirit, and her lament that she was a weak woman with a useless body. At the end was her instruction to her great-grandson to be a good person. In the autumn of that same year, a second exhibition was held at the Toyooka Folklore and History Museum. Over fifteen hundred people signed the guest register and viewed portraits, poems, the dagger she received from the heir to the Chōshū domain, the toys enjoyed by the Meiji emperor, and various artifacts lent by her descendants' families.

The year 1989 is well remembered for the death of Emperor Showa, Emperor Meiji's grandson, after a sixty-odd year reign. Historians and urban pundits focused on its vicissitudes, in particular the "dark valley" of World War Two, which was blamed on the emperor system that originated in the political settlement known as the Meiji Restoration. Less critical of the past, people in Yamamoto and Toyooka recalled that they once had a direct connection with national events through the region's most famous daughter.

Taseko's local boosters had begun their efforts to insert her into the public memory of the Restoration with the first memorial service held in her honor in 1895. Her cousin Inao's youngest son solicited poems from thirty-five people to be published "as a lasting memento of this woman's brave deeds and noteworthy achievements." Given pride of place was a poem by Shinagawa Yajirō, followed by poems from nationally famous figures, not all of whom had ever met her. The five women included Miwada Masako and Andō Kikuko. Whether written by people from the provinces or notables from the cities, the verses were rung on an extremely limited number of themes: they mourned Taseko's death, praised her unwavering fidelity, extolled the feminine equivalent of masculine loyalty, or asserted that her fame would endure for a thousand years.[2]

Taseko's elevation to posthumous court rank spurred local boosters to continue commemorating her death anniversary. The pamphlet published for the tenth was titled, "In praise of Matsuo Taseko."[3] For the twentieth, a ceremony was held at the Kumashiro Elementary School followed by a public exhibition of mementos. Ichimura Minato photographed them for publication, "to console this hero's valiant spirit."[4] Even though the fiftieth occurred during the darkest days of World War Two, the District Educational Society managed to collect enough money and paper to publish an edition of her Kyoto diaries and letters.[5] For the hundredth, the Toyooka Village Educational Committee published another pamphlet in her honor. It lists the various ways in which she has been honored and provides photocopies of newspaper articles announcing the 1989 exhibitions.[6] One describes my visit to the valley.[7] The president of the Toyooka Village Historical Association would like to see a hall built in her honor for the bicentennial of her birth, but the village government has expressed little interest.[8]

Tangible evidence of Taseko's gifts to posterity remain on stone monuments scattered across the lower Ina Valley. The first was built the year of her death for a shrine in Iida and displays a poem asking the god of food for a good harvest. In 1901 another shrine in Iida erected a second boasting a carving of Taseko's poem written upon hearing that the emperor had gone to the Kamo shrine in 1863. Three monuments went up in the super-patriotic 1930s: the first at the shrine to the four nativist teachers in Yamabuki, the second at a waterfall in what was then Kumashiro village, and the third in Yamamoto. The only monument associated with her in the postwar period gives a history of the O-tegata shrine in one Toyooka hamlet, capped by a poem written when Taseko was forty-two and in the first flush of her enthusiasm for the teachings of Hirata Atsutane.[9] A local sculptor carved her bust in bronze for an Iida middle school. A copy was given to the Hazama family of Nakatsugawa.[10] The advantage to stone and sculpture, especially in recent years, is that it says very little and requires no upkeep. With only a name, a date, or a poem to go by, people living in the locality and visitors can interpret Taseko's life for themselves. Steles and statues commemorate the past, but they do so in remarkably ambiguous and indeterminate ways.

Taseko's biographers have had to take a stand. They make much of her public role in supporting the men who brought about the Meiji Restoration at the same time that they root this role in her fundamental nature as a mother. Forgotten are her use of poetry to craft different identities for herself, her interest in the tea ceremony, her trip to Kyoto as a literary and religious experience, her enjoyment of sightseeing, and her fondness for sake. Everyone knows she fervently espoused the teachings of Hirata Atsutane; no one ever asks what those teachings might have meant to her as a woman. There is never any mention of her activities in Tokyo in 1869. Her unedifying work as a lobbyist in the scramble for political favor is so contrary to the image of her pure-minded idealism that historians and pundits cannot deal with it. Nor do they point out that for all her lamentations regarding the state of national affairs, she was apparently a cheerful woman who faced her personal prospects with considerable optimism.

A happy concatenation of external circumstances and personal attributes took Taseko to Kyoto in 1862. She was old enough to have done with child care and household management yet young enough to walk all day and talk late into the night. She had the financial resources to spend six months in an urban environment without contributing to her own upkeep. She had sufficient polish acquired through years of studying classical poetry to respond appropriately when meeting her betters in the social hierarchy. She had acquired a world view and a social network through her membership in the Hirata school that both enhanced the city's meaning for her and provided a vocabulary with which to discuss the issues of the day. In addition, she arrived at that moment when Kyoto had become the center of politics. A year or two earlier and the men who thought as she did would have been scattered across Japan; a year or two later and they would have been in domanial confinement or dead.

Fortuitous coincidences, however, do not explain why Taseko, of all her relatives and neighbors, ventured to Kyoto when she did. In her life she juxtaposed a highly unconventional audacity enlisted in the service of strictly conventional, indeed conservative notions of poetry, piety, and politics. Hints that she honored the norms of her day in the breach appear in her travels with her husband and her decision to become the Hirata school's first female posthumous disciple. The friends of her old age testify to her lack of concern with the proprieties when they describe how unlike most women she was in the way she sat and her conversation. She clearly possessed the right combination of social skills, wit, and courage to move with grace and ease across the profound cleavages of gender and status that divided men from women and commoners from the ruling class.

Taseko has achieved greater renown than her fellow Hirata disciples or indeed other commoners who tried to participate in the plethora of events resulting in the Meiji Restoration. She stands out simply because she was a woman when few women claimed a role on the public stage, giving her a secure place in the subgenre of women's history. Her work as guarantor, go-between and information conduit for the revolutionary underground depended at least in part on her sex. Given the highly developed espionage system run by the bakufu and its allies, plus all the restrictions placed on interactions between men of different classes, Taseko had the advantage of being able to slip in and out of aristocratic mansions and even the imperial palace without attracting attention. No one would ever suspect an old peasant woman of subversion, making her subsequent reputation all the more noteworthy. Did Taseko make a difference? If the focus is on the transformation of the national government, the answer is probably not.

Taseko has never achieved the fame that samurai such as Sakamoto Ryōma enjoy. This is due at least in part to a failure on the part of historians to notice her type of achievement or to assume that only achievements with lasting political consequences are worth remembering. One reason why she is so often credited with having saved the life of Iwakura Tomomi is because this is usually seen as the only kind of history that counts. Many of Taseko's concerns—the raising of silkworms, the births, illnesses and deaths of her descendants, her fascination with a landscape defined by ancient poetry—

FIGURE 25.
Bust of Taseko by
Kurasawa Kōsei.
Courtesy of Hazama Jōji.

constitute nothing but trifles in the context of reverberating public events that happened elsewhere. Some historians of women have argued that "the female world is worthy of study in and of itself, quite apart from its impact on the male world."[11] On the other hand, examining Taseko's life within the context of her times opens up the possibility of questioning the distinction between public and private, male roles and female roles and the often hazy margin between conceptual categories that mesh into one another in practice.[12] Restoring her to the history of the Meiji Restoration has to enlarge our perspective on it. Dead ends, the vision espoused by the Hirata disciples, for example, need also to be included. Insofar as the historiography of her life follows in the train of the historiography of the Meiji Restoration without becoming completely submerged and speaks to the concerns of local boosters or issues germane to women, it supplements the master narrative with extraneous material. It rewrites that narrative without replacing it, making up for its insufficiencies and demonstrating that it can never be complete.

Abbreviations

Works frequently cited have been identified by the following abbreviations:

HAz   *Shinshū Hirata Atsutane zenshū*. Tokyo: Meicho Shuppan, 1977.

HHH   Mizugaki Kiyoshi. *Hazama Hanbei Hidenori to sono gyōseki: Nakatsugawa no Hirata monjin*. Nakatsugawa-shi: by the author, 1987.

HHHs   *Hazama Hanbei Hidenori shū*. Mizugaki Kiyoshi, ed. Nakatsugawa-
shi: Hazama Kōtarō, 1976.

Iks   Murasawa Takeo. *Ina kadō shi*. Iida-shi: Yamamura Shoin, 1936.

IMz   *Ichimura Minato zenshū*, vol. 5. Ichimura Minato Zenshū Kankōkai,
ed. Iida-shi: Shimoina Kyōikukai, 1980.

Isss   Ichimura Minato. *Ina sonnō shisō shi*. Iida-shi: Shimoina-gun Kokumin Seishinsaku Kyōkai, 1929.

MTic   Ichimura Minato. *Matsuo Taseko ihō chō*. Iida-shi: Tanaka Shōten,
1918.

Sgs   Shimoina-gun Gunyakusho. *Shimoina gunshi shiryō*, vol. 2. Tokyo:
Rekishi Toshosha, 1977.

Sks   Ichimura Minato. *Shinano kyōdo sosho*, vol. 17, *Matsuo Taseko*.
Nagano-shi: Shinano Kyōdo Bunka Fukyūkai, 1930.

TnMt   *Tabi no nagusa, Miyako no tsuto: Matsuo Taseko jōkyō nikki*. Ichimura
Minato, ed. Iida-shi: Shimoina Kyōikukai, 1944.

Notes

Place of publication is not specified for university presses or where the place of publication is Tokyo.

Introduction

1. Quoted in Richard Jenkyns, "The Pleasures of Melodrama," *The New York Review of Books* 43.12 (July 11, 1996): 10.
2. Shimazaki Tōson, *Before the Dawn,* trans. William E. Naff (University of Hawaii Press, 1987). See biographical note for Taseko on p. 780. In this translation she appears on pages 176, 213, 307, 366, 431, 636.
3. William E. Naff, "Shimazaki Tōson's *Before the Dawn:* Historical Fiction as History and as Literature," in *The Ambivalence of Nationalism: Modern Japan between East and West,* ed. James W. White, Michio Umegaki, and Thomas R. H. Havens (University Press of America, 1990), p. 99.
4. "Matsuo Taseko to Meiji ishin: Jiko to jendā no Nihonshi," in *Jendā no Nihonshi,* vol. 2, ed. Wakita Haruko and Susan B. Hanley (University of Tokyo Press, 1995), pp. 176–97.
5. George M. Wilson, *Patriots and Redeemers in Japan: Motives in the Meiji Restoration* (University of Chicago Press, 1992), p. 63.
6. Four books in particular illustrate this perspective to one degree or another: Albert Craig, *Chōshū in the Meiji Restoration* (Harvard University Press, 1961); Marius B. Jansen, *Sakamoto Ryōma and the Meiji Restoration* (Princeton University Press, 1961); W. G. Beasley, *The Meiji Restoration* (Stanford University Press, 1972); Thomas M. Huber, *The Revolutionary Origins of Modern Japan* (Stanford University Press, 1981).

7. Sasaki Junnosuke, *Bakumatsu shakairon* (Hanawa Shobō, 1969); idem, *Yonaoshi* (Iwanami Shoten, 1979).

8. Miyachi Masato, *Bakumatsu ishin-ki no bunka to jōhō* (Meicho Kankōkai, 1994).

9. Herbert Bix, *Peasant Protest in Japan, 1590–1884* (Yale University Press, 1986); Donald W. Burton, "Peasant Movements in Early Tokugawa Japan," *Peasant Studies* 8.3 (1979): 162–81.

10. Wilson, *Patriots and Redeemers in Japan,* especially p. 67.

11. Harry D. Harootunian, *Toward Restoration: The Growth of Political Consciousness in Tokugawa Japan* (University of California Press, 1970), p. 17; J. Victor Koschmann, *The Mito Ideology: Discourse, Reform and Insurrection in Late Tokugawa Japan, 1790–1864* (University of California Press, 1987).

12. Harry D. Harootunian, *Things Seen and Unseen: Discourse and Ideology in Tokugawa Nativism* (University of Chicago Press, 1988).

13. My thanks to Kären Wigen for this formulation.

14. A number of Haga's books appear in the notes to this study. For his intellectual autobiography see *Henkaku-ki ni okeru kokugaku* (San'ichi Shobō, 1975), pp. 7–9.

15. Conrad Totman, *The Collapse of the Tokugawa Bakufu, 1862–1868* (University of Hawaii Press, 1980), p. 458; Beasley, *The Meiji Restoration,* pp. 33–34. Beasley points out that "social structure was not in the end the only factor that decided political allegiance." James W. White goes so far as to say, "There was no autonomous popular component in the Restoration itself at all." *Ikki: Social Conflict and Political Protest in Early Modern Japan* (Cornell University Press, 1995), p. 34.

16. Joan W. Scott, "Women's History," in *New Perspectives on Historical Writing,* ed. Peter Burke (Cambridge and Oxford: Polity Press, 1991), pp. 43–60. The quotation is on p. 49.

17. Anne Walthall, "Devoted Wives/Unruly Women: Invisible Presence in the History of Japanese Social Protest," *Signs: Journal of Women in Culture and Society* 20.1 (Autumn 1994): 106–36.

18. See, for example, Matsumura Hiroshi, *Kinsei no onnatachi* (Osaka: Tōhō Shuppan, 1989), pp. 214–33.

19. Susan J. Pharr has pointed out that the same is true for neotraditional political women in Japan today, and Tanaka Kakuei, a deceased Prime Minister, has a daughter who wins elections using his name. *Political Women in Japan: The Search for a Place in Political Life* (University of California Press, 1981), p. 104; Sally Ann Hastings, "Women Legislators in the Postwar Diet," in *Re-imaging Japanese Women,* ed. Anne E. Imamura (University of California Press, 1996), p. 295.

20. Susan N. G. Geiger, "Women's Life Histories: Method and Content," *Signs: Journal of Women in Culture and Society* 11.2 (1986): 335.

21. Anne Walthall, "The Family Ideology of the Rural Entrepreneurs in Nineteenth Century Japan," *Journal of Social History* 32.3 (Spring 1990): 463–83.

22. Donna Robinson Divine, "'Difficult Journey—Mountainous Journey'— The Memoirs of Fadwa Tuqan," in *The Female Autograph: Theory and Practice of*

Autobiography from the Tenth to the Twentieth Century, ed. Domna C. Stanton (University of Chicago Press, 1987), p. 192.

23. Edwin McClellan, *Woman in the Crested Kimono: The Life of Shibue Io and Her Family Drawn from Mori Ogai's "Shibue Chusai"* (Yale University Press, 1985).

24. Feminist biography has become a vast and self-conscious genre. For a few representative works, see Personal Narratives Group, ed., *Interpreting Women's Lives: Feminist Theory and Personal Narratives* (Indiana University Press, 1989); Kathleen Barry, "The New Historical Syntheses: Women's Biography," *Journal of Women's History* 1.3 (Winter 1990): 75–105; Laurel Thatcher Ulrich, *A Midwife's Tale: The Life of Martha Ballard, Based on Her Diary, 1785–1812* (New York: Vintage Books, 1990); Sara Alpern et al., eds., *The Challenge of Feminist Biography: Writing the Lives of Modern American Women* (University of Illinois Press, 1992); the special issue on feminism, biography, and theory in *a/b: Auto/Biography Studies* 8.2 (Fall 1993); Linda Wagner-Martin, *Telling Women's Lives: The New Biography* (Rutgers University Press, 1994), and other books and articles cited in the endnotes.

25. Sandra M. Gilbert and Susan Gubar, *The Madwoman in the Attic: The Woman Writer and the Nineteenth-Century Literary Imagination* (Yale University Press, 1979), pp. 133–34.

26. Patricia Buckley Ebrey, *The Inner Quarters: Marriage and the Lives of Chinese Women in the Sung Period* (University of California Press, 1993), p. 7.

27. Tinne Vammen, "Introduction" to "Forum: Modern English Auto/Biography and Gender," *Gender and History* 2.1 (Spring 1990): 17.

28. Joan Wallach Scott, *Only Paradoxes to Offer: French Feminists and the Rights of Man* (Harvard University Press, 1996), pp. 15–16.

29. Esashi Akiko, *Onna no isshō wo kaku: hyōden no hōhō to shiten* (Nihon Editā Sukūru Shuppansha, 1994), p. 49.

30. Muriel Bell, personal communication, 19 May 1996.

31. Esashi, *Onna no isshō wo kaku*, p. 53.

32. *Sgs*, documents section, p. 44.

33. Sakurai Ban, personal communication, 7 July 1989.

34. The other five were either noblewomen or samurai. Nomura Bōtō was a poet imprisoned for helping pro-imperial samurai; Muraoka no tsubone served as a messenger between the court nobility and the samurai; Kawase or Ikeda Kō assisted her husband in his loyalist activities; Kurosawa Toki from Mito appealed to the emperor for pardon for her daimyo; Ōe Iwashiro was the mother of Emperor Kōkaku. See Takagi Shunsuke, "Sōmō no josei," in *Nihon josei shi*, ed. Joseishi Sōgō Kenkyū Kai, vol. 3 (Tōkyō Daigaku Shuppan Kai, 1982), pp. 260–66.

35. Carolyn G. Heilbrun, *Hamlet's Mother and Other Women* (Ballantine Books, 1990), p. 44.

36. Carolyn G. Heilbrun, *Writing a Woman's Life* (Ballantine Books, 1988), p. 48 and passim.

37. Mary Elizabeth Berry, "Public Peace and Private Attachment: The Goals and Conduct of Power in Early Modern Japan," *Journal of Japanese Studies* 12.2 (Summer 1986): 237–71.

38. I thank Kären Wigen for this suggestion.

39. I take the notion of a heterogeneous public sphere from Judith R. Walkowitz, *City of Dreadful Delight: Narratives of Sexual Danger in Late-Victorian London* (University of Chicago Press, 1992), pp. 38, 45, 85.

40. Jürgen Habermas, *The Structural Transformation of the Public Sphere: An Inquiry into a Category of Bourgeois Society*, trans. Thomas Buger (MIT Press, 1989). A clear exposition of his ideas is in Sarah Maza, *Private Lives and Public Affairs: The Causes Célèbres of Prerevolutionary France* (University of California Press, 1993), pp. 13–14.

41. Marius B. Jansen, "The Meiji Restoration," in *The Cambridge History of Japan*, vol. 5, *The Nineteenth Century* (Cambridge University Press, 1989), p. 320.

42. An excellent study of rural entrepreneurs who combined a love of study with a commitment to village and self improvement is by Watanabe Susumu, *Sonraku no Meiji ishin kenkyū* (San'ichi Shobō, 1984).

43. Janet A. Walker, "Conventions of Love Poetry in Japan and the West," *Journal of the Association of Teachers of Japanese* 14.1 (April 1979): 41, 44, 47–48.

44. Vammem, "Introduction," p. 20.

45. Heilbrun, *Hamlet's Mother*, p. 29.

46. There are five editions of the Ichimura biography. The first was Shimoina-gun Gunyakusho, *Shimoina gunshi shiryō*, section 6 (Iida-shi: Shimoina-gun Gunyakusho, 1913), of which the second half contains Taseko's poetry, diaries, and a sample of her letters. The next one was *Matsuo Taseko*, a revised and expanded edition of *Shimoina gunshi shiryō*, above, but without the second half. It was published in Iida by Yamamura Shoin in 1940. *Shimoina* was then completely reprinted by Rekishi Toshosha in Tokyo in 1977 as volume 2 of *Shimoina gunshi shiryō*. Next came a reprint of *Matsuo Taseko* in modern orthography, in Ichimura Minato Zenshū Kankōkai, ed. *Ichimura Minato zenshū*, vol. 5 (Iida-shi: Shimoina Kyōiku Kai, 1980). Lastly, there is a slightly illegible photocopy edition of *Matsuo* Taseko with the addition of a useful afterword by Takagi Shunsuke, published in 1989 by Ōzorasha in Tokyo. Minato wrote a short popularized biography of Taseko with helpful *furigana* in 1930 published as volume 17 of *Shinano kyōdo sosho* in Nagano city by Shinano Kyōdo Bunka Fukyūkai. He also edited two collections of her works and relics for memorial services.

47. The book is *Ina sonnō shisō shi.*

48. Esashi, *Onna no isshō wo kaku*, p. 64.

49. Kären Wigen, *The Making of a Japanese Periphery, 1750–1920* (University of California Press, 1995), p. 191.

50. Gilbert and Gubar, *The Madwomen in the Attic*, p. 562.

51. *HHHs.*

52. Gayle Greene and Coppélia Kahn have pointed out that "describing exceptional women defines achievement according to the male, public world and appending women to history as it has been defined leaves unchallenged the existing paradigm." "Feminist Scholarship and the Social Construction of Women," in

Making a Difference: Feminist Literary Criticism, ed. Gayle Greene and Coppélia Kahn (New York: Methuen, 1985), p. 13.

53. Heilbrun, *Writing a Woman's Life,* p. 17.

54. Sidonie Smith, *A Poetics of Women's Autobiography: Marginality and the Fictions of Self-Representation* (Indiana University Press, 1987), pp. 7 – 8.

55. Heilbrun, *Writing a Woman's Life,* p. 11.

56. One exception to the rule that only men write about the Meiji Restoration is Marlene J. Mayo, "Late Tokugawa and Early Meiji Japan," in *Introduction to Japanese Civilization,* ed. J. Alfred Tiedmann (New York: Heath Co., 1974), pp. 131 – 80.

Chapter One

1. *Sgs,* documents section, p. 141. "Waga sato no oshie no mado ni yubi sashite ba wa are miyo to iishi kotoba wo."

2. Up to 1873, all dates are given according to the lunar calendar.

3. The mean household size in many regions was around five persons. Akira Hayami and Nobuko Uchida, "Size of Household in a Japanese County throughout the Tokugawa Era," in *Household and Family in Past Time,* ed. Peter Laslett (Cambridge University Press, 1972), p. 420.

4. Conrad Totman, *Early Modern Japan* (University of California Press, 1993), pp. 480, 490 – 94.

5. Herman Ooms analyzes this system of social controls in *Tokugawa Village Practice: Class, Status, Power, Law* (University of California Press, 1996), pp. 12 – 13, 131 – 34.

6. Yamamoto Sonshi Hensan Iinkai, *Yamamoto sonshi* (Iida-shi: Yamamoto Sonshi Hensankai, 1957), pp. 198 – 99.

7. Haga Noboru, *Ishin wo motomete* (Mainichi Shinbunsha, 1976), p. 211.

8. Tsuchiya Hitsutarō, *Kinsei Shinano bunkashi* (Nagano-shi: Shinano Kyōiku Kai, 1962), p. 320.

9. Murasawa Takeo, "Sonnō no shi Iwasaki Nagayo," *Shinano* no. 25 (March 1944): 3.

10. Miwada Masako, "Matsuo Taseko den," *Jokan* no. 31 (1893): 22.

11. Yamamoto, *Yamamoto sonshi,* p. 228 – 29; Ichimura, *Matsuo Taseko,* p. 269.

12. *Sgs,* narrative section, p. 14.

13. Nagano-ken Kyōiku Shi Kankōkai, *Nagano-ken kyōiku shi,* vol. 8: *Shiryō hen,* vol. 2 (Nagano-shi: Nagano-ken Kyōiku Shi Kankōkai, 1973), pp. 480 – 81.

14. Masaki Keiji, *Tōkai to Ina: shohin ryūtsū to seiji, bunka, kōryū* (Nagoya: by the author, 1978), p. 98. *Iks,* p. 232.

15. *IMz,* p. 564.

16. Kawada Jun, "Onna jobu Matsuo Taseko," *Fujin kōron* 24.9 (September 1939): 262; Iwahashi Kunie, "Matsuo Taseko," in *Jinbutsu Nihon no josei shi: Edo-ki josei no ikikata,* ed. Enchi Fumiko (Sōbisha, 1977), pp. 107, 129.

17. Haga Noboru, *Ryōsai kenbo ron* (Yūzankaku, 1990), p. 37.

18. Yamakawa Kikue, *Women of the Mito Domain: Recollections of Samurai Family Life,* trans, Kate Wildman Nakai (University of Tokyo Press, 1992), pp. xv–xvi.

19. Mark Morris, "Buson and Shiki: Part One," *Harvard Journal of Asiatic Studies* 44.2 (December 1984): 383.

20. Yabuta Yutaka, "Moji to josei," in *Iwanami kōza Nihon tsūshi,* vol. 15: *Kinsei* 5, ed. Asao Naohiro et al. (Iwanami Shoten, 1995), p. 227.

21. *Iks,* pp. 285–301, 254, 320–21, 372–73, and passim; *Isss,* pp. 65–67. In Edo she studied with Katō Chikage. Her family had fifty monks attend her funeral.

22. I am indebted to Susan Klein for this formulation.

23. Thomas J. Harper, "The Tale of Genji in the Eighteenth Century: Keichū, Mabuchi and Norinaga," in *Eighteenth Century Japan,* ed. C. Andrew Gerstle (Sidney: Allen & Unwin, 1989), p. 119.

24. Takie Sugiyama Lebra, *Above the Clouds: Status Culture of the Modern Japanese Nobility* (University of California Press, 1993), p. 18.

25. Roger K. Thomas, "Plebeian Travelers on the Way of Shikishima: Waka Theory and Practice during the Late Tokugawa Period" (Indiana University diss., 1991), pp. ix, 72. The great twelfth-century poet Fujiwara Teika established the first three imperial anthologies as the canon for would-be poets. Hiroaki Sato and Burton Watson, *From the Country of Eight Islands: An Anthology of Japanese Poetry* (Garden City, New York: Anchor Press, 1981), p. 204.

26. Robert H. Brower and Earl Miner, *Japanese Court Poetry* (Stanford University Press, 1961), p. 14.

27. Norma Field, *The Splendor of Longing in the Tale of Genji* (Princeton University Press, 1987), p. 208.

28. Akiko Hirota, "Ex-Emperor Go-Toba: A Study in Personality, Politics and Poetry" (UCLA diss., 1989), p. 340.

29. Pierre Bourdieu, *Distinction: A Social Critique of the Judgment of Taste,* trans. Richard Nice (Harvard University Press, 1984), p. 2.

30. Roger K. Thomas, "'High' versus 'Low': The Fude no Saga Controversy and Bakumatsu Poetics," *Monumenta Nipponica* 49.4 (Winter 1994): 460, 462; Kanekiyo Masanori, *Keienha kadan no kessei* (Ōfusha, 1985), p. 198.

31. Kanekiyo Masanori, *Kagawa Kageki* (Yoshikawa Kōbunkan, 1973).

32. *Isss,* pp. 131–32; *Iks,* pp. 544–46; Sensōji Nikki Heiki Kenkyūkai, *Sensōji nikki,* vol. 14 (Kinryūzan Sensōji, 1991), pp. 310, 745.

33. According to a local informant, Higuchi Mitsunaka (who was Kitahara Yorinobu's youngest son), Taseko practiced a lot of poetry with her cousin Haruki. *Sgs,* narrative section, p. 36.

34. Kanekiyo, *Keienha kadan no kessei,* pp. 496–98.

35. *Isss,* p. 167.

36. Stephen Owen, "Salvaging the Poetic: The 'Poetic' in the Qing," workshop on "Cultural Constructions and Political Norms in China," University of California, Irvine, June 17–21, 1992. There are of course notable exceptions.

37. *Iks,* p. 74. Kiyokaze evidently did not realize that the *Shinkokinshū* contains

diverse styles reflecting the taste of its chief compilers, Ex-emperor Go-Toba and Fujiwara Teika. For a fascinating discussion of their differences see Akiko Hirota, "Ex-Emperor Go-Toba," pp. 274–303.

38. Mori Keizō, *Bakumatsu kadan no kenkyū* (Rakurō Shoin, 1935), pp. 10–13.

39. *Iks*, pp. 202, 213–18.

40. Ibid., pp. 457–59.

41. Ibid., pp. 76–77.

42. Laurel Rasplica Rodd with Mary Catherine Henkenius, *Kokinshū: A Collection of Poems Ancient and Modern* (Princeton University Press, 1984), p. 297.

43. *IMz*, p. 530.

44. *Sgs*, documents section, p. 169.

45. *IMz*, pp. 586–87.

46. Kanekiyo, *Keienha kadan no kessei*, p. 494.

47. *Shinkokinshū* poem 1023. Shinhen Kokka Taiken Henshū Iinkai, *Shinhen kokka taiken*, vol. 1, *Chokusen shūhen kashū* (Kadokawa Shoten, 1983), p. 238.

48. *Shinkokinshū* poem 682, Shinhen Kokka, *Chokusen shūhen kashū*, p. 230.

49. *Sgs*, documents section, pp. 63, 95.

50. Haga Noboru has stated that Kiyokaze made many grammatical mistakes in his own poems and he did not always follow the poetic rules that he held so dear. With him as a leader, the poetry meetings held at the Kitahara house cannot have attained a very high level. *Bakumatsu kokugaku no tenkai* (Hanawa Shobō, 1963), p. 123.

51. Ichimura, *Matsuo Taseko*, p. 32.

52. Rodd with Henkenius, *Kokinshū*, p. 332.

53. *Sgs*, documents section, p. 45.

54. Shinhen Kokka, *Chokusen shūhen kashū*, p. 239, poem 1094. "Kiene tada shinobu no yama no mine no kumo kaeru kokoro no ato mo naki made." Translation by Laurel Rasplica Rodd.

55. *Sgs*, documents section, p. 47.

56. Robert E. Morrell, "The *Shinkokinshū*: 'Poems on Sākyamuni's Teachings (*Shakkyōka*),'" in *The Distant Isle: Studies and Translations of Japanese Literature in Honor of Robert H. Brower*, ed. Thomas Hare, Robert Borgen, and Sharalyn Orbaugh (University of Michigan Center for Japanese Studies, 1996), p. 307.

57. *Sgs*, documents section, p. 47. Lady Nijō received a poem containing similar allusions after she acquired a new lover. See Donald Keene, *Travelers of a Hundred Ages* (New York: Henry Holt and Company, 1989), pp. 158–59.

58. Anne Allison, *Nightwork: Sexuality, Pleasure, and Corporate Masculinity in a Tokyo Hostess Club* (University of Chicago Press, 1994), p. 197.

59. *Iks*, pp. 186–87.

60. *Sgs*, narrative section, p. 44.

61. Yaha Katsusaki, "Kinsei Shinano no shuppan mokuroku, Echigo, Sado haisho shuppan nenpyō," in *Kinsei chihō shuppan no kenkyū*, ed. Asakura Haruhiko and Ōwa Hiroyuki (Tōkyōdō Shuppan, 1993), pp. 244–88.

62. *Sgs*, documents section, pp. 50, 121, 164.

63. Taseko's daughter-in-law Tami recalled in a twentieth century interview that she had seen these books on Taseko's desk. *Sgs*, narrative section, p. 259.

64. Ibid., p. 34. The name of the commentary was *Genji monogatari kogetsu sho*, written by Kitamura Kigin in 1673. It also included the entire text and remained the standard edition of this classic for over two hundred years. Thomas Harper, "Motoori Norinaga's Criticism of Genji monogatari" (University of Michigan diss. 1971), p. 74. I am indebted to Susan Klein for this reference.

65. Helen Craig McCullough, *Tales of Ise: Lyrical Episodes from Tenth-Century Japan* (Stanford University Press, 1968), pp. 4–5.

66. Takano Yoshio, *Nihon kyōiku shisō taikei*, vol. 16, *Kinsei joshi kyōiku shisō* (Nihon Tosho Center, 1980), pp. 1–77. A copy of the notebook showing what the Kitahara house lent is in Nagano-ken, *Nagano kenshi*, vol. 4, *Kinsei shiryōhen* 3 (Nagano-shi: Nagano Kenshi Kankōkai, 1980), pp. 427–34.

67. In the sixteenth century Luis Frois remarked that unmarried women went where they pleased without answering to their parents, and even married women had the liberty to seek diversion without their husbands knowing anything about it. Pierre F. Souyri, "Luis Fróis et l'histoire des femmes japonaises," in *O Século Cristao do Japao: Actas do Colóquio Internacional Comemorativo dos 450 anos de amizade Portugal-Japao* (Lisbon, 1993), pp. 629–44.

68. Umihara Tōru, *Kinsei no gakkō to kyōiku* (Kyoto: Shibunkaku, 1988), p. 252.

69. Yabuta, "Moji to josei," p. 234. The author was Miyaoi Sadao.

70. Ichimura, *Matsuo Taseko*, p. 282.

Chapter Two

1. *Sgs*, documents section, p. 55. "Kaki kurashi yuki ge no sora mo honobono to kasumi tanabiku ochi kochi no yama."

2. Ibid., p. 54.

3. Wigen, *The Making of a Japanese Periphery*, p. 75.

4. Ichimura, *Matsuo Taseko*, p. 172.

5. Ichimura Minato, *Edo jidai ni okeru minami Shinano* (Iida-shi: Shinano Kyōdo Shuppansha, 1934), p. 43.

6. Ichimura, *Kyōdo shi danwa* (Iida-shi: Zakōji Jitsugyō Hōshū Gakkō, 1933), pp. 100–103.

7. *Sgs*, documents section, p. 147.

8. Yamamoto, *Yamamoto sonshi*, pp. 130, 131; Henshū Iinkai, *Kadogawa Nihon chimei daijiten*, vol. 20: *Nagano-ken* (Kadogawa Shoten, 1990), p. 1146. For general trends in the Ina Valley that confirm this statement, see Wigen, *The Making of a Japanese Periphery*, pp. 113–14.

9. *Isss*, pp. 131–32; *Iks*, pp. 544–46; Shiga Daigaku Keizai Gakubu Fuzoku Shiryōkan Shozō Shiryō, "Nishikawa Yoshisuke monjo shashinkan," vol. 18. 1865/10/24. The first son adopted by Jirōhachi went to Edo in the late 1830s

where he studied military science and calligraphy as well as the heterodox Confucianism taught by the Mito school. He changed his name to Yamamoto Teiichirō, became friends with Hashimoto Sanai and helped get secret imperial decrees sent to Mito. According to one story, Ii Naosuke decided to force Tokugawa Nariaki into house arrest and execute Sanai as well as Yoshida Shōin because papers carried by Teiichirō fell into the wrong hands. Owing to this debacle, the vast Kubota compound in Yamamoto was confiscated and the Kubota family had to change its name to Kameyama, though it continued to serve as the Kondō's intendant.

10. *Sgs,* narrative section, p. 47.

11. Luke S. Roberts, "The Petition Box in Eighteenth-Century Tosa," *Journal of Japanese Studies* 20.2 (Summer 1994): 423–58.

12. Kozo Yamamura, *A Study of Samurai Income and Entrepreneurship: Quantitative Analyses of Economic and Social Aspects of the Samurai in Tokugawa and Meiji Japan* (Harvard University Press, 1974), pp. 40, 205.

13. Huber, *The Revolutionary Origins of Modern Japan,* p. 215.

14. Yamamoto, *Yamamoto sonshi,* pp. 188–90.

15. Ibid., p. 209.

16. Ibid., pp. 210–11; Nagano, *Nagano kenshi,* pp. 203–89.

17. Yamamoto, *Yamamoto sonshi,* p. 213.

18. Ibid., p. 211.

19. Hirasawa Kyoto, *Kinsei minami Shinano nōson no kenkyū* (Ochanomizu Shobō, 1978), p. 38.

20. *IMz,* p. 566.

21. Conversation with Kitahara Takeo, 8 August, 1997.

22. For a synthesis of this period, see Harold Bolitho, "The Tempō Crisis," in *The Cambridge History of Japan,* vol. 5, *The Nineteenth Century,* ed. Marius B. Jansen (Cambridge University Press, 1989), pp. 116–67.

23. Ichimura Minato, *Kyōdo shi danwa,* pp. 100–101. Hori Chikashige achieved this position in the bakufu because his wife was the niece of Tokugawa Nariaki who saw himself as the shogun's informal advisor on matters of reform.

24. *IMz,* p. 543.

25. Marius B. Jansen, "Japan in the Early Nineteenth Century," in *The Cambridge History of Japan,* vol. 5, *The Nineteenth Century* (Cambridge University Press, 1989), p. 113.

26. Quoted in Haga Noboru, *Ryōsai kenbo ron,* p. 221.

27. Kurushima Hiroshi, "Hyakushō to mura no henshitsu," in *Iwanami kōza Nihon tsūshi* 15: *Kinsei* 5, ed. Asao Naohiro et al. (Iwanami Shoten, 1995), p. 97–98.

28. For a recent discussion of this period's demography, see Laurel L. Cornell, "Infanticide in Early Modern Japan: Demography, Culture and Population Growth," *Journal of Asian Studies* 55.1 (February 1996): 22–50.

29. Conversation with Kitahara Takeo, 1 July 1989.

30. Another example of how commoners used marriage connections instrumentally can be seen in Joyce Chapman Lebra's "Women in an All-Male Industry: The

Case of Sake Brewer Tatsu'uma Kiyo," in *Recreating Japanese Women, 1600–1945,*
ed. Gail L. Bernstein (University of California Press, 1991), pp. 142–45. Takie
Sugiyama Lebra has emphasized the importance of marriage as status validation in
present-day aristocratic families in "Skipped and Postponed Adolescence of Aristocratic Women in Japan: Resurrecting the Culture/Nature Issue," *Ethos* 23.1
(1995): 85.

31. Genealogy drawn up by Kitahara Takeo, Zakōji, Iida-shi.

32. "Nendaiki" Kitahara-ke monjo in the possession of Kitahara Takeo of Zakōji
village.

33. Haga, *Bakumatsu kokugaku no tenkai,* p. 126.

34. *IMz,* p. 567.

35. Genealogy drawn up by Kitahara Takeo. Inao often called himself Nobukata,
though he signed government documents Shin'emon.

36. *TnMt,* Correspondence section, p. 1.

37. For the classic statement on intravillage political conflict, see Thomas C.
Smith, *The Agrarian Origins of Modern Japan* (Stanford University Press, 1959),
pp. 180–200. See also Edward Earl Pratt, "Village Elites in Tokugawa Japan: The
Economic Foundations of the 'Gōnō'" (University of Virginia Diss., 1991), pp. 62,
64, 105, 226, 280 and passim.

38. *Zakōji rekishi shiryō shū* no. 2 (Iida-shi: Zakōji Shigakkai, 1978), pp. 34–35.

39. Ibid., pp. 36–37,

40. Matsuo-ke monjo stored in the Toyooka Rekishi Minzoku Shiryōkan.

41. Toyooka Sonshi Hensan Iinkai, *Toyooka sonshi,* vol. 1 (Nagano-ken, Toyooka-
mura: Toyooka Sonshi Kankōkai, 1975), p. 215.

42. Matsuo-ke monjo, document no. 462.

43. For a recent summation of this incident in English, see White, *Ikki,* pp. 4–6
and passim.

44. Haga Noboru, *Sōmō no seishin* (Hanawa Shobō, 1970), p. 194.

45. Kurushima, "Hyakushō to mura no henshitsu," p. 98.

46. Ibid., p. 106.

47. Lebra, "Skipped and Postponed Adolescence," p. 93.

Chapter Three

1. *Sgs,* documents section, p. 48. "Mono omou tsuma to wa nareto sayo ginu ni
narete nuru yo mo nagatsuki no sora."

2. If this incident took place, Taseko was probably guiding the animal that
trampled fertilizer into the mud. Kären Wigen has found documents stating that
horses and oxen were little used for plowing in the Ina Valley before the late 1870s.
The Making of a Japanese Periphery, p. 155.

3. Ichimura, *Matsuo Taseko,* p. 269.

4. Judith Butler, *Gender Trouble: Feminism and the Subversion of Identity* (Routledge, Chapman & Hall, 1990), p. 127.

5. Heilbrun, *Hamlet's Mother and Other Women,* p. 134.

6. Taseko was younger than most peasant brides, even in the better-off families. See Akira Hayami, "Another *Fossa Magna:* Proportion Marrying and Age at Marriage in Late Nineteenth Century Japan," *Journal of Family History* 12.1–3 (1987): 58–59.

7. *Sks,* p. 12.

8. Ebrey makes this argument for Chinese women, but it applies equally well to Taseko. See *The Inner Quarters,* p. 9.

9. Horiguchi Sadayuki, *Kinsei minami Shinano sonraku shakaishi* (Reibunsha, 1970), pp. 30, 47, 115; Mega Atsuko, "Edo zenchūki no onna hōkōnin no kon'in ni tsuite," *Josei shigaku* no. 2 (1992): 13. See also Ooms, *Tokugawa Village Practices,* pp. 29–32; 161–91.

10. The Takemura were not unique in their ability to marry back and forth with members of the ruling class. For another example, see Martha Caroline Tocco, "School Bound: Women's Higher Education in Nineteenth-Century Japan" (Stanford University diss., 1994), pp. 42–44.

11. Furushima Toshio, *Furushima Toshio chosaku shū 2: Nihon hoken nogyōshi, kazoku keitai to nogyō no hattatsu* (Tōkyō Daigaku Shuppan Kai, 1974), p. 331; Ooms, *Tokugawa Village Practices,* pp. 167–70.

12. Kitahara-ke monjo in the possession of Kitahara Takeo of Zakōji village. See Nendaiki, 1822/12/11; Min'emon nikki, 1822/1/3, 1824/1/3.

13. *Sgs,* documents section, p. 97.

14. Ichimura, *Matsuo Taseko,* p. 274. The go-between was Hara Tamon who practiced Chinese medicine.

15. *Sgs,* narrative section, p. 17.

16. The Sekiguchi family, headmen for Namamugi village between what is now Kawasaki and Tokyo spent thirty *ryō* on their eldest daughter for a dowry. Ōguchi Yūjirō, "Nōson josei no Edojo ōoku hōkō: Namamugi mura Sekiguchi Chie no baai," in *19 seiki no sekai to Yokohama,* ed. Yokohama Kaikō Shiryōkan, Yokohama Kinseishi Kenkyūkai (Yamakawa Shuppansha, 1993), pp. 256–60. The record of what was spent for Mino is in the Kitahara-ke monjo.

17. Matsuo-ke monjo, document no. 11.

18. Shōji Hiroya, "Namae no rekishi—Igirisu ni okeru myōji shūzoku no rekishiteki kenkyū," report given at the Kinsei joseishi kenkyū kai, 19 June 1994.

19. This was reported by Shiba Keiko at the Kinsei joseishi kenkyū kai, 19 June 1994.

20. In ancient Japan, this character may have been read *shi* as a mark of respect. In Chinese it is pronounced *tsu* or *tse,* as in Lao-tse. I am indebted to Susan Klein and Hu Ying for this point. Feminist logic might dictate calling the subject of this book Takemura Tase, but I have chosen the name by which she is more commonly known.

21. Yanagi Miyoko, "Josei no seikatsu kūkan: kaku kaikyū o megutte," in *Onna to otoko no jikū: Nihon joseishi saikō,* vol. 4, *Ranjuku suru onna to otoko: Kinsei,* ed. Fukuda Mitsuko (Fujiwara Shoten, 1995), p. 396.

22. *Sgs*, documents section, p. 165. See also pp. 65 and 147 and narrative section, p. 256.

23. See Rodd and Henkenius, *Kokinshu*, pp. 146–47 and Helen Craig McCullough, *Kokin Wakashū: The First Imperial Anthology of Japanese Poetry* (Stanford University Press, 1985), p. 84.

24. Dorinne K. Kondo, "Gender, Self and Work in Japan: Some Issues in the Study of Self and Other" *Culture, Medicine and Psychiatry* 9 (1985): 325; G. William Skinner, "Conjugal Power in Tokugawa Japanese Families: A Matter of Life or Death," in *Sex and Gender Hierarchies*, ed. Barbara Diane Miller (Cambridge University Press, 1993), pp. 239, 240.

25. Narita Ryūichi, "Mobilized from Within: Women and Hygiene in Modern Japan," trans. Julia Rousseau, in *Women and Class in Japanese History*, ed. Hitomi Tonomura, Anne Walthall and Wakita Haruko (University of Michigan Center for Japanese Studies, forthcoming).

26. Furushima, *Nihon hoken nōgyōshi, kazoku keitai to nōgyō hattatsu*, pp. 328, 353, 356. See also Akira Hayami, "Rural Migration and Fertility in Tokugawa Japan: The Village of Nishijo, 1773–1868," in *Family and Population in East Asian History*, ed. Susan B. Hanley and Arthur P. Wolf (Stanford University Press, 1985), pp. 123, 125.

27. Murasawa Takeo, *Shinano jinbutsushi* (Iida-shi: Shinano Jinbutsushi Kankōkai Jimusho, 1965), p. 29.

28. *Sgs*, documents section, p. 223.

29. Ibid., p. 213.

30. Ibid., p. 103.

31. Conversation with Matsuo Sen, 8 August 1997.

32. *Sgs*, narrative section, p. 17.

33. Ichimura, *Matsuo Taseko*, p. 268.

34. In China the only ancestors considered important were those immediately identifiable in kinship relation to the head of the family. From one generation to the next they would be relegated to lesser and lesser positions until they finally disappeared altogether. The Japanese did not differentiate so strongly between one generation and the next, and by the same token, distant ancestors did not disappear. Carl Steenstrup, *Hōjō Shigetoki (1198–1261) and His Role in the History of Political and Ethical Ideas in Japan* (New York: Curson Press, 1979), pp. 43–45.

35. *Sgs*, documents section, pp. 51–54.

36. Ichimura, *Edo jidai ni okeru minami Shinano*, p. 102; Ishii Ryōsuke, *Tokugawa kinrei kō* (Sōbunsha, 1959), pp. 160–61.

37. Philip C. Brown, *Central Authority and Local Autonomy in the Formation of Early Modern Japan: The Case of Kaga Domain* (Stanford University Press, 1993), pp. 232–33; White, *Ikki*, pp. 39, 43–46.

38. Mary Elizabeth Berry, *The Culture of Civil War in Kyoto* (University of California Press, 1994), p. 274 and passim; Aoki Michio, "Chiiki bunka no seisei," in *Iwanami kōza Nihon tsūshi*, vol. 15, *Kinsei* 5, ed. Asao Naohiro (Iwanami Shoten, 1995), pp. 281–82.

39. *Sgs*, documents section, p. 66. The first two lines in this poem may be found in three of the later court anthologies, the *Shokugosenshū* compiled in 1251, poem 79, the *Shinsenzaishū* compiled in 1359, poem 1661, and the *Shingoshūishū* completed in 1384, poem 1544. The last poem is in the section on celebratory poems. It declares that the practice of poetry is a sign that the country is well governed.

40. *Sgs*, documents section, p. 66–67.

41. Ibid., p. 102.

42. *TnMt*, price lists.

43. Ichimura, *Matsuo Taseko*, p. 266.

44. *Sgs*, documents section, p. 67. Two other poems expressing the pleasure she took in drinking sake are on p. 136.

45. Ibid., p. 136.

46. Constantine Nomikos Vaporis, *Breaking Barriers: Travel and the State in Early Modern Japan* (Harvard University Press, 1994), p. 184.

47. Nagashima Atsuko, "Kinsei josei no jūzoku to jiritsu wo megutte," in *Sōten Nihon no rekishi*, vol. 5, *Kinseihen*, ed. Aoki Michio and Hosaka Satoru (Shinjunbutsu Ōraisha, 1991), p. 351. Suzuki Yukiko has emphasized that money gave Taseko and her husband the leisure to travel. She goes on to say that "traveling together would of course improve the communication between couples as well as open their eyes to the larger world." *Kikikatari Nippon josei 'ai' shi* (Kōdansha, 1988), p. 207.

48. The tenth century *Tales of Yamato* told how a man was forced to abandon his aunt on this mountain. As he left, a beautiful moon rose to light his way. Keene, *Travelers of a Hundred Ages*, p. 307.

49. Toyoda Toshisada and Odagiri Tadachika, ed. and illus. *Zenkōji meisho zue*, vol. 2 (Nagayo: Minoya Iroku, 1849).

50. *Sgs*, documents section, p. 59.

51. Mark Teeuwen, "Arakida Hisaoyu (1746–1804): Poetry, Sake and Acrimony in the Kokugaku Movement," *Monumenta Nipponica* 52.3 (Autumn, 1997): 307.

52. Yabuta, "Moji to josei," p. 247.

53. Vaporis, p. 235.

54. *Sgs*, documents section, p. 59.

55. Mark Morris, "Buson and Shiki: Part Two," *Harvard Journal of Asiatic Studies* 45.1 (June 1985): 301.

56. *Sgs*, documents section, p. 59.

57. Helen Craig McCullough, trans. *Tales of Ise: Lyrical Episodes from Tenth-Century Japan* (Stanford University Press, 1968), p. 149. My thanks to Susan Klein for this reference.

58. *Sgs*, documents section, p. 1.

59. Ibid., p. 2.

60. Ibid., p. 3.

61. Vaporis, *Breaking Barriers*, pp. 14, 217–54.

62. *Sgs*, narrative section, p. 46.

63. Morosawa Yōko, *Shinano no onna*, vol. 1 (Miraisha, 1969), p. 188.

64. *Sgs,* narrative section, p. 47.

65. Ibid., p. 48.

66. *MTic,* p. 38.

67. Toyooka, *Toyooka sonshi,* vol. 1, p. 400.

68. *Sgs,* narrative section, p. 47. The third and fourth lines of this poem repeat the first two lines of *Man'yōshū* poems numbers 96 and 97.

69. *Isss,* p. 169.

70. *Sgs,* narrative section, p. 51.

71. Carroll Smith-Rosenberg, *Disorderly Conduct: Visions of Gender in Victorian America* (Oxford University Press, 1985), pp. 55–59.

72. *Sgs,* documents section, p. 214.

73. Ibid., p. 152.

Chapter Four

1. *MTic,* p. 23. "Kuni to iu kuni ni tsuranuku hikari koso waga fusou no mayu no tama no itoguchi."

2. I am indebted to Kitajima Eiko for reminding me of this point.

3. *Sgs,* narrative section, p. 18. This scenario is repeated without the hyperbole in Takagi, "Sōmō no josei," p. 273.

4. Ooms argues this point forcefully in *Tokugawa Village Practice,* pp. 72–75 and passim.

5. Edward Pratt, "Village Elites in Tokugawa Japan," p. 100 and passim.

6. Wigen, *The Making of a Japanese Periphery,* pp. 45–49.

7. Yamamoto, *Yamamoto sonshi,* p. 213.

8. Saitō Osamu, *Puroto-kōgyōka no jidai: Seiō to Nihon no hikakushi* (Nihon Hyōronsha, 1985).

9. Johannes Hirschmeier and Tsunehiko Yui, *The Development of Japanese Business, 1600–1973* (Harvard University Press, 1975), p. 34.

10. White, *Ikki,* p. 64.

11. Tetsuo Najita, "Remembering Forgotten Texts: Commoner Writings in Tokugawa Japan," Lecture at University of California, Irvine, 13 April 1993.

12. Wigen, *The Making of a Japanese Periphery,* pp. 72, 161–65.

13. White, *Ikki,* p. 46.

14. Toyooka, *Toyooka sonshi,* vol. 1, pp. 306, 382; idem., vol. 2, p. 1038; Matsuo-ke monjo, Box 1.

15. Wigen, *The Making of a Japanese Periphery,* pp. 107, 109, 113.

16. Ibid., pp. 111, 113.

17. Toyooka, *Toyooka sonshi,* vol. 1, pp. 610, 660, 662. Taseko's great-great uncle Kitahara Matsujirō who died in 1766 was the priest for the Tomono temple. The bell was melted down during World War Two.

18. Matsuo-ke monjo, unnumbered document.

19. Peter Duus, *The Rise of Modern Japan* (Houghton Mifflin Co., 1976), p. 115;

W. G. Beasley, "Meiji Political Institutions," in *The Cambridge History of Japan,* vol. 5, *The Nineteenth Century,* ed. Marius B. Jansen (Cambridge University Press, 1989), p. 655. Makoto was elected to the first prefectural assembly of 1879 and he paid property taxes of over ten yen a year according to Toyooka, *Toyooka sonshi,* vol. 2, p. 880.

20. Beasley, "Meiji Political Institutions," p. 639.

21. Toyooka, *Toyooka sonshi,* vol. 2, pp. 1000–1003. Matsuo-ke monjo, unnumbered document.

22. The prices given here are rough estimates derived from Yamamura, *A Study of Samurai Income and Entrepreneurship,* pp. 58–60.

23. *Sgs,* documents section, p. 100.

24. Haga, *Bakumatsu kokugaku no tenkai,* p. 136.

25. Toyooka, *Toyooka sonshi,* vol. 2, pp. 1004–1005. According to Kären Wigen, by 1921, the lower Ina Valley produced 30,000 koku or 1.344 million gallons of sake a year. This was for local consumption, yielding an average household consumption rate of 46.4 gallons of sake per year. *The Making of a Japanese Periphery,* p. 241.

26. Toyooka, *Toyooka sonshi,* vol. 1, pp. 477–80. Matsuo-ke monjo, document number 471. Haga, *Bakumatsu kokugaku no tenkai,* p. 136.

27. *Sgs,* narrative section, p. 161.

28. Suzanne Gay, "The Moneylenders of Medieval Kyoto: Freedom and Constraints in Urban Society," *Nichibunken Forum* no. 11 (1989): 1–23.

29. Matsuo-ke monjo, document number 4.

30. Ronald P. Toby, "Both a Borrower and a Lender Be: From Village Moneylender to Rural Banker in the Tempō Era," *Monumenta Nipponica* 46.4 (Winter 1991): 483–512. Nishijō was only half the size of Tomono in terms of population.

31. Matsuo-ke monjo, document number 5.

32. Haga, *Bakumatsu kokugaku no tenkai,* p. 136.

33. *Sgs,* documents section, p. 163.

34. The worst inflation occurred after 1859, according to Peter Frost, *The Bakumatsu Currency Crisis* (East Asia Research Center Harvard University, 1970), pp. 41, 46.

35. Ōguchi Yūjirō, "Nōmin nikki ni miru joseizō," *Rekishi hyōron* no. 479 (March 1990): 62.

36. Hirasawa Kiyoto, *Shimoina sanshigyō hattatsushi* (Nagano-ken Suwa-chō: Kōyō Shobō, 1952), pp. 49–53; Wigen, *The Making of a Japanese Periphery,* p. 82; Hanyū Masahiko, "Yokohama kaikō to Shimoina no ki-ito," *Ina* 44.7 (July 1996): 3–10.

37. Wigen, *The Making of a Japanese Periphery,* p. 83; Ichimura, *Edo jidai ni okeru minami Shinano,* p. 152.

38. Kitahara-ke monjo, *Nendaiki* for 1822, 1823.

39. Toyooka, *Toyooka sonshi,* vol. 2, p. 994; Furushima, *Nihon hoken nogyōshi,* p. 221.

40. *Sgs,* documents section, p. 239.

41. Furushima, *Nihon hoken nogyōshi*, p. 220, 223.

42. *Sgs*, documents section, p. 169.

43. *Sgs*, narrative section, p. 209.

44. Toyooka, *Toyooka sonshi*, vol. 2, p. 1050. The village created in 1875 that incorporated Tomono was named Kumashiro.

45. Ibid., pp. 1054–56; Hirasawa, *Shimoina sanshigyō hattatsushi*, pp. 136, 138, 150, 159–60; Wigen, *The Making of a Japanese Periphery*, pp. 165–66, 171–75, 194.

46. Hanyū, "Yokohama kaikō," p. 7; Nakatsugawa-shi, *Nakatsugawa shishi*, vol. 2 pt. 2 (Gifu-shi: Nakatsugawa-shi, 1988), p. 1687.

47. Hirasawa, *Shimoina sanshigyō hattatsushi*, pp. 104, 109.

48. *Sgs*, narrative section, p. 62.

49. *Sgs*, documents section, p. 149. Another long poem expressing similar sentiments may be found in *MTic*, p. 24.

50. As early as 1701, Japanese scholars had used *Kara* to refer to China instead of *Chugoku* with its connotations of "geographic extensiveness, centrality and . . . civilization." Bob Tadashi Wakabayashi, *Antiforeignism and Western Learning in Early Modern Japan: The New Theses of 1825* (Harvard University Council on East Asian Studies, 1991), p. 31.

Chapter Five

1. *Sgs*, documents section, p. 137. "Shiori naru michi fumiwakete mimakuhoshi mukashi nagara ni niou sakura wo." *Mimakuhoshi* is a pillow work found frequently in the *Man'yōshū*.

2. Kishida Sadao, "*Yoake mae* no Iwasaki Nagayo no koto," *Ina* 32.12 (December 1984): 18–20.

3. Murasawa Takeo, "Iwasaki Nagayo no shinshiryō," *Ina* 33.7 (July 1985): 16–20.

4. *Isss*, pp. 172–77.

5. Peter Nosco, "*Man'yōshū* Studies in Tokugawa Japan," *Transactions of the Asiatic Society of Japan*, 4th series, vol. 1 (1986): 109, 129.

6. Murasawa, "Sonnō no shi Iwasaki Nagayo," p. 5.

7. *Sgs*, narrative section, p. 64.

8. Itō Masao, *Kinsei no waka to kokugaku* (Ise-shi: Kōgakkan Daigaku Shuppanbu, 1979), pp. 281–82; Nakatsugawa-shi, *Nakatsugawa shishi*, vol. 2 pt. 2, p. 1559.

9. Mori Keizō, *Bakumatsu kadan no kenkyū* (Rakurō Shoin, 1935), pp. 141–51.

10. Ichimura, *Matsuo Taseko*, p. 58.

11. Ian Hideo Levy, *The Ten Thousand Leaves* (Princeton University Press, 1981), pp. 85–86.

12. Itō Tasaburō, *Kokugaku no shiteki kōsatsu* (Ōokayama Shoten, 1932, 1942), p. 237.

13. *Sgs*, narrative section, p. 55.

14. Itō Tasaburō, *Sōmō no kokugaku* (Meicho Shuppan, 1982), p. 7.

15. Ibid., pp. 3–4.

16. Ibid., p. 4; Wigen, *The Making of a Japanese Periphery*, p. 169.

17. This, at least, is the explanation given by Haga Noboru for the school's popularity in *Bakumatsu kokugaku no tenkai*, pp. 140, 144. Mori Keizō emphasizes regional rivalries in *Bakumatsu kadan no kenkyū*, p. 72.

18. *Sks*, p. 34. The village was Yamabuki. See Ichimura, *Kyōdo shi danwa*, p. 110. Atsutane himself wrote explicitly that Buddhist statues and memorial tablets should not be tossed in rivers because they had been treasured by people in the past. *HAz*, vol. 6, p. 591.

19. Miyachi Masato, "Bakumatsu Hirata kokugaku to seiji jōhō," in *Nihon no kinsei*, vol. 18, *Kindai kokka e no shikō*, ed. Tanaka Akira (Chūō Kōronsha, 1994), p. 237.

20. *Iks*, pp. 543–44.

21. *Sgs*, narrative section, p. 57.

22. The person who has done the most work on these communication networks is Miyachi Masato. See his "Fūsetsu tome kara mita Bakumatsu shakai no tokushitsu: kōron sekai no tanshoteki seiritsu" *Shisō*, no. 831 (September 1993): 4–26.

23. Huber, *The Revolutionary Origins of Modern Japan*, pp. 88, 100.

24. Ōguchi Yūjirō, "Kokka ishiki to tennō," in *Iwanami kōza Nihon tsūshi*, vol. 15, *Kinsei* 5, ed. Asao Naohiro et. al (Iwanami Shoten, 1995), p. 219.

25. *Sgs*, document section, p. 141. See also Ichimura, *Matsuo Taseko*, p. 25.

26. *Sgs*, document section, p. 142; Ichimura, *Matsuo Taseko*, p. 26.

27. *Sgs*, narrative section, p. 60.

28. Mori, *Bakumatsu kadan no kenkyū*, p. 27.

29. *Sgs*, narrative section, p. 56.

30. *Isss*, pp. 182–83.

31. Ibid., pp. 206–7.

32. Haga, *Bakumatsu kokugaku no tenkai*, p. 138,

33. Takagi, "Sōmō joseishi," pp. 270–72. For a record of the Hirata disciples in the Ina Valley see the list at the end of *Isss*. The Hirata school had a smaller percentage of women disciples than any of its nativist predecessors. Five percent of the membership in Norinaga's school was female, less than for Kamo Mabuchi. Peter Nosco, *Remembering Paradise: Nativism and Nostalgia in Eighteenth-Century Japan* (Harvard University Council on East Asian Studies, 1990), p. 208.

34. *IMz*, p. 441.

35. *Sgs*, narrative section, p. 65.

36. Ibid., p. 66.

37. Higashiyama Michihiko, "Bakumatsu ishin no senkakusha: Hazama Hidenori kōyōroku," *Mino shinbun* 1987/1/3 p. 1; 1987/1/25 p. 1; *HHH*, p. 2; Haga Noboru, *Yoake mae no jitsuzō to kyozō* (Kyōiku Shuppan Center, 1984), p. 7; *Isss*, pp. 55–56, 195–96. On the other hand, a diary from Magome says that Toshinari did not leave Nakatsugawa for Tomono until 1860. Shimazaki Tōson, *Tōson zenshū*, vol. 15 (Chikuma Shobō, 1968, 1976), pp. 426–28, 471. Tomono had eighteen dis-

ciples, Zakōji had seventeen, and Yamamoto had seven. Yamabuki, where the bakufu bannerman Zakōji Tametomo joined the school and encouraged his retainers to do so as well, had thirty-one disciples and Ono to the north had twenty-four. Despite its much larger population, the castle town of Iida had only fifty.

38. James Edward Ketelaar discusses the resurgence of this kind of prayer writing in *Of Heretics and Martyrs in Meiji Japan: Buddhism and Its Persecution* (Princeton University Press, 1990), pp. 45–46.

39. Itō, *Sōmō no kokugaku*, p. 219.

40. Ibid., pp. 221–23.

41. Harootunian, *Things Seen and Unseen*, pp. 17–18.

42. Fukaya Katsumi, "Bakuhan shihai to mura yakuninsō no kokugaku jūyō," *Shikan* no. 91 (1975): 13–23. For a recent reformulation see Nakajima Masato, "Meiji kokka to jiyū minken undō: Kindai kokumin kokka keiseiki ni okeru kokka to minshū," *Higashi Ajia no kindai ikō to minshū* no. 3 (August 1997): 2.

43. White, *Ikki*, pp. 114–15.

44. Katsurajima Nobuhiro, *Bakumatsu minshū shisō no kenkyū* (Kyoto: Bunrikaku, 1992), p. 32.

45. Ibid., pp. 55–56.

46. Miyachi, *Bakumatsu ishin-ki no bunka to jōhō*, pp. 230–31.

47. Takagi, "Sōmō no joseishi," p. 271.

48. I am indebted to Peggy Pasco and Alice Fahs for these insights.

49. Shakai Kyōiku Kyōkai, ed. *Kinnōka shikashū* (Shakai Kyōiku Kyōkai, 1940), p. 58.

50. Records show that eight imperial princesses, none of them daughters of emperors, traveled the Nakasendō to be wed to the shogun or the lord of Mito beginning in 1731. Nakatsugawa, *Nakatsugawa shishi*, vol. 2. pt. 2, p. 1415.

51. Fujita Satoru, *Bakumatsu no tennō* (Kōdansha, 1994), pp. 205–6.

52. Nakatsugawa, *Nakatsugawa shishi*, vol. 2. pt. 2, p. 1569.

53. Hirata Kanetane, *Fūun himitsu tantei roku*, vol. 1. Manuscript at the Shiryō Hensanjo, Tokyo University.

54. *Sgs*, document section, p. 102.

55. *Isss*, pp. 209–10. Inao's colleagues on this project were Maijima Masami, Katagiri Harukazu, Iwasaki Nagayo, Majima Torinari, and Hara Mayomi.

56. *HAz*, vol. 1, p. 228. The two others were Nakajima Noritake and Sasaki Yoshio from Omi village in the same district.

57. Masaki, *Tōkai to Ina*, p. 108.

58. *Isss*, p. 214.

59. *Sgs*, documents section, p. 174.

60. *HAz*, vol. 2, p. 48.

61. Three aged women living in Iida paid for volume fifteen. None of them were Hirata disciples. *HAz*, vol. 2, p. 267.

62. *TnMt*, correspondence section, p. 9.

63. *HHH*, pp. 6, 30. Masaki, *Tōkai to Ina*, p. 105–6.

64. *Isss*, Record of Hirata Disciples, pp. 3–26.

65. Masaki, *Tōkai to Ina*, p. 105.

66. Toyooka, *Toyooka sonshi*, vol. 1, p. 576.

67. *Isss*, biography section, p. 48.

68. Haga, *Bakumatsu kokugaku no tenkai*, p. 144; Haga, *Henkaku-ki ni okeru kokugaku*, p. 140, 213. For a discussion of phallic and ktenic stones, see Michael Czaja, *Gods of Myth and Stone: Phallicism in Japanese Folk Religion* (New York and Tokyo: Weatherhill, 1974), pp. 161–79.

69. The most detailed account of these festivities is in Itō, *Sōmō no kokugaku*, pp. 225–31, but see also *Isss*, pp. 237–95 for the difficulties of building the shrine and collecting the objects.

70. Itō, *Sōmō no kokugaku*, p. 231.

71. Evidence that Taseko continued to participate in festivals can be found in the poems she wrote in 1886. *Sgs*, documents section, p. 134–35. According to a history of the region published in 1901, festivals continued to held at Hongaku shrine in spring and fall. Sano Shigechika, *Nanshin Ina shiryō*, vol. 2 (Yamanashi-ken: Yōkaichiba-mura, by the author, 1901), p. 46.

72. Miyashita Misao, *Ina kyōdo shigaku ronkō* (Tokyo: Kokusho Kankōkai, 1975), p. 295.

73. Itō, *Sōmō no kokugaku*, p. 230.

Chapter Six

1. *Sgs*, documents section, p. 52. "Chitose heru matsuo no oiki ni kotowan chigaishi kami no arishi mukashi wo."

2. *IMz*, p. 426.

3. *Sgs*, narrative section, p. 259.

4. Nagano-ken, *Nagano kenshi*, pp. 427–34.

5. *Sgs*, documents section, p. 75; narrative section, p. 259.

6. Haga Noboru, *Bakumatsu kokugaku no kenkyū* (Kyōiku Shuppan Center, 1980), p. 353; Itō, *Kokugaku no shiteki kōsatsu*, p. 250.

7. Haga Noboru has emphasized what he sees as the populist intent of Atsutane's message. *Kokugaku no hitobito: sono kōdō to shisō* (Hyōronsha, 1975), p. 103. Atsutane himself said, "sometimes I have the prefaces to my books written in Chinese because some people read only that. The text itself is written in Japanese to suit the desires of old women." *HAz*, vol. 6, p. 155.

8. Haga Noboru, "Kaisetsu" *Shinshū Hirata Atsutane zenshū geppō* no. 3 (January 1977): 7.

9. *IMz*, p. 426.

10. *HAz*, vol. 6, p. 283.

11. Motoori Norinaga, "Tamakatsuma" *Nihon shisō taikei*, vol. 40, *Motoori Norinaga*, ed. Yoshikawa Kōjirō, Satake Akihiro, and Hino Tatsuo (Iwanami Shoten, 1978), p. 231.

12. Satake Akihiro, "Tamakatsuma oboegaki," in *Nihon shisō taikei*, vol. 40, *Motoori Norinaga* (Iwanami Shoten, 1978), pp. 551–55.

13. Quoted in Peter Nosco, *Remembering Paradise*, p. 225.

14. Motoori Norinaga, "Tamakatsuma," pp. 206, 214–15. The quotation is on p. 211.

15. Ibid., pp. 207–9, 215, 231.

16. Ibid., pp. 216–17.

17. For a description of this dance that emphasizes its sexuality, see Ian Buruma, *Behind the Mask: On Sexual Demons, Sacred Mothers, Transvestites, Gangsters and Other Japanese Cultural Heroes* (Random House, 1984), pp. 3, 8.

18. *HAz*, vol. 7, p. 365.

19. Ibid., pp. 367, 368, 371. One translation of this song is in Czaja, *Gods of Myth and Stone*, p. 233. Like Buruma and unlike Atsutane, Czaja emphasizes the dance's lasciviousness.

20. *HAz*, vol. 7, p. 369.

21. Ibid., p. 371.

22. For a description of the Motoori school interpretation of *miyabi*, see Harootunian, *Things Seen and Unseen*, pp. 128, 141.

23. *HAz*, vol. 7, pp. 371–72.

24. Ibid., p. 373–74.

25. Ibid., pp. 375–77. Atsutane also discussed the august achievements of this goddess in "Tamadasuki." *HAz*, vol. 6, pp. 392–414.

26. The heavy use of pillow words is one characteristic of the archaizing *Man'yō* style. See Teeuwen, "Arakida Hisaoyu (1746–1804)," p. 299.

27. *Sgs*, documents section, p. 144.

28. Susan B. Klein, "Allegories of Desire," forthcoming.

29. *HAz*, vol. 1, pp. 187, 192.

30. Ibid., p. 194, 213. For a discussion of agronomy, sex, and nativism, see Jennifer Robertson, "Sexy Rice: Plant Gender, Farm Manuals, and Grass-Roots Nativism," *Monumenta Nipponica* 39.3 (1984): 233–60.

31. This is a paraphrase of a longwinded statement at the bottom of *HAz*, vol. 1, p. 215. See also pp. 195–96. Atsutane summarized this argument in "Tama no mihashira," in *Nihon shisō taikei*, vol. 50, *Hirata Atsutane, Ban Nobutomo, Ōkuni Takamasa*, ed. Tahara Tsuguo, Seki Akira, Saeki Arikiyo and Haga Noboru (Iwanami Shoten, 1973), p. 31.

32. My interpretation of how Atsutane saw the relationship between people and gods differs significantly from Harootunian's. See *Things Seen and Unseen*, pp. 160 and 354. My thanks to Herman Ooms for pointing this out.

33. *HAz*, vol. 1, pp. 220–21.

34. Ibid., pp. 213, 216, 223.

35. Haga Noboru, "Kaisetsu" *Shinshū Hiraga Atsutane zenshū geppō* no. 6 (April 1977): 8–10.

36. Koyasu Norikuni, "'Tama no mihashira' to tama no yukikata" *Shinshū Hirata Atsutane zenshū geppō* no. 12 (October 1977): 1–3.

37. Haga Noboru has pointed out that Atsutane and his wife had an exceptionally close and intimate relationship. See *Henkaku-ki ni okeru kokugaku*, pp. 84–85 and *Kokugaku no hitobito: sono kōdō to shisō*, p. 101.

38. Haga, *Bakumatsu kokugaku no kenkyū*, p. 350.

39. Harootunian, *Things Seen and Unseen*, pp. 154 and 452; Takara Tsuguo, "'Tama no mihashira' igo ni okeru Hirata Atsutane no shisō ni tsuite," in *Nihon shisō taikei*, vol. 50, *Hirata Atsutane, Ban Nobutomo, Ōkuni Takamasa*, ed. Tahara Tsuguo, Seki Akira, Saeki Arikiyo, and Haga Noboru (Iwanami Shoten, 1973), p. 585.

40. Hirata, "Tama no mihashira," pp. 17–27.

41. Ibid., pp. 37, 38, 44, 48, 57.

42. Ibid., pp. 60, 66, 70, 72, 77–79, 96, 120 and passim.

43. Haga, *Henkaku-ki ni okeru kokugaku*, pp. 74–75.

44. Hirata, "Tama no mihashira," pp. 51–53, 125, 127.

45. Ibid., p. 128.

46. Takara, "'Tama no mihashira' igo," p. 575.

47. Hirata, "Tama no mihashira," p. 92–93. Atsutane liked the story of the tower of Babel because it showed that the entire world originally spoke Japanese; The story of Adam and Eve was a corruption of the story of Izanami and Izanagi. Ibid., pp. 32, 85.

48. Katsurajima, *Bakumatsu minshū shisō no kenkyū*, p. 57.

49. *HAz*, vol. 6, pp. 31–32.

50. Ibid., p. 65.

51. Ibid., pp. 35–36.

52. Ibid., p. 101.

53. Ibid., p. 115. See also p. 98. Arai Hakuseki is the historian who criticized Nobunaga.

54. Ibid., pp. 124–25. Another justification of the current political order may be found in "Tama no mihashira," p. 77.

55. See the chapter on "The Modern Monarch," in Carol Gluck, *Japan's Modern Myths: Ideology in the Late Meiji Period* (Princeton University Press, 1985), especially pp. 89, 93.

56. *HAz*, vol. 6, p. 443. This formulation of the emperor as a manifest god I drew from James Edward Ketelaar, *A Quiet Great Land: History of Japan's Eastern Frontier* (Princeton University Press, forthcoming).

57. *HAz*, vol. 6, pp. 436–37.

58. Ibid., p. 509. This poem is repeated in "Tama no mihashira," p. 81. Yoshida Shōin also quoted it approvingly. Horace E. Coleman, "The Life of Shōin Yoshida" *Transactions of the Asiatic Society of Japan* 45.1 (1917): 158–59.

59. *HAz*, vol. 6, p. 186.

60. Ibid., p. 467.

61. Ibid., ppp. 177–78

62. Ibid., pp. 454–59.

63. Ibid., pp. 472–77.

64. Ibid., pp. 231, 443.

65. Ibid., pp. 558–59. See also p. 413.

66. Ibid., pp. 20–30 gives Atsutane's history of Buddhism. The instruction to

parents is on p. 209. Further attacks on the religion are scattered throughout the volume. See pp. 153, 337–42.

67. Ibid., pp. 194, 317, 412. Haga Noboru, *Sōmō no seishin* (Hanawa Shobō, 1970), p. 12.

68. *HAz*, vol. 6, pp. 335–37. For another statement suggesting that a woman might go against her parents' wishes in deciding whom to marry, see p. 506.

69. Ibid., pp. 208–9.

70. Ibid., p. 490. "In China a bloodline through women is not considered a lineage at all, but in our sacred country from the time of the gods, women's blood lines were incorporated into lineages and that is in accordance with the way of the gods." See also Haga, *Sōmō no seishin*, p. 10.

71. *HAz*, vol. 6, pp. 241–47.

72. Donald L. Philippi, trans. *Kojiki* (Princeton University Press and University of Tokyo Press, 1969), pp. 244–45. Many taboos associated with pollution were formulated much later than the earliest versions of the creation myths.

73. *HAz*, vol. 6, pp. 265–71.

74. Ibid., pp. 362–64.

75. Ibid., pp. 565–66.

76. Kenneth D. Butler, "Woman of Power behind the Kamakura Bakufu: Hōjō Masako," in *Great Historical Figures of Japan*, ed. Murakami Hyoe and Thomas J. Harper (Japan Culture Institute, 1978), pp. 91–101; H. Paul Varley, *The Ōnin War* (Columbia University Press, 1967).

77. The interest in the supernatural found in Atsutane's work and those of his disciples is emphasized in Katsurajima Nobuhiro, "Hirata-ha kokugakusha no 'dokusho' to sono gensetsu," *Edo no shisō* no. 5 (Dec. 1996): 83–95.

78. Robert Darnton, "History of Reading," in *New Perspectives on Historical Writing*, ed., Peter Burke (Cambridge and Oxford: Polity Press, 1991), p. 148.

79. Haga, *Yoake mae no jitsuzō to kyozō*, p. 257.

80. Tahara Tsuguo, "'Sandaikō' wo meguru ronsō to Hirata-gaku no hōhō ni tsuite," *Shinshū Hirata Atsutane zenshū geppō* no. 12 (October 1977): 3–5.

Chapter Seven

1. *TnMt*, "Miyako no tsuto" section, p. 1. "Tabi goromo furikaerite furusato wa kiri tachi kakusu tsure nashinoyama." These diaries constitute the primary sources of information for Taseko's trip to Kyoto.

2. Ibid., p. 1.

3. *Sgs*, narrative section, p. 71.

4. *Sgs*, documents section, pp. 173–74.

5. "Whenever you go on a trip, you should always visit the tutelary deity to let him know." Hirata, "Tamadasuki," p. 313.

6. Quoted in *IMz*, p. 617.

7. *TnMt*, "Miyako no tsuto" section, p. 1.

8. Ibid., p. 2.

9. *TnMt*, "Tabi no nagusa" section, p. 1.

10. *TnMt*, "Miyako no tsuto" section, p. 2. It is 36 kilometers between Yamamoto and Nakatsugawa via the tunnel on the central expressway.

11. Nakatsugawa-shi, *Nakatsugawa shishi*, vol. 2, pt. 2, pp. 1258–95.

12. Kitakōji Ken, *Kisoji: bunken no tabi* (Geisōdō, 1970), p. 248

13. Kanekiyo, *Keienha kadan no kessei*, p. 490.

14. Ichioka Masane, *Hijimori Isō* (Nakatsugawa-shi: pub. by the author, 1987), pp. 191–202; Kanekiyo, *Keienha kadan no kessei*, pp. 482–91. Shigemasa was called Chōmon on official documents, that being the traditional name for the head of the Ichioka family. After he retired, he took the name Hijimori.

15. Satō Shigerō, *Ōmi shōnin bakumatsu ishin kenbunroku* (Sanseidō, 1990), p. 16.

16. Uchida Kusuo and Shimano Michiho, *Bakumatsu ishin Kyōto chōnin nikki: Takaki Zaichū nikki* (Osaka: Seibundō, 1989), pp. 170–79. This diary kept by a Kyoto pawnbroker contains a great deal of information about which daimyo moved into the city and where they lived.

17. Haga, *Yoake mae no jitsuzō to kyozō*, p. 240.

18. *Sgs*, narrative section, p. 80.

19. *TnMt*, "Tabi no nagusa" section, p. 2.

20. *TnMt*, "Miyako no tsuto" section, p. 3. The mention of farewell parties is in *Sgs*, documents section, p. 106. Note that the first line and a half of this poem replicates the poem she wrote on the goddess Miyabi found in chapter 6.

21. *TnMt*, correspondence section, p. 3.

22. Burton Watson, *Saigyō: Poems of a Mountain Home* (Columbia University Press, 1991), p. 8.

23. *TnMt*, "Miyako no tsuto" section, p. 3.

24. *TnMt*, "Tabi no nagusa" section, p. 3; "Miyako no tsuto" section, p. 3.

25. Alan Grappard, *The Protocol of the Gods: A Study of the Kasuga Cult in Japanese History* (University of California Press, 1992), p. 4.

26. *TnMt*, "Tabi no nagusa" section, pp. 3–4.

27. Donald Keene describes many travel diaries written expressly for this purpose in *Travels of a Hundred Ages*. See especially pp. 33, 187, 199, 219.

28. *TnMt*, "Tabi no nagusa" section, p. 6.

29. Ibid., p. 5.

30. Thomas, "Plebeian Travelers on the Way of Shikishima," p. 128.

31. *TnMt*, "Tabi no nagusa" section, p. 6.

32. *TnMt*, "Miyako no tsuto" section, p. 6.

33. *TnMt*, correspondence section, pp. 6, 3.

34. Ketelaar, *Of Heretics and Martyrs in Meiji Japan*, pp. 8, 10, 12, 44.

35. *TnMt*, correspondence section, pp. 1–2.

36. *TnMt*, accounts listed at the end of the volume. Currency exchange rates changed in the middle of the nineteenth century. Up to 1843, 4,000 *mon* in copper

equaled one gold *ryō*, but thereafter it took 6,500 *mon* or more. Frost, *The Bakumatsu Currency Crisis*, p. 8.

37. *TnMt*, "Miyako no tsuto" section, p. 6.

38. In folklore the thief takes the heavenly maiden for his wife until years later she finds her robe and escapes back to the stars. Keigo Seki ed., *Folktales of Japan* (University of Chicago Press, 1963), pp. 63–69. There are many versions of the Noh play. See, for example, Arthur Waley, *The Nō Plays of Japan* (Grove Press, Inc. 1957), pp. 217–26. The beauty of the drama cannot conceal that disrobing a woman was a serious violation of her person. Hitomi Tonomura, "Black Hair and Red Trousers: Gendering the Flesh in Medieval Japan," *American Historical Review* 99.1 (February 1994): 129–54.

39. Nihon Shiseki Kyōkai, *Takechi Zuizan kankei monjo*, vol. 1 (Tōkyō Daigaku Shuppan Kai, reprint ed., 1972), p. 139.

40. Jansen, *Sakamoto Ryōma and the Meiji Restoration*, p. 414.

41. *Sks*, p. 47.

42. Emily Grozos Ooms, *Women and Millenarian Protest in Meiji Japan: Deguchi Nao and Ōmotokyō* (Cornell University East Asia Program, 1993), p. 3; Yasumaru Yoshio, "Japan's New Religions and the Experience of Modernity," UCLA, 2 December 1996.

43. Margaret Lock, *Encounters with Aging: Mythologies of Menopause in Japan and North America* (University California Press, 1993), p. 206.

44. Lock, *Encounters with Aging*, p. 313.

45. Mary Catherine Bateson, *Composing a Life* (Penguin Books, 1989), p. 28.

46. *TnMt*, "Miyako no tsuto" section, p. 7.

47. Murai Yasuhiko, *Kyōto jiten* (Tōkyōdō Shuppan, 1993), p. 38.

48. *HAz*, vol. 6, p. 31.

49. *TnMt*, "Miyako no tsuto" section, p. 7. The quotations that follow come from the same page.

50. Keith Thomas, "The Big Cake," a review of *Landscape and Memory* by Simon Schama in *New York Review of Books* 42.14 (September 21, 1995): 10–11.

51. *TnMt*, "Miyako no tsuto" section, p. 8.

52. Ibid., p. 9.

53. Ibid., pp. 9–10.

54. The *Los Angeles Times* once ran an article on one of these Fuyachō inns. See the *Travel* section for Sunday, January 23, 1994, pp. 1 and 13 for a description of the best way to travel so long as money is no object.

55. *TnMt*, "Miyako no tsuto" section, p. 11.

56. In 1868 Hanjirō was to start calling himself Kirino Toshiaki and it was under that name that he died in the Satsuma rebellion of 1877. Nihon Rekishi Gakkai, *Meiji ishin jinmei jiten* (Yoshikawa Kōbunkan, 1981), pp. 345–46.

57. *TnMt*, "Miyako no tsuto" section, p. 10. His name was Sugawa Nobuyuki.

58. Kyōto-shi: *Kyōto no rekishi* vol. 7, *Bakumatsu no gekidō* (Kyōto: Kyōto Shishi Hensansho, 1974), p. 330. Her biography continues on pp. 331–32.

59. *TnMt*, "Miyako no tsuto" section, p. 12. Lee Johnson, "The Life and Art of Ōtagaki Rengetsu" (M.A. Thesis, University of Kansas, 1988), pp. 1–28. When the nun Nomura Bōtō, also a famous poet, paid Rengetsu a visit, she was treated quite coldly.

60. The beautiful Konohananosakuya was chosen by Ninigi no mikoto for his bride when he rejected her ugly but long-lived sister. *HAz*, vol. 6, p. 294.

61. *TnMt*, "Miyako no tsuto" section, p. 12.

62. Ibid., p. 13.

63. Murai, *Kyoto jiten*, p. 367; Takashi Fujitani, *Splendid Monarchy: Power and Pageantry in Modern Japan* (University of California Press, 1996), p. 89.

64. *TnMt*, "Miyako no tsuto" section, pp. 13–14.

65. Ibid., p. 16.

66. Ibid., p. 17.

67. Jennifer Robertson, *Native and Newcomer: Making and Remaking a Japanese City* (University of California Press, 1991), p. 25, 26.

68. Madenokōji Naofusa, *Nihon shiseki kyōkai sosho*, vol. 179, 179: *Madenokōji nikki*, vol. 3 (Tōkyō Daigaku Shuppan Kai, 1974), p. 237; Okada Yoneo, "Jingū jinja sōkenshi," in *Meiji ishin shintō hyakunenshi*, vol. 2, ed. Matsuyama Yoshio (Shintō Bunkakai, 1966), p. 87.

69. See, for example, *Sks*, p. 42.

70. Harada Tomohiko, *Nihon josei shi* (Kawada Shobō, 1965), p. 186.

71. *IMz*, p. 534. Atsutane emphasized the importance of household occupation above all else in "Tamadasuki." See Katsurajima, "Hirata-ha kokugaku no 'doku-sho,'" p. 90.

Chapter Eight

1. *IMz*, p. 442. "Anakashiko kumoi ni niou ume ga ka wo iyashiki shizu no sode ni utsushite."

2. Ōguchi Yūjirō, "Kokka ishiki to tennō," in *Iwanami kōza Nihon tsūshi*, vol. 15, *Kinsei* 5 ed. Asao Naohiro et al. (Iwanami Shoten, 1995), p. 208.

3. Ichimura, *Edo jidai ni okeru Minami Shinano*, p. 22; Craig, *Chōshū in the Meiji Restoration*, p. 11; Beasley, *The Meiji Restoration*, pp. 22–23. Tokugawa Ieyoshi, 1793–1853, was the first shogun to take the highest court rank and office. Nihon Rekishi Gakkai, *Meiji ishin jinmei jiten*, p. 658.

4. Ōguchi, "Kokka ishiki to tennō," pp. 196–97; Inoue Katsuo, "Kaikoku zengo," in *Meiji ishin*, ed. Tanaka Akira (Yoshikawa Kōbunkan, 1994), p. 59.

5. *Sks*, p. 39; *Sgs*, narrative section, p. 59. The governor was Sakai Tadaaki.

6. *TnMt*, accounts section; Yamakawa, *Women of the Mito Domain*, pp. 12, 25.

7. Inoue Yorikuni, "Shinano no retsufu: Matsuo Taseko," *Yamato shinbun*, 18 November 1911, p. 1.

8. *Sgs*, documents section, pp. 178–79.

9. Nihon Shiseki, *Takechi Zuizan kankei monjo*, p. 316.

10. Ōtsuka Takematsu, *Iwakura Tomomi kankei monjo*, vol. 1 (Tokyo: Nihon Shiseki Kyōkai, 1927), p. 1.

11. *Sgs*, document section, p. 183.

12. *TnMt*, "Miyako no tsuto" section, pp. 35, 36.

13. *Sgs*, documents section, p. 183.

14. *TnMt*, "Miyako no tsuto" section, p. 24.

15. *TnMt*, correspondence section, p. 9.

16. Miyachi, "Bakumatsu Hirata kokugaku to seiji jōhō," p. 245.

17. *Sgs*, narrative section, p. 96. The speaker is Tsunoda Tadayuki.

18. When Shimazu Hisamitsu sent his representative to meet with the emperor, Nakayama Isako, one of the emperor's attendants received ten *koku* in rice. Her diary provides an excellent record of court life. See *Nihon shiseki kyōkai sosho*, vol. 154, 154: *Nakayama Isako nikki* (Tōkyō Daigaku Shuppan Kai, 1967), especially p. 808. Another diary kept by a woman official is *Nihon shiseki kyōkai sosho*, vols. 48–50, *Oshikōji Namiko nikki* (Tōkyō Daigaku Shuppan Kai, 1968).

19. *TnMt*, "Miyako no tsuto" section, p. 23.

20. *Sgs*, documents section, p. 103.

21. Discussed in Hutcheon, *The Politics of Postmodernism*, p. 41.

22. *TnMt*, "Miyako no tsuto" section, p. 15.

23. Beasley, *The Meiji Restoration*, pp. 191–92. The envoys were Sanjō Sane-tomi and Anegakōji Kintomo.

24. *TnMt*, "Miyako no tsuto" section, pp. 26–27.

25. Ibid., p. 27.

26. *TnMt*, correspondence section, p. 11.

27. Hatanaka Ichirō, *Bunkyū sannen ichigatsu nikki: Kōmei tennō wo riyōshita hitobito no nikki* (Osaka: ASG, 1992), p. 78.

28. *TnMt*, "Miyako no tsuto" section, p. 28; Hatanaka, *Bunkyū sannen ichigatsu nikki*, p. 134.

29. *TnMt*, correspondence section, p. 10.

30. *TnMt*, "Miyako no tsuto" section, p. 32.

31. *TnMt*, correspondence section, p. 11.

32. *Sgs*, narrative section, p. 114.3

33. *TnMt*, "Miyako no tsuto" section, pp. 33–34.

34. Ibid., p. 34.

35. *Sgs*, documents section, p. 155.

36. *Nihon shisō taikei*, vol. 56, *Bakumatsu seiji ronshū*, ed. Yoshida Tsunekichi and Satō Seizaburō (Iwanami Shoten, 1976), p. 291.

37. Satō, *Ōmi shōnin bakumatsu ishin kenbunroku*, p. 22; Uchida and Shimano eds., *Bakumatsu ishin Kyōto chōnin nikki*, p. 192; Iwakura-kō Kyūseki Hozonkai, ed., *Iwakura-kō jikki*, vol. 1 (Iwakura-kō Kyūseki Hozonkai, 1903), pp. 671–74.

38. Yanase Kazuo, *Takabatake Shikibu no kenkyū* (Aichi-ken Ō-shi: By the author, 1961), p. 18.

39. Yanase Kazuo, ed., *Takabatake Shikibu zenkashū* (Toyohashi-shi: By the editor, 1958), p. 54.

40. Yanase, *Takabatake Shikibu no kenkyū*, p. 22.

41. Ōtsuka Takematsu, *Ishin nichijō sanshū*, vol. 4 (Nihon Shiseki Kyōkai, 1927), p. 12. The retainer's name was Ono Gonnojō. See also Hatanaka, *Bunkyū sannen ichigatsu nikki*, p. 309.

42. Uchida and Shimano, *Bakumatsu ishin Kyōto chōnin nikki*, p. 185. The date was 1862/11/15. Homma Seiichirō, himself the victim of assassination, had hated Imaki Shigeko so much for her role as a maid of honor in promoting Kazunomiya's marriage that he plotted to kill her father, then attack her when she returned home to mourn his death. Hatanaka, *Bunkyū sannen ichigatsu nikki*, p. 88.

43. *Sgs*, narrative section, p. 122.

44. Yanase, *Takabatake Shikibu zenkashū*, p. 351.

45. Ibid., p. 352–53.

46. *TnMt*, "Miyako no tsuto" section, p. 35.

47. Ibid., pp. 52–53.

48. Ōguchi, "Kokka ishiki to tennō," pp. 192, 218; Inoue, "Kaikoku zengo," pp. 59–62.

49. Fujita, *Bakumatsu no tennō*, pp. 6, 130–32, 242. For a discussion of how the posthumous name Kōkaku was bestowed on Kōmei's grandfather, see Herschel Webb, *The Japanese Imperial Institution in the Tokugawa Period* (Columbia University Press, 1968), pp. 125–26.

50. Fujita, *Bakumatsu no tennō*, p. 5.

51. Wilson, *Patriots and Redeemers in Japan*, p. 43, 46.

52. Robert Young criticizes master narratives in *White Mythologies: Writing History and the West* (Routledge, 1990), pp. 21–23, 56–58, 63. Peter Burke has called for a micro-narrative that "moves back and forth between public and private worlds," celebrating the "'mediocre hero' . . . whose ordinariness allows the reader to see the life and social conflict of the time more clearly." "History of Events and the Revival of Narrative," in Peter Burke, ed., *New Perspectives on Historical Writing* (Cambridge and Oxford: Polity Press, 1991), pp. 243, 245.

Chapter Nine

1. *TnMt*, Correspondence section, p. 12. "Ima sara ni ika de yamu beki naka-naka ni omoi noborishi Yamato kichigai."

2. Ibid., p. 8.

3. Thomas M. Huber, "Men of High Purpose and the Politics of Direct Action, 1862–1864," in *Conflict in Modern Japanese History: The Neglected Tradition*, ed. Tetsuo Najita and J. Victor Koschmann (Princeton University Press, 1982), pp. 112–14.

4. Quoted in Craig, *Chōshū in the Meiji Restoration*, p. 198. See also a long poem

by Morooka Masatane in which he boasts of having won over "the crazy men."
Haga, *Bakumatsu kokugaku no kenkyū*, p. 469.

5. Nihon Shiseki, *Takechi Zuizan kankei monjo*, vol. 2, pp. 308–29. Zuizan met a number of the people Taseko later got to know, Lord Ōhara for example, but also Oka Mototarō, Nakajima Masutane, and Fukuba Bisei.

6. Haga Noboru, *Ishin wo motomete* (Mainichi Shinbun, 1976), p. 225.

7. *TnMt*, Correspondence section, p. 8.

8. Huber, *The Revolutionary Origins of Modern Japan*, pp. 76, 86; Haga, *Sōmō no seishin*, pp. 7–8.

9. *Sgs*, narrative section, p. 121; *IMz*, p. 475.

10. Mary Hamer, *Signs of Cleopatra: History, Politics, Representation* (Routledge, 1993), p. 30. She is commenting on Boccaccio.

11. Smith-Rosenberg, *Disorderly Conduct*, pp. 44, 140, 157–8; Mary P. Ryan, *Womanhood in America: From Colonial Times to the Present* (New Viewpoints, 1975), pp. 42, 74.

12. Quoted in David L. Barnhill, "Bashō as Bat: Wayfaring and Antistructure in the Journals of Matsuo Bashō," *Journal of Asian Studies* 49.2 (May 1990): 276.

13. Gilbert and Gubar, *The Madwoman in the Attic*, p. 174.

14. Joan Wallach Scott, *Gender and the Politics of History* (Columbia University Press, 1988), p. 73.

15. *Sgs*, narrative section, p. 93–94.

16. *TnMt*, "Miyako no tsuto" section, p. 15.

17. Nihon Rekishi Gakkai, *Meiji ishin jinmei jiten*, p. 846.

18. *TnMt*, "Miyako no tsuto" section, p. 22.

19. *Sgs*, narrative section, p. 113.

20. *TnMt*, "Miyako no tsuto" section, p. 17. Okamura Bunsuke was thirty-three when Taseko met him. In 1867 he would change his name to Katori Motohiko.

21. *TnMt*, "Miyako no tsuto" section, p. 18.

22. Nihon Rekishi Gakkai, *Meiji ishin jinmei jiten*, p. 283.

23. *TnMt*, "Miyako no tsuto" section, p. 19.

24. Nishikawa Tajirō, *Nishikawa Yoshisuke* (Shiga-ken Ōtsu-shi: Ōmi Shinhōsha, 1904), pp. 2–8.

25. *Sgs*, narrative section, p. 113.

26. Ibid., p. 136.

27. Shinhen Awa Sosho Henshū Iinkai, *Shinhen Awa sosho*, vol. 2 (Rekishi Toshosha, 1977), p. 309; Kobayashi Masakage, *Nishikawa Yoshisuke* (Ōmi-Hachiman: Nishikawa Yoshisuke Kenshōkai, 1971), pp. 85–86; *TnMt*, "Miyako no tsuto" section, pp. 19–20.

28. *TnMt*, "Miyako no tsuto" section, p. 22.

29. Watanabe Genpo, "Matsuo Taseko-den Genpo-kun bengi," *Shidankai sokkiroku* no. 93 (Shidankai, 1900), p. 27.

30. *Sgs*, narrative section, p. 100.

31. Walkowitz, *City of Dreadful Delight*, p. 68.

32. Jansen, *Sakamoto Ryōma*, p. 98.

33. Nagashima Atsuko, "Bakumatsu nōson josei no kōdō no jiyū to kaji rōdō," in *Ronshū kinsei joseishi*, ed. Kinsei Joseishi Kenkyū Kai (Yoshikawa Kōbunkan, 1986), p. 168.

34. Heilbrun, *Writing a Woman's Life*, pp. 126–28.

35. *Sgs*, narrative section, p. 100.

36. *Sgs*, documents section, p. 116.

37. Quoted in Haga, *Bakumatsu kokugaku no kenkyū*, p. 463. The five men were Miyawada Tanekage, Morooka Masatane, Miwada Mototane, Ishikawa Hajime, and Tatebe Ken'ichirō. They were soon joined by three others.

38. *TnMt*, "Miyako no tsuto" section, pp. 22–23.

39. *TnMt*, Correspondence section, p. 5.

40. Ibid., p. 5.

41. Ibid., p. 6.

42. Tamamushi Sadaiyū, *Zoku Nihon shiseki kyōkai sosho*, vols. 17–18, *Kanbu tsūki* (Tōkyō Daigaku Shuppan Kai, 1976). See vol. 18, pp. 534–49 for biographical information.

43. *Sgs*, narrative section, p. 96.

44. *TnMt*, Correspondence section, p. 9.

45. Tanishima Kazuma, "Noshiro Hirosuke kankei shiryōshū," *Ichihara chihōshi kenkyū* no. 16 (March 1990): 36–45. The doctor was Gonda Naosuke.

46. Ibid., pp. 46, 80.

47. Miyachi, *Bakumatsu ishin-ki no bunka to jōhō*, p. 214; Asai Shōji, "Ashikaga shōgun mokuzō kyōshu jiken," in *Kyōdō kenkyū: Meiji ishin*, ed. Shisō no Kagaku Kenkyū Kai (Tokken Shoten, 1967), pp. 307–8, 316.

48. *TnMt*, Correspondence section, pp. 11–12, 14.

49. *TnMt*, "Miyako no tsuto" section, p. 30. Kawada Jun, "Onna jobu Matsuo Taseko" *Fujin kōron* 24.9 (September 1939): 265.

50. Ichimura, *Matsuo Taseko*, p. 137; for an account of this day, see *TnMt*, "Miyako no tsuto" section, pp. 30–32.

51. Siân Reynolds, "Introduction," in *Women, State and Revolution: Essays on Power and Gender in Europe since 1789*, ed. Siân Reynolds (University of Massachusetts Press, 1987), p. xiv.

52. *TnMt*, "Miyako no tsuto" section, p. 34.

53. *IMz*, p. 474.

54. Watanabe Tamezō, *Ishin shishi shōki shū* (Min'yūsha, 1911), pp. 230–31; *TnMt*, "Miyako no tsuto" section, pp. 35–36.

55. *TnMt*, "Miyako no tsuto" section, pp. 38–39; Ōtsuka, *Ishin nichijō sanshū*, pp. 21–36.

56. Ōtsuka, *Ishin nichijō sanshū*, p. 38.

57. *TnMt*, "Miyako no tsuto" section, pp. 39–40.

58. For an entertaining account of what Takauji did and why he has been treated as a villain in Japanese history, see Ivan Morris, *The Nobility of Failure: Tragic Heroes in the History of Japan* (Holt, Rinehart and Winston, 1975), pp. 107, 140–42. For Hirata Atsutane's version, see *HAz*, vol. 6, pp. 63–102.

59. *Sgs,* narrative section, p. 116.

60. Tanaka Zen'ichi, "Atsuta Daigūji Tsunoda Tadayuki ōden," in *Atsuta fudoki,* ed. Ikeda Chōsaburō (Nagoya: Kyūchikai, 1980), p. 95.

61. There are many accounts of this incident. See for example, Haga, *Bakumatsu kokugaku no kenkyū,* pp. 441–89, or Anne Walthall, "Off with Their Heads! The Hirata Disciples and the Ashikaga Shoguns," *Monumenta Nipponica* 50.2 (Summer 1995): 137–70.

62. Nishikawa, *Nishikawa Yoshisuke,* p. 10.

63. This text appears in numerous places. An easy-to-find annotated version is in Yoshida and Satō, ed., *Bakumatsu seiji ronshū,* p. 292.

64. Ibid., p. 293.

65. Uchida and Shimano, *Bakumatsu ishin Kyōto chōnin nikki,* pp. 193–94.

66. *Sgs,* narrative section, pp. 121–22,124. A manuscript in Tsunoda Tadayuki's own hand in which he takes full credit for instigating the incident states baldly that Taseko "had not the slightest connection with it." "Mokushu shimatsu tsuki yūshi shika." Manuscript in Mukyū Toshokan, Machida-shi, Tokyo.

67. Barry, "The New Historical Syntheses: Women's Biography," p. 77.

68. Satō, *Ōmi shōnin bakumatsu ishin kenbunroku,* p. 22.

69. Haga, *Bakumatsu kokugaku no kenkyū,* p. 453; Nishikawa, *Nishikawa Yoshisuke* section 2, p. 9.

70. Berry, *The Culture of Civil War in Kyoto,* p. 9.

71. Bob Takashi Wakabayashi, "Imperial Sovereignty in Early Modern Japan," *Journal of Japanese Studies* 17.1 (Winter 1991): 29–30.

72. Tōyama Shigeki and Kaneko Mitsuharu, eds., *Kyōto shugoshoku shimatsu,* vol. 1 (Heibonsha, 1965), pp. 74–75; Tokutomi Iichirō, *Kinsei Nihon kokuminshi: Sonnō jōi hen* (Min'yūsha, 1936), p. 267.

73. *TnMt,* "Miyako no tsuto" section, p. 40.

74. Inoue Yorikuni, "Shinano no retsufu: Matsuo Taseko" no. 2, in *Yamato shinbun,* 18 November 1911, p. 1.

75. "Dai Nihon ishin shiryō kōhon," vol. 32, p. 87 (left). Manuscript in the Shiryō Hensanjo.

76. *Sgs,* documents section, p. 113.

Chapter Ten

1. Shakai Kyōiku Kyōkai ed., *Kinnōka shikashū* (Shakai Kyōiku Kyōkai, 1919), p. 268. "Furusato ni kaeru mo oshiki tabigoromo Ōuchi yama ni hikarete hikarete."

2. *Sgs,* narrative section, p. 118.

3. Tamamushi, *Kanbu tsūki,* p. 3–4; Asai, "Ashikaga shōgun mokuzō kyōshu jiken," pp. 320–21.

4. Conrad Totman, *The Collapse of the Tokugawa Bakufu, 1862–1868* (University of Hawaii Press, 1980), p. 56.

5. Nishikawa, *Nishikawa Yoshisuke*, section 2, p. 1; Tokutomi, *Kinsei Nihon Kokuminshi Sonnō jōi hen*, p. 261.

6. Nishikawa, *Nishikawa Yoshisuke*, section 2, pp. 23–28.

7. *TnMt*, "Miyako no tsuto" section, p. 41.

8. Fujita, *Bakumatsu no tennō*, p. 220.

9. *TnMt*, "Miyako no tsuto" section, p. 41.

10. Craig, *Chōshū in the Meiji Restoration*, p. 142.

11. Iwakura-kō Kyūseki, *Iwakura-kō jikki*, vol. 1, pp. 678–79.

12. Ibid., p. 679.

13. Ibid., pp. 680–81.

14. Tanishima, "Noshiro Hirosuke kankei shiryō shū," pt. 1, p. 63.

15. Watanabe, *Ishin shishi shōki shū*, p. 48.

16. Koizumi Tōzō, *Ishin shishi kinnō shika hyōdan* (Kyoto-shi: Ritsumeikan Shuppanbu, 1939), pp. 145–46.

17. Nishikawa, *Nishikawa Yoshisuke*, section 2, pp. 44–45.

18. The British perspective on these negotiations may be found in Sir Rutherford Alcock, *The Capital of the Tycoon*, vol. 2, pp. 103, 107.

19. *TnMt*, "Miyako no tsuto" section, p. 41.

20. Herman Ooms, *Tokugawa Ideology* (Princeton University Press, 1985), pp. 42, 107.

21. *TnMt*, "Miyako no tsuto" section, p. 41.

22. Ibid.

23. Sir Ernest Mason Satow, trans. *Japan 1853–1864 or Genji Yume Monogatari* (Naigai Shuppan Kyōkai, 1905), pp. 82–83.

24. *TnMt*, "Miyako no tsuto" section, p. 41.

25. A similar refusal to accept the Tokugawa shoguns' attempt to mystify their origins may be found in Ooms, *Tokugawa Ideology*, p. 107.

26. *TnMt*, "Miyako no tsuto" section, p. 43. This poem was later carved on a stone erected in the shrine precincts for Kami Iida village. *Sgs*, narrative section, p. 26.

27. *HAz*, vol. 6, p. 521; *Sks*, p. 76.

28. *Sgs*, narrative section, p. 129.

29. *HHH*, pp. 1–2; Higashiyama Michihiko, "Bakumatsu ishin no senkakusha: Hazama Hidenori kōyūroku," *Mino shinbun*, 1 January 1987, p. 1; 2 January 1987, p. 1; 3 January 1987, p. 1.

30. *HHH*, pp. 2, 6, 30; Higashiyama, "Bakumatsu ishin no senkakusha," *Mino shinbun*, 1 January 1987, p. 1.

31. For the arguments between the moderates and Kido Takayoshi, see Craig, *Chōshū in the Meiji Restoration*, pp. 181–84. For the Nakatsugawa meetings, see *HHH*, pp. 7–8.

32. Ichioka, *Hijimori isō*, p. 117.

33. *HHHs*, p. 94.

34. Ichioka, *Hijimori isō*, p. 119.

35. *HHHs*, p. 98.

36. Ibid., pp. 98–105.

37. Ibid., pp. 106–8.

38. Ichioka, *Hijimori isō*, p. 128.

39. Ibid., pp. 128–30; *HHHs*, pp. 108–9. Hidenori said the priests were traitors. For a brief discussion of the Iyo petition, see Walthall, "Off with Their Heads," p. 167.

40. Ichioka, *Hijimori isō*, p. 131; *HHHs*, p. 110; *TnMt*, "Miyako no tsuto" section, p. 44.

41. Ichioka, *Hijimori isō*, p. 132; *TnMt*, "Miyako no tsuto" section, pp. 44–45.

42. *TnMt*, "Miyako no tsuto" section, p. 45; *HHHs*, pp. 118–19.

43. Ichioka, *Hijimori isō*, p. 137. Guide books for this area typically portray the pleasures of boating in balmy spring weather. See Akatsuka Kiyoshi, *Yodogawa ryōgan ichiran* (Edo: Yamagiya, 1861).

44. Ichioka, *Hijimori isō*, pp. 138–40; *TnMt*, "Miyako no tsuto" section, pp. 45–47; *HHHs*, pp. 120–21.

45. *HHHs*, pp. 123–25; *TnMt*, "Miyako no tsuto" section, p. 47.

46. Ichioka, *Hijimori isō*, pp. 143–44; *TnMt*, "Miyako no tsuto" section, p. 48; *HHHs*, pp. 127–30.

47. Ichioka, *Hijimori isō*, p. 146; *TnMt*, "Miyako no tsuto" section, p. 49.

48. Satow, *Genji Yume Monogatari*, pp. 88–89.

49. *TnMt*, "Miyako no tsuto" section, p. 49.

50. Ibid., p. 49.

51. Ibid., p. 50. There is a variant version of this poem in *Sgs*, documents section, p. 151.

52. *TnMt*, "Miyako no tsuto" section, p. 51.

53. Ibid., pp. 51–52.

54. *Sgs*, documents section, p. 184; Ichioka, *Hijimori isō*, p. 152.

55. Sugima Akijirō, *Gifu-ken kyōdo ijinden* (Nagoya: Gifu-ken Kyōdo Ijinden Henshū Kai, 1933), p. 583.

56. A light-hearted explanation of postmodernism and the individual can be found in David Lodge, *Nice Work* (London: Penguin Books, 1988), pp. 39–40. For more serious assessments see Joan Wallach Scott, *Only Paradoxes to Offer*, and Dorinne K. Kondo, *Crafting Selves: Power, Gender, and Discourses of Identity in a Japanese Workplace* (University of Chicago Press, 1990).

57. Esashi, *Onna no isshō wo kaku*, pp. 49, 218, 262.

58. *Sgs*, documents section, p. 71.

Chapter Eleven

1. *TnMt*, frontispiece to "Miyako no tsuto." "Taoyame no mi wo kuiakashi hiru no ko no ashi tatanu mi wo kui tsutsu sooru."

2. See Ronald J. DiCenzo, "The Yamato Incident of 1863," *Princeton Papers in East Asian Studies*, vol. 1, *Japan* 1 (1972): 57–87.

3. *MTic*, p. 37.

4. Kobayashi, *Nishikawa Yoshisuke*, pp. 207–13.

5. "Nishikawa Yoshisuke monjo shashinkan," vol. 6, 1864/11/5. Taseko also included this poem in her own poetry collection, published in *Sgs*, documents section, pp. 115–16.

6. Darnton, "History of Reading," p. 142.

7. Lynne Miyake, "Gender and Perception in Heian Literature," talk given 11 October 1991, University of California, Irvine.

8. For examples of this usage in *Man'yōshū* poems, see Gary L. Ebersole, *Ritual Poetry and the Politics of Death in Early Japan* (Princeton University Press, 1989), pp. 175, 193, 196, 210, 217.

9. Thomas, "Plebeian Travelers on the Way of Shikishima," p. 170.

10. McCullough, *Tales of Ise*, p. 78.

11. See Sugimoto Tsutomu, *Onna no kotoba shirushi* (Yūzankaku, 1985), p. 191 for a history of the term and pp. 170, 171, 181, 188 for examples of women's speech.

12. Tahara, "'Tama no mihashira' igo," p. 580.

13. *Sgs*, documents section, p. 121.

14. I am indebted to Helen Hardacre for this insight.

15. For a vivid account see Sharon L. Sievers, *Flowers in Salt: The Beginnings of Feminist Consciousness in Modern Japan* (Stanford University Press, 1983), pp. 33–47.

16. Nishikawa Yūko, "Diaries as Gendered Texts," in *Women and Class in Japanese History*, ed. Hitomi Tonomura, Anne Walthall, and Wakita Haruko (University of Michigan Center for Japanese Studies, forthcoming).

17. Levy, *The Ten Thousand Leaves*, pp. 350–52.

18. Philippi, trans. *Kojiki*, pp. 51, 399.

19. Ketelaar, *A Quiet Great Land*. For a more extended discussion of the meanings behind the leech child, see Jane Marie Law, *Puppets of Nostalgia: The Life, Death and Rebirth of the Japanese Awaji Ningyō Tradition* (Princeton University Press, 1997), pp. 63-4, 122–24, 158.

20. *Sgs*, documents section, p. 121.

21. Itō Masao, *Kinsei no waka to kokugaku* (Ise-shi: Kōgakkan Daigaku Shuppanbu, 1979), p. 209; *HAz*, vol. 6, p. 39.

22. Heilbrun, *Hamlet's Mother*, p. 34.

23. Patricia Fister, "Female Bunjin: The Life of Poet-Painter Ema Saikō," in *Recreating Japanese Women: 1600–1868*, ed. Gail L. Bernstein (University of California Press, 1991), p. 129.

24. Smith, *A Poetics of Women's Autobiography*, p. 53.

25. *Sgs*, documents section, p. 150.

26. Dea Birkett and Julie Wheelwright, "How Could She? Unpalatable Facts and Feminists' Heroines," *Gender and History* 2.1 (Spring 1990): 50.

27. Thomas, "Plebeian Travelers on the Way of Shikishima," p. 170.

28. Irene Coltman Brown, "Mary Wollstonecraft and the French Revolution or Feminism and the Rights of Men," in *Women, State and Revolution: Essays on Power and Gender in Europe since 1789,* ed. Siân Reynolds (University of Massachusetts Press, 1987), p. 11.

29. Marysa Navarro, "Of Sparrows and Condors: The Autobiography of Eva Peron," in *The Female Autograph: Theory and Practice of Autobiography from the Tenth to the Twentieth Century,* ed. Domna C. Stanton (University of Chicago Press, 1987), p. 184.

30. Letter to Kitahara Inao in *Sgs,* documents section, p. 215.

31. Ibid., p. 186.

32. Koschmann, *The Mito Ideology,* pp. 152–71.

33. Seinaiji Sonshi Hensan Iinkai, *Seinaiji sonshi,* vol. 1 (Nagano-shi: Seinaiji Sonshi Kankō Kai, 1982), p. 442. Nishikawa Yoshisuke's record includes drawings of these banners that he got from Hazama Hidenori.

34. Yamamoto, *Yamamoto sonshi,* p. 236.

35. Kitakōji, *Kisoji: Bunken no tabi,* pp. 211–12.

36. Shimazaki, *Tōson zenshū,* vol. 15, p. 475.

37. Nakatsugawa-shi, *Nakatsugawa shishi,* vol. 2, pt. 2, pp. 1664–70.

38. *IMz,* p. 550.

39. Kitakōji, *Kisoji: Bunken no tabi,* pp. 228–31. The leader was Takeda Kōun. For a depiction of what happened to the families of the Mito warriors, see Yamakawa, *Women of Mito Domain,* pp. 119–20.

40. "Nishikawa Yoshisuke monjo shashinkan," vol. 19.

41. Itō, *Sōmō no kokugaku,* p. 261.

42. According to Matsuo Sen, Tsunoda Tadayuki kept a diary from this period that frequently mentions Taseko. His heirs were trying to transcribe it, but one died and the other is ill. 8 August 1997.

43. *Tsunoda Tadayuki okina koden* (Nagoya: Atsuta Jingu Guchō, 1989), pp. 127, 148.

44. Hirasawa and Kobayashi, *Shimoina sanshigyō hattatsushi,* p. 113.

45. Masaki, *Tōkai to Ina,* pp. 473–74

46. Tanishima, "Noshiro Hirosuke kankei shiryōshū," pt. 1, pp. 36, 37.

47. *Sgs,* documents section, p. 187.

48. Tanabe Katsuya, comp. *Inoue Yorikuni okina koden* (Tokyo: Tanabe Katsuya pub. 1921), pp. 40–41.

49. "Nishikawa Yoshisuke monjo shashinkan," vol. 22, 1866/2/2; Higashiyama Michihiko, "Bakumatsu ishinki no senkakusha: Hazama Hidenori kōyūroku," *Mino shinbun,* 23 January 1987, p. 1.

50. *Sgs,* narrative section, p. 148.

51. Ibid., p. 149.

52. Tanishima Kazuma, "Noshiro Hirosuke kankei shiryōshū," pt. 2, *Ichihara chihōshi kenkyū* no. 17 (March 1992): 41.

53. *Sgs*, narrative section, pp. 159–60.

54. Ibid., pp. 161–62.

55. Fujita, *Bakumatsu no tennō*, pp. 224–40.

56. *Sgs*, documents section, p. 76.

Chapter Twelve

1. *Sks*, p. 86. "Kagamiyama kokoro no sumi mo hare ni keri tachi kaeru yo no omokage wo mite."

2. For a detailed account of the negotiations and infighting, see Beasley, *The Meiji Restoration*, pp. 273–92.

3. Ichioka, *Hijimori isō*, p. 169.

4. *Sgs*, narrative section, p. 171.

5. Ichimura, *Matsuo Taseko*, p. 168.

6. Catharine R. Stimpson, "The Female Sociograph: The Theater of Virginia Woolf's Letters," in Stanton, ed., *The Female Autograph*, pp. 168–69.

7. *MTic*, p. 26.

8. Ichioka, *Hijimori isō*, p. 174.

9. Ueda Mannen, *Kokugakusha denki shūsei*, vol. 2 (Meicho Kankōkai, 1978), pp. 1496–1501.

10. Kanzaki Shirō, *Kannagara no michi no kyūkōsha Gonda Naosuke-ō* (Kanagawa-ken, Ōma-chō: Aburi Jinja Shamusho, 1937), pp. 81–82.

11. Uchida and Shimano, *Bakumatsu ishin Kyōto chōnin nikki*, p. 282; Nishikawa, *Nishikawa Yoshisuke*, p. 79.

12. Kanzaki, *Kannagara no michi no kyūkōsha*, pp. 75–80; Beasley, *The Meiji Restoration*, pp. 296–97.

13. Hasegawa Noboru, *Sagara Sōzō to sono dōshi* (Shinshosetsusha, 1943, 1968), pp. 87–99.

14. Ichimura, *Matsuo Taseko*, pp. 179–80.

15. Takagi Shunsuke, *Sorekara no shishi: mo hitotsu no Meiji ishin* (Yūzankaku, 1985), pp. 19–22.

16. Shinano Kyōikukai Suwa Bukai, *Sagara Sōzō kankei shiryōshū* (Seishikai, 1975), p. 23.

17. *Sgs*, narrative section, p. 182.

18. Kitakōji Ken, *Zoku Kisoji: bunken no tabi* (Geisōdō, 1971), p. 189.

19. Haga Noboru, *Nise kangun to Meiji ishin seiken* (Kyōiku Shuppan Center, 1992), p. 137. For accounts of Sōzō and his men, see Hasegawa, *Sagara Sōzō to sono dōshi*, pp. 461–612; Takagi, *Sorekara no shishi*, pp. 40–55; Ōba Masami, *Sōmō no keifu* (San'ichi Shobō, 1970), pp. 188–98, and Miyachi Satohide, "Kōto shishite sōku nirareru: Sekihōtai jiken no tenmatsu ni miru seiji rikigaku no hijō," *Nihon oyobi Nihonjin* no. 1618 (April 1995): 112–17.

20. Takagi, *Sorekara no shishi*, p. 84.

21. *Sgs*, documents section, p. 191.

22. Haga, *Nise kangun to Meiji ishin seiken*, pp. 17, 23, 104

23. Eiko Ikegami, *The Taming of the Samurai: Honorific Individualism and the Making of Modern Japan* (Harvard University Press, 1995), p. 144.

24. Kanzaki, *Kannagara no michi no kyūkōshā*, pp. 89–90.

25. Haga, *Yoake mae no jitsuzō to kyozō*, p. 83; Shinano Kyōikukai, *Sagara Sōzō kankei shiryōshū*, pp. 98–99. According to a sign erected by the local commemorative association, a festival is held in Sōzō's honor every year at the grave, located about a mile below the Suwa shrine in a well-marked square.

26. Quoted in Haga, *Nise kangun to Meiji ishin seiken*, p. 46.

27. *Sgs*, narrative section, p. 176.

28. *Sgs*, documents section, pp. 188–89.

29. Totman, *Early Modern Japan*, p. 545.

30. *Sgs*, documents section, pp. 190–92.

31. Ibid., pp. 189, 193, 197.

32. *Isss*, p. 351.

33. Ibid., pp. 400–401.

34. Ichimura, *Matsuo Taseko*, p. 178.

35. Beasley, *The Meiji Restoration*, pp. 286–92.

36. Masaki, *Tōkai to Ina*, p. 484.

37. *Isss*, pp. 29, 402–7; *Sgs*, documents section, p. 192. Masatoshi spent the rest of his life a Shinto priest in Yamamoto.

38. *IMz*, p. 437; *Sgs*, documents section, pp. 37, 201.

39. *Sgs*, documents section, pp. 189, 192, 193.

40. Ibid., pp. 188–89, 192; narrative section, pp. 173–74. The third man was Morooka Masatane.

41. Unpublished letter written to Kakehi Genzō in 1892. I am grateful to Yoshida Saburō of Nakatsugawa for showing me a copy.

42. *Sgs* documents section, p. 191. Taseko's nephew Ōzawa Akitada begged for an official position so he could serve the emperor, but to no avail. *Iks*, pp. 185–86.

43. *Isss*, p. 380, for example.

44. *IMz*, pp. 489–90.

45. *Isss*, pp. 382–86.

46. *HHHs*, pp. 152–60, 176.

47. Hatanaka, *Bunkyū sannen ichigatsu nikki*, p. 301; Ketelaar, *Of Heretics and Martyrs in Meiji Japan*, pp. 44–45. John Breen argues that Tsuwano and Bisei simply wanted to clarify the relationship between Buddhism and Shinto, not obliterate Buddhism. "Shintoists in Restoration Japan (1868–1872): Towards a Reassessment," *Modern Asian Studies* 24.3 (1990): 593–95.

48. Shimazaki, *Tōson zenshū*, vol. 15, pp. 406–53.

49. *Iks*, p. 216, 438.

50. Toyooka, *Toyooka sonshi*, vol. 1, p. 663.

51. On my 1997 trip to the Ina Valley, I saw the *rei-i* for Taseko, her husband,

son, grandson, and great-grandson as well as other family members. The most recent was dated 1994. Kitahara Takeo's mother who died in 1991 is also remembered with a *rei-i*.

52. *Sgs*, documents section, p. 35.

53. Fujitani, *Splendid Monarchy*, pp. 95–97.

54. *Sgs*, documents section, p. 34.

55. *HHHs*, p. 153; *Isss*, pp. 368–70.

56. *Sgs*, documents section, p. 34.

57. *HHHs*, p. 172. There is a Nagasawa Sekijō who spied on Aizu for the Nagaoka domain. He died in battle a month after Taseko's summons. Shimonaka Kunihiko, *Nihon jinmei daijiten*, vol. 4 (Heibonsha, 1979), p. 541.

59. Uno Shun'ichi, Ōishi Manabu, Kobayashi Tatsuo, Satō Kazuhiko, Suzuki Yasutami, Takeuchi Makoto, Hamada Takashi and Mitaku Terumasa, *Japan Chronik: Nihon zenshi* (Kōdansha, 1991), p. 910.

60. *Sgs*, documents section, p. 198, 199, 202–3.

61. *Sgs*, narrative section, p. 196.

62. Ibid., p. 194–95.

63. Marius B. Jansen and Gilbert Rozman, eds., *Japan in Transition from Tokugawa to Meiji* (Princeton University Press, 1986).

Chapter Thirteen

1. *Sgs*, documents section, p. 123. "Kasunaranu kusa no sueba ni iya takaki kotoba no tsuyu no kakaru ureshisa." ("Having received a letter from a lady-in-waiting at the Iwakura mansion.")

2. Tomomi's correspondence for the six months that Taseko resided in his compound is published in Ōtsuka Takematsu ed., *Iwakura Tomomi kankei monjo*, vol. 4 (Nihon Shiseki Kyōkai, 1930). His aunt Chikō-in is mentioned once; other women appear not at all. Yajirō's papers are still being published. So far nothing has appeared regarding Taseko. Shoyu Kurabu Shinagawa Yajirō Kankei Monjo Hensan Iinkai, *Shinagawa Yajirō kankei monjo* (Shoyu Kurabu, 1993).

3. Kodama Masatō, *Bakumatsu kuge shūsei* (Shinjinbutsu Ōraisha, 1993), pp. 398–403.

4. This paraphrase of a memorial prepared by Tomomi is in Beasley, *The Meiji Restoration*, p. 174.

5. Iwakura-kō, *Iwakura-kō jikki*, p. 651–52.

6. Ibid., p. 655.

7. Ōtsuka Takematsu, *Iwakura Tomomi kankei monjo*, vol. 1 (Nihon Shiseki Kyōkai, 1927), p. 1.

8. *Sgs*, narrative section, p. 108–10.

9. Ibid., p. 85

10. Ibid., p. 172; *HHHs*, 170.

11. *Sgs*, documents section, p. 195.

12. Ibid., pp. 35, 195, 198.

13. Haga Noboru et al., eds., *Nihon josei jinmei jiten* (Nihon Tosho Sentā, 1993), p. 134.

14. *Sgs*, documents section, p. 201.

15. Kodama, *Bakumatsu kuge shūsei*, p. 545.

16. *Sgs*, documents section, pp. 74, 131.

17. Ibid., p. 131.

18. Shinhen Kokka, *Shinhen kokka taikan*, vol. 2: *Shisen shūhen kashū*, p. 371 poem 49: "michitose no kazu ni mo megure haru wo hete taenu yayoi no hana no sakazuki."

19. Carl Sesar, trans. "The Queen Mother of the West," in *Twenty Plays of the Nō Theatre*, ed. Donald Keene, (Columbia University Press, 1970), pp. 254–63. I am indebted to Susan Klein for this information.

20. *MTic*, p. 36.

21. *Sgs*, narrative section, p. 250.

22. *Sgs*, documents section, p. 74.

23. Ibid., p. 123.

24. Ibid., pp. 74–75, 132.

25. Ibid., p. 75 I thank Marjorie Beale for suggesting this translation of *fundoshi*.

26. *HAz*, vol. 6, p. 18.

27. *Sgs*, documents section, p. 73.

28. Ibid., p. 129.

29. Ibid., p. 35, 201.

30. Ibid., pp. 35, 198, 199.

31. Gluck, *Japan's Modern Myths*, p. 73. Many years ago John W. Hall pointed out that the people themselves tried to bring the emperor into their lives. "Their willingness to submerge in him their political and private interests were as much their making as his." "A Monarch for Modern Japan," in *Political Development in Modern Japan*, ed. Robert E. Ward (Princeton University Press, 1968), p. 54. My thanks to Sally Hastings for this citation.

32. *Sgs*, documents section, p. 200

33. For a map showing the Iwakura residence's proximity to the palace, see Fujitani, *Splendid Monarchy*, p. 80.

34. *Sgs*, documents section, p. 207.

35. Ibid., p. 39.

36. Ibid., p. 233.

37. Ibid., p. 219.

38. *Sgs*, narrative section, p. 209–10.

39. Ibid., p. 250.

40. *Sgs*, documents section, p. 220.

41. Ibid., p. 122.

42. *Sgs*, narrative section, p. 210.

43. Ibid., p. 211.

44. Ibid., p. 253.

45. Ichimura, *Matsuo Taseko*, p. 270.

46. *Sgs*, documents section, p. 231.

47. *MTic*, p. 32.

48. Mizue Renko, *Kinsei no naka no onnatachi* (Nihon Hōsō Shuppankai, 1983), pp. 224–25; Seki Tamiko, *Edo kōki no joseitachi* (Aki Shobō, 1980), pp. 169–73.

49. Miwada Yoshiko, *Baika no fu: Miwada Masako den* (Miwada Masako Sensei Gojūnensai Kinen Shuppankai, 1977), p. 18 and passim. For a brief biography of Kōran see Patricia Fister, *Japanese Women Artists, 1600–1900* (Lawrence Kansas: Spencer Museum of Art, 1988), pp. 104–5.

50. Miwada Masako, "Shinano no retsufu: Matsuo Taseko" no. 4 *Yamato Shinbun*, 22 November 1911, p. 1.

51. *Sgs*, narrative section, p. 241.

52. Miwada, "Shinano no retsufu," p. 1.

53. Miwada, *Baika no fu*, pp. 65–68.

54. Ibid., pp. 69–80.

55. Ibid., pp. 81–85.

56. Miwada, "Shinano no retsufu: Matsuo Taseko" no. 6 *Yamato shinbun*, 25 November 1911, p. 1

57. *Sgs*, narrative section, p. 194. See also the poem *Iks*, p. 492.

58. See, for example, Don Roden, "Taishō Culture and the Problems of Gender Ambivalence," in *Culture and Identity: Japanese Intellectuals during the Interwar Years*, ed. J. Thomas Rimer (Princeton University Press, 1990), p. 41.

59. Miwada, *Baika no fu*, pp. 86–136, 194–98.

60. Miwada, "Matsuo Taseko den," p. 32.

61. Kyoto-shi, *Bakumatsu no gekidō*, p. 360. For details of this social movement see Wilson, *Patriots and Redeemers.*

62. *Sgs*, documents section, p. 239; *Sks*, p. 100.

63. *MTic*, p. 33.

64. *Isss*, pp. 6–7, 156–59.

65. Takahara Tomimochi, "Takahara bunko tsūshin," *Minami Shinshū shinbun*, 20 June 1989, p. 5.

66. Tanaka Akira takes a cynical view of these excursions, seeing them as a device used by the oligarchs to manipulate popular opinion in *Mikan no Meiji ishin*, pp. 42–43.

67. *IMz*, pp. 479–84.

68. Ibid., pp. 486–89; Ichimura, *Matsuo Taseko*, pp. 234–36. A copy was kept by Gotō Naoto, who happened to be a shrine priest in Ajima village just downstream from Tomono.

69. *IMz*, p. 486.

70. Ibid., p. 487.

71. Ibid., p. 488.

1. *Sgs*, documents section, p. 105. "Mi ni tsumoru oi wa wasurete kimi ga yo ni nami tatanu hi wo inori kurashitsu."

2. Ibid., p. 206.

3. Ishii Ryōsuke, *Edo bakufu hatamoto jinmei jiten* (Hara Shobō, 1989), vol. 2, p. 302; vol. 3, pp. 470–71; vol. 4, p. 317, 569.

4. Masaki, *Tōkai to Ina*, pp. 121–22.

5. *Sgs*, documents section, pp. 197, 199.

6. Masaki, *Tōkai to Ina*, pp. 123–24.

7. *Sgs*, documents section, pp. 204–5. This letter is unsigned and undated, but from the contents it is clear that it was written in the third month of 1869, and it was sent to her closest friend in the Iwakura house, Miwada Masako.

8. Ibid., p. 204.

9. *Sgs*, narrative section, p. 211.

10. *MTic*, p. 26.

11. Masaki, *Tōkai to Ina*, p. 126.

12. Tasaki Kimitsukasa, "Meiji shonen no gōnōsō: Fukushima-ken Aizu chihō o jirei ni," *Higashi Ajia no kindai ikō to minshū* no. 3 (August 1997): 26.

13. *Sgs*, documents section, p. 206.

14. *HHHs*, pp. 180–92.

15. Ibid., pp. 193–95.

16. *Sgs*, documents section, pp. 37, 159.

17. *HHHs*, pp. 195–96.

18. *Sgs*, documents section, p. 37.

19. Stephen Vlastos, "Opposition Movements in Early Meiji, 1868–1885," in *Cambridge History of Japan*, vol. 5, *The Nineteenth Century*, pp. 368–70.

20. Wigen, *The Making of a Japanese Periphery*, pp. 169–70.

21. *Sgs*, documents section, p. 209.

22. Ibid., p. 209.

23. Ibid., p. 38.

24. F. G. Notehelfer, ed., *Japan through American Eyes: The Journal of Francis Hall Kanagawa and Yokohama 1859–1866* (Princeton University Press, 1992), p. 515.

25. W. G. Beasley, "The Foreign Threat and the Opening of the Ports," in *The Cambridge History of Japan*, vol. 5, *The Nineteenth Century*, p. 305.

26. *Sgs*, documents section, p. 38, 208.

27. Ibid., p. 243.

28. Ibid., p. 39; *Sgs*, narrative section, p. 202; *HHHs*, pp. 205–31.

29. Nishikawa, *Nishikawa Yoshisuke*, pp. 84–86.

30. Fujitani, *Splendid Monarchy*, p. 40.

31. For translations of these two poems, see Levy, *The Ten Thousand Leaves*, pp. 127, 236.

32. Ibid., pp. 56–57.

33. *Sgs,* documents section, p. 114.

34. Levy, *The Ten Thousand Leaves,* p. 349.

35. Ketelaar, *Of Heretics and Martyrs in Meiji Japan,* p. 67.

36. Miyachi, *Bakumatsu ishin-ki no bunka to jōhō,* pp. 235–37.

37. This biographical sketch is based on Maruyama Yoshihiko and Maruyama Masahiko, *Maruyama Sakura den* (Tokyo: pub. by the authors, 1899); Maruyama Sueo Ikōshū Kankōkai, *Kokugaku shijo no hitobito* (Tokyo: Yoshikawa Kōbunkan, 1979); Nagasaki Kenritsu Nagasaki Toshokan, *Kyōdo no senkakusha tachi: Nagasaki-ken jinbutsuden* (Nagasaki-shi: Nagasaki-ken Kyōiku Iinkai, 1968).

38. *Sgs,* documents section, p. 41.

39. Maruyama, *Maruyama Sakura den,* p. 57.

40. Rodd with Henkenius, *Kokinshū,* pp. 310–11.

41. Breen argues persuasively that Bisei and his faction "ran early Meiji Shinto affairs and not the Hirata faction—who by comparison were powerless." "Shintoists in Restoration Japan," p. 581.

42. Tanishima, "Noshiro Hirosuke kankei shiryō shū," pt. 1, p. 37.

43. Ketelaar, *Of Heretics and Martyrs in Meiji Japan,* pp. 91–95.

44. John Lawrence Breen, "Emperor, State and Religion in Restoration Japan" (Cambridge University diss., 1992), p. 43.

45. Haga Noboru, *Kokugaku no hitobito: sono kōdō to shisō* (Hyōronsha, 1975), p. 196.

46. Haga, *Henkaku-ki ni okeru kokugaku,* pp. 250–51.

47. Haga, *Bakumatsu kokugaku no tenkai,* p. 209.

48. Haga, *Yoake mae no jitsuzō to kyozō,* pp. 122, 124.

49. Haga, *Bakumatsu kokugaku no tenkai,* p. 220.

50. Takagi, *Sorekara no shishi,* pp. 149–86.

51. Kanzakī, *Kannagara no michi no kyūkōsha,* p. 105.

52. *Sgs,* documents section, pp. 206, 209, 211–12.

53. Ibid., p. 120; *MTic,* p. 22.

54. *Sgs,* documents section, p. 147.

55. Ichimura Minato states that Taseko said nothing more about national affairs after she returned to Tomono in 1882, but he neglects the evidence of her poems that he had published. *Sgs,* narrative section, p. 223.

56. *Sgs,* documents section, p. 139.

Chapter Fifteen

1. *MTic,* p. 32, "To be read at the grave of Matsuo Taseko."

2. *Sgs,* documents section, p. 217.

3. Toyooka, *Toyooka sonshi,* vol. 2, pp. 745–66.

4. Ibid., pp. 843–73.

5. Wigen, *The Making of a Japanese Periphery*, p. 298.

6. Ichimura, *Matsuo Taseko*, p. 266.

7. Ibid., p. 266–67.

8. Ibid., p. 266–67.

9. Ibid., p. 267.

10. *Sgs*, narrative section, p. 258.

11. Kanekiyo Masanori, "Keishū kajin Andō Kikuko," *Ina* 41.8 (August 1993): 3–8.

12. Kanekiyo, "Keishū kajin Andō Kikuko," *Ina* 41.9 (September 1993): 11–16.

13. *Sgs*, narrative section, pp. 255–56.

14. Kanekiyo, "Keishū kajin Andō Kikuko," *Ina* 41.10 (October 1993): 13–19; *Ina* 41.11 (November 1993): 14–19; *Ina* 41.12 (December 1993): 3–7; *Ina* 42.2 (February 1994): 26–31; *Ina* 42.3 (March 1994): 16–22; *Ina* 42.5 (May 1994): 18–25; *Ina* 42.7 (July 1994): 30–37. See also Murasawa Takeo, "Yanagita Kunio to Iida," *Ina* 24.1 (January 1976): 23–29. Kikuko died in her sleep at the age of eighty-seven. Yanagita Kunio published a volume of her poems, and Miwada Masako wrote the preface for her autobiography.

15. *Sgs*, documents section, p. 234.

16. Ibid., pp. 237–8, 244. The first letter is too fragmentary to explain much about what the supplicant wanted.

17. Robert J. Marra, "Social Relations as Capital: The Story of Yuriko," in *Re-imaging Japanese Women*, ed. Anne E. Imamura (University of California Press, 1996), p. 113.

18. *Sgs*, narrative section, pp. 252–53.

19. Ibid., p. 253.

20. Ibid., p. 258

21. Ibid., pp. 252–53.

22. *Sgs*, documents section, p. 245.

23. Ibid., p. 225.

24. *Sgs*, narrative section, p. 258.

25. Ichimura, *Matsuo Taseko*, p. 268.

26. In contemporary Japan, second cousins are not considered relatives. See Marra, "Social Relations as Capital," p. 107. In Tokugawa Japan, however, even third cousins might have to take responsibility for family members. Ooms, *Tokugawa Village Practice*, p. 32.

27. *Sgs*, documents section, p. 206.

28. *IMz*, pp. 535–36, 554

29. *Sgs*, documents section, p. 212.

30. Ibid., p. 218.

31. Ibid., pp. 239–40.

32. "Kin work" is a term I learned from Gail L. Bernstein, who got it from Micaela di Leonardo, *The Varieties of Ethnic Experience: Kinship, Class and Gender among California Italian-Americans* (Cornell University Press, 1984).

33. Ōshika Sonshi Hensan Iinkai, *Ōshika sonshi,* vol. 3 (Ōshika sonshi Kankō Iinkai, 1984), pp. 115–17.

34. *Sgs,* documents section, p. 143–44.

35. Ibid., p. 226.

36. Murasawa Takeo, *Shinano jinbutsu shi* (Iida-shi: Shinano Jinbutsushi Kankō-kai, 1965), p. 362. This was Fukuzawa Noriharu.

37. *HHH,* pp. 3–5.

38. Higashiyama, "Bakumatsu ishin no senkakusha: Hazama Hidenori kōyū-roku," *Mino shinbun* no. 14, 14 January 1987, p. 1.

39. *Iks,* p. 493.

40. Toyooka, *Toyooka sonshi,* vol. 2, pp. 787–89. See also Wigen, *The Making of a Japanese Periphery,* p. 177 for a slightly different assessment of this fund.

41. Haga, *Yoake mae no jitsuzō to kyozō,* p. 90.

42. *IMz,* pp. 524–25.

43. Haga, *Ryōsai kenbo ron,* p. 37.

44. *Sgs,* documents section, p. 127.

45. Ibid., p. 223.

46. Ibid., p. 224.

47. Rodd with Henkenius, *Kokinshū,* p. 79.

48. Ichimura, *Matsuo Taseko,* p. 262.

49. Murasawa Takeo, "Iida jiken zengo," *Ina* 12.12 (December 1964): 2.

50. *Sgs,* documents section, p. 90.

51. Robertson, *Native and Newcomer,* p. 172.

52. Toyooka, *Toyooka sonshi,* vol. 1, p. 586. The local notable was Watanabe Chiaki, who started life as a retainer to the Takashima domain lord and rose to become a member of the nobility through bureaucratic service. He died in 1921 at the age of 73. Murasawa, *Shinano jinbutsu shi,* p. 490.

53. Matsuo-ke monjo, document no. 475.

54. *Iks,* pp. 340–41.

55. Toyooka, *Toyooka sonshi,* vol. 2, pp. 1290–306.

56. Ibid., pp. 1307–32; *Sgs,* narrative section, pp. 225–26.

57. *MTic,* p. 22.

58. Yoshikawa Shōichi, "Matsuo Chiburu shōtokuhi ni yosete," *Ina* 39.10 (October 1991): 42.

59. *Sgs,* documents section, p. 140.

60. *TnMt,* preface, pp. 3–4.

61. *Sgs,* narrative section, pp. 230–32.

62. Kitahara Chizan, *Ina-dani jinja no rekishi* (Iida: Yamamura Shoin, 1938), p. 196. Aizawa Seishisai had argued as early as 1825 that imperial cloth offerings once sent to all shrines throughout the realm "conveyed the meaning behind the emperor's ritual acts . . . his service to heaven, reverence for the ancestors, and love of the people." Wakabayashi, *Anti-foreignism and Western Learning in Early Modern Japan,* pp. 267–68.

63. *Sgs,* documents section, pp. 227–30. The curtain in Yamamoto continued to grace the shrine through the years leading to World War Two. Kitahara, *Inadani jinja no rekishi,* p. 197.

64. *Sgs,* documents section, p. 157.

65. *Sgs,* narrative section, p. 215.

Chapter Sixteen

1. *Sgs,* narrative section, pp. 238–39.

2. Ichimura, *Matsuo Taseko,* p. 241–42.

3. *Sgs,* narrative section, p. 234.

4. Taseko's biography first appeared in a biographical dictionary in 1903 as well. Kawaguchi Ukichi, *Dai Nihon jinmei jisho,* 5th ed. (Keizai Zasshisha, 1903), p. 1849. In 1936 she was included in the first dictionary of Japanese women published by Takemura Itsue, *Dai Nihon josei jinmei jishō* (Kōseikaku, first. ed. 1936, reprint ed. Shinjinbutsu Ōraisha, 1980), pp. 504–5.

5. Tajiri Tasaku, *Zōi shokenden,* vol. 1 (Kondō Shuppansha, 1927), pp. 490–91; Takagi Shunsuke, "Meiji ishin to josei—Matsuo Taseko wo chūshin ni," in *Shinshū no kindaika to josei: rekishi bungaku geijutsu ni saguru,* ed. Kamijō Hiroyuki, Nishimura Shin'ichi and Nishina Tsutomu (Nagano-shi: Ginga Shobō, 1987), p. 28.

6. *Sgs,* narrative section, p. 207.

7. Ibid., p. 222.

8. Tanabe, *Inoue Yorikuni okina koden,* pp. 113, 116.

9. Ibid., pp. 1–31, 132–33, 146.

10. Fukuchi Gen'ichirō, *Bakufu suibōron* (Min'yūsha, 1892).

11. Wakabayashi, *Antiforeignism and Western Learning,* pp. 101, 124.

12. Kenneth B. Pyle, "Meiji Conservatism," in *The Cambridge History of Japan,* vol. 5, *The Nineteenth Century,* pp. 676–79.

13. *MTic,* p. 31.

14. Miwada, "Matsuo Taseko den," p. 27. The aim of this journal was to resist the deterioration of womanly virtues by promoting the ideology of good wife, wise mother and denigrating notions of women's independence or equal rights for men and women. Haga, *Ryōsai kenbo ron,* p. 107.

15. Miwada, "Matsuo Taseko den," p. 30.

16. For the government's intent in founding this school, see Martha C. Tocco, "School Bound: Women's Higher Education in Nineteenth-Century Japan" (Stanford University diss., 1994), pp. 125–28

17. Miwada, "Matsuo Taseko den," pp. 22, 26.

18. See for example, Watanabe Tamezō, *Ishin shishi shōki shū* (Min'yūsha, 1911); Shakai Kyōiku Kyōkai ed., *Kinnōka shikashū* (1919: Shakai Kyōiku Kyōkai, reprint ed., 1940).

19. More examples: Koizumi Tōzō, *Ishin shishi kinnō shika hyōdan* (Kyoto: Ri-

tsumeikan Shuppanbu, 1939); Shida Nobuyoshi, *Bakumatsu kinnō kajin shū* (Kyōgaku Kyoku, 1939).

20. Watanabe Genpo, "Matsuo Taseko den Genpo-kun bengi," *Shidankai sokkiroku* no. 93 (1900): 26 – 34.

21. Kathy Ragsdale, "Popular Ideology and the Literary Marketplace: The Late Meiji katei shōsetsu," forthcoming in *Journal of Japanese Studies*.

22. Inoue Yorikuni, "Shinano no retsufu: Matsuo Taseko" *Yamato Shinbun*, 17 November 1911, p. 1; *Yamato Shinbun*, 18 November 1911, p. 1; *Yamato Shinbun*, 20 November 1911, p. 1. Miwada Masako then continued this series with her own recollections of life in the Iwakura mansion, *Yamato Shinbun*, 22 November 1911, p. 1; *Yamato Shinbun* 24 November 1911, p. 1.

23. Eimei was born in 1868 to a former samurai in Iida and died in 1930. Oya to Ko no Furusato to Hyakka Kankōkai ed., *Shimoina bunka jiten* vol. 5, 5: *Kyōdo bunka wo hagukunda hitobito* (Iida-shi: Shin'yōsha, 1992), p. 140.

24. Hanyū Eimei, "Oko Matsuo Taseko toji," *Nanshin shinbun*, 19 November 1903, p. 1.

25. For what this code meant for women, see Gail Lee Bernstein, "Introduction," in *Recreating Japanese Women, 1600 – 1945*, p. 8 and Sharon H. Nolte and Sally Ann Hastings, "The Meiji State's Policy Toward Women, 1890 – 1910" in the same volume, pp. 151 – 52.

26. See, for example, Beasley, *The Meiji Restoration*, pp. 2 – 12; Jansen, "The Meiji Restoration," pp. 360 – 66.

27. Sano, *Nanshin Ina shiryō*, p. 180; Shimizu Kin'ichi, *Matsuo no homare* (Kōronsha, 1904), p. 6. "Zōshō goi Matsuo Taseko," *Nanshin*, 17 November 1903, p. 1; Shimoina Kyōikuhin Kenkyūjo, *Shimoina annai* (Tokyo: Bunseidō, 1911), pp. 67 – 69; Shinano Shidankai, ed., *Shinano no hito* (Nagano-shi: Kyūkōkaku Shoten, 1915), p. 387.

28. Shinano, *Shinano no hito*, p. 385.

29. Hagiwara Shōtarō, *Kinnō resshiden* (Tokyo: Kinnō Resshi Shōkō Kenpi Jimusho, 1906), p. 258; Nagano-ken Kyōsan Kai, ed. *Nagano ken annai* (Tokyo: Nagano-ken Kyōsan Kai, 1908), unpaginated; Kumaya Keitarō, *Nihon retsujo den* (Tokyo: Meiji Shuppansha, 1913), pp. 430 – 31.

30. Nihon Rekishi Gakkai, *Meiji ishin jinmei jiten* (Yoshikawa Kōbunkan, 1981), pp. 823 – 24.

31. Shimizu, *Matsuo no homare*, p. 32; Watanabe Tamezō, *Ishin shishi ihōchō* (Tokyo: Kokumin Shinbunsha, 1910), p. 155; Watanabe, *Ishin shishi shōki shū*, pp. 274 – 75.

32. Watanabe Mokuzen, "Rekishi jitsuwa Matsuo Taseko," *Fujin sekai* 6.1 (January 1911): 122 – 28; 6.2 (February 1911): 90 – 96; 6.3 (March 1911): 116 – 22.

33. *IMz*, p. 619.

34. Sogawa Gyorō, "Shinfujin kokki Nagano-ken no fujin," *Fujin sekai* 7.5 (May 1912): 118 – 25. The journal may have been forced to print this more sedate account as an apology to its Ina Valley readers.

35. Mizuno Toshio, *Ina-dani kyōdo shika retsuden* (Iida-shi: Iida Bunkazai no Kai, 1972), pp. 14–15.

36. Takagi Shunsuke, "Kaisetsu," in Ichimura Minato, *Denki sosho*, vol. 59, *Matsuo Taseko* (Tokyo: Ōzorasha, 1989), pp. 1–3.

37. Watanabe, "Matsuo Taseko den Genpo-kun bengi," p. 34.

38. Haga, *Ryōsai kenbo ron*, p. 18.

39. Quoted in Ibid., p. 62.

40. Kumaya Keitarō, *Nihon retsujo den* (Meiji Shuppansha, 1913), p. 428.

41. Quoted in Ichimura, *Matsuo Taseko*, pp. 281–82.

42. Laurel Rasplica Rodd, "Yosano Akiko and the Taishō Debate over the 'New Woman,'" in *Recreating Japanese Women*, pp. 175–78.

43. Shinano, *Shinano no hito*, p. 394.

44. Ōkura Tōrō, "Kinnō monogatari: Matsuo Taseko," *Fujokai* 41.2 (February 1929): 133–42; 41.3 (March 1929): 133–43; 41.4 (April 1929): 161–71; 41.5 (May 1929): 117–27; 41.7 (July 1929): 165–74; 41.8 (August 1929): 147–57; 41.9 (September 1929): 123–32; 41.10 (October 1929): 139–48; 41.11 (November 1929): 115–25; 42.1 (January 1930): 153–63; 42.2 (February 1930): 147–57.

45. Ōkura Tōrō, "Kinnō monogatari: Matsuo Taseko," *Fujokai* 41.10 (October 1929): 140.

46. See Miriam Silverberg, "The Modern Girl as Militant," in *Recreating Japanese Women*, pp. 239–66. A lengthy description of how Tokyo changed in the 1920s is in Edward Seidensticker, *Tokyo Rising* (New York: Alfred A. Knopf, 1990), pp. 21–87.

47. Fumura Yasuhiro, *Meiji ishin to josei* (Tokyo: Ritsumeikan Shuppanbu, 1936), p. 37.

48. Yoshikawa Eiji, "Aikoku no josei emonogatari," *Shufu no tomo* 22.2 (February 1938): 49–57.

49. Ibid., pp. 54–55.

50. Yasuma Kōken, *Bakumatsu no aikoku josei: Matsuo Taseko no shogai* (Tokyo: Ikuseisha, 1938), pp. 1, 5.

51. Ibid., pp. 115, 124.

52. Iwasaki Chōshi, "Ishin no joryū kinnōko," pt. 1 in *Nihon josei bunka shi*, ed. Miwada Motomichi, vol. 2 (Zenkoku Kōtō Jogakkōchō Kyōkai, 1938), pp. 753–97. Similar views are expressed by Shimizu Fuichi, "Kinnō joketsu: Matsuo Taseko," *Jogakusei* 3.1 (January 1941): 36–39; Ogawa Enson, *Kinnō retsujo* (Ryōkokuminsha, 1943), pp. 103–20; Maezawa Engetsu, "Miyako no tsuto: Matsuo Taseko," in *Yamazakura: Shinshū no hitobito* (Tokyo: Hōgaku Shoin, 1942), pp. 168–202.

53. Mizushima Ayame, "Kinnō no haha: Matsuo Taseko," *Shōjo kurabu* 17.3 (February 1939): 66–74.

54. Kawada, "Onna jōbu Matsuo Taseko," pp. 258–67. The quotation is on p. 262.

55. Hayashida Tatsusaburō, *Kō to kon: Nihon joseishi* (Asahi Shinbunsha, 1966), pp. 530–33.

56. Akagi Shizuko, *Nihonshi shōhakka*, vol. 2, 2: *Josei* (Kondō Shuppansha, 1977), p. 241.

57. Morosawa Yōko, *Shinano no onna*, vol. 1 (Miraisha, 1969), pp. 183.

58. Suzuki Yukiko, *Kikikatari Nippon josei 'ai' shi* (Kōdansha, 1988), pp. 196–213.

59. Morosawa, *Shinano no onna*, pp. 183–202.

60. Hashida Sugako and Yoshimi Kaneko, "Bakumatsu ishin no josei tachi," in *Taidan Nihon no joseishi* (Akita Shoten, 1981), pp. 268–91.

61. Ibid., pp. 86–291.

62. Anne E. Imamura, *Urban Japanese Housewives: At Home and in the Community* (University of Hawaii Press, 1987), p. 65.

63. Anzai Atsuko, "Ishin wo horu jojin gunzō," *Bungei shunjū*, special edition (January 1973): 169–170; Nishioka Masako, *Edo no onna banashi* (Kawada Shobō Shinsha, 1993), pp. 198–201.

64. Takahara Sumiko, "Nichinichi oriori," *Shinano Mainichi shinbun*, 29 May 1989, p. 1.

65. Yanagi, "Josei no seikatsu kūkan," p. 398.

66. Saotame Takami, "Ina-dani no joketsu," *Rekishi kenkyū* (May 1968): 16–19; Kitakōji Ken, *Zusetsu Yoake mae no shiori: kyozō to jitsuzō wo saguru* (Kokusho Kankōkai, 1973), pp. 67–68; Igarashi Tomio, *Nihon josei bunkashi* (Azuma Shoten, 1984), pp. 148–50; Shinano no Joseishi Kankōkai, *Shashin kiroku: Shinano no joseishi* (Matsumoto-shi: Kyōdo Shuppansha, 1994), p. 34.

67. Iwahashi Kunie, "Matsuo Taseko," pp. 98–132; Haga Noboru, "Kokuji ni honsō shita onna shishi: Matsuo Taseko," *Rekishi yomihon bekkan: Bakumatsu ishin wo ikita 12 nin no onna tachi* (1979): 31–40; Naramoto Tatsuya, "Matsuo Taseko," in *Zusetsu jinbutsu Nihon no josei shi*, vol. 9, *Ishin-ki no saijo tachi*, ed. Ōga Tetsuo (Shōgakkan, 1980), pp. 53–70; Kitakōji Ken, "Matsuo Taseko: Sonjō undō no onna jōbu," in *Nihon josei no rekishi* vol. 10, *Bakumatsu ishin no josei*, ed. Konishi Shirō (Akatsuki Kyōiku Tosho Kabushiki Kaisha, 1978), pp. 48–49; Enchi Fumiko, ed., *Nihon joseishi jiten* (Sanseidō, 1984), p. 211.

68. Konishi Shirō, "Jidai geisetsu," in *Nihon josei no rekishi* vol. 10, *Bakumatsu ishin no josei*, pp. 133–37.

69. Shinano Mainichi Shinbunsha Kaihatsukyoku Shuppanbu, *Ishin no Shin-shūjin* (Nagano-shi: Shinano Mainichi Shinbunsha, 1974), pp. 273–314; Tai Yukiko, *Nihon no joseishi 6: Meiji onna hyakkafu* (Kai Shobō, 1979), pp. 2–5.

70. Komatsu Asayuki, *Onna tachi no Meiji ishin* (Ben'ensha, 1986), pp. 186–233; Kusudo Yoshiaki, *Ishin no onna* (Mainichi Shinbunsha, 1992), pp. 89–92.

71. Iwahashi Kunie, "Matsuo Taseko," p. 106; Tai Yukiko, *Meiji onna hyakkafu*, p. 5.

72. Furukawa Chieko, *Akaki kokoro wo: onna kinnō shishi: Matsuo Taseko* (Shiode Shuppansha, 1990), p. 251.

73. Ibid., p. 86.

74. Ibid., p. 199.

75. Toyooka-mura Kyōiku Iinkai, *Taseko botsugo hyakunen: Minami Shinano no*

sanga ga unda bakumatsu no joryū kinnōka: Matsuo Taseko no shōgai (Toyooka-mura; Toyooka-mura Kyōiku Iinkai, 1994), p. 76.

76. Noriko Hayakawa, "Feminism and Nationalism in Japan, 1868–1945," *Journal of Women's History* 7.4 (Winter 1995): 117.

Epilogue

1. *Sgs*, documents section, p. 119. "Toshi wo furu oi mo wakayagu kokochi seri hi kazutsumoranu haru wo mukaete."

2. *Sgs*, narrative section, pp. 217–21.

3. Shimizu, *Matsuo no homare.*

4. *MTic*. See also Yakezaki Kenji, *Shinano ijin ihō chō* (Nagano-shi: Nagano Shinbun Kabushiki Kaisha, 1918), pp. 47–48.

5. *TnMt*.

6. "Shinkō no shōzōga hakken," *Minami Shinshū shinbun*, 5 May 1989, p. 3; "Bakumatsu no josei: Matsuo Taseko" (Iida-shi: Iida Shin'yō Ginkō Yamamoto Shiten, 1989).

7. Toyooka, *Taseko botsugo hyakunen.*

8. Conversation with Shioda Ken, 11 June 1995.

9. Toyooka-mura, *Taseko botsugo hyakunen*, pp. 61–64.

10. The sculptor was Kurasawa Kōsei, 1895–1980.

11. Harriet Bodgett, *Centuries of Female Days: Englishwomen's Private Diaries* (Rutgers University Press, 1988), p. 1.

12. Linda Wagner-Martin, *Telling Women's Lives: The New Biography* (Rutgers University Press, 1994), p. 11.

Index

Noh, 101, 155, 197, 267, 272
Nomura Bōtō, 12, 227, 347, 357n. 34
Nonoguchi Masashiki, 172–173, 216
Nonomiya, 158
Noro Kyūzaemon, 189, 196, 198; arrest of, 204–205
Noshiro Hirosuke, 192–193, 197, 207, 214

Ochiai Naoaki, 246, 250
Oda Nobunaga, 133
Offense against National Affairs Incident (*Kokuji ihan jiken*), 300–301
Office (Ministry) of Rites, 256, 294
Ogino Ginko, 332
Oka Mototarō, 189, 194, 198
"One hundred poems by one hundred virtuous women" (*Retsujo hyakunin isshū*), 36
onna masurao (manly woman), 185
Ono no Komachi, 152
Opium War, 49
Otamura Bunsuke, 187
Owari domain, 250, 253, 285–294
Ōba Kyōhei, 198, 204, 207
Ōhara Chigura, 194
Ōhara Shigetomi, 168–169
Ōhara Yūgaku, 104
Ōkawara, 50, 309
Ōkubo Toshimichi, 247, 298, 300
Ōkuni Masatane, 172
Ōkuninushi, 131, 132, 137, 151, 228
Ōmoto-Kyō, 104, 156
Ōnin war, 159, 163
ōsei fukko, 237
Ōshio Heihachirō, 49
Ōtagaki Rengetsu, 12, 160, 178, 190, 233, 311, 346

people and gods, 214, 282, 296, 327, 374n. 32
Peron, Eva, 233
Pillow Book, 35
poetry writing circles, 27–31, 71, 103, 106; and women, 29–31
political jurisdictions, 41–42, 44
Popular Rights Movement, 298
posthumous court rank, 10, 330, 350
Pratt, Edward, 83

"The Precious Sleeve Cord" (*Tamadasuki*), 121–122, 130, 132–138, 218, 231, 282, 321; and Matsuo Taseko, 121, 145, 197, 210, 217, 227, 268
protoindustrialization, 84, 85
public space, 10, 11, 109, 114, 185, 353

Queen Mother of the West, 266–267

Retsujo hyakunin isshū ("One hundred poems by one hundred virtuous women"), 36
return of land registers, 289
revere the emperor, expel the barbarians, 3, 143, 153, 168, 170, 184, 191, 226, 234
Reynolds, Siân, 194
Robertson, Jennifer, 163, 323
rōnin, 204
rural entrepreneurs: and economic activities, 82–83, 99; erudition of, 11, 21, 25–26, 104; and Hirata school, 104–105, 300; and Meiji Restoration, 3–5; and moneylending, 91; and politics, 2; as political activists, 185; and status, 290
ryōsai kenbo. See "good wife, wise mother"

"The Sacred Pillar of the Soul" (*Tama no mihashira*), 122, 130–132
Sagara Sōzō, 247–250, 292
Sagitsuchō, 175
Saigō Takamori, 247, 249, 250, 254
Saigyō, 150
saisei itchi. See Unity of Rites and Rule
Sakamoto Ryōma, 244, 352
Sakamoto Ryōma and the Meiji Restoration, 3
Sakhalin (Karafuto), 297
Sakurai Chie, 25–26, 28, 109, 311
Sakurai family, 42
Sakurai Haruki, 27, 109, 311, 319
Sanjō, Emperor, 159
Satsuma, 148–149, 169, 202, 225; and Meiji Restoration, 244–245, 255
Satsuma-Chōshū alliance, 244, 279
Sawa family, 251, 258
Sawa Nobuyoshi, 251, 297
Sawa Tamekazu, 251, 259
Sawa Yoshitane, 316